# SOCIOCULTURAL THEORY AND THE PEDAGOGICAL IMPERATIVE IN L2 EDUCATION

From its inception in the early 1970s the field of second language acquisition (SLA) has struggled to overcome the dichotomy between theory/research and classroom practice. Explicating clearly and concisely the full implication of a praxis-oriented language pedagogy, this book argues for an approach to language teaching grounded in a significant scientific theory of human learning—a stance that rejects the consumer approach to theory and the dichotomy between theory and practice that dominates SLA and language teaching. This approach is based on Vygotsky's sociocultural theory, according to which the two activities are inherently connected so that each is necessarily rooted in the other; practice is the research laboratory where the theory is tested. From the perspective of language education, this is what is meant by the "pedagogical imperative."

*Sociocultural Theory and the Pedagogical Imperative in L2 Education:*

- Elaborates a new approach to dealing with the relationship between theory and practice—an approach grounded in praxis—the dialectical unity of theory and practice
- Presents an analysis of empirical research illustrating praxis-based principles in real language classrooms
- Brings together cognitive linguistics and sociocultural theory—the former provides the theoretical knowledge of language required of praxis and the latter furnishes the theoretical principles of learning and development also called for in a praxis approach
- Offers recommendations for redesigning teacher education programs.

Its timely focus on the theory–practice gap in language education and its original approach to bridging it put this book at the cutting edge of thinking about Vygotskian sociocultural theory in applied linguistics and SLA.

**James P. Lantolf** is the George and Jane Greer Professor in Language Acquisition and Applied Linguistics in the Department of Applied Linguistics at Penn State University, USA.

**Matthew E. P** LIVERPOOL JMU LIBRARY ram Director of the K-12 teacher certification p and Applied Linguistics in the Department of te University, USA.

# ESL & Applied Linguistics Professional Series

*Eli Hinkel, Series Editor*

**Christison/Murray** • *What English Language Teachers Need to Know Volume III: Designing Curriculum*

**Turner** • *Using Statistics in Small-scale Language Education Research: Focus on Non-parametric Data*

**Hong/Pawan** • *The Pedagogy and Practice of Western-trained Chinese English Language Teachers: Foreign Education, Chinese Meanings*

**Lantolf/Poehner** • *Sociocultural Theory and the Pedagogical Imperative in L2 Education: Vygotskian Praxis and the Research/Practice Divide*

**Brown** • *Pronunciation and Phonetics: A Practical Guide for English Language Teachers*

**Birch** • *English Grammar Pedagogy: A Global Perspective*

**Liu** • *Describing and Explaining Grammar and Vocabulary in ELT: Key Theories and Effective Practices*

**deOliviera/Silva, Eds.** • *L2 Writing in Secondary Classrooms: Student Experiences, Academic Issues, and Teacher Education*

**Andrade/Evans** • *Principles and Practices for Response in Second Language Writing: Developing Self-Regulated Learners*

**Sayer** • *Ambiguities and Tensions in English Language Teaching: Portraits of EFL Teachers as Legitimate Speakers*

**Alsagoff/McKay/Hu/Renandya, Eds.** • *Principles and Practices of Teaching English as an International Language*

**Kumaravadivelu** • *Language Teacher Education for A Global Society: A Modular Model for Knowing, Analyzing, Recognizing, Doing, and Seeing*

**Vandergrift/Goh** • *Teaching and Learning Second Language Listening: Metacognition in Action*

**LoCastro** • *Pragmatics for Language Educators: A Sociolinguistic Perspective*

**Nelson** • *Intelligibility in World Englishes: Theory and Practice*

**Nation/Macalister, Eds.** • *Case Studies in Language Curriculum Design: Concepts and Approaches in Action Around the World*

**Johnson/Golumbek, Eds.** • *Research on Second Language Teacher Education: A Sociocultural Perspective on Professional Development*

**Hinkel, Ed.** • *Handbook of Research in Second Language Teaching and Learning, Volume II*

**Nassaji/Fotos** • *Teaching Grammar in Second Language Classrooms: Integrating Form-Focused Instruction in Communicative Context*

**Murray/Christison** • *What English Language Teachers Need to Know Volume I: Understanding Learning*

**Murray/Christison** • *What English Language Teachers Need to Know Volume II: Facilitating Learning*

**Wong/Waring** • *Conversation Analysis and Second Language Pedagogy: A Guide for ESL/EFL Teachers*

**Nunan/Choi, Eds.** • *Language and Culture: Reflective Narratives and the Emergence of Identity*

**Braine** • *Nonnative Speaker English Teachers: Research, Pedagogy, and Professional Growth*

**Burns** • *Doing Action Research in English Language Teaching: A Guide for Practitioners*

**Nation/Macalister** • *Language Curriculum Design*

**Birch** • *The English Language Teacher and Global Civil Society*

**Johnson** • *Second Language Teacher Education: A Sociocultural Perspective*

**Nation** • *Teaching ESL/EFL Reading and Writing*

**Nation/Newton** • *Teaching ESL/EFL Listening and Speaking*

**Kachru/Smith** • *Cultures, Contexts, and World Englishes*

**McKay/Bokhosrt-Heng** • *International English in its Sociolinguistic Contexts: Towards a Socially Sensitive EIL Pedagogy*

**Christison/Murray, Eds.** • *Leadership in English Language Education: Theoretical Foundations and Practical Skills for Changing Times*

**McCafferty/Stam, Eds.** • *Gesture: Second Language Acquisition and Classroom Research*

**Liu** • *Idioms: Description, Comprehension, Acquisition, and Pedagogy*

**Chapelle/Enright/Jamieson, Eds.** • *Building a Validity Argument for the Test of English as a Foreign Language™*

**Kondo-Brown/Brown, Eds.** • *Teaching Chinese, Japanese, and Korean Heritage Language Students: Curriculum Needs, Materials, and Assessments*

**Youmans** • *Chicano-Anglo Conversations: Truth, Honesty, and Politeness*

**Birch** • *English L2 Reading: Getting to the Bottom, Second Edition*

**Luk/Lin** • *Classroom Interactions as Cross-cultural Encounters: Native Speakers in EFL Lessons*

**Levy/Stockwell** • *CALL Dimensions: Issues and Options in Computer Assisted Language Learning*

**Nero, Ed.** • *Dialects, Englishes, Creoles, and Education*

**Basturkmen** • *Ideas and Options in English for Specific Purposes*

**Kumaravadivelu** • *Understanding Language Teaching: From Method to Postmethod*

**McKay** • *Researching Second Language Classrooms*

**Egbert/Petrie, Eds.** • *CALL Research Perspectives*

**Canagarajah, Ed.** • *Reclaiming the Local in Language Policy and Practice*

**Adamson** • *Language Minority Students in American Schools: An Education in English*

**Fotos/Browne, Eds.** • *New Perspectives on CALL for Second Language Classrooms*

**Hinkel** • *Teaching Academic ESL Writing: Practical Techniques in Vocabulary and Grammar*

**Hinkel/Fotos, Eds.** • *New Perspectives on Grammar Teaching in Second Language Classrooms*

**Hinkel** • *Second Language Writers' Text: Linguistic and Rhetorical Features*

Visit **www.routledge.com/education** for additional information on titles in the ESL & Applied Linguistics Professional Series.

# SOCIOCULTURAL THEORY AND THE PEDAGOGICAL IMPERATIVE IN L2 EDUCATION

## Vygotskian Praxis and the Research/Practice Divide

*James P. Lantolf*
*Matthew E. Poehner*

Routledge
Taylor & Francis Group

NEW YORK AND LONDON

First published 2014
by Routledge
711 Third Avenue, New York, NY 10017

and by Routledge
2 Park Square, Milton Park, Abingdon, Oxon OX14 4RN

*Routledge is an imprint of the Taylor & Francis Group, an informa business*

© 2014 Taylor & Francis

*Library of Congress Cataloging in Publication Data*
Lantolf, James P.
  Sociocultural theory and the pedagogical imperative in L2 education: Vygotskian praxis and the research/practice divide/James P. Lantolf, Matthew E. Poehner.
    pages cm.—(ESL & applied linguistics professional series)
  Includes bibliographical references and index.
  1. Second language acquisition—Social aspects.   2. Vygotskii, L. S. (Lev Semenovich), 1896–1934.   I. Poehner, Matthew E.   II. Title.
  P118.2.L3685 2014
  418.0071—dc23                                            2013028397

ISBN: 978-0-415-89417-3 (hbk)
ISBN: 978-0-415-89418-0 (pbk)
ISBN: 978-0-203-81385-0 (ebk)

Typeset in Bembo
by RefineCatch Limited, Bungay, Suffolk, UK

Printed in Great Britain by TJ International Ltd, Padstow, Cornwall

# DEDICATION

Jim Lantolf to my grandchildren: Harrison, Henry, Jackson, Samson.

Matt Poehner to my extraordinary wife, Priya, and to our two little treasures, Bella and Leo.

# CONTENTS

*Preface*                                                                       *xi*

*Acknowledgements*                                                              *xvi*

**1   Theory/Research–Practice Gap in Applied Linguistics            1**
*What to Do About the Gap? 3*
*Reconceptualizing Theory and Practice 5*
*The Pedagogical Imperative 6*
*Overview of Sociocultural Theory 8*

**2   Sociocultural Theory and the Dialectic of Praxis:
An Alternative to the Theory/Research–Practice Gap            14**
*Vygotsky's Response to the Crisis: A Unified Psychology 15*
*Praxis: The Theory–Practice Dialectic 26*
*Macro Cultural Psychology: A Neo-Vygotskian Theory of
  Higher Mental Processing 32*
*Conclusion 36*

**3   Psychology of the Social Environment                           39**
*Environment as a Source of Development 40*
*Conclusion 52*

**4   A Theory of Developmental Education                            56**
*Orders of Mediation 57*
*Systemic Theoretical Instruction 61*
*Pre-Understanding and Its Negation 68*
*Defining Concepts for L2 Developmental Education 70*

*STI and the Explicit/Implicit Interface 72*
*L2 Neuroscience Research and STI 74*
*Conclusion 79*

**5    L2 Systemic Theoretical Instruction: Experimental-
      Developmental Studies**                                          **82**
*STI and the Sociopragmatics of L2 French 83*
*STI and L2 Sarcasm 93*
*Topicalization in Chinese: Testing the Teachability Hypothesis 99*
*Conclusion 117*

**6    L2 Systemic Theoretical Instruction: Intact
      Classroom Studies**                                             **119**
*Spanish Verbal Aspect: Connecting Language and Literature 119*
*The Chinese Temporal System 130*
*English Phrasal Verbs 136*
*Conclusion 143*

**7    The Zone of Proximal Development and
      Dynamic Assessment**                                            **146**
*Interpreting the ZPD 147*
*Feuerstein's Mediated Learning Experience as a Framework for DA 159*
*Conclusion 167*

**8    Dynamic Assessment and L2 Development**                        **170**
*Quality of Mediation in L2 DA 171*
*DA in an Intact Elementary L2 Spanish Classroom 174*
*DA and L2 Listening Comprehension: An Experimental-
   Developmental Study 181*
*L2 DA Beyond the Classroom 186*
*Concluding Remarks and Ongoing Challenges 199*

**9    Conclusion**                                                   **206**
*The Role of Teachers in Developmental Education 208*
*L2 Teacher Education 211*
*Developing Expertise in Pre-Service L2 Teacher Education 213*
*In-Service L2 Teacher Education Through Praxis 220*

*References*                                                          *225*
*Index*                                                              *243*

# PREFACE

The primary goal of this volume is to address what many in second language acquisition (SLA) research perceive as the problematic gap between theory/research on the one hand and classroom practice on the other. SLA researchers such as R. Ellis (2005b, 2010), Erlam (2008), and Long (2009), among others, propose to find ways of bridging this gap, which means, in large measure, translating the implications of the findings of SLA research in ways that are useful for teachers. The proposal the authors of the present volume offer is to argue, on the basis of sociocultural theory (SCT) as formulated by L. S. Vygotsky and his colleagues, that a theory/research–practice gap need not exist in the first place and to explore the research that has been carried out to date on L2 teaching and learning in the classroom setting that supports the "non-gap" position. To achieve this goal, we first discuss the foundations of SCT in the critical writings of Vygotsky as well as in the writings of contemporary neo-Vygotskian scholars, in particular, Carl Ratner (2012). We then consider how the current version of the theory has been extended to L2 educational practice, with specific attention to Gal'perin's (1992) theory of developmental education known as Systemic Theoretical Instruction (STI) and the concrete realization of Vygotsky's concept of the Zone of Proximal Development (ZPD) as Dynamic Assessment (DA) (Luria, 1961).

## The Intended Audience

The primary audience for this book is all those in the field of applied linguistics directly or indirectly concerned with understanding language development in the educational setting. This includes researchers, teachers, teacher educators, as well as those preparing to join the professional and academic communities, including graduate students interested in pursuing a career in applied linguistics or language education. The book is also intended for those working in Vygotskian psychology, and in particular those concerned with language and education.

## Overview

The book comprises nine chapters in total. The goal is to present our argument for the pedagogical imperative as it relates to L2 development in educational settings.

Chapter 1 outlines the nature of the theory/research–practice gap and briefly traces its history. It also initiates the discussion of a dialectical and praxis-based approach to overcoming the gap, not by bridging it but by eliminating it. Finally, it reviews the major relevant concepts and principles of sociocultural theory.

Chapter 2 fleshes out Vygotsky's theory of psychology, with specific focus on its grounding in materialist dialectical philosophy. In Chapter 2, we argue that to fully appreciate the significance of Vygotsky's theory necessitates recognizing that he was first and foremost a dialectical thinker and that as a consequence the principles and concepts of the theory he proposed are dialectical in nature. Thus, while we do not present an in-depth analysis of Marxist theory, we maintain that it is difficult to fully apprehend the unified nature of Vygotsky's proposals without some consideration of dialectical materialism. We are especially concerned with *praxis*, or the dialectical unity of theory and practice, which Vygotsky argued forms the basis of developmental education. As we explain in Chapter 2, it is important to keep in mind that SCT is not a theory restricted to explaining L2 development, as such. Rather, SCT is a general psychological theory that attempts to account for higher order consciousness, and, as Vygotsky himself (1987) pointed out, this includes language development. Therefore, the same principles and concepts that account for the development of memory, perception, attention, planning, and rational thought should also account for language development, and, most immediately, L2 development.

Chapter 2 also includes a discussion of the research methodology proposed by Vygotsky. His overall approach is often referred to as the *genetic method*, the goal of which is to understand and explain development by tracing its formation, or history, over time. A component of his general program is what he called the *experimental-developmental* method (Vygotsky, 1978), which is normally conducted in laboratory settings and involves observing the effect of introducing a mediational artifact into a task at the point where the task becomes difficult for the participants to complete. This is done on the theoretical grounds that higher forms of human development (i.e., cultural development) are mediated by tools and social interaction. An essential feature of Vygotsky's research program is to connect the findings of laboratory work to research in real-world settings, including schools. This approach to research forms the basis for the L2 studies considered in Chapters 5 through 8.

Chapter 3 continues this discussion and brings into focus a central tenet of Vygotsky's theory, namely his position that the sociocultural environment is the primary source of human development. Chapter 4 then connects this understanding of the relationship between the environment and development back to education. The logic is that if the sociocultural environment shapes development then intentionally and systematically organizing educational praxis in specific ways creates the conditions for development to take place rather than waiting for it to arise spontaneously as in the everyday world.

Arguably the two most important pedagogical frameworks derived from Vygotsky's theory are Gal'perin's (1992) *Systemic Theoretical Instruction* (STI) and Davydov's (2004) *developmental instruction*. Beginning from Vygotsky's contention that effective developmental education entails presentation of well-organized conceptual knowledge of the object of study linked to concrete practices, both approaches propose ways of materializing conceptual knowledge so that it can be appropriated by learners and used to mediate their performance in goal-directed activity. To date, most of the L2 research on developmental instruction has been informed by Gal'perin's approach (Ferreira, 2005 is a notable exception). Consequently, our major focus, beginning in Chapter 4, is on Gal'perin's educational model. A central theme of the chapter concerns how scientific knowledge, connected to everyday knowledge, may be effectively introduced into educational activity. In the case of L2 education, we make the case for cognitive linguistic research as a source of high quality scientific knowledge of language. We also consider neuroscience models that support a central role of explicit knowledge in developmental education.

Chapters 5 and 6 explore research that implements STI in L2 educational environments. In Chapter 5 we discuss three studies carried out that adopt an experimental-developmental approach, which involved engaging volunteer adult L2 learners in instruction carried out in accordance with principles of STI. One study addressed French negation (*pas, ne ... pas*), 1st person plural pronouns *on* and *nous*, and 2nd person formal and informal pronouns *tu* and *vous*. The second study focused on teaching learners of L2 English how to identify and interpret spoken sarcasm. The third study was the pilot for an in-progress study on topicalization in L2 Chinese. The study was designed to test the Teachability Hypothesis of Pienemann's Processability Theory. Chapter 6 moves to research conducted in intact classrooms. Again it focuses on three studies: one dealing with STI and L2 Spanish verbal aspect, another that examines the effects of STI on development of L2 Chinese temporal grammar, and the third reports on an STI instructional program designed to develop learner ability with English phrasal verbs formed with the particles *over, out,* and *up*.

Chapters 7 and 8 shift focus to another, and equally important, aspect of Vygotsky's theory—the Zone of Proximal Development (ZPD)—and how it has been brought into education through Dynamic Assessment (DA). Chapter 7 essentially complements Chapter 4 in that its focus is on the social interaction between instructors and learners aimed at promoting development, whereas Chapter 4 is more concerned with the role of conceptual knowledge in language development. We argue that the ZPD may be appropriately understood as cooperative activity undertaken by teachers and learners that allows individuals to function beyond their actual capabilities. From this perspective, the quality of mediation during such interactions performs a dual function by promoting learner development and providing insights into abilities that have not yet fully emerged but are in the process of forming. The chapter includes discussion of the Mediated Learning Experience approach to DA proposed by Reuven Feuerstein (Feuerstein, Feuerstein, & Falik, 2010; Feuerstein, Rand, & Hoffman, 1979), whose work with learners with special needs bears striking similarities to Vygotsky's approach to "defectology." Moreover, Feuerstein's DA framework has strongly influenced L2 DA research in that he eschews the standardization required for producing test scores that adhere to traditional psychometric criteria in favor of open-ended dialogue between mediators and learners that allows for joint regulation as they cooperatively complete tasks, explore questions, reflect on performances, and consider problems.

Chapter 8 surveys recent L2 DA studies that illustrate how Vygotsky's conceptualization of ZPD activity and Feuerstein's elaboration of DA have been pursued in L2 educational contexts. Although numerous studies of L2 DA have appeared over the last several years, we limit our discussion to representative projects that reflect collaborations with L2 classroom teachers and that afford insights into processes of L2 development that help to further refine our understanding of the underlying theoretical concept (i.e., the ZPD). The selected DA projects may be understood as instantiations of Vygotskian praxis. Similar to the organization of studies in Chapters 5 and 6, the DA research reported on in Chapter 8 includes one project conducted in an intact classroom and another project carried out in an experimental-developmental setting. The classroom study documents how a teacher adapted DA to meet the needs and constraints of her unique environment without compromising the principles of the theory. The experimental-developmental study included university learners and its focus was on L2 French listening comprehension, a component often overlooked in L2 instructional programs.

The third study examined in Chapter 8 was a project that developed listening and reading comprehension DA tests in Chinese, French, and Russian delivered in an on-line format. An innovative feature of this project is the introduction of a *learning potential score* that takes account of differences between mediated and non-mediated learner performance. Part of this study included a series of one-on-one DA interactions between mediators and learners aimed at developing the prompts used in the on-line tests. One of these interactions revealed insights that enhanced our understanding of DA. We therefore include a discussion of this component of the broader project in the chapter.

Chapter 9 concludes the book with discussion of the implications of the theory/research–practice dialectic for L2 teacher education. The chapter pays special attention to the forms of expertise required of L2 teachers if they are to undertake praxis activities such as STI and DA. We argue that teachers need to have in-depth and systematic knowledge of a coherent theory of development, such as SCT, in order to understand the potential for their practices to intervene in and indeed shape learner L2 development. Equally important, high quality linguistic knowledge is required if teachers are to move beyond rule-of-thumb accounts of language grammar in favor of organizing their L2 curriculum around abstract or scientific conceptual knowledge of language. This is an aspect of teacher preparation that has been, in our view, neglected, particularly in programs that prepare teachers of languages other than English. As part of this discussion, the chapter surveys a number of current L2 teacher education programs in the US with regard to course requirements relating to language knowledge for teachers. Together, expert knowledge of a theory of development and their object of study (i.e., language) positions L2 teachers to overcome the theory/research–practice divide by engaging in praxis, that is, theoretically guided, practical activity that elaborates and refines our understanding of the processes of L2 development. In our view, the L2 field has reached a turning point wherein praxis is imperative both for researchers as well as educators.

# ACKNOWLEDGEMENTS

We would like to thank the current and former graduate students whose dissertations, as instantiations of praxis, provided the empirical foundation for this work. We also thank them for their exceptional and insightful conversations about Vygotskian theory. Among these we single out Rimma Ableeva, Kristan Davin, Jiyun Kim, Wei Lai, Hyewon Lee, Adam van Compernolle, Carmen Yáñez-Prieto, and Xian Zhang. We thank Kimberly Buescher, whose research summaries and work on a teacher education survey were indispensable for our project. We thank Naomi Silverman for her unending patience and tolerance as we slowly produced the manuscript. We would also like to thank our colleagues, Karen Johnson, Rick Donato, Eduardo Negueruela, Carl Ratner, Merrill Swain, Steve McCafferty, and all those who regularly attend the annual meeting of the Sociocultural Theory and L2 Working Group for their inspiration and their criticisms of our ideas. Finally, we would like to acknowledge Leo van Lier, a special colleague who passed away this year, and who as a regular contributor to the SCT-L2 Working Group was always willing to engage us in intellectual conversations to challenge and mediate our thinking.

# 1

# THEORY/RESEARCH–PRACTICE GAP IN APPLIED LINGUISTICS

Before second language acquisition (SLA) was recognized as an independent field, scholars such as S. Pit Corder (1973, 1978) argued that applied linguistics, as the field most directly concerned with the teaching of second and foreign languages, was a consumer, rather than generator, of theories. In other words, applied linguists assumed the task of bringing into relevance theories of language for the purpose of improving intentional language instruction. This ranged from first-order application that entailed descriptions of a particular language (Corder, 1973, p. 145); to second-order application, whereby material from first-order description was selected for inclusion in a pedagogical syllabus (p. 150); to third-order application where specific instructional techniques and materials were implemented relative to the second-order syllabus (p. 155). Researchers soon began to ask questions about the nature of L2 acquisition that were not directly related to classroom instruction. Long (2009, p. 376, italics in original), for instance, described the separation between SLA and language teaching, as follows: "the goal of a theory of language teaching is a maximally *efficient* approach, not, as in the case of a theory of SLA, one which is primarily concerned with what is *necessary* and *sufficient* for language acquisition to occur."

The SLA branch of applied linguistics began to grow its own theories and eventually emerged as a discipline without direct connections or interests in classroom instructional practice. Even though SLA emerged as an independent field, researchers continued to cast an eye toward the classroom setting and to wonder if and how the findings of their work might be relevant for teachers. Indeed, Crookes (1998, p. 6) noted that "If the relationship [between research and practice] were simple, or not a source of concern, I do not think it would come up so often." Bygate (2005, p. 568) captured the ambivalence of the field when he noted that although by the 1980s SLA had established itself as an independent "academic discipline in its own right," many continued to view SLA "as synonymous with an approach to language teaching." R. Ellis (2010, p. 183), for example, commented that despite its interest in language acquisition as such, SLA is "still at its heart an applied rather than a pure discipline."

One of the recurring worries regarding the relationship of SLA and language pedagogy has been the perception among some researchers that the field has not yet reached the level of maturity where it can with confidence make recommendations to language teaching. For example, Tarone, Swain, and Fathman (1976, p. 19) remarked that "second language acquisition research is still in an infancy stage, and hence cannot yet provide the classroom teacher with the kind of valid and reliable guidelines needed to effect curriculum change." At about the same time, Hatch (1978, p. 140) made her famous comment that the findings of research either should not be applied at all, or if they are to be applied, we should do so "with caution." About a decade later, Lightbown (1985, p. 173) expressed the belief that SLA was still not in a position to offer teachers concrete guidance on what should be done in classrooms, although the field might be in a position to highlight some expectations for what teachers and learners can achieve through classroom instruction. Fifteen years later, Lightbown (2000, p. 452) noted that SLA research had established a robust compilation of findings that not only offered teachers guidance on what was achievable in classrooms but that the field could also "provide valuable clues to effective pedagogical practice." However, she once again echoed Hatch's admonition to apply with "caution." Even more recently Gass and Mackey (2007, p. 190) continued to worry about the application of the findings of research on the interactionist hypothesis to the classroom as potentially "premature."

A particularly revealing manifestation of the ambivalence toward the application of SLA research to classroom practice is documented in *TESOL Quarterly* (2007) where five SLA researchers debated the merits of the editorial policy of the journal at the time whereby its aim was to publish papers that contribute to bridging the theory and practice gap to the extent that practical submissions must be grounded in theory and theoretical articles much show their relevance for practice. Magnan (2007), then outgoing editor of the *Modern Language Journal*, remarked that she had revised the journal's editorial policy to encourage submissions that did not avow any "immediate pedagogical applications" (p. 401). Chapelle (2007) adopted the alternative view that strongly supported the stated policy of *TESOL Quarterly* (p. 405). Han (2007, p. 391) argued that "excessive concern" with trying to force a connection between empirical research and classroom practice when one is not clearly present could result in misplaced applications as well as failure to pursue interesting research because it does not have clear practical implications. For her part, Belcher (2007) adopted a more neutral stance that pointed to the theory and practice gap as reflected in the pedagogically oriented programs of the annual TESOL Convention (we would include the annual ACTFL Convention) and the strongly theory/research bias of AAAL conference programs. She did suggest, however, that given the high number of journals in applied linguistics today (approximately 50), authors should be able to identify an appropriate outlet for their research. According to Belcher (2007), for those wishing to submit to *TESOL Quarterly* they should recognize its editorial policy aimed at bridging the theory–practice gap early on in their research and well before the pedagogical implications of their work must be addressed (p. 399).

## What to Do About the Gap?

A number of solutions have been proposed to overcome the gap between theory/ research and practice. Some have been more radical than others. Among the more radical proposals is an early recommendation by Jakobovits and Gordon (1974) that surfaced even before the field of SLA was firmly established. They insisted that if teaching is to result in successful learning outcomes it must free itself from "the tyranny of irrelevant expertise," which they claimed understands virtually nothing about the "individual qualities" of teachers or their students (p. 85). Their criticism is directed at so-called basic research of the kind supported by Krashen and other early SLA scholars, and which represents one side of the gap. The authors, however, did not reject all research and instead called for an increase in applied classroom research. More than 30 years later, Allwright (2005, p. 27) adopted a less incendiary stance that nevertheless made the same point as Jakobovits and Gordon in his comment that academic research "is of negligible value to current classroom participants, who need their understandings now."

M. A. Clarke (1994) offered two suggestions for dealing with the gap, one of which meshed with Jakobovits and Gordon's position—for teachers to engage in "small actions" that resist the advice of experts "except on their own terms in order to solve problems of direct interest" to their practice (p. 18). The other suggestion was to invert the assumed researcher/practitioner hierarchy whereby teachers are on top with the experts and administrators below them and in their service (p. 18). Stewart (2006) proposed that another way to overcome the hegemony of the researcher, which is maintained even in proposals calling for collaborative research, is for teachers themselves to conduct classroom research for their own benefit and without concern for what is happening in so-called basic research (p. 425).

R. Ellis has had a long-standing concern regarding the theory/research–practice gap. In Ellis (1997) he reflected Hatch's (1978) recommendation to apply the findings of SLA research with caution because the field was still in a stage of "relative infancy" (p. 70). However, Ellis (2005b), continuing to espouse the view that SLA was "still a very young field of study" (p. 209), nevertheless asserted that it had "to bite the bullet and proffer advice" to language teachers, provided the advice be understood as "tentative" and "provisional" (p. 210). With the requisite caution, he offered a set of ten principles for teachers to reflect upon. The principles that are relevant for the current work are that "Instruction needs to be predominantly directed at developing implicit knowledge of the L2 while not neglecting explicit knowledge" (p. 214), that it "needs to take into account the learner's 'built-in syllabus'" (p. 216), and to be successful "instructed language learning requires extensive L2 input" (p. 217).

R. Ellis (2010) continued his efforts to connect SLA and language teaching, this time asserting that the field had finally achieved the status of "an established discipline" (p. 182) as attested by the existence of numerous graduate programs, journals, and conferences where research findings are presented, discussed, and passed on from one generation of scholars to the next. Reviewing past and current proposals to (re-)connect research and practice, he offered eleven principles for a graduate-level SLA course concerned with language teaching (presumably designed for teachers, teacher educators, and classroom researchers). These principles seem to be sensitive to some of the skepticism and resistance to basic SLA research reflected in the positions taken by Clarke, Stewart, and perhaps even Jakobovits and Gordon, as illustrated by the following sample: "The topics covered in an SLA course need to be demonstrably relevant to teaching" (p. 195); "The texts selected for an SLA course need to be comprehensible to teachers who lack technical knowledge about SLA" (p. 195); "Any proposals emanating from the SLA 'ideas' examined in the course or from the pedagogical implications of research articles should be viewed as 'provisional', to be evaluated in the light of teachers' own classrooms and experiences of learning and teaching an L2. This process of evaluation needs to be conducted explicitly" (p. 196).[1]

Long (2009) pointing out that while SLA is "(much) less developed" than fields such as medicine and engineering, it nevertheless has a responsibility to at least recommend best practices to teachers based on "what is known or thought to be known at the time" (p. 375). He provided a set of ten principles intended as "design features, motivated by theory and research findings ... which show them either to be necessary for SLA or facilitative of it" (p. 376). Some of Long's principles parallel those proposed by Ellis, including "respect 'learner syllabus'/ developmental processes" and "provide rich (not impoverished) input" (p. 387). The principles are intended to be implemented at "the classroom level" through a "potentially infinite range of pedagogic procedures" (p. 376).

In Chapters 5 through 8 we consider SCT research that addresses a subset of the principles proposed by R. Ellis and Long, respectively; specifically that instruction must be directed at implicit knowledge, that it must respect the learner's built-in syllabus that is presumed to guide development, and that it requires extensive input. Our immediate concern here is to respond to Ellis's (2010) misconstrual of the SCT perspective that the theory–practice gap is a result of the dualistic stance common in Western science and that the gap can be eliminated through a praxis-based orientation. Ellis (2010, p. 186) argued that the SCT position is ultimately untenable because the activity and interests of researchers diverges from the activity and interests of teachers in a fundamental way. According to Ellis (p. 186) academic theories (and presumably affiliated research) are explicit and framed in "technical language," while teacher theories are implicit, "action based," and derived from "practical knowledge." Ellis's assertion that there is "a world of difference between studying and acquiring technical knowledge and developing and using practical knowledge" (p. 184) makes a great deal of sense when the relationship between theory and practice is construed dualistically. The SCT position sustains however an approach wherein theory/research and practice do not constitute different discourses; rather, they are two sides of the same coin, not different coins. In other words, Kurt Lewin's laconic aphorism, alluded to by Ellis (2010, p. 186), that there is nothing as practical as a good theory, is but one side of a new kind of coin, in which the reverse side carries the following inscription: there is nothing more "theoretically rich than a good practice" (Stetsenko & Arievitch, 2004, p. 76).

The relationship between theory and practice can be reciprocal rather than a one-way street whereby theory informs, or is applied to, practice, but practice does not inform, or apply to, theory. In fact, from a praxis-based perspective, which is at the foundation of Vygotsky's theory, the relationship is cyclic: theory–practice–theory, etc. or indeed, practice–theory–practice, etc.

## Reconceptualizing Theory and Practice

The traditional understanding of theory is rooted in one strand of Greek philosophy that eventually came to dominate Western European thinking during the Enlightenment. The strand, espoused by Plato and Aristotle, postulated a fundamental distinction between mind and matter, neither of which had anything to do with the other (Novack, 1978, p. 402). Theory was conceived of as abstract ideal knowledge "derived mostly through contemplation," whereas practice was taken to mean concrete activity in the material world (Stetsenko & Vianna, 2009, p. 39). Theory was also seen as having virtually no practical relevance and practice was considered to have no role in advancing theory, which could only happen through pure, or basic, research (p. 39). Furthermore, priority was assigned to basic research with application to practical circumstances proceeding in a linear fashion once scientists had sufficient confidence in their findings, not unlike the situation in SLA described earlier.

However, an alternative conceptualization of knowledge and practice also emerged from Greek philosophy and it too had an impact on Enlightenment thought. At the end of the 6th century BC Heraclitus of Ephesus developed a philosophy which held the world to be in a constant state of flux consisting of the dialectical unity of opposing forces (Novack, 1978, p. 410). The two conflicting understandings of the world (dualistic vs. dialectical) were captured "in the positions on the problem of knowledge put forward by Spinoza and Hegel on the one hand and Hume and Kant on the other" (Novack, 1978, p. 273). Essentially, one approach, represented by Hume and Kant, sustained the Aristotelian schism between the material world and the ideal world epitomized in human thinking; the other, represented by Spinoza and Hegel, rejected the schism and argued instead for a world unified in diversity and transformed through "mutual contradictions" (Valsiner, 2012, p. 89). This is the essence of the materialist dialectic that Vygotsky relied on to formulate his scientific psychology.

As we will discuss in Chapter 2, Vygotsky, following Marx, and in contra-distinction to many of his contemporary Western European and North American colleagues (e.g., Piaget, Freud, Stern, Watson, Thorndike, Titchner), undertook to construct a psychology grounded in a dialectical understanding of the material world. His theory, discussed in Chapter 2, connects scientific knowledge with practical activity, as the two together "form inherent aspects (or dimensions) of one and the same process of people collaboratively engaging with their world" (Stetsenko & Vianna, 2009, p. 46). On this view, there is a "reciprocal link between human involvement in the making of scientific knowledge, including theory, and the sciences' involvement in the making of human life and history" (p. 41). This orientation to theory–practice unity, or praxis, was at the heart of Vygotsky's thinking and as such forms the foundation of what we call the *pedagogical imperative*, outlined in the following section and argued for throughout the book.

## The Pedagogical Imperative

The final two chapters of Lantolf and Thorne (2006) address the question of how the principles and concepts of SCT can be concretized in second language education. At the time, the vast majority of SCT-informed L2 research had used the theory as a lens through which to understand classroom interactions between teachers and students and between students (see Lantolf & Beckett, 2009). However, beginning with Negueruela's (2003) dissertation and Poehner's (2005) dissertation, SCT-L2 research began to engage in language instruction in accordance with the concepts and principles of the theory. Negueruela's work reported on an instructional program carried out in a university Spanish course where Vygotsky's notion of conceptual knowledge served as the primary unit of explicit instruction implemented in line with principles of Systemic Theoretical Instruction (STI) (see, Gal'perin, 1967, 1970, 1979; Haenen, 1996). Poehner's project extended the earlier work of Aljaafreh and Lantolf (1994) on the effect of mediation in the Zone of Proximal Development (ZPD). His research was conducted within a Dynamic Assessment (DA) framework where instruction and assessment interact as a seamless, dialectical, process to simultaneously diagnose and promote learner development.

Following the appearance of Negueruela's and Poehner's respective dissertations and relevant publications emanating from each study (e.g., Negueruela, 2008; Poehner, 2008b), an increasing number of dissertations, periodical publications, book chapters, edited volumes, and conference presentations have appeared in the SCT-L2 literature that have been directly or indirectly influenced by their original studies. This newly emerging research does not employ SCT as a theoretical lens to understand L2 learning and teaching; rather it undertakes to deploy specific principles and concepts of the theory in order to intentionally promote L2 development through appropriately organized instructional practice. The scope of the present work is to crystalize and synthesize the new approach to SCT-L2 research that emanates from a dialectical approach to theory and practice in a particular social context—the language classroom. We will focus exclusively on the consequences for learning of introducing concrete educational practices derived from the theory.

Interestingly, at about the same time that SCT-L2 research was beginning to concentrate on how to promote classroom language development, applied cognitive linguists also began to manifest a similar interest in exploring ways of bringing the theory to bear on classroom practice (see Tyler, 2012). Given that SCT, as a psychological theory, and cognitive linguistics, as a linguistic theory, both foreground the importance of meaning (rather than structure), we believe that it is worth considering how the theories might be integrated in the service of language education. This constitutes an additional goal of the present work and will be addressed in Chapters 5 and 6.

A further goal of the volume is to make the case once and for all that SCT is not a social or sociolinguistic theory. It is instead a theory that explains human psychology, including L2 development, as the dialectical unity of a biologically endowed brain functioning with socially generated forms of mediation that give rise to what Vygotsky called "higher" forms of thinking where humans deploy mediation appropriated through social activity to control (i.e., regulate) their mental functions. As Ratner (2012) argued, culture is not a variable factor to be correlated with psychology, nor is it an "add on" (p. 25) to psychology; it is the "impetus" (p. 89) for psychology. In other words, culture produces the human mind.

The new orientation to SCT-L2 research we refer to as *the pedagogical imperative*. The motivation for this will be more fully explained in Chapter 2, where we present in some detail Vygotsky's philosophical argument for proposing a unified approach to psychology. At this point, however, we point out that the term is intended to reflect Vygotsky's position that to be successful, psychology cannot be a science limited to observation of human psychological processes and their development, but it must become a science that takes seriously the obligation stated succinctly in Marx's *Eleventh Thesis on Feuerbach*: "The philosophers have only *interpreted* the world in various ways; the point is to *change* it" (Marx, 1978b, italics in original). Vygotsky argued that the true test of a science, including psychology, is determined by the extent to which the efforts of its adherents result in change. For this reason, Vygotsky directly participated in the educational reforms that were carried out during the years immediately following the Russian Revolution, which were unfortunately abandoned once Stalin assumed full control of the Soviet Government (see van der Veer & Valsiner, 1991).

For Vygotsky educational practice is a form of scientific research. It is the laboratory where the principles of the theory are to be tested. Unlike in dualistic science where failure to achieve success in practical real-world activity does not necessarily falsify the theory, Vygotsky, as we will discuss, argued that the ultimate test of a theory is to be found in the real world, where people engage in all of the various social activities sanctioned by their respective cultures, not in the experimental laboratory where variables are controlled and predictions are made on the link between dependent and independent variables. Widdowson (1990, p. 25), in his insightful work on language teaching, offered the following commentary on the issue of academic research and classroom practice: "experimental subjects are only partially real people" because experiments "induce" them "to behave in a certain way within the idealized limits of experimental control." Vygotsky's theory is interested in what people know and do when they are fully real people and this means being fully social.

## Overview of Sociocultural Theory

Although we present a detailed discussion of the relevant features of SCT for L2 education in the chapters that follow, we feel it is useful for the reader, especially for anyone not familiar with the theory, to offer an overview in the introductory chapter. The central principle of Vygotsky's theory is that human consciousness arises through the dialectical unity of our biologically endowed brain and "auxiliary stimuli" appropriated during participation in social practices. The stimuli enable us to intentionally control, or regulate, our mental functioning. They are most often arbitrary in the sense that they bear no direct connection to the process they are used to regulate. For example, in order to remember to do something, we may tie a string around one of our fingers, or to borrow an example from Gordon Wells (personal communication, October 20, 2012), we may drive a shovel into the ground to remember where to renew the planting of tomatoes in our garden when interrupted by a phone call. While these examples are relatively simple, they nevertheless make the point that humans can use such devices to influence our psychological and even our physical behavior. It is also important to note that all of these stimuli are human creations (i.e., cultural artifacts) that were originally designed for some other purpose; that is, strings and shovels are not for remembering. However, humans are able to purpose and repurpose our cultural creations in seemingly arbitrary ways (e.g., using a butter knife as a screwdriver), and one of these ways is to regulate through artificial means, our mental functioning. Another term used by Vygotsky to describe the capacity humans manifest to regulate not only themselves but each other is *mediation*. In fact, the self-regulatory capacity is derived from the capacity to regulate, or mediate, others as well as to be mediated by others.

Auxiliary stimuli that are more complex and more powerful means of mediation are comprised of symbols, diagrams, numbers, music, art, and the like. These are all human creations and all can be used to mediate our mental and physical behavior. Consider for example the use of drumbeats to regulate marching of military personnel, and jazz music to mediate the movements of a couple engaged in dance. Diagrams are frequently used by scientists, architects, and engineers to model an object of interest (e.g., atom, solar system), to design buildings, or plan an electric grid for a city. Art, whether verbal (e.g., poetry) or visual (e.g., painting), as Vygotsky showed in his dissertation (Vygotsky, 1971), can evoke, or regulate, powerful human emotions. Numbers are used in a wide array of daily and scientific life to mediate how we think and act ranging from carpenters measuring pieces of lumber, to assessing profits and losses of stock market investments, to measuring mental aptitude and language proficiency.

The most pervasive and powerful of human symbolic creations is language, and it is language, as the quintessential human signification system, that Vygotsky situated at the heart of his psychological theory. He reasoned that through the meaning making and meaning communication system that we use to mediate the thinking and behavior of con-specifics (Tomasello, 1999) during social interaction, we also mediate our own thinking. The principle Vygotsky proposed to capture this process of mediation through linguistic means is *signification*—the process of regulating our mental activity through the use of signs (Vygotsky, 1997b, p. 59). In other words, although the human brain is equipped to attend to, perceive, and remember objects and events in the world, and to impel or inhibit our actions in the world, through the creation of sign-based auxiliary stimuli we are able to voluntarily control these activities in far more effective ways than is possible by any other life form. Voluntary attention, perception, and memory, along with the intentional will to act or not, taken together, comprise the higher functional system of human consciousness (Vygotsky, 1997b, p. 59).

## Illustrating the Theory

### Concepts and Development

The first illustration of the theory is based in large part on Vygotsky's writings on conceptual knowledge. Human cultures create categories for organizing events and objects in the world. These categories, or concepts, are by and large represented in linguistic signs passed on from one speaker to another and from one generation to the next. (To be sure, as signs circulate in social interaction they can be modified both in form and in meaning; however, we leave this matter aside for the time being.) As children are brought into their culture through interactions with parents and other members of relevant social classes they appropriate the concepts of their particular social group. According to Vygotsky (1987), when children initially appropriate a word such as *flower* in English they do not imbue it with the same meanings that the word carries for adults. At first they assume that the word refers only to specific concrete manifestations of the botanical category. In other words, children are not able to distinguish between flowers and roses, in the way adults are. For adults, while flower can indeed be used to refer to a specific member of the category, as in the utterance "there is a flower on the table" (where the adult does not feel it necessary to profile the specific member of the category, say a rose), for children flower is the label for rose and for daisy and for tulip, not as members of the category but as discrete entities that are all called by the same name. What the child needs to develop as they grow up is the realization that flower is a superordinate culturally created concept that includes roses, tulips, daisies, etc. Once this realization occurs, children are able to perceive roses, tulips, etc. as manifestations of the category flower. In terms of the natural world, flowers as such, do not exist. What exist are discrete concrete entities. Human culture through human language creates categories that endow us with greater flexibility in our dealings with the natural world. In other words, at times we treat roses, tulips, and the like as flowers and at other times we treat them as separate instantiations of the category, depending on our specific intentions.

Vygotsky's point is that not only do we operate on the world according to the categories offered by our cultures, we also perceive and therefore think about the world according to those same categories. Thus, in what he at times called the "cultural development" of children (Vygotsky, 1987), their perceptions of the world are shaped by the categories made available to them as they appropriate their language and as a consequence develop their psychology. On this view, cultures with different conceptual categories should be expected to perceive and therefore think about the world differently from other cultures (this also applies to social groups within a particular culture, see Ratner, 2012). Indeed, Vygotsky argued in his writings on the development of perception that once children appropriate the conceptual system of a culture, perception loses its zoo-logical character and becomes "historical"; that is, it takes on the qualities of mediated adult perception whereby it is restructured as "verbalized perception" (Vygotsky, 1999, p. 29). In other words, perception (as are attention and memory) is restructured through cultural means and takes on a "mediated character" (p. 31).

Luria and Vygotsky (1992, p. 63) point out that many indigenous languages of Australia have no words for superordinate categories such as tree, fish, or bird and instead use words that refer specifically to each species of each category. While children in European communities eventually learn not only to talk but to think in terms of superordinate groupings such as "trees," "fish," and "birds," indigenous children in Australia learn to talk and think about particular species of tree, fish, and bird. In other words, while visual biology enables members of Australian and European communities to see the same woody objects growing out of the earth their culturally organized minds push them to perceive different categories of objects: trees in one case and specific species of tree in another.

## Vygotsky and Whorf

Although Vygotsky's theory of the human psyche stated that the creation and use of signs was the species-specific vehicle through which people organized themselves socially and psychologically, the kinds of signs people create at the micro-level, and how, when, and for what purpose they use them, "is historically unique" (Valsiner, 2012, p. 161).Vygotsky recognized the importance of postulating a universal law regarding signs and the need to investigate the concrete impact of the law at the local (i.e., group and individual) level.

The reader will recognize Vygotsky's position as tantamount to a Whorfian orientation on thinking, which of course it is. However, we do not believe that Vygotsky espoused what is often taken as the "strong version" of the Whorfian stance. For Vygotsky, education, when properly organized (as we will discuss in Chapters 3 and 4), can indeed alter our conceptual systems in profound ways. On this view, education is not merely a matter of acquiring new knowledge (i.e., learning); rather it is a new process of development that results in new ways of conceptualizing the world. Luria's (1976) research with educated and non-educated Uzbek adults carried out under Vygotsky's guidance, as well as more recent cross-cultural research by Scribner and Cole (1981) and Tulviste (1991), support this view of education as a developmental process. It also demonstrates that while culture mediates thinking, it does not determine it once and for all.

In our view, Vygotsky's thinking here concurs with what Agar (1994) calls "languaculture," his term to capture the unity of language and culture that was torn asunder by Saussure in linguistics and by Wundt in psychology. Agar, using an agricultural metaphor, suggests that while languacultures create furrows, which shape and restrict our view of reality, it is possible with some effort to extricate ourselves from the furrows and appropriate alternative ways of conceptualizing the world created by other languacultures. A similar view is espoused by Slobin (1996, 2003) in his "thinking for speaking" hypothesis, which holds that the conceptual categories of a language (e.g., how motion events are organized) influence a speaker's thinking during on-line speaking activity, a weaker version of the Whorfian perspective.

## Planning

As the human mind emerges during ontogenesis, children develop the all-important adult capacity to plan their own mental and physical behavior. According to Vygotsky, this ability is organized and regulated primarily through the use of signs. A plan can be complex, detailed, and fully externalized as in the case of an architect's blueprint for a building, or it can be fairly simple, vague, and constructed completely on the mental plane, as when someone decides how they want to respond to an interlocutor's utterance. To be sure, even in the case of the architect's blueprint, much of the planning takes place on the mental plane or between the mental plane and the physical plane of paper and pencil or computer; however, the external artifacts, or auxiliary stimuli, that the architect uses are themselves components of the thinking process. They have psychological status (see Lantolf & Thorne, 2006). It is not the objects, as objects, that have this status; rather it is their use, their involvement in the activity of planning a building, that is imbued with psychological qualities.

Luria's (1982) research showed that planning is not a capacity that emerges all at once in children; rather it develops over time as speaking gradually expands from its original interactive social function to include a private psychological function. A crucial feature of planning is the timing of the integration of speaking into a particular activity. Luria demonstrated that the planning process develops through a series of phases where a child's behavior is first regulated by someone else's (usually a parent's) plan. Eventually, as the psychological function of speech emerges, children are able to plan and direct their own behavior through auxiliary means. For this to happen, however, requires that the timing relationship between speaking and acting be properly sequenced. At first children act and then describe what they have done after the fact. To plan necessitates a shift whereby speaking precedes acting, as this enables the person to formulate a plan; but this also requires the ability to use auxiliary stimuli to inhibit action until a plan is developed, something children have a difficult time doing.

## Social Interaction

Sign-based mediation does not arise from nowhere. It arises from the interactions that occur in the social relationships that are the *sine-qua-non* of human life. As we will discuss in more detail in Chapter 2, social relationships are culturally organized at both a macro and micro level of granularity. The macro level includes specific institutional arrangements that include education, work, religion, family, leisure activity, political organizations (e.g., government structures, political parties), legal systems, economic structure, etc. (see Ratner, 2012). The macro-level structures shape the kinds of social interactions that occur at the micro level. For example, while conversations are considered micro-level social activities, how they are conducted is constrained by the macro-level structural framework in which they occur. Thus, a conversation in a tavern between friends is a very different kind of conversation from what occurs in a classroom between a teacher and students. Both of these are different from conversations that occur in families, religious organizations, or political systems.

In Chapter 7, we will focus on conversations that occur in educational settings and consider how they relate to, and influence, learning. Vygotsky (1978) recognized that particular types of conversations are especially effective at promoting the development of students. He tried to capture this in the concept of the *ZPD*—a social relationship conducted largely through language in which individuals undertake to help other individuals to appropriate and gain control over available forms of mediation in the service of mental and emotional growth. Although schools are not the only cultural institutions in which the ZPD is relevant, Vygotsky stressed its importance in this setting because, he argued, education promotes a special and vital type of development that expands and even changes the understandings children develop of the world prior to entering school.

Vygotsky makes an important distinction between the kind of knowledge children have access to in the everyday world and the knowledge available in more structured macro-cultural institutions, in particular, education. As children are integrated into their social communities, they appropriate the knowledge (usually empirically grounded) of those communities. Our vision and our language tell us the sun rises in the east, moves across the sky, and sets in the west. Science, appropriated in school, tells us something quite different. Once this happens, it changes our psychological perspective of reality. Although in this case it does not change the language we use in our everyday life to talk about the sun and earth, it does affect the meaning of the terms we use to describe the circadian cycle. The rising and setting sun are no longer literal but metaphorical concepts.

The function of educational activity is to modify the understandings students have upon entering school and change them so they align with the best scientific knowledge available at any given time in human history. In Chapters 5 and 6 we focus on the relevance of conceptual knowledge for language development in educational activity and in Chapters 7 and 8 we address the details of how the ZPD figures into language education.

## Note

1   If and how the eleven principles proposed by R. Ellis (2010) relate to the principles given in Ellis (2005b) is unclear. It could be that the early set of ten principles is intended to provide the content of the SLA course; Ellis makes no mention of this possibility.

# 2

# SOCIOCULTURAL THEORY AND THE DIALECTIC OF PRAXIS

## An Alternative to the Theory/Research–Practice Gap

Most people familiar with the work of L. S. Vygotsky have at least a passing acquaintance with his most widely cited publication *Thinking and Speech* (Vygotsky, 1987). This volume, published in its original Russian version in 1934, discusses and synthesizes research focusing on what have become the well-known constructs and principles of his theory of human consciousness (e.g., mediation, concept development, word meaning, imitation, egocentric and inner speech, ZPD). As important as this work is, it is arguably an earlier work, with the English title *The Historical Meaning of the Crisis in Psychology: A Methodological Investigation* (Vygotsky, 2004/1926), that established the theoretical and methodological foundation for Vygotksy's approach to psychology. Although written sometime between 1926 and 1927, the manuscript did not appear in print until the Russian edition of his collected works was published in 1982 (Rieber & Robinson, 2004, p. 222). According to Veresov (1999, p. 145), *The Crisis*, as it is usually abbreviated, is one of Vygotsky's "most important and most significant works." In it Vygotsky identifies the nature and origins of the crisis and proposes a way of resolving it.

Vygotsky's response to the crisis and its implications for developmental education are derived from a Marxist theory of historical materialism. Although works such as Lantolf and Thorne (2006) have discussed the connection between Vygotsky's psychology and Marxist theory to a limited degree, the case has not been made as forcefully as it should be. As a result, we believe that Vygotsky's theory of higher mental functions tends to be viewed through the dualistic lens that dominates Western approaches to psychology. Evidence for this is seen in R. Ellis's (2010) reaction to the SCT perspective on the theory–practice gap mentioned in Chapter 1. When theory and practice are dichotomized the perception that researchers and practitioners operate in different discursive worlds is not surprising. Moreover, applied linguists continue to see SCT as a social or even sociolinguistic theory rather than as a psychological or even psycholinguistic theory, as intended by Vygotsky. For instance, in many of the recent handbooks on applied linguistics and SLA, the chapter on SCT is usually included under the heading of social approaches, or language in context (see Gass & Mackey, 2012). To our knowledge it is never grouped with chapters on "psycholinguistic" approaches to SLA, despite the fact that Lantolf and Thorne (2006, p. 6), following Leontiev (1981, p. 99), characterize the theory as third generation psycholinguistics, concerned with the relationship between communication and psychological processes.

To make the case that Vygotsky's theory is a psychological and not a social theory and that SCT-L2 is a psycholinguistic theory we first provide an overview of the crisis and Vygotsky's response to it. In so doing we explicate the principles of Marxist theory that Vygotsky drew on to build his psychology, including dialectics, praxis, and the central role of culture and social activity in the formation of consciousness. In addition we incorporate the recent neo-Vygotskian work of Ratner (2002, 2006, 2012) and Stetsenko (Stetsenko, 2010; Stetsenko & Arievitch, 2004; Stetsenko & Vianna, 2009) to flesh out the implications of Vygotsky's theory for developmental education.

## Vygotsky's Response to the Crisis: A Unified Psychology

By the 1920s, psychology had bifurcated into two "separate and independent sciences" (Vygotsky, 1997a, p. 7). How much responsibility for the split can be laid at Wundt's doorstep remains to be determined (see Cole, 1996). It is, nevertheless, the case that two of Wundt's major publications, if nothing else, fortified the wall between two distinct approaches to the study of the human psyche. In his 1904 work, *Principles of Physiological Psychology* (1904a), Wundt undertook to create a scientific rather than a philosophical approach to the study of human con-sciousness. Recognizing that the stuff of science is material he established a set of methodological principles, the application of which would allow psychologists to uncover the physiological substrates of consciousness through proper experi-mental (i.e., reaction to various stimuli) procedures. In 1904 Wundt (1904b) published the inaugural volume of what would become a ten-volume work, *Völkerpsychologie* (*Ethnic/Social Psychology*), in which he "recognized that certain forms of cognition, emotion, and behavior are oriented to the represented cognition, emotion, and behavior of members of social groups ... e.g., other family members, Democrats, Catholics, bankers, or gang members" (Greenwood, 2003, p. 70). Consequently, Wundt legitimized social formations such as language, religion, mythology, customs, law, and art as constituting objects of study for a second branch of psychology. Aside from a challenge raised by Greenwood (2003), historians of psychology have generally agreed that Wundt considered the comparative-historical method as the appropriate research methodology for the second psychology rather than experimentation.

Vygotsky (1997a, p. 304) described one of the opposing branches of psychology as idealistic, intentional, or "understanding psychology" and concerned with the spirit (*Geist*) and the other as materialistic, causal, or explanatory. Representatives of the first branch include Dilthey, Freud, and Husserl, while the second include Pavlov, Watson, and Titchener, among others. Essentially, the first approach to psychology reduced mental processes to social factors and the second reduced them to purely material bodily reactions (Valsiner & van der Veer, 2000). The problem was how to reconcile the two branches, each comprised of subfields with their own viewpoint, explanatory principles, and research methodologies, into a single psychology that maintained a legitimate claim to scientific standards (Vygotsky, 1997a, p. 284).

Psychologists, recognizing the crisis, proposed three solutions to the problem: do nothing and allow the field to continue in crisis mode; create an eclectic psychology that cobbled together features from the various subdisciplines according to the interests of particular researchers without concern for potential contradictions; create a new psychology based on a politically motivated selection of quotes from Marx's writings. Vygotsky rejected all three options. Instead he undertook to build a materialist psychology that drew from Marxist principles rather than discovering it "ready-made in the haphazard psychological statements of the founders of Marxism" (1997a, p. 312). Instead, he wanted "to learn from Marx's whole method how to build a science, how to approach the investigation of the mind" (p. 331).

Dialectical materialism maintains that dialectical principles operate in all three domains of nature: the physical world, the social world, and the world of human consciousness. However, it also recognizes that each of these domains is subject to its own laws, principles, and categories and therefore requires intermediary theories to fully understand and explain the object of study. For example, in the physical domain biology operates with concepts such as cells, amino acids, molecules and genes; processes such as osmosis, action potential, and binary fission; and laws such as mass action and absolute fitness. In the social domain Marx and Engels operated with such concepts as use value, exchange value, surplus value, class, commodity, capital, means of production, private property; processes such as relations of production, wage labor, alienation, and technological progress; and laws such as the law of value, the law of labor power, and the accumulation of capital. Vygotsky proposed to overcome the crisis in psychology by building an intermediary theory of scientific psychology that sought to uncover how dialectical principles functioned in the domain of human consciousness. He argued, however, that just as theories of the physical and social domains require their own concepts, laws, and principles, these are also needed in psychology to explain humans' ability to use symbols to mediate their psyche (Mahn, 2009, p. 307). Vygotsky understood that he could not accomplish his task by relying only on Marx's concepts and principles; he therefore also drew from the work of scholars such as Piaget, Baldwin, Janet, Stern, Sapir, and others to formulate the domain-specific aspects of his theory. We have outlined these in Chapter 1 and will have more to say about them in the chapters that follow. For now, we limit our dis-cussion to general laws of dialectical materialism, which form the foundation of Vygotsky's psychology.

## Materialism and Dialectics

### Materialism

As we pointed out in Chapter 1, materialism has as long a history in Western philosophy as does idealism. However, there can be little doubt that idealism, which originated in the writings of Plato, has had a broader impact on Western thinking, particularly since the time of the Enlightenment. The basis of idealism is Plato's distinction between forms, which are universal and timeless, and extensions of these forms that we encounter in the world (Boivin, 2008, p. 14). The task of philosophy is to discern the universal forms as the ultimate source of what we perceive in the concrete world. Since we cannot perceive the universal forms directly, we must use rational thought to gain access to the eternal forms. Given that this thought is directly accessible to us, it is considered to have "more reality than things" (p. 15). Thus, idealism "subordinates nature to mind/spirit" (Novack, 1978, p. 119) and as such it is "the essence of reality" (p. 336). What defines humans from other life forms under idealism is our capacity to symbolize (through language and other systems) and to create "a unique cultural order" (Boivin, 2008, p. 15).

Descartes, perhaps the most influential idealist thinker of the Enlightenment, argued that the mind and the world are comprised of distinct substances. The substance of mind is thought and the substance of the world is matter that is extended in space. Given this essential distinction between mind and world, Descartes wondered how it would be possible for humans to know the world with certainty. Even use of mathematical models left room for doubt regarding explanations of natural phenomena, because, for one thing, mathematics, like ordinary language, is a human creation (Bakhurst, 1991, p. 204). Kant's response to Descartes's mind–world conundrum was to assert that humans could at least know the world as it appears to us filtered through preexisting mental categories, a proposal that does not ameliorate Cartesian skepticism (p. 196).

Although "the highest expression" of materialism is dialectical materialism (Novack, 1978, p. 119), it is helpful to begin the discussion with a definition of materialism itself as a contrasting position to idealism. According to Novack (p. 119), *materialism* is the philosophical position that nature, "based on matter in motion, has a self-sufficient existence" and that "everything in human life [culture, society, thinking] is derived from and dependent upon the objective world." Thus, nature is objective and exists prior to, and independent from, humans.

Marxism, as a materialist philosophy, begins from the position that material reality exists with or without humans and humans as such are part of reality.

Importantly, thinking is not a process in which "people passively receive sensations and preceptor mirror images of objects" (Novack, 1978, p. 129). This is because humans are neither spectators of the world nor reactors to stimuli, as in the case of animals; they are "doers, inquirers, and strugglers who engage in labor and other practical activities directed by their ideas, and who have developed their conceptual equipment in accord with changing historical circumstances and social relationships" (p. 129). Moreover, the brain more or less accurately reflects the objective world; if it did not provide humans with "reliable information about the phenomena, conditions and laws of reality, the process of cognition would be worse than useless; it would have no practical value in orienting us to what is happening or in dealing with difficult situations and changing them" (p. 129).

Vygotsky (1997a, pp. 327–328) explained the connection between reality and thinking using a mirror analogy, which had been used by other psychologists, but which he modified to suit his particular project. The reflection of a table in a mirror generates an image of the table. The question Vygotsky posed is how many of the three "objects" mentioned in this sentence, table, mirror, image, are real? According to Vygotsky, an idealist response would include all three objects, the mirror, the table, and the image, although the image would be comprised of a different substance from the table and mirror. For Vygotsky, however, the image is not real, but ideal—one cannot, for example, place books on the image of a table. What is material, and therefore real, is the refraction of light waves in the mirror; thus, there are indeed three material entities involved in the statement— the table, the mirror, and the movement of light—all three of which exist independent of the image. Vygotsky points out that a science of mirror images, as such, is not possible, but a science of light and "the things which cast and reflect it" is (p. 327).

Although there is clearly a place for the ideal in materialist theory, it is not a separate substance. It is a reflection of material object-oriented activity of humans in their equally material brain that is "consistent with the form of the thing outside the head, outside the brain" (Ilyenkov, 2012, p. 162). Said another way, the ideal is the image of material human activity and objects in the world reflected by the material brain. However, the mirror analogy can only take us so far, because the brain is not a "stamping machine" that merely duplicates its object, as happens in (perfect) mirrors; it actively processes human activity in and on the material world.

However, materialism recognizes that brains as such do not think, people think. Indeed, the relationship between humans and brains is the same as between humans and hands: work is done not *by* the hand but *with* the hand and thinking is done not *by* the brain but *with* the brain (Ilyenkov, 2012, p. 162). Just as the hand is the material, anatomical tool, par excellence, that enables humans to engage in physical labor in the world, the brain is "the material, anatomical-physiological organ of this labor, mental labor, that is to say, intellectual labor" (p. 162). The product of this special labor is precisely the ideal.

Materialism offers a way out of the mind–body dualistic conundrum. It rejects the idea that the mind and the body are two different objects comprised of different substances, but are instead "one single object, which is the thinking body of living, real man [sic]" (Ilyenkov, 1977, p. 31). Although the single object can be observed and studied from two different perspectives (body or mind), it does not follow that two separate and distinct objects are involved—"thought lacking a body and a body lacking thought" (p. 31.) Thinking is not a reality that exists independently of the physical body, but is instead a mode of existence of the body itself. Just as the mode of action of the legs is walking, the mode of action of the human body is thinking (p. 35). Given that the human body is essentially composed of the same material as the objects about which it thinks, there is no basis for the Cartesian skepticism.

Moreover, humans do not act as isolated beings; rather, they are "entwined in a net of social relations, always mediated by material objects, created by man [sic] for man [sic]" (Ilyenkov, 2012, p. 162). Accordingly, in the absence of the nexus of social relations humans are no more capable of thinking than is "a brain isolated from the human body" (1977, p. 252). Thus, acting in the world, unlike in the Cartesian ontology, is not the *result* of thinking (an exclusively 'inside the head' mental activity), but is an intimate component of the thinking process itself (p. 171). In other words, for Ilyenkov as for Marx, an acting human body is a thinking body. This now prepares us for a discussion of dialectics and dialectical materialism.

## Dialectics

Materialism, as espoused by thinkers such as Feuerbach, held that humans, as material beings, are the products of the material conditions in which they are raised and live, and that if these conditions change humans subsequently change. Feuerbach said nothing about how the conditions themselves change. Marx, however, fused Feuerbach's materialist perspective with Hegel's dialectical logic, but which he turned on its head, and in so doing was able to show that humans, unlike any other living species, through (goal oriented) socially organized practical activity, create and change the material conditions in which they live and in so doing change themselves. Marx expressed this argument succinctly in *Theses on Feuerbach* (Marx, 1978b, pp. 144–145).

The concept of dialectics in Western culture originates in Greek philosophy, and in particular with Heraclitus, as we mentioned in Chapter 1. Perhaps its most famous instantiation among the Greeks, however, was in the so-called Socratic dialogue, the purpose of which was not for one interlocutor to persuade the other that only one viewpoint was correct, nor was it to point out the flaws in the other's argument; it was to establish truth through a synthesis of opposing points of view.[1] While dialectic reasoning occurs in a variety of cultural traditions, our concern is with the specific form it took in Marxist theory as historical materialism, and eventually in Vygotsky's materialist psychology.

The dialectical laws that operate in nature were not invented by Hegel; rather they were they uncovered by him through close analysis of processes of movement and change (Mahn, 2009, p. 305). These laws include the following: change of quantity into quality, development through contradiction, negation of negation, conflict of content and form, and interruption of continuity (see Mahn, 2009, pp. 305–306). Marx and Engels integrated the dialectic laws that Hegel uncovered with Feuerbach's materialism and extended them to the analysis of human society, history, and consciousness.

## An Example

At this juncture, it is useful to introduce an admittedly simple, but what we believe to be an effective, example of how dialectic principles operate. Consider a fairly simple-looking object—a pencil with a sharpened point at one end and an eraser at the other. As an object, or more appropriately, a socially created technical tool, it is completely without value. Its value resides in the use that humans make of it; that is, its value is derived from the fact that it is used for the activity of writing (and perhaps drawing)—the creation of symbolic texts. In creating such texts, humans do not merely convert (i.e., objectivize) their preformed ideas into entities that are simultaneously symbolic and objective/physical, they also form their ideas through the dialectical interaction of mind, hand, pencil, and paper (inspiration for this analysis comes from John-Steiner & Mahn, 1996). However, to achieve this act of creation, most people use both ends of the pencil—the pointed end to create symbolic marks and the eraser end to eradicate (i.e., negate) the marks and replace them (using the pointed end again) with other marks—negation of negation. This activity continues until writers feel their expressive/communicative intent has been met. A pencil, then, is a dialectical tool that enables humans to generate meaningful texts by creating, eliminating, and recreating objective material symbols.

Another important aspect of dialectical principles illustrated in the pencil example is what Hegel referred to in the German term *Aufhebung*—a concept which does not have a good English equivalent. Its meaning is in fact dialectic in that it conveys a sense of removal or rejection but at the same time preserving or saving something of what has been removed (see Vygotsky, 1997b, p. 81). When we create texts, we produce and remove symbols from the page, but when we remove what had been previously created we normally do not start the process from scratch; rather, we build upon what had been there before. We preserve traces of what we had originally produced and partially removed. Hence, a key component of dialectical processes is development through generation and removal/rejection with preservation. Consider Marx's (1978a, p. 230) example of biological and cultural hunger: "the hunger gratified by cooked meat eaten with a knife and fork is a different hunger from that which bolts down raw meat with the aid of hand, nail and tooth." The former is a cultural hunger mediated by, among other things, the production–consumption process and the other is a biologically driven instinctual hunger typical of brute animals. In humans, the biological need to consume calories in order to sustain life remains but is controlled and reshaped by cultural processes. The notion of *Aufhebung* fulfills a key role in Vygotsky's psychology. For instance, as he points out in *Thinking and Speech* (Vygotsky, 1987), human consciousness is built upon the foundation of biological mental processes that are retained but restructured by culture in the creation of higher mental functions.

In addition to the use value of a pencil in the activity of producing a text, we can also consider the creation of the tool itself from a dialectical perspective. The tool is simultaneously a natural object, comprised of wood, graphite, and rubber, and a social object, consisting of the objectification of a human idea imposed on natural material through planned activity in the service of a human need. Therefore, the ideal does not exist only in the head of the individual(s) who constructed the pencil but in the pencil itself. That is, the pencil came into existence through the integration of two contrary activities, one ideal and the other practical, which objectified the ideal and made it real. The ideal is then given significance through the object as it is "incorporated into our life activity in a certain way," but this significance includes "not a single atom of the tangible physical substance that possesses it" (Bakhurst, 1991, p. 182). In other words, it is not the object as such that has value, it is the use to which the object is put that imbues it with value and significance. Marx (1978a, p. 229, italics in original) asserted that "a garment becomes a real garment only in the act of being worn; a house where no one lives is in fact not a real house; thus the product, unlike a mere natural object, proves itself to be, *becomes*, a product only through consumption." This distinction shows up in Voloshinov's (1973) approach to linguistic analysis whereby sentences are analogous to unworn garments, while utterances are real products because they are garments that are worn. Bakhurst (1991, p. 186) cogently captured this important point with regard to language when he stated that "a symbol plucked from the real process of exchange between social beings and nature, stops being a symbol ... its soul vanishes from its body."

## Psychological Materialism

To highlight its materialist foundation Vygotsky referred to his theory as psychological materialism. At other times, depending on which aspects of the theory he wished to emphasize, he used terminology such as cultural psychology, cultural-historical psychology, and sociocultural psychology. The concepts, principles, and laws that Vygotsky incorporated into the domain-specific theory include mediation, inner and egocentric speech, signification, conceptual knowledge, ZPD, internalization, imitation, psychological predicate/subject, and genetic method.

Vygotsky proposed that a materialist psychology seeks to explain the precise nature of the relationship between brain, body, human practical activity, and consciousness. To carry out this project, he recognized the need to establish a unit of analysis. For Vygotsky this unit is provided by language, or rather in Marxian terms, *languaging*,[2] an activity that is simultaneously material (acoustic waves and neuronal connections in the brain) and symbolic (i.e., it has conceptual content determined by the activity of humans in their natural habitat—society).

Language is an appropriate unit because of its bi-directional quality; that is, it is outwardly directed as social speech at influencing other members of society and it is inwardly directed as private or inner speech (i.e., dialogue with the self) at influencing one's own psychological activity. On this view, language mediates thinking in the same way that human hands coupled with physical tools mediate human activity in the world of objects. Mahn (2009, p. 304) points out that an extremely important quote on the relationship between language and consciousness from Marx's *The German Ideology* is missing from the English translation of *Thinking and Speech*. According to Mahn, Soviet censors removed the quotation marks in the 1934 original Russian version of the work in order to attribute to Vygotsky rather than to Marx what was at the time "deemed" to be an "unMarxist" understanding of human consciousness.[3] Because the quote reflects Vygotsky's own position, we cite it in full here:

> Language is as old as consciousness, language *is* practical consciousness, that exists also for other men, and for that reason alone it really exists for me personally as well; language, like consciousness, only arises from the need, the necessity, of intercourse with other men. . . . Consciousness is, therefore, from the very beginning a social product, and remains so as long as men exist at all.
>
> *(Marx & Engels, 1978, p. 158, italics in original)*

## The Dialectics of Brain and Culture

Vygotsky understood that the human brain, as a natural biological organ, comes endowed with natural mental capacities—involuntary memory, attention, and perception, along with connections to sensory input systems (e.g., vision, audition, olfaction, etc.), which provide direct access to the material world, along the lines of other higher forms of animal life. During infancy, the relationship between humans and the environment is generally unidirectional; that is, reactive. As children mature and are gradually brought into their culture by caretakers (e.g., parents, siblings, other relatives, peers, teachers, etc.), they appropriate cultural forms of mediation, most especially signification. Signification refers to culturally created artifacts that carry meaning and are used as artificial auxiliary stimuli to regulate the behavior of others and the self. These stimuli also create "new connections in the brain" (Vygotsky, 1997b, p. 55). Consequently, "culture creates special forms of behavior, it modifies the activity of mental functions, it constructs new superstructures in the developing system of human behavior" (p. 18). This formed the basis of Vygotsky's (p. 55) "new regulatory principle of behavior, a new concept of determinacy of human reaction which consists of the fact that man [sic] creates connections in the brain from outside, controls the brain and through it, his own body."[4]

Human thinking is comprised then of two sets of interconnected structures: the first is dependent on the biology of the brain; the second comprises higher and more complex structures arising from cultural development of the person. It is important to point out that the concept of *Aufhebung*, introduced earlier in the chapter, comes into play in Vygotsky's proposal. Recall that the term entails what appear to be two contradictory processes: simultaneous rejection/removal and saving. Cultural development does not mean that biological processes are completely rejected; instead they are the basis on which the higher voluntary structures are built. For example higher (voluntary) memory is intentionally remembering through the use of signs in which a temporal connection is created in the brain "using an artificial combination of stimuli" (Vygotsky, 1997b, p. 59). Nevertheless, eidetic memory is still available as for example happens when one experiences a particularly salient event, such as winning the lottery. Under such circumstances people often remember where they were, who they were with, what they were wearing, etc. when they received the potentially life-changing news. One does not have to try to voluntarily remember the event. On the other hand, as one of the present authors was in the process of writing the current chapter, he often found it necessary to write down on scraps of paper in almost shopping-list format the ideas he wanted to include in the discussion. He then rehearsed and expanded upon these in his thinking throughout the day in order not to forget. The same occurs with regard to attention, where we can intentionally prepare ourselves to attend to a particular upcoming sequence in a musical composition, or to particular linguistic features in a spoken or written text, etc. On the other hand, when we hear a sudden loud noise we do not normally tell ourselves to pay attention. Our natural reflex kicks in and we involuntarily focus our attention to locate the source of the noise.

Although humans everywhere by virtue of biological evolution come equipped with more or less the same natural mental capacities, they do not share the same social relationships and cultural forms of mediation. All cultures share a capacity to create and use symbol systems, including language, to create and share tools, and to create and live in social organizations. These capacities provide the basis for reorganizing and asserting intentional control over nature and our biology, including the brain. However, it is also the case that not all cultures and social groups within cultures create and share the same symbolic systems, tools, or social organizations. While all human societies communicate with each other through language, the meanings they create and make available to individual members of their respective communities are not the same.

Materialist psychology, according to Vygotsky, has three general goals: to distinguish natural from voluntary psychological processes, to understand the psychological differences that emerge across different sociocultural communities and how these differences developed over the course of history, and to understand how thinking develops in individual members of sociocultural communities over the course of the person's life history.

## Research Methodology

To carry out the research agenda of materialist psychology, Vygotsky required a new research methodology. Here it is important to distinguish the overarching methodological approach required for analysis in all domains addressed by the theory and specific research methods that could be implemented in each domain. In this regard we quote one of the most important passages in Vygotsky's writings:

> The search for method becomes one of the most important problems of the entire enterprise of understanding the uniquely human forms of psychological activity. In this case, the method is simultaneously prerequisite and product, the tool and the result of the study.
>
> (Vygotsky, 1978, p. 65, italics in original)

Vygotsky based his analytical methodology for a materialist psychology on principles of dialectical materialism. As a first principle he proposed that analysis must be genetic (i.e., historical), because only through a historical analysis was it possible to disentangle the two sources of human thinking: biology and culture. He further argued that analysis must seek to uncover the processes rather than the product of thinking, and it must be explanatory in seeking out causes (i.e., origins) rather than descriptions of the processes. Given the historical orientation of Vygotsky's methodological proposal, he believed it was inappropriate to study mental processes in fully formed adult thinking, because the biological and cultural strands have become blurred (Vygotsky, 1978, p. 62). For example, he (p. 64) pointed out that by studying attention when fully formed in adults, one could erroneously conclude that voluntary and involuntary attention function the same way and emerge from the maturation of the biological process alone. Only in genetic analysis can the origin and cause of a process be revealed. Thus, paralleling Marx in his analysis of human society, Vygotksy proposed that the general methodological approach for materialist psychology had to be historical or genetic in its orientation, which means to analyze the process as it changes, because in "movement" a phenomenon reveals its nature and this is "the dialectical method's basic demand" (p. 65).

Historical movement (i.e., dialectical development) is a complex process "characterized by periodicity, unevenness in the development of different functions, metamorphosis or qualitative transformation of one form into another, intertwining of external and internal factors" (Vygostky, 1978, p. 73). Development is revolutionary rather than smoothly passing from one predictable stage to the next in a straight line, as in classic Piagetian psychology. There certainly can be times when the process proceeds in a straightforward evolutionary way, but at other times it consists of upheavals and backsliding or even a complete cessation (at least for a while). The point is that smoothness and abruptness are not incompatible processes from the dialectical perspective; they are "mutually related and mutually presuppose each other" (p. 73).

All domains of psychological research must be guided by principles of the historical development of whatever process is under study. In laboratory settings, Vygotsky criticized reaction-time studies for what he saw as their mechanical approach to analysis. In Vygotsky's view, the problem with the method is that it "substitutes relations existing between stimuli for the real relations underlying the process of choosing." In other words, "experimental procedures become surrogates for psychological processes" (1978, p. 67).

To overcome the problem with reaction-time analysis Vygotsky and his colleagues proposed what they called the *experimental-developmental* method. The method "artificially provokes or creates a process of psychological development" (Vygotsky, 1978, p. 61). Vygotsky and his colleagues achieved this by making what were at the outset simple tasks into increasingly complex tasks that were beyond the ability of most adults to carry out. At this point, they introduced auxiliary stimuli through which the adults were able to mediate their behavior in order to complete the task. In one study adults were given a choice reaction task, which required them to press a button with their left hand upon seeing a red light and press with their right hand when a green light was flashed. This was easy for adults to master. However, the researchers then introduced a variety of different colored lights and required the participants to respond sometimes by pressing a button and sometimes by raising a finger, depending on the light color. In addition, no pre-training was provided; instead the task was initiated immediately following minimal instructions. According to Vygotsky most adults refused to even attempt the task, indicating instead the problems they had remembering what was required of them. When the researchers placed auxiliary stimuli on the response buttons the adults immediately understood that they could use the additional stimuli to mediate the memory of the required stimuli–response connections (e.g., if this light, then press the button with the left hand, but if this light, raise the index finger on the right hand, etc.). Adults understand how to use auxiliary stimuli to mediate their thinking because, in a sense, this is what it means, psychologically, to be an adult.

With children, the experiment followed a completely different, and far more complex, trajectory. While 6–8-year-old children had little difficulty with the initial button-pressing task, when the complications were introduced, the children, unlike the adults, launched into the task without much hesitation; however, they immediately ran into problems. The children operated on the local level and once they mastered a specific stimulus–response relationship they would ask about another, an indication that they dealt with each task separately rather than as an integrated set and that they were unable to use mediated memory, relying instead on their natural memory. In other words, for the children there was no difference between simple and complex tasks (Vygotsky, 1978, p. 71). The adults, on the other hand, did not even attempt to deal with individual stimuli in the complex task, but when the auxiliary stimuli were introduced they were able to use these to master "all the necessary relations" (p. 70) required in the task.

The researchers next introduced specific kinds of auxiliary stimuli to assist the children in the complex task. Initially the auxiliary stimuli were related to the primary stimuli; thus, if the primary were a horse to which the child was to carry out a key press with the left index finger, the auxiliary, pasted on the appropriate key, would be a sleigh. Something similar was done for the primary stimulus bread for which the auxiliary was a knife pasted onto the correct response key. The children were able to make the correct response choices without much difficulty under this condition; an indication that they were at the beginning of the restructuring of their memory toward adult voluntary mediated memory.

A further indication that the children had not yet fully developed mediated memory comes from the next stage of the experiment where the researcher switched the stimulus–response pairings (e.g., horse–knife, bread–sleigh), a condition that was not a problem for the adults. The children, however, were unable to utilize the new pairings to respond correctly because they relied on episodic knowledge of how the primary stimuli objects related to the auxiliary stimuli objects rather than on the general notion that a stimulus could arbitrarily mediate a response to another stimulus, the basis of sign-mediated remembering typical of adults.

As the experiment continued, the children were given the opportunity to create their own primary–auxiliary stimuli–response pairings. At first they continued to rely on episodic connections but the researchers pushed them to break from this type of pattern and to invent completely new patterns that were novel and arbitrary. Once the children achieved this they were eventually able to operate with true signs to mediate their memory. Gradually the children were able to internalize the operation whereby they no longer needed the external stimuli to successfully carry out the tasks. Vygotsky described the process as follows: "in its most developed form, this internal operation consists of the child grasping the very structure of the process, learning to understand the laws according to which external signs must be used. When this stage is reached, the child will say, 'I don't need pictures anymore. I'll do it myself'" (Vygotsky, 1978, p. 72).

## Praxis: The Theory–Practice Dialectic

Although Vygotsky and his colleagues carried out numerous experimental-developmental studies in their laboratory, they also understood, again following

Marxist theory, that the true test of their theory is not to be found in performance of "partially real people" (Widdowson, 1990, p. 25) under laboratory conditions, but was determined by the power of the theory to make a difference in the practical behavior of a community.[5]

Vygotsky concluded that a new relationship between theory and practice was required in a materialist psychology. On this view, theory no longer functioned independently of practice and practice was no longer "the application" of theory that took place "outside of science and came after science" (Vygotsky, 1997a, p. 305). Practice was to be drawn into the scientific enterprise in a profound way, whereby it was to become an equal partner with theory as it "sets the tasks and serves as the supreme judge of theory, as its truth criterion" (pp. 305–306). The dialectical unity of theory and practice is referred to as *praxis*, in which theory guides practice but at the same time practice influences, and if need be, changes theory. Theory–practice interdependence emerges from Marx's *Theses on Feuerbach*, in particular the Eleventh Thesis, which states that the purpose of philosophy (i.e., theory) is not to observe or contemplate the world, but to change it.

Sowell (2009) provides a mundane, but nevertheless helpful, illustration of how to conceptualize the theory–practice dialectic. Sowell contrasts the activity of Vince Lombardi, the legendary coach of one of the most successful franchises in American professional football, the Green Bay Packers, with how academics expound and elaborate their theories. The latter are evaluated on the basis of internal criteria; that is, whether they are consistent (p. 6), whereas Lombardi's theory of how to play and win football games is assessed on the basis of external criteria on the concrete material field where the game is actually played. This is precisely the perspective on the relationship between theory and practice that Vygotsky argued for—validity of the theory is determined by external, objective criteria rather than by theory-internal criteria. If Lombardi's theory of how the game should be played is verified then we would expect consistent successful outcomes on the playing field (provided of course the team has quality players who are able to adequately instantiate the theory). If the theory is not valid then we would expect unsuccessful outcomes and hopefully the theory would be revised or rejected entirely in favor of a different theory. How well the theory is implemented during practice sessions (perhaps analogous to the experimental laboratory, a controlled environment) cannot be its true test; this comes only under game conditions where the outcome matters and where the opposing team is doing its best to counter Lombardi's theory.

Vygotsky also believed that though the practice field of the experimental laboratory was certainly important, he insisted—as noted by Luria in his intellectual autobiography—that research ultimately could not be "divorced from the real world" (Cole, Levitin, & Luria, 2006, p. 53). Vygotsky dedicated a significant component of his research to educational innovation and to rehabilitation research in his institute for *defectology* (see Vygotsky, 1990). In both domains, he was committed to the theoretical principle that "higher mental functions cannot be understood without sociological study, that is, that they are a product not of biological but of social development of behavior" and that if this behavior changes so too will the higher mental functions (1997b, p. 18). In the spirit of this principle, Vygotsky believed that with the proper forms of mediation it was possible to overcome, to some degree at least, problems such as deafness (which at the time was considered a serious detriment to normal functioning), schizophrenia, children raised in cultural deprivation (e.g., street children), and children born with various types of mental disabilities. Following Vygotsky's death and the censorship of his writings by the Stalinist regime, Luria continued to surreptitiously work within the theory as he sought to heal individuals suffering from brain damage due to war injuries, stroke, or other forms of cerebral trauma. In most cases, he was able to successfully alleviate internal problems through external forms of mediation. One of the most important outcomes of Luria's practice with brain-damaged individuals was confirmation of Vygotsky's theoretical claim that the brain is a functional system in which processes such as memory, perception, imagination, generalization, and attention involve different neurological areas and that language indeed plays a central role in these processes (see Luria, 1973). In the next subsection we will discuss an especially important research project carried out by Luria in the 1930s that corroborated the dialectical principle that changes in social activity affect cognitive processing.

## A Natural Experiment

The decision of the Stalinist regime to collectivize the traditional communities of Soviet Central Asia during the early 1930s provided Vygotsky and his colleagues with the opportunity to conduct a sociocultural experiment that would demonstrate the consequences of social change on cognitive processing. The project took place in remote areas of Uzbekistan and Kirghizia. Vygotsky and Luria reasoned that the introduction of formal education, in accordance with the directive from Moscow, would create "new structures of cognitive functioning" and "advance human consciousness to new levels" (Luria, 1976, p. 163). Specifically formal schooling would result in "the transition from situational to taxonomic conceptual thinking" (p. 52). Specific research questions for the project included whether individuals (i.e., adult members of rural communities) who have been to school retain a "habitual approach to generalization" or if exposure to activities "inculcated in education, produce a radical change" in the preferred method of generalization (p. 53). In other words, will formal education result in a change from functional to taxonomic thinking?

The study is well known and we have written about it on a number of occasions (see Lantolf & Thorne, 2006, pp. 35–42). Nevertheless, it will be useful to consider a few examples of the data presented by Luria (1976). In one experiment, Luria's team showed the participants drawings of a *hammer, saw, log,* and *hatchet* and asked them which of the items could be referred to using a single word. Individuals who had not been to school by and large had a difficult time responding with the superordinate term *tool* to categorize hammer, saw, and hatchet. One such participant acknowledged that hammer, saw, and hatchet "work together" but also insisted that the log had to be included in the grouping as well (p. 56). Even when the researcher informed another participant that the three items were all tools, the participant continued to respond functionally stating "Yes, but even if we have tools, we still need wood—otherwise, we can't build anything" (p. 56).

Shown four other items, *glass–saucepan–spectacles–bottle* and asked to eliminate any item that did not belong, another non-schooled villager first grouped glass, saucepan, bottle together but on further thought decided that the spectacles also belonged in the group, reasoning that "if a person doesn't see too good, he has to put them on to eat dinner" (Luria, 1976, p. 57). Another villager rejected the option of grouping the saucepan, bottle, and glass together with the superordinate term *vessel*, on the grounds that the bottle was harmful because it appeared to contain vodka; he further insisted on including the spectacles on the grounds of their utility (pp. 57–58). When the researcher persisted that the spectacles cannot be called a vessel, the participant responded with "If you're cooking something on the fire, you've got to use the eye-glasses or you just won't be able to cook" (p. 58).

In a final example from the grouping task Luria's team attempted to explain to a non-schooled villager the principle of taxonomic classification with only minimal success (see Luria, 1976, pp. 65–67). The team began by showing the man pictures of an *ax* and a *sickle* and asking him to choose a similar item from a second group consisting of a *saw*, a *log*, and an *ear of grain*. The man chose ear of grain and paired it with the sickle. When asked if the ax, sickle, and grain are the same type of object, the man responded that the ax was not as similar to the grain as the sickle and added that ax belonged with the log because it could chop it. When reminded that he had to select one thing from the second group so that all three were alike, he insisted that it had to be the grain, leaving the saw and the log in the second group, which in his view belonged together. In response to the researcher's repeated question: "Are those things really alike?" the man said "no," adding that the grain had to be moved closer to the sickle and the ax closer to the log. The researcher then speculated about what situation would hold if the ax were not close to the log, to which the villager responded: "then they wouldn't be alike. But if you put them next to each other, the ax can chop the log. They'll be very much alike then and very handy." This was followed by an even more explicit question: "Is an ax like a sickle in some way—is it the same type of thing?" The man's answer that they are both tools and that the saw could also be called by the same term seemed to indicate that he finally understood superordinate categorization.

To assess if the participant had indeed developed an understanding of categorical taxonomy, the researchers presented another set of objects with the reminder that the same rule of categorization applied. The first set of objects consisted of a *tree* and an *ear of grain* and the second set was comprised of *bird–rosebush–house*. The man selected rosebush to fit with the first set of objects, explaining that they are all trees, but then added that the bird could belong in the group as well because it could keep "an eye on the trees." Luria points out that the man had finally adopted abstract classification but followed it with "*situational thinking.*" As a final task, the researchers presented the same villager with a set comprised of *horse–ram* and a second set consisting of *camel–bucket–house*, and once again reminded him to rely on the tool-grouping strategy. The man immediately included the camel with the horse and ram saying they were animals. However, he then shifted to situational thinking saying that the bucket belongs with house because it is useful.

Villagers with one to two years of schooling at the time of the interviews had little difficulty categorizing objects taxonomically. One participant presented with *glass–saucepan–spectacles–bottle* quickly responded that saucepan did not belong because the other items were all made of glass and the saucepan was metal (Luria, 1976, p. 76).

## Conceptual Thinking and Deduction

According to Luria (1976, pp. 100–101), conceptual thought and deduction are important because they demonstrate the ability to derive inferences "from given premises without having to resort to immediate graphic-functional experience, and make it possible to acquire new knowledge in a discursive and verbal logical fashion"; in other words, it shows the ability to think theoretically. To assess theoretical thinking, the team presented the villagers with a series of syllogisms and asked them to reproduce in their own words the relation between the major and minor premise and to provide an appropriate response to the resultant question without relying on practical experience (p. 103).

When presented with such syllogisms as "*Precious metals do not rust. Gold is a precious metal. Does it rust or not?*" (Luria, 1976, p. 104, italics in original), the non-schooled villagers had a difficult time even repeating the major and minor premise. In other cases, participants refused to even attempt an inference for syllogisms such as "*In the Far North, where there is snow, all bears are white. Novaya Zemlya is in the Far North. What color are bears there?*" on the grounds that "they had never been in the North and had never seen bears" and followed up with the revealing comment that "to answer the question you would have to ask people who had been there and seen them" (p. 107). One villager remarked that "we always speak only of what we see; we don't talk about what we haven't seen" (p. 109). Even if pushed to reach a conclusion solely on the basis of the words of a syllogism, the non-schooled participants continued to insist that if they had not experienced the object or circumstance in question they could not reach a conclusion: "If a man was sixty or eighty and had seen a white bear and had told about it, he could be believed, but I've never seen one and hence I can't say. That's my last word. Those who saw can tell, and those who didn't see can't say anything" (p. 109).

Of fifteen non-schooled villagers, nine were able to solve syllogisms associated with direct experience immediately and without prompting from researchers, while six could do so only with prompts (e.g., "on the basis of my words"). Of the same group, two were able to immediately solve some syllogisms on discursive grounds alone and another four were able to do so with extensive prompting, while another eight could not do so even under prompting conditions (Luria, 1976, p. 116). On the other hand, all fifteen villagers who had been to school were able to solve experiential and discursive syllogisms immediately without prompting from researchers.

## A Replication

Although Luria points out that the research project was conducted under "unique and non-replicable conditions" (Luria, 1976, p. 161), it turns out that nearly 60 years after the original study, Tulviste (1991) reports on a project that comes quite close to replicating the earlier research with a larger number of participants. Seventy individuals from Kirghizia participated in Tulviste's study. Of these, eighteen had no formal schooling, while the remaining fifty-two individuals had attended school for an average of 4.5 years. Those between the ages of 25 and 30 had achieved at least 7 years of formal education and those over seventy had no schooling at all. Tulviste found a strong statistically significant correlation between years of education and ability to solve both empirical and discursive syllogisms and, more importantly, those with higher levels of education were far more likely to immediately solve the latter type of reasoning problem than were those with fewer years of education (p. 133). Moreover, and just as important, is Tulviste's finding that individuals who had been away from school and engaged in non-school-based occupations for a lengthy time period, were more likely to approach syllogisms from an empirical rather than a theoretical stance. A similar finding was also reported in Scribner and Cole's (1981) Liberia study. In our view, findings of this type lend even more support to the materialist position that mental processing depends "utterly on the basic forms of social practice" (Luria, 1976, p. 164) that operate in a culture.

The changes in thinking brought about as a consequence of the radical cultural shifts that took place under collectivization in the former Soviet Union are perhaps easier to observe than are the effects of societal differences at work in technologically developed cultures such as the U.S. Nevertheless, the principle that material reality and changes in that reality impact on higher forms of thinking is expected to operate, given that these forms of consciousness are

> the essence of internalized relations of a social order, a basis for the social structure of the individual. Their composition, genetic structure, method of action—in a word, their entire nature—is social; even in being transformed

into mental processes, they remain quasisocial. Man [sic] as an individual maintains the functions of socializing.

*(Vygotsky, 1997b, p. 106)*

In the next section we will discuss some of the implications of this argument for an early 21st-century society such as the United States as formulated in Ratner's (2012) neo-Vygotskian theory.

## Macro Cultural Psychology: A Neo-Vygotskian Theory of Higher Mental Processing

Macro cultural psychology is a continuation and expansion of Vygotskian theory that takes as its starting point Vygotsky's (1987, p. 212) argument that mental processing is not only a consequence of social relationships, but because it is socially based, it is constructed on the basis of social class. As Ratner (2012, p. 19) explains, modern psychology, in contradistinction to Vygotskian theory, explains mental processes as "natural and universal" with society having little effect on these processes within the individual, who is free to construct his or her own personality, thoughts, feelings, desires, and motives. When disorders in these processes occur the problem is located within the individual, who is often treated with drugs, rather than in society, which might well require substantial restructur-ing of social relationships in order to alleviate the source of the problem, as we explain below.

Macro cultural psychology asserts that all aspects of human psychology are cultural, or as Ratner (2012, p. 29) states: "it is culture all the way down." As with Vygotsky, for Ratner, this does not mean that biology is off the stage. What it does mean, however is that biology is acculturated and therefore loses its "purely biological character that it retains in nonhumans, who have no culture" (p. 29). Essentially, Ratner's agenda is to move psychology out of the "domain of animal and child biology where innate processes determine behavior" (p. 37)[6] and into the domain of culture, where culture and not "brain circuitry" creates the human mind (p. 96). In other words, "psychology must necessarily proceed from the fact that between individual consciousness and objective reality there exists the 'mediating link' of the historically formed culture, which acts as the prerequisite and condition of individual mental activity" (Ilyenkov, 2012, p. 189). Even when culture is smuggled into psychology through variables such as socialization, and age and gender differences, they remain local and "cut off from broader macro cultural factors" (Ratner, 2012, p. 37). Indeed for Ratner, culture is not simply an environment in which humans reside; it is a new life form, "a new order of biological existence" (p. 93).

Macro cultural psychology proposes that while social relationships matter, as Vygotsky argued, these need to be "congruent with macro factors" (Ratner, 2012, p. 139) that include institutions (e.g., family, schools, government, health care institutions, economic enterprises, spiritual organizations, leisure time organizations, etc.), artifacts (tools, clothing, eating and cooking utensils, housing, etc.), and cultural concepts (time, wealth, man, woman, mortality, health, nature, sex, etc.). Crucially, these factors are "governed by particular interest groups and benefit the well-being of those interest groups" (p. 17). This means that while the institution "family," for example, may be found in all cultures it is constructed, and therefore thought about, differently in different cultures. This notion also applies to social groups within a given culture. For instance, the debate currently underway in the U.S. regarding the definition of a family, and the related institution of marriage, is a socially motivated struggle for how the culture will construe these institutions in the future and therefore how the psychology of family and marriage will be constituted.

## Culture in Mind

Throughout his work, Ratner provides rich illustrations of how psychological concepts derive from cultural formations. The concept of "self" in Western industrialized societies, for instance, resulted from economic changes that took place in England between the 16th and 17th centuries. During this period, businessmen made decisions based on their own judgment and initiative in order to maximize profits, which was a break from traditional consultative practices where the good of the community had priority (Ratner, 2012, p. 142). The notion of the individualistic self, making decisions for one's own benefit, was enhanced during the industrial revolution and the rise of capitalism in the 18th and 19th centuries when "business required an individualistic self that took individual initiative and responsibility for actions" (p. 143) that was "necessary to implement capitalism" (p. 145).

Another informative example is the cultural organization of the sense of smell. Although all humans are able to detect odors through their olfactory system, how we conceptualize these (i.e., assign meaning) and therefore psychologize them is decidedly culturally organized. Natural odors, in themselves, are value free and in themselves do not carry sociocultural meaning. However, in early modern Europe, "odors became a proxy for social standing" whereby "smells associated with racial and ethnic minorities and working class (bodies, home, labor) were evaluated negatively as belonging to activities that were socially disparaged," while the wealthy bathe themselves in perfumes to "distinguish themselves socially" from the masses (Ratner, 2012, p. 147).

Without looking into the historical construction of a concept, we risk reification as if it were a natural rather than a historical human (i.e., sociocultural) kind. The individualistic self is thus understood as an atemporal and universal concept. One dislikes manual labor because "it results in foul smelling bodies" and not because it signifies working class, and therefore, inferior individuals (Ratner, 2012, p. 148). A task of macro cultural psychology is to negate "the reification of psychological and social categories by explaining the cultural practices, status, and values" that define them as historical human kinds rather than natural kinds.

As a final example, consider how important speed is in psychological measurement and in school evaluation. IQ and various memory tests incorporate speed as an indicator of success: "Psychological importance is defined in terms of speed of response" and if a response is slow it is "deemed to be meaningless psychologically" (Ratner, 2012, p. 173). Students who rapidly master new concepts and abilities in schools are more highly rewarded and valued than are students who take more time to do so. Some psychologists, according to Kozulin (2011), go so far as to conflate speed of learning with intelligence.

Ratner proposes that the reason speed is assigned significance in psychology and education relates to its value in capitalist society, which "strives for rapid turnover of capital to generate profit" (2012, p. 173). Moreover, "behavior is geared toward speed so people will be accustomed to working faster, getting to work faster, and deciding to spend money faster" (p. 173). A dominant metaphor in U.S. culture is TIME IS MONEY. The pecuniary advantage accruing from speed is then built into psychology, where it is assumed that if one is not capable of rapid production or reproduction of information one does not have it, and in education slow performing students are labeled as less intelligent than faster learners. What is more, there are often dire consequences that impact people for a lifetime arising from the value of speed. The three examples considered here, from among many others discussed by Ratner, underscore the importance of Vygotsky's genetic approach to psychological research.

## Working Memory and Macro Cultural Psychology

The case for the nexus of macro cultural factors and psychological processing is forcefully made with regard to working memory (WM), an area that has become particularly relevant in SLA research. J. N. Williams (2012, p. 427) characterizes WM as a cognitive system used for "temporary maintenance of task-relevant information whilst performing cognitive tasks." He further points out that individuals can be expected to manifest considerable variation in WM capacity (p. 427). The earliest model of WM, proposed by Baddeley and Hitch (1974), comprises two components: a domain-specific short-term memory store consisting of a phonological loop for verbal information and a visuo-spatial "scratch pad" for storing visual and spatial information (J. N. Williams, 2012, p. 427), and a central executive that selects and maintains attention on relevant information (Holmes, Gathercole, & Dunning, 2009, p. F9). Williams cites research that shows a relationship between phonological short-term memory and second language vocabulary and even grammar learning, particularly under conditions of explicit instruction (p. 437). We will have more to say about WM and language learning in Chapter 3. For now we are interested in the fact that evidence shows WM is influenced by experience (p. 437). The issue, however, is what kind of experience?

Neurologically, WM is located primarily in the prefrontal cortex with some interaction both with the hippocampus and amygdala (Evans & Schamberg, 2009, p. 6545). Psychologists had assumed until very recently that WM was a "highly heritable" capacity that was "relatively impervious to substantial differences in environmental experience and opportunity" (Holmes et al., 2009, p. F9). This conclusion found support in initial training studies that failed to produce lasting effects or to generalize across learning circumstances (p. F10). However, more recent studies have reported lasting and generalizable effects for training, especially for children (e.g., Mezzacappa & Buckner, 2010; Klingberg, 2010). Klingberg (2010) in particular reports neurological changes in brain activity as a consequence of training, an illustration of environmental conditions impacting brain function, as claimed by Vygotsky and Ratner.

Klein and Boals (2001) established a connection between stress and WM capacity. Their argument was that individuals "trying to suppress cognitions related to stressful life events will be at a disadvantage on WM tasks that compete for the same mental resources," because the effort required to inhibit the unwanted stressful thoughts uses the same cognitive resources as WM (p. 566). A series of studies carried out with college students found significant relationships between participants reporting stressful life events such as a recent death of a close family member, anxiety about obtaining a job, etc., and diminished performance on WM tasks. Their general conclusion was that "stressful events are analogous to a secondary task that shares WM resources with the primary operation-word span task" (p. 576).

If stressful life events can inhibit performance on WM tasks for college students, one can imagine the effect of living in an environment where stressful life events are experienced virtually on a daily basis. It turns out that this is precisely what occurs in individuals raised in poverty. People who experience chronic life stress that results from living in poverty exhibit a significantly diminished WM when compared with individuals from the middle class (Evans & Schamberg 2009). Evans and Schamberg (2009) show that chronic stress results in an increased allostatic load, which negatively impacts the functioning of the hippocampus and prefrontal cortex, areas responsible for WM. Allostatic load indexes the wear and tear on the body that results from constant mobilization of the body's response systems (neuronal, endocrine, cardiovascular) triggered by environmental stressors (p. 6545).[7]

Children raised in poverty have a significantly greater allostatic load compared with children who are not, and the longer the period of poverty the greater the load. Increased load contributes not only to early death, but if chronically increased it impacts on neurological processes, "particularly in the hippocampus and prefrontal cortex, that are capable of disrupting cognitive function" (Evans & Schamberg, 2009, p. 6545). In this way, poverty, the result of macro cultural factors, penetrates the body and the brain (p. 6545). The consequences are that adults raised in poverty have a diminished WM when compared with adults from middle-income families. There is also a suspected relationship among "chronic poverty, allostatic load, and long-term, declarative memory, which [also] resides in the hippocampus" (p. 6548).

## What Is To Be Done?

If particular configurations of material life result in particular kinds of cognitive processing, it follows that changing the circumstances will change how people think. This is the point of Marx's *Theses on Feuerbach* and it is the foundation of Vygotsky's materialist psychology and Ratner's macro cultural theory. We have to keep in mind that by material life, we mean social institutions in which people live. How these are configured and the kinds of activities people have access to in these institutions shape how they think. For Vygotsky, education was a major instrument for bringing about cognitive change. His project in this regard was to find appropriate ways of restructuring education in order to maximize the developmental potential of all students, and, in particular, for those from deprived sociocultural backgrounds. If a function such as WM significantly contributes to successful educational outcomes then short of eliminating poverty (Ratner's preferred solution) the macro cultural institution of education must make a commitment to enhance this capacity for individuals and members of socioeconomic groups who enter the institution in a disadvantageous position. This would comprise a far better and equitable solution to the problem than to place students into instructional programs according to their WM capacity and where they would receive instruction "tailored to their cognitive abilities" (see J. N. Williams, 2012, p. 437). To rephrase the comment by Evans and Schamberg (2009)—if poverty can enter the brain, so can education.

## Conclusion

In this chapter we have made the case that sociocultural theory is a cognitive theory of mind inspired by Marx's historical materialist philosophy. As such, it holds that consciousness arises from the dialectical interaction of the brain, endowed with biologically specified mental capacities, and socially organized activity determined by macro cultural institutions, artifacts, and concepts. The interaction between two material substances (i.e., brain and culture) humanizes the brain's functions so that psychological processing "embodies the social structure in form and content"; in other words, "social structure is *in* psychology" (Ratner, 2012, p. 159, italics in original). Social structure is not a variable; it is the source of human psychology.

The relationship between the material and the ideal that vexed philosophers (and psychologists) for centuries is no longer a problem, because in historical materialism and in the intermediary theory of materialist psychology, the ideal and the material are not two distinct substances. The ideal is the consequence of the interaction between two material substances: brain and human social activity. More accurately, thinking and acting are both behaviors of the same material body. The ideal changes under changing conditions of life. Moreover, development is an uneven and revolutionary process, typical of dialectical change in all material domains, including nature, society, and of course thought. It moves in fits and starts and often in unanticipated directions. The most important point, however, is that it is shaped by the sociocultural circumstances in which it occurs. For this reason, Vygotsky assigned an especially important role to education as a leading activity of development.

In idealist theories, this is far less likely to happen, given that the mind and the body/world are comprised of fundamentally different substances. Even though it may not be overtly stated, we suspect that the distinction goes a long way to explaining why psychological theories assume universal patterns of development that are pretty much impervious to outside (i.e., social) forces. Chomskian theory, for instance, assumes that all knowledge needed to acquire language is pre-specified in the brain with the environment playing only a minimal role as trigger. Pienemann's Processability Theory of SLA similarly argues that the environment, including education, cannot affect the sequencing of processing procedures development for particular features of language such as topicalization, question formation, negation, word order, and the like.

Above all, with regard to the gap between theory and practice, Vygotsky's theory of materialist psychology not only eliminates the mind–world dualism, because of its emphasis on praxis, but it closes the theory/research–practice gap that has worried SLA researchers for decades. It does so because of its commitment to the *Eleventh Thesis on Feuerbach*. The implications of this, as we have argued, is profound: a theory is no longer an instrument for observing the object of study, it is, instead, the instrument for changing the object of study. Said in another way— to study something means to change it. Here it is important to keep in mind that while the laboratory is a place where change happens, it is the site where theory testing begins not where it ends. Vygotsky understood this principle of Marxist philosophy and consequently required that materialist psychology be brought into the human world in order to make things better. This was for him the true test of the theory. It explains his concern to help people suffering from the consequences of biological and sociological pathologies (see Vygotsky, 1990). It explains Luria's (1973) commitment to bring the principles of the theory to bear in healing people suffering from the ravages of stroke and cerebral traumas caused by World War II. Most importantly, for our purposes, it explains the commitment of the theory to providing people with full access to development through formal education. All of this is demanded of a theory that places praxis at its core—there is nothing as practical as good theory and there is nothing as theoretical as good practice. Beginning with Chapter 4, we explore the consequences of praxis for second language development. First, however, we want to make the case stronger for the role of the social environment in psychological development, the topic of Chapter 3.

## Notes

1 If we bring dialectic dialogue into contact with SLA research, it would, for example, try to find a way of synthesizing debates over whether implicit or explicit feedback is more effective. It would approach the problem from the perspective that perhaps both types of feedback are needed depending on learner development and responsiveness to mediation.

2 Although Swain (2006) introduced *languaging* into SLA research, it has a long history in Marxist theory, see for example R. Williams (1977). For convenience, we continue to use the term language rather than *languaging*, although unless otherwise specified, we intend it as activity rather than structure.

3 During Stalin's rule, Vygotsky's works were heavily censored, as were his educational activities in collaboration with Lenin's widow, Nadya Krupskaya. Some even speculate that had Vygotsky not expired from tuberculosis in 1934, he most likely would have ended up in the gulag if not worse (van der Veer & Valsiner, 1991).

4 A. R. Luria, considered by most to be the founder of neuropsychology, and Vygotsky's most influential colleague, provides evidence of the reorganization in the research he conducted on brain-damaged individuals (Luria, 1973). More recently, research such as Clark (2008), Sutton (2008), and Boivin (2008) in also arguing for the nexus of thinking, material body and material world, provide additional evidence of the impact of social activity on the brain, and Schumann and his colleagues (Schumann et al., 2004) investigate the effect of external events relating specifically to L2 acquisition on the chemical processes at work in the brain.

5 Atkinson (2002, pp. 535–536) captured the difference between laboratory and real-world settings in the following comment:

> I frequently find the reading of SLA research to be almost an exercise in surrealism— based, I believe, in the just-mentioned contradictory 'present absence' of human beings. Human beings as I know them whether people on the street, students I teach and work with, professional colleagues, or those I am close to and love, appear to act, think and feel in ways and for reasons entirely different than those most typically featured in SLA research.

6 Vygotsky (1997a, p. 234) used the term "zoopsychology" to capture the same idea.

7 Allostatic load is measured using six risk factors: systolic and diastolic blood pressure; body mass index; hormonal secretions, including cortisol, which breaks down glucose in muscles and the liver; epinephrine, which regulates heart rate and controls the fight-or-flight response; and norepinephrine, a neurotransmitter that affects attention and is also involved in fight-or-flight.

# 3
# PSYCHOLOGY OF THE SOCIAL ENVIRONMENT

The previous chapter introduced the central principle of sociocultural psychology regarding the influence of the social environment on psychological processes. We illustrated this relationship with Luria's research showing the effects of education on the psychology of rural populations in Central Asia and with research documenting the consequences of poverty for WM. In this chapter we specify the principles and processes postulated by Vygotsky to account for the transformation of biologically endowed mental behaviors into human psychology.

Cognitive psychology operates from the general assumption that the key to explaining cognitive processes resides inside of the mind/brain. While thinking individuals live in social environments these contexts are generally assumed to play, at most, a minor role in influencing mental processes. This perspective is mirrored in what Atkinson (2012) calls "cognitivist SLA." While cognitivist SLA recognizes that SLA takes place in social settings, it nevertheless assumes that the "secrets" to the process itself are to be found "in the mind brain" (Long & Doughty, 2003, p. 866). Long (2007, p. 145) characterizes the cognitivist stance to SLA as follows:

> change the social setting altogether (e.g., from street to classroom), or from a foreign to a second language environment and, as far as we know, the way the learner acquires does not change much either (as suggested, e.g., by a comparison of error types, developmental sequences, processing constraints, and other aspects of the acquisition process in and out of classrooms).

As we explained in Chapter 1, in sociocultural psychology, the brain, as the biological pole of mental processing, is not the only site that matters when explaining human cognition. The social environment, as the other pole in the dialectical formation that is the human mind, is the "the *source* of development"

(Vygotsky, 1994b, p. 349, italics added). Stetsenko and Vianna (2009, p. 45, italics in original) expand on this perspective in the following comment:

> cultural-historical practices (or activities) are neither ancillary nor complementary to development ... they are *the very realm* (or the very "matter" and fabric) that these processes serve, stem from, belong to, and are carried out in, with no ontological gap posited between people actively engaging their world on the one hand, and their knowing, learning, and becoming on the other.

The goal of this chapter is to examine the contention that the social environment is not merely the context where learning happens, but it has profound psychological relevance. On this view, then, SLA is not the same process wherever it occurs. Change the environment and the process changes.

## Environment as a Source of Development

Vygotsky (1994b) offered an explanation along with examples of how he conceptualized the environment. The proper environment for human life is not the physical but the social world. This is the world, as discussed in Chapter 2, created by human activity over the course of history. By creating and changing the world, and not merely adapting to it, as proposed in Piagetian psychology, humans change not just the social circumstances in which they live, but these very circumstances shape their psychology. However, Vygotsky (1994b, p. 338) cautioned that sociocultural psychology is not interested in the "study of the environment as such," but in its "role, meaning and influence" in development. In other words, what matters is the relationship between individuals and their environment, and this relationship changes not only as the environment changes but as the individual emerges as a psychological being over the course of ontogenesis.

Consider the case of a newborn infant. The only aspects of the world that matter as far as the infant is concerned are the phenomena most immediately surrounding her and in some way connect to her body. As the child grows, however, features of the environment that did not matter at the outset are brought into contact with the child and in this sense begin to exist for the child and to influence her development. Vygotsky (1994b, p. 339) pointed out for example that although the language surrounding children at 6 months is the same as when they are 18 months or even 3 years old it assumes a different meaning for them as their comprehension improves.

### Illustrating the Role of the Environment

Vygotsky (1994b) provided a concrete example of child–environment interaction when he recounted the case of three children from the same family brought to his clinic for observation and treatment. He pointed out that the objective circumstances within the family were the same for the three children. Their mother was an alcoholic, who also suffered from other psychoses (p. 340). When inebriated she frequently beat the children and on one occasion even attempted to throw one of them out of a window. Vygotsky determined that each child presented "a completely different picture of disrupted development, caused by the same situation" (p. 340). The youngest child developed neurotic tendencies that resulted in episodes of feelings of helplessness and "incomprehensible horror" (p. 341). At times he was unable to speak and suffered from depression. The second child experienced the situation as a conflict between simultaneous strong attachment and feelings of hatred, fear, and hostility (p. 341). The oldest child oriented to the situation as a family misfortune that required him to take on the responsibility "to mitigate the misfortune and to help both the sick mother and the [other] children" (p. 341). Vygotsky concluded that the same set of circumstances influenced the children's psychological development in different ways. In other words, the source of development existed in the environment but its effect on development was experienced differentially by the three children. Changing the circumstances by helping the mother overcome her alcohol abuse or by removing her from the life of the children would also be expected to have differential effects on the psychological development of each of them.

In a more recent study on environment–person interaction conducted in the macro cultural domain of education, but with influences from the sociopolitical domain, Steele and Aronson (1995) investigated the effect of the "*stereotype threat*" (p. 797) in a university testing environment. According to Steele and Aronson, when performing explicit academic tasks, African-American students "face the threat of confirming or being judged by a negative societal stereotype—a suspicion—about their group's intellectual ability and competence" (p. 797). The researchers hypothesized that the "self-threat" would potentially interfere with the students' performance on standardized tests, because under such a circumstance their attention would be redirected onto "a concern with the significance of one's performance in light of a devaluing stereotype" (p. 798). They further suggested that the stereotype would be particularly relevant to performance when the test itself was "frustrating" because it would raise "the possibility that they have an inability linked to their race" (p. 798).

Although three connected studies were carried out, our direct concern is with the first. It involved a total of 114 White and Black undergraduates enrolled at Stanford University. The students were asked to take a 30-minute test constructed of items drawn from the verbal Graduate Record Exam. The items were sufficiently difficult to generate frustration among most of the testees. The test was administered under three separate conditions, determined by what the participants were told the purpose of the test was. In the first condition they were informed that the test was intended as a diagnostic of their intellectual ability, which was the stereotype-threat condition for the Black participants. In the second, they were told that the identical test was a non-diagnostic problem-solving task, which was hypothesized to make irrelevant the racial stereotype threat. In the third condition, the students were told the test was non-diagnostic but challenging and they were therefore urged to do their best. In all three conditions the participants were told that they were unlikely to get many items correct and that in the diagnostic condition the difficulty level was "justified as a means of providing a 'genuine test of your verbal abilities and limitations so that we might better understand the factors involved in both'" (p. 799). In the two non-diagnostic conditions the participants were told that their ability was not being evaluated because the test was part of a research project investigating "'psychological factors involved in solving verbal problems'" (p. 799).The students were encouraged to make a sincere effort to do well so that the researchers would be better able to analyze that process (p. 799).

Using an ANCOVA with students' self-reported verbal and quantitative SAT scores (higher for Whites than for Blacks) as the covariate, the researchers reported a significant main effect for condition with participants in the non-diagnostic-challenge condition outperforming students in the non-diagnostic-only and diagnostic conditions (p. 800). They also reported a significant main effect for race with the White students doing better than the Black students. Most importantly, however, the performance of the Black participants in the diagnostic condition was significantly below the performance of Black students in either non-diagnostic condition, but the performance of Black participants was not significantly lower than Whites in either of the non-diagnostic conditions. Moreover, when the participants in the three conditions were asked to assess their performance, the Black students in the diagnostic condition estimated their performance as poorer than did Black students in either of the non-diagnostic conditions. No effect was found for White students across the three conditions.

With regard to our primary concern in this section, Steele and Aronson's study clearly showed that individuals with different sociocultural histories in ostensibly identical objective environments behave differently. Clearly, the significance of "diagnostic test" as a way of framing the test-taking activity was radically different for Black students than for White students; consequently, their respective performances on the test varied accordingly. For the African-American students, characterizing the test as diagnostic of intellectual ability had the effect of fulfilling the racial stereotype threat, thus depressing their performance relative to White students as well as to Black students in the other test conditions.

In sociocultural psychology it is the dynamic nature of the dialectical relationship between individuals and environment that is of interest, and while the environment serves as the source of development, its effects are not always the same; rather it exerts its influence in different ways on different individuals and on the same individuals at different times (Vygotsky, 1994b, p. 347). This is an especially relevant point for the educational environment. Children from lower socioeconomic backgrounds, for example, may not be prepared to deal with an educational environment organized on the basis of middle and upper class language, norms, and expectancies of learning outcomes. The interaction between such children and the educational environment can be expected to vary radically from the interaction between the same objective environment and children from middle and upper class backgrounds. Consequently, to provide lower SES children with the opportunity to develop in accordance with the expectations of the educational program would necessitate different kinds of social relationship and cultural artifacts to mediate their development.

Head Start programs in the United States are designed specifically to enhance the opportunities for the cognitive development of children from lower SES prior to their entrance into the established educational environment. In addition, special schools have also been established to assist such children even beyond the pre-school years. The East Side Institute in New York City, for instance, among its various components has designed a curriculum based in large part on Vygotskian developmental principles (see Holzman, 2009). With regard to second language development, Aljaafreh and Lantolf (1994) demonstrated how social inter-action mediation could be modified to provide developmental support for adult learners with objectively similar language difficulties. This topic will be addressed specifically in Chapters 7 and 8 that deal with the ZPD and DA. At this point, however, we wish to consider the role of the *ideal* as an aspect of the environment as conceptualized by Vygotsky.

## The Ideal

All developmental processes, whether associated with language, cognition, emo-tion, or personality, depend to a large extent on the final, or ideal, version of what is possible to attain as a consequence of development. The ideal "acts as a model for what should be achieved at the end of the developmental period" (Vygotsky, 1994b, p. 348). This does not mean, however, that the model will be duplicated; rather it serves to influence and shape the developmental process. As an example, Vygotsky mentioned child language acquisition where adults and, in particular, parents, provide the ideal final form of development for the child. In addition to the linguistic features of a language, its psychological function is also modeled in the environment. Although in this case, it is modeled as communicatively oriented social speech. Higher psychological functions that are specifically human in nature, as we have stated more than once in our discussion, originate as cooperative social behavior between children and adults. What was com-municative speech becomes first egocentric speech (external speech directed at self-regulation) and later in ontogenesis develops into non-vocal inner speech, which lacks the formal structure of communicative speech but which maintains aspects of its original social meanings—the meanings that were in the environ-ment while the speech was still communicative. Thus, speech as a means of regulating thinking comes from "speech as a means of communication" (Vygotsky, 1994b, p. 353).

In the absence of an environmental model with which individuals can interact, development will be highly aberrant if not completely inhibited, especially in the case of language (Vygotsky, 1994b, p. 349). In circumstances where a model is available, but not a final, adult model, Vygotsky argued that development will occur in "an extremely peculiar way" (1994b, p. 350). Courtin (2000) provided empirical evidence to support Vygotsky's thesis. He studied the situation in which Deaf children of hearing parents were placed in a school environment whose goal was to teach them to use oral, rather than sign, language. Even though adults were present in the environment and interacted with them the children had a difficult time achieving full access to adult spoken language due to their diminished auditory capacity. Likewise, at home the children did not have access to adult models of sign language as used by a Deaf community. When the children then undertook to communicate with each other in the absence of adults, they often used a sign system that was in no way as linguistically developed and as lexically rich as adult sign language (Courtin, 2000, p. 269). Children reared in such an environment not only tended to have language problems, they also displayed cognitive deficits. Courtin's (2000) study, for example, compared (1) signing children of Deaf parents, (2) signing Deaf children of hearing parents, (3) oral Deaf children of hearing parents, and (4) hearing children of hearing parents on theories of mind (TOM) tasks. He found that group (1) outperformed all other groups (they were on average 15 months older than the hearing group); group (2) outperformed group (3) and were not significantly different from group (4); and group (4) did better than group (3). Hence, the Deaf children whose parents were hearing and whose primary language was oral were the least effective group in dealing with the TOM tasks. This is because, as predicted by Vygotsky, they were denied full access to an adult model of language and therefore their psychology was also impaired.

## Internalization

The primary processes which allow the environment to function as the source of higher forms of consciousness are internalization and imitation. We have discussed both of these in relation to language development in previous publications (Lantolf & Thorne, 2006; Lantolf, 2006), and therefore will not repeat that discussion here. Instead, we will flesh out a bit more our understanding of the processes in light of research that has appeared in the intervening years. In this section we focus on internalization and in the next on imitation.

Internalization (also translated as interiorization, or in-growing) was proposed by Vygotsky as a way of explaining the formation of the dialectical unity between social activity and higher mental functions. According to Luria (1979, p. 45), "it is through interiorization of historically determined and culturally organized ways of operating on information that the social nature of people comes to be their psychological nature as well." In other words, *inter*personal communication, whereby individuals regulate and are regulated by other individuals, shifts to *intra*personal communication in which the cultural artifacts that emerge interpersonally are appropriated and reshaped to meet the needs of the individual. Intrapersonal communication through private and inner speech (i.e., a conversation between "I" and "me" rather than between "I" and "you") is the means proposed by Vygotsky (1987) through which humans regulate their mental life, paralleling how humans regulate their social life.

Some have criticized the concept of internalization on the grounds that it "suggests a simplistic transfer of societal into personal meaning" (Holodynski, 2013, p. 21). The criticism crucially, though mistakenly, assumes that something gets directly transmitted from a cultural expert (or old-timer) to a novice (or newcomer) whole cloth as the correct way of doing things or of using "conventionalized signs" (Holodynski, 2013, p. 21) with no flexibility or creativity allowed. This, however, is not what Vygotsky proposed. He recognized that the process is transformative rather than transmissive and that what occurs, therefore, in movement from interpersonal to intrapersonal communication is that societal conventions are imbued with personal sense in accordance with an individual's motives and goals carried out in concrete practical, or intellectual, activity.

Vygotsky (1986) incorporated into his psychology the distinction between the Russian terms *znachenie* (conventional meaning) and *smysl* (personal sense). Accordingly, while meaning is stable and corresponds to what is found in a dictionary, sense emerges when conventional meanings are brought into concrete practical activity by individuals in the service of specific motives and goals. Consequently, sense is "a dynamic, fluid, and complex whole, which has several zones of unequal stability" and, crucially, "it changes in different minds and situations and is almost unlimited" (Vygotsky, 1986, p. 245). Thus, we might argue that meaning is social, but sense is psychological, and "reaches its peak" in inner speech (Vygotsky, 1986, p. 247), which Lantolf and Appel (1994, p. 4) described as a "semantic black hole" that accumulates previous encounters with a word. Importantly, however, people do not create sense from nothing; instead, they rely on "the appropriation and use of conventionalized signs when they want to communicate successfully and satisfy their motives in social interaction" (Holodynski, 2013, p. 22), but the signs are at the same time imbued with personal sense—in other words, they have psychological status.

Holodynski (2013, p. 22) provided a useful example to illustrate the distinction between meaning and sense, which we borrow and modify somewhat for our present purposes. In a conversation two interlocutors might use propositional utterances to talk about "dogs." As such they are likely to agree on the conventional meaning of the word (i.e., *znachenie*); however, at the same time the psychological sense (i.e., *smysl*) of the word could be markedly different for each person. If one was raised around friendly canine family pets and the other experienced dogs as large and aggressive animals that evoked feelings of fear and trepidation, their respective senses of "dog" shaped by their concrete relationships with the animals are quite different. Hence, as a psychological concept at the level of inner speech, "dog" is a very different entity for the two interlocutors, despite their conventional understanding of the word.

Vygotsky did not limit the distinction between conventional and personal meanings to words, although word meaning plays an important role in the theory. He also distinguished between social and psychological grammar (Vygotsky, 1986, p. 211), which recognized that "the structure of speech does not simply mirror the structure of thought . . . thought undergoes many changes as it turns into speech" . . . "it finds its reality and form" in speech (Vygotsky, 1986, p. 219). Vygotsky argued that the grammatical subject and predicate of an utterance do not necessarily correspond to what he called the psychological subject and predicate of the utterance (p. 221). To get a sense of Vygotsky's claim, consider an imagined interaction between guests and a host at a dinner. The host observes that one of the guests has finished her serving of carrots and asks: "Would you like more carrots?" In this case, the grammatical subject and predicate correspond to the psychological subject and predicate. However, the host immediately notices that a second guest also has finished his carrots. The question directed at the second guest is likely to be different: "Would you (as well)?" In this case, the grammatical subject and predicate and their psychological counterparts are reversed. That is, the grammatical subject "You" is now the psychological predicate since it is the focus of the host's thinking and "like more carrots" functions as the psychological subject, contextually given and therefore unsaid. In fact, in a very informal dining situation say between a mother and her children, the interaction might have unfolded as follows: the mother turns to one child and asks "More?" and then turns to the other child, but this time she asks "You?" In the first utterance "more" is the psychological predicate, indicting the focus of the mother's attention. The psychological subject, which is backgrounded and therefore assumed to be contextually given, need not be overtly stated. The second question reverses the contextually assumed and the unassumed. The mother understands and assumes her child also understands that the given, or psychological subject, is that she is dishing out carrots. The focus of her attention this time, and psychological predicate, is "you", the likely grammatical subject of a more expanded utterance (Would you like more carrots?). Finally, consider the possibility that the mother could choose to gaze at one of the children holding the plate of carrots and make the offer of more carrots without uttering anything. She could then turn to the second child and make the same offer. For Vygotsky in each situation, the psychological predicates and subjects would be the same as those reflected in the spoken versions of the interactions.

While psychological, or inner, speech, originates in social speech that individuals internalize from others in their environment, it is not subject to the constraints of socially conventional speech. However, when individuals wish to communicate their inner order through linguistic means (rather than through other channels, such as gesture) they must convert what "appears disconnected and incomplete" (Vygotsky, 1986, p. 235) into social speech that adheres to the conventions of the community's language. This, according to Vygotsky (1986, pp. 248–249), "is a complex, dynamic process involving the transformation of the predicative, idiomatic structure of inner speech into syntactically articulated speech intelligible to others." *Smysl* (sense) must be converted into *znachenie* (meaning).

Because of the complexity involved and the frequent mismatch between psychological subject and predicate, on the one hand, and their grammatical counterparts on the other, spontaneous utterances do not always adhere to the constraints of conventional grammar, and this is not limited to subject and predicate but also includes case, gender, number, tense, grammatical categories, etc. "which also have their psychological doubles" (Vygotsky, 1986, p. 221).

For example, Hopper (1997, p. 100) argued that the category Verb in real English discourse is far from the "discrete category" assumed in linguistic theory. Referencing J. R. Firth's "observation that the English verb is typically not a simple word, but is strung out over several parts of a 'verbal expression'" (Hopper, 1997, p. 95), Hopper analyzed the verbal expressions in a written narrative produced by a member of a U.S. bomber squadron that operated over Germany during World War II. The writer's goal, according to Hopper, was not to produce a literary text but to present to relatives and to other members of the squadron his account of the missions as he remembered them several decades after the war had ended.

Without going into the details of Hopper's analysis we would like to highlight the fact that according to Hopper expressions such as "I [took fast evasive action]," "I [was just beginning to get acquainted]," "we [were getting set to attack]," we [took a chance and dived down]," and "30 fighters really [give us a going over]" (Hopper, 1997, pp. 96–97) proliferated in the portions of the text where the narrative was recounting emotional events that the narrator had personally participated in. In contrast, the narrator used single-word verbs to relate events that were "distant, depersonalized" and "removed from any intimate context of personal experience," which in Hopper's view could account for why the traditional notion of verb "figures so prominently in the sentences constructed by philosophers and linguists" (p. 99).

The point we want to make is that internalization is not the result of direct transmission from old to new members of a community. Cultural artifacts, and even physical tools, can be manipulated by members of the community to fulfill their communicative and expressive needs, once they have been appropriated.[1] Moreover, internalization does not necessarily require that a feature or process "disappears" inside of an individual's head. There are many processes that are distributed between head and hand, as usually occurs in mathematical calculations of multiple digits; between head and machines, such as computers, calculators, and the like; or between individuals, as for instance occurs when piloting commercial jetliners or large ocean-going vessels (see Hutchins, 1995). The key aspect of internalization is where the locus of control resides: in others, in the self, or distributed between the self and others (including the artifacts they have created).

During ontogenesis children control the behavior of their caregivers through the non-linguistic sounds they emit, including those that indicate distress, disgust, fright, interest, and endogenous pleasure (Holodynski, 2013, p. 12). When in distress because of hunger or pain, for instance, infants are incapable of performing "motive-serving actions" to eliminate the source of the distress (Holodynski, 2013, p. 14). They are, however, able to emit natural responses such as crying, which is interpreted as an "'intentional' appeal'" by caregivers who commit to the necessary motive-action on the child's behalf in order to alleviate the problem through feeding or removing the source of pain (p. 14). While the locus of control for indicating distress resides with the child, the locus of control for the motive-serving action resides crucially with the caregivers. Eventually, children as they mature, appropriate from caregivers how to carry out their own motive-serving actions when they experience hunger and pain. The locus of control for this behavior shifts from caregivers to children. When hungry, for example, children might reach for a cookie or piece of candy. Alternatively, once they have appropriated sufficient language, they might use linguistic sounds to request, or demand, a motive-action from the caregiver (e.g., "I want a peanut butter sandwich"). In this case, the locus of control for motive-action is distributed between the child and the caregiver. The difference between an infant crying when in distress and a child verbally requesting to be fed is intentionality. The crying infant is operating purely as a biological entity, while the interpreting parent is operating as a cultural entity to take appropriate motive-serving action. When children produce linguistic sounds to indicate distress when hungry or in pain, they are operating as intentional cultural entities and, therefore, are sharing in the motive-serving action to some extent. Over time, children internalize how to conduct their own culturally appropriate motive-serving actions and the locus of control shifts from caregivers to offspring.

Figure 3.1 graphically represents our interpretation of Vygotsky's proposal on the environment as the source of development. It takes into account the discussion in this section as well as that included in Chapter 2 regarding the dialectical unity of culture and body/brain. As is indicated in the diagram, culture penetrates the body/brain and, as it does, a conscious mind emerges. The mind is not intended to be co-terminus with the brain but includes the entire person (brain and body) as a psychological organism. Moreover, the diagram captures the fact that the relationship between environment and person is a two-way rather than a one-way street, whereby the person, whose consciousness is organized through the internalization of cultural artifacts and social relationships, also contributes (see Stetsenko & Arievitch, 2004) to, and affects, the development of the environment.

Although the diagram in Figure 3.1 captures the fact that environment and person are dialectically connected, because of the constraints of representing

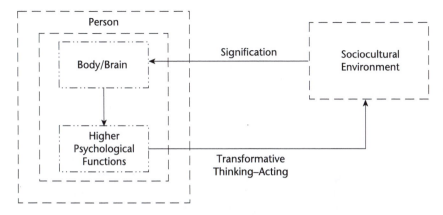

FIGURE 3.1 The dialectical interpenetration of environment and consciousness

things in two-dimensional space, it looks as if environment and person are two completely separate phenomena. As we have been arguing, however, this is not the case. To capture this unity we would like to supplement Figure 3.1 with Figure 3.2, which is intended to depict Ratner's (2012) argument that reconceptualizes human psychology as a culturally formed phenomenon; that is, psychology is enveloped by, and immersed in, culture. Again, the bi-directional arrows are intended to show the two-way flow between culture and psychology. The figure also represents the notion that the environment, although sociocultural, is the source of psychology and that, as Vygotsky argued, psychology is, because of its genesis, always quasi-social.

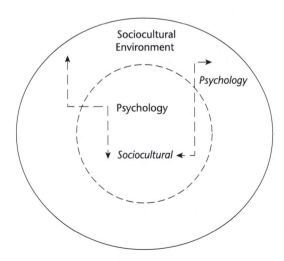

FIGURE 3.2 Psychology as a sociocultural phenomenon

## Imitation

Vygotsky proposed that "all the specifically human characteristics of consciousness" (this includes language) develop as a result of imitation (Vygotsky, 1987, p. 210). Along with instruction (formal and informal), imitation forms the basis of the ZPD. Vygotsky reasoned that if an individual is unable to imitate what is provided through cooperative instruction it is not within the individual's ZPD. If, on the other hand, the person is able to imitate a feature of behavior, under the guidance of another, it is in the process of "ripening" and will eventually come under full and independent control of the person (Vygotsky, 1986, p. 188). Reflecting the ideas of James Mark Baldwin (1915), Vygotsky characterized imitation as a complex and transformative process rather than simple copying or emulation. According to Baldwin, imitation is "a means for further ends, a method of absorbing what is present in others and of making it over in forms peculiar to one's own temper and valuable to one's own genius" (cited in Valsiner & van der Veer, 2000, p. 153).

Under the influence of the cognitive revolution headed up in large part by Chomsky and his generative theory of language, psychologists by and large lost interest in imitation, considering it, no doubt, to be a holdover from the days of behaviorist psychology. With the discovery of mirror neurons by Giacomo Rizzolatti and his colleagues at the University of Parma toward the end of the 20th century, psychologists and neuroscientists once again began to focus on the function of imitation in mental behavior (see Meltzoff, 2002). Echoing Baldwin's and Vygotsky's orientation to imitation, Hurley and Chater (2005a, p. 1) summarizing recent work on imitation, characterized it as "a rare ability that is fundamentally linked to characteristically human forms of intelligence, in particular language, culture and the ability to understand other minds." According to Goldman (2005, p. 89) the activity of mirror neurons provides the "neural substrate of an intention, or plan, to execute a goal-oriented action."

The key features of imitation are the human ability to read the intentions of other human beings and the ability to recognize the specific means that humans deploy as they direct their intentions toward specific goals. Tomasello, Carpenter, Call, Behne and Moll (2005, p. 680) remarked that in imitative learning "the observer must perform a means-ends analysis of the actor's behavior and say in effect 'When I have the same goal I can use the same means (action plan)'." The ability to engage in what they call "rational imitation" emerges very early in human ontogenetic development with children as young as 9 months of age showing some ability to imitate in a specifically human way (p. 680). Indeed, Tomasello (1999, p. 159) noted that even though under the right conditions some chimps have been observed to engage in real imitation rather than emulation,[2] which they are rather adept at, children are "imitation machines."[3]

This is not the place to enter into an extended discussion of the complex research on mirror neurons and of the array of human capacities in which imitation has been implicated (e.g., moral development, imitation of violence, emotions, tool use, etc.). The interested reader can consult the excellent two-volume survey of research edited by Hurley and Chater (2005b) and a more recent volume edited by Pineda (2010). Our immediate concern, of course, is with the relationship between imitation and language development. Arbib (2002) has made a case for an evolutionary connection between the mirror system and language, given the presence of mirror neurons in Brocca's and Werneke's areas, which would provide for a "common code for the actions of self and other" including production and comprehension of language (Hurley & Chater, 2005a, p. 6). Moreover, according to Arbib (2002, p. 275) the fact that human imitation is flexible and complex regarding ends–means relationships may implicate it in specific features of grammar, including recursivity.

Imitation, along with other processes (e.g., pre-emption, entrenchment, and analogy) plays a significant role in Tomasello's (2003) usage-based theory of language acquisition. To appropriate the language models available in the environment requires the ability to read ends–means relationships. However, in the case of language a particular variant of imitation is needed; what Tomasello (2003, p. 27) calls "role reversal imitation", which entails understanding the complex relationship between the "I/you" pattern in discourse. Thus, when a child attempts to imitate an adult utterance such as "I want you to put your toys away" the child needs to understand that the referent of the "I" and "you" must reverse. Through role reversal imitation children learn that in conversations interlocutors produce and comprehend the same forms and in this way establish intersubjectivity, an important aspect of social interaction.

Through imitation of frequently occurring forms and patterns children assemble grammatical schemas that mitigate the need to construct utterances from scratch as for example in the template *Gimme-the* X, *I (don't) wanna* X, *Where's the* X? (Tomasello, 2003, pp. 306–307). Reliance on templates and prefabricated chunks is not only important in language development, but it is a feature of adult language use as well (see Hopper, 1997). Use of chunks also plays an important role in adult L2 language development and use (see N. Ellis, 2009, p. 147).

Importantly, imitation does not only take place in direct linguistic interaction, it also occurs through eavesdropping on interactions that do not include learners directly. Saville-Troike (1988) documented several instances of *vicarious* (see Ohta, 2001) imitation by young, non-native-English-speaking children as they apparently eavesdropped on conversations among their American classmates. Moreover, as Meltzoff and Gopnik (1989) noted, imitation of an environmental model need not occur immediately and may be deferred for more than a day; a behavior that would allow learners the luxury of offline analysis and therefore afford the opportunity to pay closer attention to the model. Speidel (1989, p. 163) argued that deferred imitation may be situated on a continuum between immediate imitation and spontaneous speech with the former functioning as "essential building blocks for spontaneous speech." Speidel and Nelson (1989, p. 5) even consider *observation* to be a form of imitation. Research reported in Goldman (2005, p. 89) documents that mirror neurons in monkeys and in humans fire when they observe goal-directed actions performed by others.

To conclude the discussion on imitation, we call attention to the "ratchet effect" discussed by Tomasello (1999) in which imitation, possibly along with intentional instruction, serves to establish a "platform" for innovation over time in accordance with shifting cultural and individual needs (p. 39). As each generation appropriates the cultural artifacts of the previous generation through imitation (and instruction), it has the opportunity to modify the artifacts to meet social and individual needs (p. 37). The ratchet effect applies to physical tools such as hammers (whose development has been documented in archeological records) as well as "cultural conventions and rituals," including language (p. 37). With regard to language one can point to grammaticalization whereby lexical words have, through frequent use across generations, lost their meaning and have taken on grammatical functions (e.g., English auxiliary verbs *do* and *will*). Imitation at the individual level can also serve the ratchet effect as L1 and L2 learners increase their proficiency in a language.

## Conclusion

Based on our discussions in Chapters 1, 2, and 3, it should be clear by now that SCT is not a social or sociolinguistic theory, it is a full-fledged theory of human psychology that seeks to understand its origins, functioning, and development. Unlike other psychological theories, however, it argues that the factors that shape mental activity are social in origin. Humans do not merely react to the world, as other animals do, they intentionally change it; however, change is a social rather than an individual act. For this reason, Vygotsky rejected behaviorist theory and behaviorist research methodology because it assumed that humans only react to, rather than change, the world. Although he sought to build a materialist psychology that was based on a foundation of rigorous scientific analysis, he also recognized that it would not be feasible to rely on the same research methodologies used in the natural sciences to study processes that were in themselves not naturally sociocultural. Following Marx, Vygotsky proposed a historical research methodology—a methodology designed to understand human psychology by uncovering its origins and tracing its change over time in at least five different temporal domains: phylogenesis, where humans diverged from primates; sociocultural history of humanity as such that entailed cross-cultural analysis of the psychological effects of different modes of life on thinking; the consequences of changes in the modes of living within a particular culture (e.g., the introduction of formal schooling in rural communities); ontogenesis of individuals; and the development of specific psychological processes over time (e.g., acquisition of a second language). Thus, Vygotsky established a completely new methodology for psychology—a historical, or genetic, method that seeks to understand how humanly created artificial forms of mediation (auxiliary stimuli) enter into, and reshape, the thinking process.

One of the challenges that those of us working within SCT-L2 research have confronted over the past 25 years is a general and persistent misunderstanding of the theory. Therefore, instead of summarizing the discussion in the current chapter, we would like to conclude by addressing Fulcher's (2010) recent misinterpretation of the scope and nature of SCT. Although Fulcher directs most of his commentary at DA, several of his remarks relate to the theory in general. We respond to the latter remarks here and we reserve our reactions to his critique of DA for Chapter 8.

The following are what we see as Fulcher's construal of SCT: it is a social constructivist theory that forgoes any claims to generalizability beyond a given context (2010, p. 75); it assumes that learning "is a progression along a known pathway" even though very few theories of SLA (e.g., Krashen's natural order hypothesis and Pienemann's Processability Theory) provide evidence of "regular and predictable development" (p. 77); yet, it "explicitly rejects any view of second language acquisition that posits a universal process that is regular and predictable" (p. 78); and it "rejects any general learning theory, like Piaget's, that posits a developmental sequence," which, according to Fulcher, is a major problem because it would mean that the theory cannot make testable predictions about acquisition and that only the mediator "is able to influence the acquisitional path of the learner, so that the next stage is decided by the current intervention" (p. 78).

We begin with the inconsistency in Fulcher's perspective regarding the predictability of developmental sequences. He first criticizes SCT for requiring developmental sequences because learning is assumed to proceed along a "known pathway" (2010, p. 77), when in fact, in his view, very few developmental sequences have been identified and then only for languages such as English and German.[4] He then criticizes the theory for arguing against developmental sequences, pointing out that Lantolf (2009) specifically rejects regular and predictable developmental paths.

To some extent we accept the findings of Pienemann's (1998) research regarding the processability hierarchy in untutored settings where learners are unlikely to have access to the kind of support/mediation needed to overcome processing constraints. The issue of concern from our perspective, as discussed in Chapter 6, is whether or not properly organized instruction can promote development that overcomes the processing constraints posited by Pienemann's theory. The problem we see with Fulcher's position is his assumption that SLA, and by implication, SCT, is expected to make predictions of the type made in the natural sciences. We recall our discussion of intermediary theories in Chapter 2 where we explained that each domain requires its own laws, principles, and concepts, including research methodologies. Vygotsky strongly criticized psychology for naively importing concepts and assumptions from the natural sciences:

A concept that is used deliberately, not blindly, in the science for which it was created, where it originated, developed and was carried to its ultimate expression, is *blind*, leads nowhere, when transposed to another science. Such blind transpositions, of the biogenetic principle, the experimental and mathematical method from the natural sciences, created the appearance of science in psychology which in reality concealed a total impotence in the fact of studied fact.

*(1997a, p. 280)*

Nevertheless, Vygotsky argued that psychology could be a science on a par with the natural sciences, but that it required its own methodology corresponding to its ontological assumptions on the nature of human consciousness. His solution, as we have noted, was the genetic method designed to trace the historical development of psychological processes.

Under appropriate mediation, SCT does allow for predictions; however, they are based on individual learner responsiveness to mediation rather than on a priori natural processes. Thus, as we will see in Chapters 7 and 8, and as predicted by the general law of genetic development, what learners are able to carry out under mediation at a particular point in time is an empirically based prediction of what they will be able to carry out independently at a future point in time.

More perplexing is Fulcher's assertion that SCT is a social constructivist theory interested exclusively in local findings. In light of what we have said so far it should be clear that SCT is most definitely not a theory of the local. For instance, we saw that its laws, principles, and concepts explained the impact of education on the psychology of rural peoples in Central Asia. The same principles were brought to bear in Vygotsky's (1990) work with individuals suffering from psychological disorders, including schizophrenia. We noted Luria's (1973) successful implementation of these principles to remediate patients experiencing a variety of neurological traumas. Finally, in Chapters 5, 6, and 8 we will discuss the research in education where the same principles and laws are employed to enhance L2 development. This is hardly a theory with a local scope.

As for the charge of social constructivism, we ask how can a theory grounded in dialectical materialism—a view that posits an independent reality as its fundamental starting point—qualify as such a theory? Ratner (2012), arguing from his neo-Vygotskian perspective, offers a scathing critique of constructivism as manifested in the work of psychologists such as Harré (2009) and Gergen and Gergen (2002). Briefly, Ratner's critique focuses on constructivism's goal of reducing society to a conversation, which Harré (2009) believes offers people greater individual freedom to live their lives as they wish. They clearly would be unable to do so if constrained by structured macro cultural institutions (Ratner, 2012, p. 35). The danger inherent in Harré's position is clear. To claim that humans are free to do as they please in a society where the reality is that institutions determine how they live only leads to deeper mystification of the very forces that are the problem in the first place. What has to occur, according to Ratner (2012), is to demystify the constraints—make them visible to people and make people aware of the consequences of the constraints on individual freedom. This is a task that should be carried out by education.

For their part, Gergen and Gergen (2002) argue that all ways of knowing are equally valid and acceptable therefore none can be privileged over any other. Furthermore, no opinion can be challenged because what is believed is what is real and not the other way around. If a belief is challenged as wrong then the reality derived from that belief must be false. Thus, beliefs in a flat world, a geocentric universe, a divinely created world, are as valid as what scientific research tells us (Ratner, 2012, p. 36). There is no need to test "opinion against an independent reality," and, as a consequence, people become susceptible to the consequences of being wrong (p. 36).

SCT starts from the premise that the material world exists independently of people and recognizes that in humanizing that world through social activity people at the same time create their own psychology. The task of the theory is to contribute to the formation of sociocultural environments and activities that optimally promote psychological development. For Vygotsky and Ratner education is a primary macro cultural environment where systematic development ought to occur through intentional and well-organized instruction (i.e., *obuchenie*). The test of the theory therefore resides not in its capacity to generate a priori predictions but in its ability to fulfill the responsibility required of a praxis-based theory of developmental education. In the next chapter we present a framework for implementing this pedagogical imperative.

## Notes

1  Vygotsky's proposal for internalization is counter to the apprenticeship model supported by Lave and Wenger (1991) in which oldtimers transmit practices to newcomers, therefore resulting in replication of cultural patterns rather than innovation change. Lantolf and Thorne (2006) provide a critique of apprenticeship particularly as it has been extended to education.

2  Emulation is the ability to achieve the same attractive goal attained by another individual by whatever means possible, including through trial-and-error (Hurley & Chater, 2005a, p. 15). Unlike in imitation, emulation does not involve the ability to read means–ends, but only ends.

3  H. Moll and Tomasello (2007) point out an important distinction between intention reading in human infants and other primates. Human intention reading entails cooperation and communication, while in primates communication is missing and instead of cooperation one finds competition.

4  The research of Pienemann and his colleagues has uncovered developmental sequences in a wide array of languages, well beyond English and German (see Pienemann, 1998, 2005; Pienemann & Kessler, 2011).

# 4
# A THEORY OF DEVELOPMENTAL EDUCATION

This chapter presents a theory of developmental education grounded in Vygotsky's materialist psychology and fleshed out in the work of Piotr Gal'perin. As we discussed in Chapter 2, the general theory of psychology proposed by Vygotsky contends that higher forms of human consciousness arise from the dialectical interaction of elementary biological mental processes and culturally shaped forms of life (i.e., tools, concepts, institutions). Education, as a salient macro cultural institution, plays a central role in his theory of development. That is, formal education for Vygotsky is not a place where one learns, it is an activity where one develops in ways that are not normally available in the everyday world. Vygotsky specifically stated that education "not only influences certain processes of development, but restructures all functions of behavior in a most essential manner" (1997a, p. 88).

We begin with a discussion of the key statements that Vygotsky provided with regard to developmental education, especially as they relate to the central principle of the theory that the social world is the source of higher forms of consciousness. We will include in the discussion the recent interpretation of Vygotsky's writings on education offered by Miller (2011). Then we present Gal'perin's theory of developmental education with particular focus on those aspects of the theory that are relevant to the research to be discussed in Chapters 5 and 6. Although our concern in this and the following chapters is the influence of systematic, or academic concepts (also called scientific concepts), as the source of development in educational activity, it is necessary to stress that mediation in the ZPD also plays a central role in the process. For purposes of presentation only, however, we deal with each of the key components of development in separate chapters, with the ZPD being treated in Chapters 7 and 8.

What we present in this chapter is not a theory of (language) teaching as for example has been proposed by Larsen-Freeman (1990), Widdowson (1990), and Ur (2012). In outlining a framework for a theory of language teaching, the three authors addressed the relevance of SLA theory for what should transpire in the classroom. Larsen-Freeman (1990, p. 267), for her part, noted that she had not yet resolved the matter of "how it [the theory] would interface with a theory of SLA." Widdowson (1990) expressed a degree of caution, if not skepticism, with regard to the relevance of SLA research and theorizing for a theory of language pedagogy. He believed that findings from basic research can only have pedagogical value if "they can be carried through into the classroom context" (p. 6). Ur (2012), in her discussion of the theory–practice interface in grammar teaching, acknowledged the argument that teaching that is not sensitive to developmental sequences is "useless" even though instruction might be able to help learners "move ahead," but not avoid "the inevitable intermediate stages" on their way to internalization of the target feature (p. 89). A fundamental difference between such theories of teaching and a theory of developmental education is that the latter does not subscribe to the view that development is, or should be, the same regardless of social environment. A theory of developmental education begins from the assumption, as we argued in the previous chapters, that the social environment has a significant impact on development and this includes appropriately organized L2 classrooms.[1]

A key feature of Vygotsky's theorizing with regard to education is that teaching and learning should not be treated as separate activities (see for example R. Ellis (2012) where separate chapters are devoted to teachers and learners) but must be brought together in a dialectical unity to exploit "their complementary effects" (Stetsenko & Vianna, 2009, p. 47). Vygotsky captured the unity in the Russian expression *obuchenie*, i.e., "teaching–learning" (Cole, 2009) which does not follow development "like a shadow follows the object which casts it" (Vygotsky, 1994a, p. 355), but prepares the way and promotes development. However, because teaching–learning–development are dialectically interconnected, as development unfolds it at the same time opens up opportunities for future teaching–learning, which in turn leads to further development. How this occurs is not only the topic of the remainder of this chapter but of the remainder of this book. We begin our presentation of the theory with a discussion of orders of mediation as framed by Miller (2011).

## Orders of Mediation

Even though we anticipate differences in the specifics of developmental processes due to variations in the material circumstances under which second languages are acquired, the overarching principle of mediation is what ultimately shapes the process in all environments. Miller (2011) identifies three orders of mediation in Vygotsky's writings. A characteristic of all orders of mediation is "the interception of the self by the other" (p. 404). That is, one enters a particular macro cultural system (family, political, legal, sports, religion, education) as an actor, whose behavior, mental and physical, is temporarily surrendered to others. Through mediation one develops a new understanding of, and way of acting in, relevant circumstances and in so doing the actor becomes a self-regulated agent (p. 404).

### First-Order Mediation

First-order mediation, also referred to by Karpov and Haywood (1998, p. 27) as *metacognitive mediation*, originates in interpersonal communication where, for example, parents tell their child not to do something that might bring the child harm (e.g., inserting a screwdriver into an electrical outlet). The parents are at the same time "regulating the child's behavior and supplying the child with a tool of self-regulation" (p. 27). The child eventually begins to self-regulate by appropriating (often through imitation, see below) the language of the adults and subsequently using it to resist the temptation to do something proscribed by the family. Of course children also appropriate the utterances of adults to guide their way through activities that are encouraged and valued by the family.

   In school, first-order mediation becomes more systematic than it usually is in the everyday world. Pre-school children, for instance, are engaged in games that teach them to develop self-control over their bodies by first reacting to variations in the tempo of music (e.g., walk slow when the tempo is slow and fast when the tempo is fast) and then by verbalizing the "rule" to regulate the movements of other children as well as their own bodies (Karpov & Haywood, 1998, p. 29). For older children first-order mediation can be carried out in subject-matter classes through group work and task-based activities, or in a particularly interesting approach developed by Ann Brown and her colleagues known as "reciprocal teaching" (Palincsar & Brown, 1984; Palincsar, Brown, & Campione, 1993). In this approach, students are given the opportunity to conduct class discussions and as such clarify, summarize, question, monitor, evaluate, and regulate, the problem-solving activity of their classmates. The students also carry out tasks in collaboration with other students in which one student guides, observes, and corrects the actions of another student whose responsibility it is to implement the procedures required to complete the task. These activities reflect Vygotsky's principle that self-regulation develops not only through surrendering to others but also through guiding others who surrender to you. First-order mediation is the major topic of Chapters 7 and 8, which focus on mediation in the ZPD and DA.

### Second-Order Mediation

Second-order mediation, and the one that is the primary concern of this and the next two chapters, deals with culturally constructed tools; that is, artifacts that are "surrogate form[s] of consciousness" as the "concrete embodiments of other minds" and which serve to "facilitate certain actions and inhibit others" (Miller, 2011, p. 398). Karpov and Haywood (1998, p. 28) refer to second-order mediation as "cognitive mediation." As with first-order mediation there are differences between the forms of second-order mediation made available in the everyday world and in the educational environment. Of particular relevance for the present discussion is the difference between unsystematic empirical knowledge that predominates in the everyday world and systematic abstract knowledge that is the basis of developmental education.

Wertsch, del Rio, and Álvarez (1995, p. 23) stress that artifacts in themselves are "powerless" and have no impact unless and until they are integrated into human activity. For one thing, this means that analyzing artifacts outside of human activity cannot tell us how the artifacts are taken up and used to carry out an activity— studying artifacts outside of activity can at best inform us of their potential to shape activity. To be sure, this is not a trivial matter, but without use the potential is only that—potential. For another thing, when artifacts are used "they do not determine or cause action in some kind of static, mechanistic way" (p. 23), they enter into a dialectical relationship with the user. In other words, as humans take up artifacts to carry out activities, the artifacts influence and shape the activity, while at the same time, humans shape and influence the artifacts.

As an example, consider the case of a potter shaping a piece of clay into a finished pot (this example is inspired by an observation made by Diane Larsen-Freeman, April, 19, 2013). The potter most likely begins the process of shaping the clay with a plan in mind, but the plan and the realization of the plan through her hands as they come into contact with the clay on the potter's wheel are influenced by the physical properties of clay. Thus, the potter's plan is influenced by the fact that clay cannot be drawn into an infinite variety of shapes and sizes (otherwise it is likely to collapse). Moreover, the potter's hands must at the same time be sensitive to how the clay responds to her movements as she seeks to carry out her plan that does take account of the properties of clay. The clay by itself does nothing, while, at the same time, the potter cannot create without the clay. Through their interaction the potter shapes the clay and the clay, through its physical properties, influences the shapes that the potter is able to generate.

Moreover, the importance of second-order mediation in general is that it compels a reanalysis of what it means to be a thinking person. Perkins (1993, p. 94) questioned the appropriateness of the traditional assumption of psychology and education that thinking is the behavior of the "person-solo." He pointed out that in experiments participants are rarely if ever offered tools, including something as simple as paper and pencil, to support their thinking, and even though education allows students to use paper and pencil, texts, computers, and even other people when studying, when it comes time to "demonstrate learning" most of these tools are proscribed other than perhaps paper and pencil, which function as "a hopper into which the person-solo can pour concrete evidence of achievement" rather than as "components of the thinking process" (p. 95). Nickerson (1993, p. 243), also supporting the notion of thinking as a functional system, or the person–plus perspective, argued that "many activities in which we engage would be impossible without the artifacts that mediate them." As an example he noted how difficult it is for him to read without a pen, which he uses to mark up and make notes in the margins of texts, which in turn affect his thinking and serve as intellectual resources and extensions of his memory (p. 253).

Wertsch (1998) offered an even more compelling example of what he characterizes as "agent-acting-with-mediational-means" (p. 24).[2] To arrive at the correct solution to the following multiplication problem, 343 × 822, most people would align the numbers vertically one under the other and proceed to multiply single digits in order to generate three vertical columns of numbers, which they would then add to arrive at the correct answer: 281,946. Wertsch (1998, p. 29) asks two questions with regard to the problem's solution: did "I" really solve it alone and what would "I" do if required to multiply the same numbers without arranging them vertically? The answer to the second question is that without the vertical arrangement it would be difficult if not impossible for most people to carry out the calculation and even if the rare few were able to calculate the answer using a horizontal arrangement, if we increased each number by one additional digit (e.g., 3,345 × 8,229), it would most likely rule out everyone. The vertical arrangement of the numbers is a second-order mediational means, which we appropriated from our experience in a third-order macro cultural institution (i.e., education). Someone else instructed us in how to arrange the numbers in order to carry out the calculation. Without this culturally created knowledge, it would be virtually impossible for most of us to arrive at the correct answer.

With regard to the first question, Wertsch (1998, p. 29) suggests that the syntax of the numbers does "some of the thinking." Most of us are unaware that the vertical arrangement is even a cultural tool and how much our performance depends on it until it is unavailable. Wertsch concludes that the answer to the first question then is that "I" did not carry out the calculation alone; rather it was "I" and the cultural tool together that did. We would add that the individual(s) who directly (or indirectly) taught us how to multiply with the use of the cultural tool are also implicated in the calculation; hence, agency in this case entails "I," the numerical syntax, and the person(s) who provided the necessary instruction.

By far the most important cultural tools available as second-order mediational means are spontaneous and scientific concepts. They play a central role in sociocultural theory. Vygotsky dedicated two major chapters of *Thinking and Speech* (Vygotsky, 1987) as well as several other independent texts to their discussion. Scientific concepts, as we will see, are the foundation of the process of developmental education. For now, we highlight the basic distinction between spontaneous and scientific concepts, which is that the former are empirical in nature and derived from appearance (e.g., a whale is a fish because it appears to have fins and it lives in oceans; tomatoes are vegetables), while the latter reveal the essential qualities of an entity or process (e.g., whales are mammals because they breath air and suckle their young, which are born alive; tomatoes are fruits because they are the means through which flowering plants disseminate seeds by encasing them in ovaries). Concepts are relevant for the formation of consciousness because they shape how we perceive, understand, and act in and on the world.

With regard to language, if we think of it as the potter's clay, while analyzing its properties, physical as well as symbolic, can tell us something of its potential (i.e., possibilities and constraints), it cannot tell us how it is actually brought into concrete communicative activity. A dialectal relationship is established when a user takes up the artifact and uses it to achieve specific communicative goals. As with the potter, the user develops a communicative plan that is sensitive to the potential that resides in the artifact and remains sensitive to this potential as the plan is implemented. Even though communities imbue their communicative systems with constraints, they can at times also violate these constraints in order to fulfill their communicative intentions. Language, as a humanly created artifact, is far more flexible than clay.

### Third-Order Mediation

Third-order mediation, according to Miller (2011, p. 400), includes "institutions, social structures or cultural forms constituted by bundles of relations between people and between people and their products." It comprises the systems and super-systems of society as constructed over the course of history. In Ratner's (2012) theory third-order mediation is comprised of the macro cultural institutions that we noted in Chapter 2 (i.e., education, politics, religion, work, economy, work, leisure, family, science, etc.). These are relevant to human psychology because they influence the nature of first- and second-order mediational means. Vygotsky (1978) dedicated a substantial portion of his writings to third-order mediation, or what he called *leading activities*—among the most important for his project are play and education, the latter of which is the focus of our book.

## Systemic Theoretical Instruction

Although Vygotsky did not work out in full detail a theory of developmental education, he did lay the foundation for such a theory that was expanded upon by Gal'perin in his theory of Systemic Theoretical Instruction (STI), at times referred to as Concept Based Instruction (CBI) in the L2 literature. Gal'perin and his colleagues, in cooperation with teachers, tested and modified the theory through more than 800 classroom studies in virtually all school subjects (including foreign languages) and general cognitive ability (e.g., attention, problem solving, systematic thinking) (Arievitch & Stetsenko, 2000, p. 76).

## Mental Action

According to Gal'perin (1992), teaching–learning entails action of some kind directed at specific objects in the service of an intended goal. An action can be a concrete physical activity such as digging a hole in order to plant seeds or a mental activity such as planning the layout of a garden. The important point is that actions can be carried out with support at four different levels of abstraction: *material/materialized*, with the support of physical objects or their representation in the form of models, diagrams, or pictures; *perceptual*, carried out without support of external objects but with the support of visualized or imagined objects; *verbal*, performed with the support of external speech; *mental*, carried out internally without the support of artifacts or speech (Haenen, 2001, p.161).

The first two types of action require the presence of an object (the real thing or a representation of the real thing), whereas the third and fourth types of action are carried out in the absence of any kind of object. The key point is that for Gal'perin mental actions do not begin as mental actions; they begin as material/materialized action and are converted into mental actions as they pass through the phase of verbal actions. Development occurs as mental actions emerge (Gal'perin, 1992; Arievitch & Haenen, 2005). It involves "expanding the potential for meaningful action" with "resources for acting, speaking, and thinking that enable the learner to participate effectively and creatively in further practical, social, and intellectual activity" (Wells, 1994, p. 84).

To illustrate the differences among the four types of support, consider the case of a person wishing to rearrange the furniture in her living room. Carrying out the action at the material/materialized level requires either physically moving the furniture or manipulating a model (e.g., computerized virtual model or perhaps toy furniture) that represents the actual pieces of furniture and their current arrangement into a new configuration. Perceptual action would be carried out with the person physically present in the living room, looking around and imagining the movement process. Verbal and mental actions could be performed while the person is sitting in her office at work rather than in her living room. In the first case, the action would be externalized in private speech, or perhaps even through communicating with a colleague, while in the second the person would manipulate the furniture in her mind's eye in the absence of any exterior speech. Gal'perin's theory also takes account of the quality of a given action characterized according to three indicators: *generalization* indicates the extent to which the properties of an action are stable and essential rather than non-essential and variable, as such the action is context independent and therefore can be implemented in a wide array of environments; *abbreviation* indicates if the original components of an action are executed or are reduced, or "telescoped" as usually happens as a consequence of rehearsal and practice; *mastery* indicates that an action can be carried out independently without support from another person (e.g., the teacher), a diagram, or model (Haenen, 2001, p. 160).

Gal'perin's theory of mental action captures a more fine-grained understanding of the process of internalization than is described in Vygotsky's writings. He concentrated on formulating a strategy to integrate his theory into educational praxis to promote student development through the internalization of domain-specific scientific (sometimes called academic by Vygotsky) concepts. This does not mean that students are merely expected to memorize and store "inert facts"; on the contrary, in Gal'perin's theory, and in line with Vygotsky's psychological principles, to know something is to be able to

> carry out, participate in, continue, and ultimately contribute to collaborative practices through ones' actions ... knowledge is an alive, generative, and deeply historical process that is engendered by and itself engenders active engagement in collaborative sociocultural practice.
>
> *(Stetsenko & Vianna, 2009, p. 46)*

## Educational Praxis

Gal'perin's theory of developmental education, in line with the principles of Vygotsky's materialist psychology, reverses the traditional view on the relationship between instruction and development, whereby instruction is assumed to be effective only when learners are developmentally ready to learn. This has been the general orientation of SLA theorizing (see, however, Larsen-Freeman & Cameron, 2008). Krashen (1981, 1982) and Pienemann (1984, 1989) are among the most notable advocates of the development first perspective; a topic that we will return to in Chapter 6.

Gal'perin's theory specifies that for teaching–learning to promote and lead development it must "integrate high-quality cultural tools that embody the most efficient ways of solving problems" (Stetsenko & Vianna, 2009, p. 44). Moreover, because the theory recognizes the dialectical unity of theory and practice (i.e., praxis), as discussed in Chapters 1 and 2, it also calls for learners to engage in subject-matter appropriate classroom practices mediated by relevant cultural tools that empower learners to explore and transform their environment (p. 44) rather than acquiesce to a pedagogical model dominated by right and wrong answers. It also rejects, as inefficient and too tenuous, constructivist approaches to education where through discovery learning students either independently or in collaboration with their teacher or other students construct their own knowledge in a particular subject area.

The theory comprises three general phases and two subphases organized in a spiral designed to stimulate development of the mental actions described above in the service of active learner participation in (communicative) practices. According to Haenen (2001, p. 161), Gal'perin originally proposed the phases or levels as the "'stepwise procedure'," a label that implied a rigid sequential procedure to be followed regardless of the learning environment. One of the outcomes of his extensive research program, however, was the abandonment of the rigid sequence in favor of a more flexible "blueprint" where levels may potentially be combined, abbreviated, or skipped entirely depending on concrete classroom conditions, including the specific mental action to be internalized, the practices to be implemented, and current learner knowledge (Arievitch & Haenen, 2005, p. 159).

## First Phase: Orienting Basis of Mental Action

This is the most important phase of the process because it presents learners with as complete a picture as possible of the relevant concept that learners can appropriate to guide mental action in a particular domain. The concept is formulated in what Gal'perin calls a SCOBA, or Schema of a Complete Orienting Basis of an Action (Gal'perin, 1989, 1992). The SCOBA provides a cognitive map that serves to orient learners whenever they engage in activities relative to the concept.

Gal'perin argued that verbal explanations of concepts alone are potentially problematic for learners, particularly at the early stages of developmental education. This is because verbal accounts are sequential and often entice learners to memorize them without deep understanding of the concept. SCOBAs, which generally take the form of a model, diagram, picture, or some other non-linguistic representation of the relevant concept, are holistic and do not lend themselves to memorization. They serve as materialized reminders of the knowledge required to engage in a particular action. Although SCOBAs can include stretches of language, we have found them to be more effective if verbal information is kept to a minimum (see Lantolf & Thorne, 2006). When learners use SCOBAs as representations of systematic conceptual knowledge to guide their performance (along with guidance provided by teachers) they are, from a psychological perspective, imitating the knowledge materialized in the SCOBA. See Figure 6.1 in Chapter 6 for a sample SCOBA used in Yáñez-Prieto (2008).

As Vygotsky (1987, Chapter 6) proposed, developmental education must be centered on high quality conceptual knowledge of the object of study. This knowledge should take account of the best available information generated by specialists through the systematic analysis of a particular domain. Vygotsky characterized this knowledge as scientific (1987) or, at times, as academic (Vygotsky, 1994a); the important point, however, is that this knowledge is systematic, abstract, and generalizable, and therefore not empirically linked to specific contexts of use. It is contrasted with so-called spontaneous knowledge that we appropriate, often, though not always, unconsciously as we participate in daily life. Spontaneous knowledge does not usually capture the essence of an object or activity; instead, it is often derived from the superficial aspects of the object or activity; and it is often connected to empirical contexts. We have discussed the distinction between scientific and spontaneous concepts at length in previous publications (e.g., Lantolf & Poehner, 2008; Lantolf & Thorne, 2006) and will therefore forego an in-depth analysis here. We will, however, repeat one example that comes from Davydov that makes the distinction clear.

Davydov (2004, p. 82) points out that there are at least three ways to conceptualize *circle*. One is typical of everyday knowledge and is based on a comparison of things that are round, such as coins, buttons, cakes, etc. The other two are based on abstract scientific understanding of the concept. The first comprises a verbal definition, as follows: "circle is a shape comprising those points in a plane that are at a constant distance, called the radius from a fixed point called the center" (p. 82). The second is also verbal, but it is of a different type: "a figure described by the rotation of a line with one end free [moving] and the other fixed" (p. 82). The first definition is far more likely to result in what Vygotsky described as "a meaningless acquisition of words, mere verbalization" that is "educationally fruitless" (1994a, p. 356) than is the second, which enables learners to capture the essence of a circle—constancy of radius—by understanding actions that generate circles.

The challenge is to formulate pedagogically effective SCOBAs that capture the systematic essence of a concept in ways that are not only understandable for learners but that at the same time allow them to deploy the concept in a broad array of concrete goal-directed activities. We will address this issue with regard to language development a bit later in the chapter, once we have completed our discussion of Gal'perin's educational theory. For now it is important to reiterate that the initial phase of the developmental process calls for the systematic presentation of high quality conceptual knowledge that can be readily deployed in concrete practice supported by the materialization of the concept either in the form of a chart, diagram, or model, and if possible material objects that can be directly manipulated by students (e.g., a compass to generate circles). The advantage of materializing a concept over providing a purely verbal definition is that the latter lends itself to memorization without understanding, while the former is difficult to memorize without understanding. In addition, verbal definitions and descriptions are sequential, which makes the information less accessible as a mediational tool during practical activities than is the case for holistic materializations of a concept. Moreover, the opportunity to physically manipulate objects has been shown to enhance performance on tasks such as mathematical calculations (Gibbs, 2005, p. 193). In Chapter 6, we will discuss a study that documented the effects on the development of Chinese word order as a consequence of learner manipulation of Cuisenaire rods associated with Silent Way pedagogy (see Gattegno, 1963).

## Second Phase: Verbal Action

Once students show a high level of control in using a concept supported by a SCOBA and/or concrete material activity, "it is necessary to tear the action away from its previous material support" (Gal'perin, 1969, p. 257). According to

Gal'perin, while a student may, on occasion, achieve this important step toward internalization and independent performance spontaneously, they generally require a shift in external support from the SCOBA to support provided by external speech (p. 259). In accordance with the principle that speaking is a reflexive activity (i.e., it is directed at interlocutors in social interaction as well as at the self) and functions as a transition phase between material and mental actions (see Vygotsky, 1987, Chapter 7 for a full discussion), Gal'perin (1969) incorporated an overt speaking phase into his theory of developmental education. In speaking about an action either to another (i.e., social communication) or to one-self (i.e., private speech) an action is liberated from control by materialized SCOBAs or material objects as occurs in the first phase of internalization. The second phase then represents developmental progress in gaining control over a concept and its use.

Gal'perin allowed for two subphases of verbal action: one that Haenen (2001, p. 163) characterizes as "communicated thinking" and another that he calls "dialogic thinking." In the former, learners are required to carry out an action linguistically in order to make it comprehensible to others and not just themselves (Gal'perin, 1969, p. 260). In the latter, students are encouraged to speak to themselves covertly about what they are doing when understanding and deploying a concept. Reliance on verbal support in order to appropriately use a concept in practical activity is an important step in transferring the knowledge and how to use it from the material to the mental plane. This is because verbal action is simultaneously material and symbolic and therefore serves as the transition phase between action that relies on purely material or materialized support and action that "leads to the formation of a new object of action, namely, abstraction" (p. 261). Abstractions enable learners to free themselves from concrete empirical contexts of concept use and empower them to deploy a concept in a wide array of contexts linked to a broad scope of goals.

The subphase of dialogic thinking is especially important because it represents a shift from speech directed at others to speech directed at oneself. In other words, shifting from communicated to dialogic thinking entails a shift from "I"/"You" conversations typical of social interaction to "I"/"Me" conversations essential for speech to become psychological (Vocate, 1994) and therefore takes on features of psychological speech (e.g., abbreviation and directed at regulating one's own behavior). Through continued engagement in dialogic thinking, activity becomes increasingly routinized and moves closer to becoming purely mental (Haenen, 2001, p. 164).

In the L2 field most SCT studies have incorporated dialogic thinking and only Swain and her colleagues have on occasion used communicated thinking. We are however, not aware of any studies that integrate both forms of verbal thinking as intended by Gal'perin. Negueruela (2003) incorporated dialogic thinking into his research on the teaching of temporal aspect and verbal mood in Spanish as a foreign language. We have already discussed this research in some detail in Lantolf and Thorne (2006) and will not repeat the discussion here. Swain and several of her colleagues have explored the effects of verbal thinking in their research on *languaging*. Languaging, according to Swain (2006, p. 96), is "the process of making meaning and shaping knowledge and experience through language" and as such is a central component in the process of learning. Swain and Lapkin (2007) examined the effects of dialogic thinking on attention, understanding and knowledge consolidation in a single learner during a writing task in which the learner was asked to compare his original essay with a remodeled version of the essay. In Brooks and Swain (2009) the researchers engaged ESL students in a collaborative writing task and recorded instances of what they identified as languaging as communicated thinking that spontaneously occurred throughout the activity as well as during a stimulated recall.

In Lapkin, Swain, and Knouzi (2008), and in Swain et al. (2009) they deliberately engaged students in dialogic thinking with regard to their understanding of the concept of passive voice in French. An important feature of the studies is that among other things the researchers reported significant correlations between the quantity and quality of languaging produced by learners and their performance on post-tests designed to assess their ability to identify the correct voice of French verbs and to produce in writing the correct forms for expressing this feature of the language.

A study by Ganem-Gutierrez and Harun (2011) of six L2 learners of English tense-aspect included both communicated and dialogic thinking in its design. In this case, however, some learners engaged in communicated thinking in dyads and others engaged in dialogic thinking individually. None of the participants was afforded the opportunity to engage in both kinds of languaging, as called for in Gal'perin's theory. Learner scores on the post-test were higher than on the pre-test with regard to their understanding of the concept of tense-aspect; however, they did not show as much improvement in their ability to explain specific instances of tense-aspect use. Unfortunately, no attempt was made to compare the effects of communicated thinking with those of dialogic thinking either on conceptual understanding or on explanation of concept use.

## Final Phase: Inner Speech

As learners gain mastery over the concept through dialogic speech, the process itself transfers to the "highest form" of speech for the self, inner speech (Gal'perin, 1969, p. 263). At this point, understanding and use of the concept becomes completely mental and any connection with a material component fades away. The individual is now able to use the concept with facility in different contexts and often in creative ways (see Chapter 5). In Gal'perin's words, the learner "just knows that's how it is" (1957, p. 221). A plan of action can be developed on the mental plane so that individuals are able to anticipate the likely effects of their actions on others, modify their behavior to fit variations in the situation, and monitor and evaluate the effectiveness of their performance (Haenen, 2001, p. 165). In other words, the orienting basis of behavior is now psychological rather than material.

## Pre-Understanding and Its Negation

A critical issue that developmental education must confront is the prior knowledge that students bring to the current instructional situation. Vygotsky (1987) pointed out that when children enter school for the first time they do so with spontaneously appropriated knowledge of various aspects of the world in which they have been integrated by members of their community. This knowledge is, as we have said, largely experientially based and frequently reflective of particular empirical contexts. When asked for instance what an "uncle" is, children usually respond with the names of their own uncles—Uncle Fred, Uncle Joe, etc.

Formal education is the activity in which learners are presented with scientific knowledge of both that part of the world they may have experienced directly as well as that part of the world that they may never directly experience. The fact that learners come to school with everyday knowledge is important, according to Vygotsky, because this knowledge forms the basis on which scientific knowledge can build. Vygotsky (1986, p. 194) discusses the relationship between the two types of knowledge in terms of the ZPD where spontaneous concepts indicate a student's actual level of development and scientific concepts represent their future development that is the goal of educational activity. The former often, though not always, arise from our immediate experiences of the world and the latter develop from "a mediated relationship" to the world and therefore trace a different path from concept to world (Miller, 2011, p. 125).

To illustrate the interaction between spontaneous and scientific concepts, Vygotsky (1986, p. 195) uses the example of learning a foreign language in school, which he asserts is "conscious and deliberate from the start," compared to learning one's native language, which is by and large acquired unconsciously while one is involved in culturally organized forms of daily life. In instructed language learning, at least as it was apparently practiced during Vygotsky's time, metaknowledge is appropriated before fluency develops, whereas for native language acquisition, the situation is reversed with schooling making the language visible and open to conscious inspection and analysis and with this students achieve greater control over how they use their language, especially in the case of literacy activities. The most important similarity between foreign language study and the development of scientific concepts is that they are both mediated by prior knowledge. According to Vygotsky (1986, p. 197), in learning a word in a foreign language a connection between the word and its object is not direct, as it is in one's native language; rather it is mediated by the meanings already established in the native language. Similarly, the development of scientific concepts is mediated by previously appropriated spontaneous knowledge of the world.

While spontaneously acquired knowledge in its mediating function is considered by Vygotsky to be a contributing factor in developmental education, Miller (2011) raised the prospect that previous knowledge, or what he calls *pre-understanding*, can be an impediment to development, particularly if it is not dealt with appropriately by educators. He illustrates the importance of pre-understanding with a simple example of a child's understanding of what chairs are for. If the child wants to retrieve an object from a high shelf he may have no idea that it would be possible to stand on a chair, if his pre-understanding of chair is that it is an object for sitting and not as something that could be used to elevate (p. 376). An adult may instruct the child with an utterance such as "use the chair," in which case the child may proceed to sit rather than stand on the chair, again because his pre-understanding is that chairs are for sitting. In this case, the adult's instructional move is insufficient to change the child's understanding of the object. The adult must inform the child that it is possible to get closer to the desired object by placing the chair under the object and then standing on it. If the child then successfully retrieves the object the "performance can serve as a model for solving similar tasks in the future using the required tool" (p. 376), because now the child's pre-understanding of chair has been modified through the adult's speech and the child's behavior.

According to Miller, repeated performance under pre-understanding or as a result of inadequate or incomplete instruction will serve to "entrench the existing understanding" (2011, p. 378). Consequently, one of the important responsibilities of an educator is to bring to the fore (i.e., make visible) a learner's current understanding of a particular topic. The task is to then confront this knowledge with systematic academic knowledge in order to generate "dis-coordination" (Gallego & Vasquez, 2011, p. 215) within the learner. This is the essence of praxis where theoretically informed knowledge and action confronts knowledge and action typical of everyday life (p. 215). The goal of resolving dis-coordination is to dislodge pre-understanding and replace it with new understanding. The process does not happen through direct transfer of knowledge but through mediated performance of the student guided by conceptual knowledge materialized in SCOBAs and by the teacher herself. The dislodging of pre-understanding and the new understanding do not come directly from the teacher or from the SCOBA but from the meaning of the actions (including communicative actions) learners carry out on the basis of materialized knowledge and teacher mediation.

Negueruela (2003) has documented the problems encountered by language learners and teachers as a consequence of learner pre-understandings of features of the target language based on rules of thumb provided in their previous learning experiences. Rules of thumb are closer to everyday knowledge than they are to scientific knowledge. They are at best descriptively appropriate for specific contexts of use and at worse they are often misleading. The problem is that, especially for learners who have a few years of experience studying languages in classroom settings, rules of thumb tend to become entrenched and consequently are not easily dislodged and replaced by new systematic knowledge. As we will see in Chapter 5, however, one of the ways of helping this process along is through communicated and dialogic thinking linked to student understanding of a concept and its use. This process enables learners to confront their pre-understanding overtly and in so doing to recognize that the rule is not adequate.

## Defining Concepts for L2 Developmental Education

In the evaluation of sociocultural perspectives on L2 learning that appeared in the first edition of their book on second language theories, Mitchell and Myles (1998, p. 161) justifiably critiqued the research that had been produced to that point as lacking "a very thorough or detailed view of the nature of language as a formal system."[3] In the second edition of their book, Mitchell and Myles (2004) again pointed out that sociocultural research on L2 has failed to offer a "thorough or detailed view of the nature of language as a system" (p. 220). They further noted that the orientation toward language, such as it was at the time, was incommensurable with the view of language as an "autonomous and abstract system acquired through specialized mechanisms" (p. 222). In the third edition of their work (Mitchell & Myles, 2013), however, the authors correctly pointed out that more recent work within the SCT-L2 framework is aligned with "meaning-based, functional perspectives on language" or what Thorne and Lantolf (2006, p. 177) call "linguistics of communicative activity." Sociocultural theory has always been aligned with meaning- and usage-based theories of language; unfortunately, those of us working within the theory failed to make this perspective explicit.[4]

Beginning with Negueruela's (2003) dissertation, SCT-L2 research began to make explicit the fact that it is closely allied with meaning-based theories of language. While Negueruela's work did not align itself with a particular theory of language, it did foreground meaning over form in presenting specific features of Spanish grammar to university students of the language. Following Negueruela's dissertation several dissertations were completed that either directly or indirectly drew on Cognitive Linguistics (henceforth, CL) as the foundation for presenting systematic and pedagogically useful knowledge to students. At about the same time that SCT-L2 research was looking to CL as a theory of language, researchers in CL were extending their theory into language pedagogy. Frank Boers and Andrea Tyler and their respective associates have been arguably the two most active applied CL scholars over the past several years. To be sure, others such as Holme (2009) and Littlemore (2010) have also been forceful advocates for applied CL; however, Boers (Boers & Lindstromberg, 2008) and Tyler (2012) have carried out a substantial number of classroom studies designed to assess the effectiveness of the theory for L2 instruction. Our goal in discussing CL is not to survey the applied research that has been carried out under its auspices; Tyler and Littlemore do an excellent job in this regard. Rather, we would like to make a case for the relevance of CL as a source of systematic concepts for STI.

## CL for STI

In our view, several features of CL make it an especially attractive theory of language for L2 STI to use for its conceptual base. Unlike generative theories, that assume an autonomous and modular language organ, CL explains language development through the same processes that account for general cognitive development. In foregrounding meaning over form, CL views language as motivated rather than arbitrary. This is especially important for instructed language development because it means that domains of language that had been considered to be difficult or perhaps impossible to teach through direct instruction (e.g., prepositions and particles verbs in English) are "amenable to instruction" through presentation of "schematic patterns with central tendencies and extended more peripheral (but usually motivated) exemplars" (Tyler, 2012, p. 62).

One of the consequences of understanding language as motivated is that patterns, including syntax, that might otherwise seem "to express the same propositional content" are in fact alternative ways of presenting "various construals on an event and on the roles participants play in the discourse" (Tyler, 2012, p. 67). For example, the English sentences *Mary gave George a cake* and *Mary gave a cake to George* are not propositionally equivalent and therefore one is not "derived" from the other as had been claimed in previous versions of generative linguistics. The constructions are motivated by different pragmatic meanings (p. 176). The first sentence reflects a **Cause to Receive** instruction, in which *George* is the semantic **recipient** and cake is the semantic **patient**, whereas the second is a **Transfer-Cause Motion** construction, in which cake is **patient** and George is **goal** (p. 176). In the first sentence, the cake is pragmatically in focus and in the second, George is in focus. An additional important difference in the patterns is that in **Cause to Receive** constructions, the recipient must be animate (p. 177), which explains the incongruity of "*Mary tossed the pond the ball," but in **Transfer-Cause Motion** constructions the goal may be animate or inanimate, as in *Mary tossed the ball to George* or *Mary tossed the ball into the pond*.

The fact that CL explains language patterns as motivated by meaning and that use is based on the way users construe events and states and how they subsequently wish to profile various aspects of events for interlocutors is particularly significant for STI. Keep in mind that the goal of STI is not the acquisition of inert knowledge, which results in what Vygotsky (1986, p. 148) called "verbalism" or knowledge that is "de-humanized" and lacking "human meaning" (Stetsenko, 2010, p. 14). It is rather for knowledge to become a meaningful tool that students can actively reconstruct in order to achieve their own activity. Lantolf (2008) calls this process "active reception" of knowledge; perhaps an even more effective characterization of the process is captured in Stetsenko's (2010, p. 14) terminology "creative reconstruction" whereby learners make systematic knowledge relevant for their specific purposes. We believe that CL provides precisely the kind of conceptual knowledge of language that can be humanized by learners to give voice to their concrete communicative needs.

The shortcoming we perceive in applied CL, however, is that it does not have a sound theory of developmental education. Consequently, how the conceptual knowledge is presented to learners and how it is internalized has been inconsistent across the various studies that have been carried out within the CL framework. This could explain why several of the studies reported on in Tyler (2012) have produced uneven, and in some cases, less than robust outcomes. We believe that STI can provide the developmental theory that CL lacks, while at the same time, CL can provide the linguistic theory that SCT-L2 research has been lacking. In terms of sociocultural theory, CL provides systematic meaning-based analysis of language, or what Vygotsky, in Russian called *znachenie*, and STI provides learners with the procedures for converting this knowledge into personally relevant meaning or *smysl*.

An especially attractive aspect of CL for STI is that it seeks to explain linguistic concepts through diagrams, schemas, and visual models. As we have argued earlier in the chapter, these represent the all-important initial phase of STI—high quality materialization of scientific concepts. Care must be taken, however, as Tyler (2012) indeed pointed out, not to import diagrams and visualizations of concepts from theoretically oriented CL research directly into pedagogical practice. Sensitivity to learner needs must be exercised, while at the same time not compromising the quality of the concept under study. Gal'perin understood the importance of the nature of materializations of concepts and therefore dedicated a substantial component of his research agenda to working out pedagogically effective SCOBAs (see Talyzina, 1981).

## STI and the Explicit/Implicit Interface

In the final section of this chapter we consider research on the material basis of L2 development that has been carried out within the framework of cognitive neuroscience and its implication for STI. As is evident from the preceding discussion, STI is very much an explicit approach to promoting developmental education. It relies on systematic conceptual knowledge presented to learners through materialized and, if possible, material activity. It requires learners' conscious understanding of concepts and of how these may be brought into their own communicative practices. The debate with regard to implicit/explicit instruction and implicit/explicit learning has been a leitmotif in SLA research for several decades. Among the issues addressed is whether or not explicit instruction can give rise to automatized and non-conscious linguistic knowledge (i.e., language acquisition), or whether this type of knowledge can only be developed through implicit instruction. In other words, is there, to some degree at least, an interface between explicit and implicit knowledge or must each type of knowledge be developed independently of the other? A related question is whether or not explicit knowledge can be used effectively in spontaneous communicative activity, a possibility proscribed in models such as Krashen's, or whether such performance can only occur as a consequence of implicitly developed knowledge.

## SLA Positions on the Explicit/Implicit Interface

SLA researchers have adopted three general positions on the matter: non-interface, strong interface, and weak interface. The non-interface position holds that implicit and explicit knowledge are stored in different regions of the brain that are not interconnected and therefore one type of knowledge cannot convert into the other. This is the position argued for by Krashen (1981, 1982) and more recently supported by Hulstijn (2002) and by Paradis (2009).

The strong interface position asserts that each type of knowledge can convert to the other. It is conversion of explicit to implicit knowledge through appropriate types of practice that is relevant for the current discussion. According to R. Ellis (2005a, p. 144), DeKeyser (1998) supports the strong interface position; however, in our view, DeKeyser's position is more nuanced than Ellis allows for. DeKeyser approaches the matter from a skills development perspective and as such casts the problem in terms of automatization (p. 56) rather than implicit knowledge per se. According to DeKeyser (p. 57) declarative knowledge, which is explicitly presented to learners in classroom settings can become proceduralized through appropriate forms of practice and therefore can be accessed automatically in spontaneous performance. However, DeKeyser (p. 57) notes that in this sense proceduralization is "incompatible with implicit learning." DeKeyser (2003, p. 329) allows for the possibility that explicit knowledge can become implicit, or at least the functional equivalent of such knowledge, if it becomes automatized and "learners eventually lose their awareness of the rules."

The weak interface position is represented in three different versions. In one, explicit knowledge can become implicit as a result of appropriate practice but only when a learner is developmentally ready to acquire the feature (Ellis, 2005a, p. 144). A second version proposes that explicit knowledge contributes to implicit acquisition by making salient to learners any differences that may exist between their current linguistic knowledge and the input they are exposed to. A third version proposes that output produced by the explicit knowledge system can serve as "auto-input" (p. 144) to the implicit system.

Recently, DeKeyser proposed three rather than two types of knowledge in skill-based learning: declarative, procedural, and automatized (DeKeyser & Criado, 2013a). Declarative knowledge is "knowledge or information about things and facts," including knowledge of the rules of language and word meanings stored in long-term memory (p. 1). This kind of knowledge can result from explicit instruction and can usually be brought into consciousness. Procedural knowledge is knowing how to carry out a process or behavior and, according to DeKeyser and Criado (p. 1) comprises "if-X-then-do-Y rules, and is associated with implicit, unconscious knowledge." Automatized knowledge results from "restructuring and fine-tuning of procedural knowledge" and enables "relevant (linguistic) behavior" to be "displayed correctly and rapidly" (p. 1).

The process through which declarative knowledge becomes automatized entails three stages, according to DeKeyser, with each requiring a particular kind of practice for consolidation to occur. Declarative knowledge is consolidated through traditional form-focused activities, including fill-in-the blank and translation exercises (DeKeyser & Criado, 2013a, p. 4). Proceduralization occurs as a consequence of communicative practice that might include question and answer exercises where learners have to pay some attention to meaning while at the same time manipulating formal features of the language (DeKeyser & Criado, 2013b). Procedural knowledge has an advantage over declarative knowledge in that it greatly reduces the burden on working memory because such knowledge is stored in prefabricated patterns that are accessible when needed and therefore avoid the need to assemble the structure from scratch (DeKeyser, 2007, p. 98). Procedural knowledge requires additional practice for it to become automatized and accessible in a rapid and error-free way. To achieve this degree of processing ease requires extensive practice in spontaneous communicative activities in both spoken and written formats (DeKeyser & Criado, 2013a, p. 4). According to DeKeyser (2003), adults have a more difficult time developing implicit knowledge than do younger learners and children and therefore are likely to require more extensive and intensive communicative experiences (e.g., study abroad) in the new language to convert declarative to procedural knowledge and to eventually automatize this knowledge.

It would appear that DeKeyser leans more toward the strong rather than the weak interface position. Explicit declarative knowledge can become proceduralized and automatized, although with some difficulty, as long as opportunities are provided for sufficient learner engagement in appropriate forms of practice in communicative activities. In personal communication with Lantolf (DeKeyser, April 11, 2005), DeKeyser expressed the opinion that the interface issue is ultimately an empirical one that might better be resolved through neuroimaging research rather than behavioral studies. In the next section we discuss research in neuroscience that addresses this question and consider its implications for STI.

## L2 Neuroscience Research and STI

Paradis (2009) and Ullman (2005), based on research in cognitive neuroscience, have independently argued for a model of adult language acquisition that supports the non-interface position, originally proposed by Krashen. In our view, they make a strong case, which we believe is compatible with Gal'perin's theory of developmental education. Ullman refers to his model as the Declarative/ Procedural model (DPM), while Paradis, as far as we can determine, does not attach a specific rubric to his hypothesis. He does stress, however, that it "*is a*

Declarative/Procedural model, even though it lacks some of the granularity of Ullman's model," in particular with regard to the role of hormones (i.e., estrogen and dopamine) and some details of the "neuroanatomical underpinnings of the distinction between implicit linguistic competence and explicit metalinguistic knowledge" (2009, p. 12, italics in original).

## Declarative and Procedural Memory

Declarative memory is the brain system that underlies semantic (i.e., facts, including word meaning) and episodic knowledge of events in the world (Ullman, 2005, p. 143). This knowledge is in part explicit and therefore available to consciousness. Procedural memory, on the other hand, is the neurological system involved in learning and control of motor and cognitive skills, in particular those that involve sequences (Ullman, 2005, p. 146). It underlies implicit knowledge and as such is not accessible to conscious inspection.

According to Paradis (2009, p. 115) the period from birth to roughly 5 years of age constitutes an optimal time span in which to acquire a language with "nativelikeness" in all components of the language, including prosody, phonology, morphology, and syntax. The ability to learn vocabulary is not included in the so-called "optimal period" in which full acquisition of a language is possible. Lexical learning is subserved by declarative memory. In Ullman's model lexical learning not only includes semantic–phonological mapping, it also includes the syntactic and collocational features associated with a word (e.g., the English verb *give* requires two object arguments, as in "John gave Mary a book" vs. "*John gave Mary").[5] Paradis, however, distinguishes between sound–meaning pairings, which he claims are learned through declarative memory, and the syntactic features associated with words, which he contends are subserved by procedural memory.

Around the age of five the optimal period for implicit acquisition begins to diminish first with regard to prosody, followed by phonology, morphology, and syntax in that order (Paradis, 2009, p. 114). Beyond the age of five full implicit acquisition of all of the components is rare, although it is possible to achieve native ability in one or two of the components but not all of them.

Paradis and Ullman agree that the neurological system that subserves implicit language acquisition is procedural memory. It is a slow process that requires extensive amounts of exposure to language. Once language enters procedural memory, however, it is processed automatically and with a high degree of accuracy. According to Paradis (2009, p. 32) once acquisition (i.e., unconscious procedural learning) occurs the language is accessed automatically. That is, automatic processing is not the result of practice; it is a consequence of acquisition by the procedural memory store. Moreover, procedural learning does not entail attention or noticing with regard to either "intent to learn," or "what is acquired" (p. 27). Most importantly, however, with regard to the current discussion, Paradis and Ullman agree that declarative and procedural memory are independent systems, which means that declarative knowledge cannot enter into procedural memory (i.e., become proceduralized) no matter how much practice one engages in. It is, however, possible for something to be learned by both systems but this must be accomplished by each system independently of the other—there is no neurological pathway connecting one system to the other. As Paradis (p. 26) states: "there is no continuum between implicit competence and explicit knowledge, declarative memory and procedural memory, incidental acquisition and attentional learning, or automatic and controlled processing."[6]

If Paradis is correct then adults attempting to learn languages after the optimal period are more likely to rely on declarative memory to accomplish the task. Again, Ullman and Paradis agree on the likelihood of this happening. The fact that late learners rely on declarative memory to learn an L2 does not, in Paradis's (2009, p. 117) view, mean that adults cannot attain a high level of mastery in an L2. It does mean, however, "that their achievement is mainly the result of conscious learning and conscious control of their output" (p. 117) through use of their declarative memory system. Mastery can be achieved through appropriate practice, which does not convert controlled, conscious processing to automatic, proceduralized processing. Instead, through practice "controlled processing may be speeded-up"; nevertheless, "it remains qualitatively different from automatic processing (which admits of no degree of conscious control whatsoever and is subserved by different neural structures)" (p. 26).

Having said this, it is important to note that both Paradis and Ullman allow for the possibility that adults are capable of acquiring an L2, at least in part, through use of procedural memory. This is because "the decline in *the use* of procedural memory when appropriating a second language is not necessarily due to a deficiency in procedural memory for language per se (though it may be at least partially so)" (Paradis, 2009, p. 118, italics in original). Paradis speculates that the shift from one memory system to the other may be because as we age we generally rely on declarative memory as our primary learning resource, especially in educational settings.[7] In addition, the L1 system, already acquired through use of the procedural system, may in some way interfere with use of the same system a second time around (p. 118). However, given sufficient exposure and for a sufficient amount of time, as for example in immersion situations as when someone immigrates into a new speech community where contact with the L1 is diminished, it would be conceivable for adults to access the procedural system to acquire an L2, although acquisition through procedural memory "becomes less efficient and takes longer with increasing age" (p. 119). For his part Ullman (2005, 2012) provides evidence through research on the learning of an artificial language that at high levels of proficiency in the language learners appear to rely on the procedural memory system given that they display ERPs that are quite similar to native speakers of a language.

## An Example

Gillon Dowens et al. (2009) report on an ERP study of the type of learners that Paradis believes could well rely on their procedural system to acquire advanced proficiency in the L2. The participants were late adult learners of L2 Spanish living in an immersion environment in Spain. Their L1 was English and they had all begun to learn Spanish after the age of twenty. They had on average 20 years of immersion experience with a minimum of 12 and a maximum of 33 years. Native speakers of English and Spanish judged all 23 participants to be at a high level of proficiency in speaking and listening comprehension in both languages. All participants reported using Spanish on a daily basis. No information is provided on their use of English and therefore it is not possible to determine if they were completely cut off from regular exposure to their L1. The ERPs generated by the participants were compared with those produced by native speakers of Spanish when exposed to a series of Spanish sentences involving the manipulation of gender and number agreement features. Leaving aside the details, the study found that the bilinguals' ERPs matched those of the native speakers for number concord but diverged from the native speakers for gender agreement. The researchers hypothesized that the variation between the groups could be attributed to differences in depth of processing for number versus gender agreement (p. 1884). Given that English marks number agreement, the bilinguals had in all probability acquired this feature earlier as part of their L1 and therefore processed at a deeper level than gender agreement, which is not a grammatical feature of English. The researchers conclude that even though late immersion learners are able to acquire an L2 at a high level of proficiency, there continue to be "lasting effects of L1 feature transfer" that have an impact on working memory capacity during L2 processing (p. 1885). In terms of Paradis's hypothesis it could be that the L1 Spanish speakers had acquired full nominal concord through procedural memory while the L2 speakers had acquired number agreement procedurally, but gender concord was learned using their declarative memory system.

Paradis and Ullman appear to support the non-interface position in that they argue that declarative knowledge cannot convert into procedural knowledge. This is because there is not a neurological connection between the two memory stores in the brain. The researchers also agree that it is possible for someone to learn a language through both systems later in life. According to Paradis, however, if the procedural system is involved it is likely to be restricted to subcomponents of the language rather than the entire language as is the case for L1 acquisition (p. 125).

## DPM and the Implicit/Explicit Divide in SLA

One of the assumptions often made in the SLA literature regarding implicit versus explicit learning and knowledge is that the former is necessary for spontaneous communication, while the latter can be pressed into service when a user has time to access the knowledge, as for instance when writing without time pressure or when taking a paper-and-pencil test that requires focus on the formal properties of a language. R. Ellis (2005a) attempted to develop a series of tests to independently measure implicit and explicit L2 knowledge. Acknowledging that even if a test created conditions for use of one type of knowledge rather than the other, there is no guarantee that a given test would result in "pure measures" of each type of knowledge, Ellis at least hoped to be able to design tests that would "predispose learners to access one or the other type of knowledge only probabilistically" (p. 153).

Ellis and his research team developed five tests, three of which (oral narrative, elicited imitation, and timed grammaticality judgment) were designed to access implicit knowledge and two of which (untimed grammaticality judgment and a task that engaged participants' metalinguistic knowledge) targeted explicit knowledge. Although Ellis proposed seven hypotheses to be tested in the study, we would like to focus on only one of these that is most directly relevant to the current discussion: time-pressure tests will elicit implicit knowledge, while non-timed tests will allow for access to explicit and implicit knowledge (p. 163).

Using factor analysis, Ellis (p. 163) uncovered two principal factors, one for the timed tests (i.e., imitation, oral narrative, and timed grammaticality judgment) and one for the untimed tests (i.e., metalinguistic test, untimed grammaticality judgment). Moreover, learner performance on the timed grammaticality judgment was significantly worse than performance on the untimed equivalent with the same test items. On this basis, Ellis concluded that "the tests provide relatively separate measures of implicit and explicit knowledge" (p. 166). The problem, however, is that following our discussion of the DP model, it is impossible to determine which of the two underlying memory systems accounts for performance on the tests of implicit knowledge. Recall that according to Paradis access to declarative memory, which underlies explicit knowledge, can be speeded up through practice. If so, this could mean that the two factors uncovered by Ellis might not be implicit knowledge (procedural memory) and explicit knowledge (declarative memory) but speeded up and slowed down access to declarative knowledge. On the other hand, it is conceivable that we are dealing with two distinct memory systems, since the DP model and Paradis's hypothesis allow for the possibility of late acquisition through procedural memory under appropriate immersion circumstances. However, according to Ellis (2005a, p. 154), the 94 NNS (non-native speaker) participants in his study had been studying English for an average of 10 years but in a largely foreign language setting with only 1.9 years on average of English immersion experience. To determine which system is being used by learners one would need to compare response times for NSs with those of the NNSs and/or compare the ERPs of both groups, as Ullman has done, or alternatively and more effectively, carry out an fMRI study to observe which brain areas are activated during the various tasks.

The implications of the DP model, which for the sake of discussion we assume to encompass Paradis's line of argument as well, are clear. Older learners heavily favor learning through the declarative memory system, which stores knowledge that can, through practice, be accessed quickly, although not as quickly as knowledge stored in procedural memory. As Paradis (2009, p. 103) points out, efficient use of speeded up access to declarative knowledge for all intents and purposes is more than adequate for learners to communicate effectively in a second language. According to the DP model to attempt to teach an L2 through procedural memory would mean finding a way to provide learners with extensive and intensive exposure to input and to isolate them from use of their L1. Assuming that this were even feasible in the educational setting, it would still take an inordinately long period of time for the procedural system to work out the complexities of the new language.

Privileging the declarative memory system through provision of high quality conceptual knowledge of the new language, along with appropriate communicative practice, as is proposed in Gal'perin's theory, is a more efficient means of developing proficiency in the L2 in the educational environment. If at some later point in life learners find themselves in appropriate immersion environments they then might be able to build up their procedural memory store relative to the L2. In the meantime through STI we undertake to promote language development through the neurocognitive system that should most effectively serve the communicative needs of learners. Ellis (2012, p. 301) states that explicit instruction is "by and large, only of value to the extent that it assists the acquisition of implicit knowledge" on the assumption that implicit knowledge, presumably subserved by procedural memory, is the only means to engage in spontaneous communicative activity. The argument made in this section is that explicit knowledge subserved by declarative memory is a viable, if not primary, alternative for instructed adult learners to achieve this ability.

## Conclusion

In this chapter we presented the theory of developmental education proposed by Gal'perin. To fully appreciate the relevance of the theory for the educational set-ting, we first discussed the major principles and concepts of Vygotsky's theory of sociocultural psychology. Perhaps the most important aspect of the discussion is the notion that education is a particular kind of development that is intentionally designed (i.e., artificial) to bring learners into contact with high quality systematic (i.e., scientific) knowledge of the object under study. Developmental education does not seek to replicate the processes at work in everyday settings. Along these lines we argued that the social environment is not merely the site where develop-ment occurs—it, in fact, plays a central role as the source of the development of higher forms of conscious functioning. The social environment includes school as a site that promotes a special kind of development not readily available in the everyday world.

Gal'perin's theory of Systemic Theoretical Instruction begins with high quality systematic knowledge (i.e., scientific concepts) and seeks to help learners not merely to understand the concepts, but to appropriate them for use in concrete practical activity, including communicative activity, in the case of language. Given its focus on meaning rather than form, we proposed that Cognitive Linguistics is a theory of language that interfaces effectively with STI and with sociocultural theory in general. Moreover, this theory fulfills an important criterion of STI in that it formulates its theoretical concepts in coherent visual schemas although adjustments need to be made in some cases for the sake of pedagogical effectiveness.

Following Vygotsky's general principle that the interaction between individuals and social environments is not identical in each instance, STI recognizes two orders of mediation as discussed by Miller (2011). The first order, mediation through cultural artifacts, is provided by theoretically grounded SCOBAs designed to represent the relevant concepts. The second order, mediation through other regulation in a learner's ZPD, takes account of the potential variation between individuals and their environments. Said another way, second-order mediation is intended to provide learners with equal access to the necessary conceptual knowledge presented in first-order artifacts, and equal access cannot mean the same treatment for all individuals (see Lantolf & Poehner, 2013). Teachers must be prepared to adjust the nature and degree of interpersonal mediation they provide to learners in order to maximally help their development. We address second-order mediation in Chapters 7 and 8.

STI is a very explicit approach to developmental education. It features well organized theoretical knowledge intended to enhance learner understanding and performance. Again, following Vygotsky's general theory of psychological development, STI incorporates verbalization (i.e., communicated and dialogic thinking) as an important component to foster learner understanding of relevant concepts and of their use in practical activity. According to STI real understanding consists not merely in comprehending concepts as such, but in finding ways of using the concepts in practical activity. For this reason, STI integrates appropriate communicative activities into its framework. However, there is no sanctioned set of activities; rather, they are determined by the instructor and depend on the communicative needs and expectations of learners. Activities that have been used in various STI studies will be discussed in the following chapters.

Finally, we proposed that STI promotes development through the declarative memory system, which is more efficient and results in faster learning for adults than development subserved by the procedural system. We believe that it is a more effective approach for the educational setting, because with appropriate practice it results in accelerated use of declarative memory. Even though declarative memory might not be accessed as quickly as automatized procedural memory, it serves communicative ability effectively.

## Notes

1  Vygotsky produced a relatively short essay on childhood multilingualism where he emphasized that social context plays a key role in the learning process (Vygotsky, 1935/1997b). He mentioned learning the phonological and grammatical properties of an L2, but was primarily concerned with the role of lexical meaning and conceptual differences between the L1 and the L2 in the thinking process and of the crucial role that inner speech plays in verbal and non-verbal thinking. John-Steiner (1985) conducted a pilot study of adult immersion learners of English as a second language from a sociocultural perspective where focus was on learning strategies and the relationship between verbal thinking in the L1 or L2. Vygotsky (1987) also dedicated several pages of *Thinking and Speech* to the teaching of foreign languages in elementary school, although he did not present anything like a full theory of L2 developmental education.

2  Lantolf and Thorne (2006) contend that from the perspective of SCT there can be no such entity as person-solo. Indeed to become a person is to act with mediational means. This is what higher human consciousness is—mediated psychological functioning. The problem is, as Wertsch (1998) pointed out, we do not have adequate terminology to capture this concept and for this reason he and his colleagues proposed the awkward, though appropriate, hyphenated expression.

3  To be fully accurate, Wells (1994) attempted to integrate Halliday's meaning-based theory of language with Vygotsky's theory of psychology. For whatever reasons his discussion of the two theories and arguments for why they should be brought into contact did not carry over to SCT-L2 research.

4  Mitchell and Myles's (2013) continuing observation that SCT-L2 research has not addressed the matter of rate and route of acquisition is a topic that we will return to in Chapter 6.

5  Sentences such as "I gave at the office" call into question the theoretical assumption that *give* is categorized as a ditransitive verb. To pursue the implications of this point is beyond the scope of the current discussion.

6  Schumann et al. (2004, p. 70), on the other hand, suggested that there might indeed be an anatomical pathway connecting the declarative to the procedural memory store. They pointed out, however, that for evolutionary reasons the conversion process is "difficult and time consuming" (p. 71).

7  Both researchers also agree that some time during middle age, roughly around the age of 45, declarative memory capacity begins to decline. According to Ullman (2005, p. 148) this may be linked to the decline in levels of estrogen in the body of men as well as women, although women have it in greater quantity throughout life relative to men.

# 5

# L2 SYSTEMIC THEORETICAL INSTRUCTION

## Experimental-Developmental Studies

R. Ellis (2012) remarked that "there are relatively few sociocultural studies that have investigated learning (as opposed to 'participation') inside the classroom." Most of the SCT-L2 studies have involved learners "withdrawn from their normal classroom to complete the various tasks in order to facilitate data collection" (p. 241). These studies, in fact, have implicitly and explicitly followed the experimental-developmental method introduced into psychology by Vygotsky (1978). In Chapter 2 we noted that the goal of this method is to explain psychological processes by provoking their development through the introduction of auxiliary stimuli (i.e., mediation). Ellis (2012, p. 248) further pointed out that even though some of these studies (e.g., those conducted by Swain and her colleagues and by Ganem-Gutierrez mentioned in Chapter 4) have incorporated pre- and post-tests, the tests have not been designed to determine if learners can transfer, and therefore, generalize, learning to new activities and new contexts (p. 248).

Lantolf and Thorne (2006) dedicated the final two chapters of their book to two studies that represented an initial step in redressing both concerns expressed by Ellis above. Negueruela's (2003) dissertation was a study of learning using STI in an intact L2 classroom and Poehner's (2005) experimental-developmental study incorporated tasks designed to assess learners' ability to transfer what they had learned through DA. Since that time a number of additional studies have been carried out both in intact classrooms and in experimental-developmental formats and some have included transfer tasks. In this chapter and the next we focus on six studies framed by STI, three of which followed an experimental-developmental format using pre- and post-tests and three of which were conducted in intact classrooms. One of the studies conducted in an intact classroom discussed in Chapter 6 did incorporate a transfer task as part of its design. Chapter 8 includes a discussion of both intact-classroom and experimental-developmental studies concerned with promoting L2 development through DA. Both studies include transfer tasks and one includes pre- and post-tests as well as transfer tasks.

The L2 studies considered in this chapter followed Vygotsky's experimental-developmental approach in order to investigate the effects of STI on the development of two areas of language that have not received extensive attention in L2 research: sociopragmatic variation in the use of 2nd person nominative pronouns *tu/vous*, 1st person plural pronoun *on/nous*, and the negation markers *ne . . . pas/. . . pas* and the ability to detect and interpret sarcasm in L2 English. The third study, while not new in terms of its language focus—topicalization in L2 Chinese—is innovative in the sense that it directly challenged Pienemann's (1984, 1987, 1989) "teachability hypothesis" from an SCT perspective. Of course, Vygotsky also understood that laboratory research is not the end point of praxis. For him the true test of psychological theory, as we said in Chapter 2, resides in its capacity to effect significant change in non-laboratory environments such as classrooms—the domain of the three studies discussed in Chapter 6. We recognize therefore that in future work the implications of the experimental-developmental studies will need to be tested under real classroom conditions.

## STI and the Sociopragmatics of L2 French

Van Compernolle (2012) conducted a project designed to orient learners of L2 French to the underlying conceptual knowledge that guides speakers in their use of three pragmatic features of the language (2nd person address forms *tu/vous*, 1st person plural pronoun *on/nous*, and negation *ne . . . pas/. . . pas*) and to be able to deploy this knowledge to guide their own use of the features in communicatively appropriate contexts. In specific terms the goal of the study was to help learners to "map conceptual meanings onto forms, which reverses more traditional approaches to SLA and L2 pragmatics, which seek to map acquired forms onto meanings" (p. 32). Van Compernolle pointed out that the three sociopragmatic features are highly frequent in an array of contexts and therefore "learners are likely to hear and have to use one or more of them in any interaction in which they participate" and that violating the conventions of use "can result in negative consequences" (p. 32). He stated that while converging with, or diverging from, the conventions of use may not be "undesirable," learners need to have an understanding of "the effect such choices may have on their interlocutors" (p. 32).

The study was carried out over a 6-week period and included eight student volunteers who were enrolled in a fourth-semester university French course in oral communication and reading comprehension. According to van Compernolle (2012, p. 54), students at this level are "communicatively capable," but their general experience with the language is limited to classroom contexts and they therefore do not have much awareness of "sociolinguistic and pragmatic variants" available in the language. None of the students had experience in immersion settings.

Each student met individually with the tutor/researcher once per week for a total of 6 weeks. Included in the instructional program were awareness interviews, judgment questionnaires that asked learners to assess appropriateness of use of each of the features, spoken-interactive tasks modeled on Di Pietro's (1987) strategic interaction methodology, and conceptual explanations and SCOBAs designed to promote learner understanding of how the features in focus can be used to reflect culturally appropriate social behavior along with the consequences of choosing to flout the conventions.

Van Compernolle argued that sociopragmatic capacity entails understanding the choices available, the consequences of those choices with regard to the reaction and uptake of an interlocutor, and the meaning that a user wishes to convey. He referred to this capacity as *"sociolinguistic agency"* (p. 22, italics in original). This does not mean that conventional patterns are to be ignored entirely, but that relying on these "exclusively" in pedagogical practice risks missing "a great deal of the local, contextualized, and discourse-sensitive aspects of language" (p. 22). This is because language users do not "draw from a sociolinguistic toolkit but ultimately have the potential to transform the patterns and meanings in and through discourse" (p. 53). Van Compernolle (p. 53) notes that this is reminiscent of Vygotsky's (1987) distinction between *znachenie* "stable meaning" and *smysl* "contextual meaning" that arises in communicative interaction.

## Conceptual Meanings and SCOBAs

Van Compernolle (2012, p. 60) noted that traditional pedagogical explanations for use of *tu/vous* are "simplistic rules of thumb" based on factors such as "relative age" and "interlocutor status." Although some immersion learners with significant daily exposure to French in a variety of communicative settings "begin to notice the more subtle complexities of the system ... their knowledge is often not very systematic" (p. 60). While learners may develop some sense that the *tu/vous* distinction is variable, they have virtually no understanding of the social variation associated with *on/nous* without immersion experiences. They do not generally appreciate the fact that in modern French, *nous* is the more formal and *on* the more informal variant of the 1st person plural pronoun, let alone understanding the more nuanced differences between the forms. Again, this is because instructional programs assign *nous* status as the general 1st person plural pronoun and *on* is usually translated to English as the general impersonal pronoun "one." Similarly, for verbal negation, traditional pedagogy requires use of pre- and post-verbal particles *ne* and *pas* and, as with the other features, learners with immersion experience tend to decrease their use of pre-verbal *ne*, but without full realization of the sociopragmatics of negation (p. 64).

To develop the necessary conceptual knowledge, van Compernolle (2012) drew on the dialectical concept of *orders of indexicality* proposed by Silverstein (2003); however, he translated these into pedagogically functional categories that were presented to learners as "concept cards" (van Compernolle, 2012, p. 65). Each card defined in a straightforward way one of Silverstein's three orders of indexicality. In van Compernolle's scheme, for the first order learners were informed that "Conventions of language use are observable based on: geographic location, formality of context, age of speaker, level of education, social class, other groups of people"; for the third order they were told that "Stereotypes are formed as judgments are made about noticeable speech traits: regional accents/expressions, proper vs. improper/slang language, stereotypes about age, group, social class, level of education, and language use"; and for the second order students were informed that "People can use conventions and stereotypes to: sound local or not, sound formal or not, sound younger or older, sound more educated or less, sound more high class or less, sound like any other group" (p. 66). Five specific SCOBAs were then designed to illustrate "how the concept of orders of indexicality plays out in actual language use" (p. 66). We forgo reproduction of the SCOBAs here, and will instead briefly describe the content depicted in each.

The first SCOBA introduced the concept of *self-presentation* visualized as pictures of two sets of individuals. One set depicted a young man and a young woman each wearing a t-shirt and blue-jeans. The caption under the picture included the three terms associated with informal usage: *tu, on, Ø . . . pas.* The second picture showed a somewhat older man and woman each wearing a business suit, and underneath the words *vous, nous,* and *ne . . . pas* appear. The individuals wearing t-shirt and jeans were intended to suggest meaning associated with "youthfulness, informality, coolness," whereas the individuals in suits manifested an image of "conservatism, professionalism, formality" (p. 68).

The choice of self-presentation, however, is more complex and therefore additional SCOBAs were developed. For *tu/vous* social distance is also a factor influencing symmetrical use of the pronouns. The SCOBA depicted two individuals situated in close physical proximity each uttering *tu* and two additional individuals separated by some physical distance, each uttering *vous.* A third SCOBA dealt with issues of power and showed two people located on the same physical level with an equal sign between them and each uttering the same pronoun, either *tu* or *vous.* Two additional individuals were situated at different physical levels relative to each other with ≠ positioned between them. The lower person was uttering *vous* and the higher person *tu.* The fourth SCOBA focused on negation and was designed to show that when negation is emphasized the dual particle *ne . . . pas* is used and when something is not emphasized only post-verbal *Ø . . . pas* is used. Moreover, in communicative circumstances where preverbal *ne* is frequently used "its emphatic potential is diminished since it likely does not draw attention to the negation" (p. 71). A small yellow triangle typical of traffic signs was used to represent non-emphatic use of *Ø . . . pas* and a much larger triangle was use to represent the emphatic meaning of *ne . . . pas* (p. 71).

The final SCOBA materialized the meaning of *on/nous.* This SCOBA is difficult to accurately describe textually and therefore we present a version of

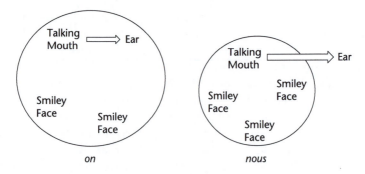

Include or exclude hearer?

**FIGURE 5.1** Inclusion and exclusion (based on van Compernolle, 2012, Figure 2.8, p. 72)

it in Figure 5.1, using words in place of some of the pictures in the original SCOBA.

Van Compernolle (2012, pp. 71–72) explained that *on* is the unmarked form of "we" in modern French. It includes the interlocutor in the scope of the pronoun, as illustrated in the first drawing, whereas *nous* is used to indicate that the interlocutor is excluded from the pronoun's scope, as shown in the second drawing. The researcher also explained that, as in the case of negation, there are contexts where *nous* occurs with high frequency (e.g., more formal writing) and therefore the excluded status of the interlocutor is not emphasized.

## Outcomes

Instruction focused on developing students' understanding of the following concepts: orders of indexicality (involving awareness of conventions and stereotypes), self-presentation, social distance, emphasis, and inclusion/exclusion. The goal was to orient them to the available options for pattern manipulation in order for them to be able to fulfill their communicative goals rather than to duplicate native-speaker performance. In the following subsections we will present a synopsis of the study's outcomes paying attention to the participants' comments in the interviews regarding pre- and post-instruction understanding of the concepts, to their performance on the appropriateness judgment questionnaire (AJQ), and to their communicative performance during the strategic interaction scenarios. We will not be able to include a discussion of the two verbalization activities (i.e., dialogic thinking) conducted during the 4-week instruction phase of the program.

### Interviews: Pre- and Post-Instruction Understanding

Generally, the participants' pre-understanding of the 2nd person address forms during the pre-instruction interview reflected rules-of-thumb knowledge regarding the grammatical features of the verbs that co-occurred with each pronoun (i.e., singular for *tu* and plural or singular for *vous*) and the assumption that the primary distinction between the forms with regard to usage was informal/formal (van Compernolle, 2012, p. 84). The general pre-understanding is reflected in the commentary from Susan (pseudonym): "like if I wasn't sure if I know what to do, I would probably just go with *vous*" (p. 85). When asked by TR (tutor/researcher) what she would do when meeting someone for the first time, she responded: "I would automatically just go with *vous*, just to show that I am not being disrespectful of their standing or who they are" (p. 85).[1] Susan also mentioned that if the interlocutor were a 5-year-old child she would probably use *tu*, but if the interlocutor were someone her own age, she would still "probably go with *vous*" (p. 85). The last remark is important because it shows a lack of sensitivity to the sociopragmatics displayed in the SCOBA for forms of address.

In the post-instruction interviews, the participants demonstrated a more nuanced understanding of the sociopragmatic factors that influence pronoun use. Laurie's (p. 87) remarks are fairly typical of this set of interviews:

> well now I know that using *tu* and *vous* is not just for plural or singular, and also it's not just for if you don't know the person. Which is what I think I was taught pretty much. But using *tu* and *vous* can also decide what kind of situation you want to present yourself as, how close or far you want to present yourself between the other person, and just the rank the like their authority. Like do you want to show your authority or not.

As for the remaining features, prior to instruction the students were unaware that *on* could be used as a 1st person plural pronoun; nor did they know that *ne* deletion was an option. Again, Susan's interview confirms this understanding: "*nous* for the most part is like us, I guess. Like we're doing something, or like mostly us. If I'm talking about myself and a group of people, and then *on*, I've always associated with like one, kind of. Like one does his homework, or one takes his dog for a walk" (p. 90). Leon's comment on negation shows a commitment to the need for both components to properly mark negation: "you can't really have one without the other" (p. 91).

Following instruction, it was clear that the students had developed an understanding of pronoun use and negation that reflected sensitivity to the sociopragmatics of communicative situations. Mary (p. 92), for instance, provided the following explanation of *on/nous* in her post-instruction interview:

> Well *nous* is kind of like more proper kind of suit-and-tie way to say us. And then *on* is would be more informal. If you just want to be relaxed. Tee-shirt-and-jeans type of thing. And then for emphasis, you can I guess you can use *nous* as exclusive and *on* as inclusive.

As for negation, Nikki's (p. 94) commentary is typical of the change in the participants' understanding of the concept:

> The tee-shirt-and-jeans is negation without the *ne*, and the business is negation with the *ne*, but also if you use the *ne* and you have a tee-shirt-and-jeans, like relationship, like where you have a close relationship, you're emphasizing, the negation.

### Appropriateness Judgment Questionnaire

A total of three AJQs were designed for the study. Two of these were used during instruction and one was administered as a pre- and post-instruction test. We will consider learner performance on the latter tasks only. The AJQs presented the students with a brief description of a situation and asked them which of the relevant features they would likely use. The following example is taken from the pre-instruction/post-instruction AJQ: "You are at a local café one evening and a friend of yours, Jean, comes in. He walks over to your table and greets you" (p. 212). Each of the five tasks took account of power, social distance, and formal/informal context (p. 96). In some cases each feature was clearly signaled, while in others it was ambiguous and therefore the students needed to consider carefully their self-presentation style for each of the variables. For instance, two of the situations involved a professor but in one case the encounter occurred in the professor's office and related to an academic issue and in the other the professor, described as friendly and a student favorite, was encountered casually on the street. We reproduce van Compernolle's (p. 96) Table 3.1 as Table 5.1 below. The table indicates the power, distance, and degree of formality assumed to operate in each situation in the AJQ. The students, of course, did not have access to this information.

Tables 5.2 and 5.3, derived from van Compernolle's Tables 3.2 to 3.4 (pp. 98, 103, 104), capture the students' pre- and post-instruction understanding of the sociopragmatics relating to the three relevant features. Prior to instruction the students heavily favored the formal variant of each feature with the notable exception of situation (1) where they unanimously selected *tu*, and situation (2)

**TABLE 5.1** Situation information (van Compernolle, 2012, p. 96, Table 3.1)

| Situation | Power | Distance | Context |
| --- | --- | --- | --- |
| Situation 1: Jean (friend) | − | − | Informal |
| Situation 2: Sophie (friend's girlfriend) | − | ? | Informal |
| Situation 3: M Robinet (professor) | + | + / ? | ? |
| Situation 4: Administrative assistant | ? | + | ? |
| Situation 5: Mme Triolet (professor) | + | + | Formal |

*Note:* A question mark (?) indicates ambiguity and/or probable interindividual variation.

**TABLE 5.2** Pre-instruction performance on Appropriateness Judgment Questionnaire (adapted from van Compernolle, 2012)

|  | *Tu* | *Vous* | *On* | *Nous* | $\emptyset$ . . . *pas* | *Ne* . . . *pas* |
|---|---|---|---|---|---|---|
| Situation |  |  |  |  |  |  |
| 1. Friend | 8 | 0 | 1 | 7 | 1 | 7 |
| 2. Friend's Girlfriend | 4 | 4 | 1 | 7 | 1 | 7 |
| 3. Professor on Street | 1 | 7 | 0 | 8 | 0 | 8 |
| 4. Admin. Assistant | 0 | 8 | 0 | 8 | 0 | 8 |
| 5. Professor Office | 0 | 8 | 0 | 8 | 0 | 8 |

**TABLE 5.3** Post-instruction performance on Appropriateness Judgment Survey (adapted from van Compernolle, 2012)

|  | *Tu* | *Vous* | *On* | *Nous* | $\emptyset$ . . . *pas* | *Ne* . . . *pas* |
|---|---|---|---|---|---|---|
| Situation |  |  |  |  |  |  |
| 1. Friend | 8 | 0 | 8 | 0 | 8 | 0 |
| 2. Friend's Girlfriend | 8 | 0 | 8 | 0 | 8 | 0 |
| 3. Professor on Street | 1 | 7 | 8 | 0 | 8 | 0 |
| 4. Admin. Assistant | 0 | 8 | 3 | 5 | 3 | 5 |
| 5. Professor Office | 0 | 8 | 7 | 1 | 7 | 1 |

where they were equally divided between *tu* and *vous*. In the latter case, half of the students appeared to follow the rule of thumb, which states that *vous* is used for strangers, as reflected in Susan's (p. 99) comment to TR:

> I would probably say *vous*. Just because I haven't met her before, and it goes back to the whole respect thing, I think, and even though, she's my age, and the girlfriend of my friend, I still just because I'm meeting her for the first time, I feel like I would just default to *vous*.

As for the other two features, only one student expressed awareness of the possibility of using *on* and $\emptyset$ . . . *pas*, which he characterized as "slang" (p. 134).

Following instruction, the students' performance change dramatically. All of them opted for *tu* in situation (2). With regard to *negation* and *on/nous* all students selected $\emptyset$ . . . *pas* and *on* for situations (1) through (3); however, for situation (4) five of the eight students preferred *ne* . . . *pas* and *nous*. Situation (4), according to van Compernolle (p. 104), was fairly ambiguous for all of the students because it involved an older woman working in an academic office that students were to approach for the first time regarding a scheduling issue. All of the students selected *vous* as the pronoun for addressing the interlocutor; however, they were not unanimous in their preferences for the other two features. The majority opted for formality, choosing *nous* and *ne . . . pas* over the informal options in each case. Steph (p. 108) explained that

> I would definitely use *vous*. Because she's older so might expect that from students as well. Same with *nous* and *ne pas*, I would stick with those just to make sure I don't like in some way insult her by using the like more casual laidback conversation.

The students were also somewhat conflicted about situation (5) where they chose *vous* to address their professor but showed a preference for informal variants of the remaining features, as explained by Leon (p. 101):

> it doesn't necessarily mean like that we're very close or there's still that sort of like professional distance. He's my teacher and I'm the student but you know I am with my friends. It's Saturday afternoon, there's no reason for me to be overly formal. So I think I would still use the *on* and . . . *pas.*

Leon, along with the other students, understood that the choices were not categorical and that even though he felt he should show respect toward his teacher, at the same time he felt comfortable using informal variants for the other two features during a street conversation.

## Scenario Performance

By far the richest data elicited during STI were generated by learner performance during the eight scenarios, the methodology that was also used by Negueruela (2003). The concept of *scenario* was developed by Di Pietro (1987) as a means of engaging students in conversation where performance is motivated by the "dramatic tension" that arises in "human interaction" (p. 3). Scenarios normally entail interaction between a minimum of two individuals, each with a concrete vested interest in the outcome of the interaction. The dramatic tension is created by the fact that the interactants are not aware of each other's interest and level of commitment to the scenario's outcome. The following is an example of a simple scenario involving two individuals:

> Role A: You must return a defective toaster to the department store. Unfortunately, you have lost the purchase receipt and you have only your lunch hour to take care of the matter. Prepare yourself for an encounter with the salesclerk.

> Role B: You are a salesclerk in the hardware department of a large store. You have been ordered to be careful in accepting returns of merchandise

that may not have been purchased at the store. Prepare yourself to deal with someone who is approaching you with a toaster.

*(pp. 48–49)*

Each participant in the above scenario is provided with a description of his/ her role only and therefore has no idea how the other participant's role is defined at the outset of the interaction. Students are given the opportunity to prepare and rehearse possible scripts for how they intend to implement their role. However, because neither participant is aware of the other's role description, they cannot be certain that their plan can be implemented successfully. This allows for an element of spontaneity and is the source of the tension that sustains the interaction once it begins.

In van Compernolle's study, the students were provided with a description of their roles and, with the TR, had the opportunity to plan a script for the interaction. Importantly, the TR did not determine how the learners should play their roles in terms of self-presentation and selection of appropriate sociopragmatic features. This was decided by the students themselves. However, he did ask them during the planning phase how they intended to present themselves in the interaction (e.g., tee-shirt-and-jeans, or suit-and-tie), which enabled him to mediate their performance during the interaction. This was important during the instruction phase of the program where four of the eight scenarios were implemented. In each scenario the interlocutor role was played by the TR, and, unlike in classroom scenarios, he knew both roles, while the students only were provided with descriptions of their roles. Scenarios in each phase of the project were implemented in pairs—one formal and one informal.

A pair of scenarios was implemented prior to instruction and a similar pair with slight variations was implemented following instruction. Table 5.4 compares the collated performance data for the three sociopragmatic features during the pre- and post-instruction scenarios. The table combines data from several of van Compernolle's tables (pp. 121–122).

In Table 5.4 the total number of occasions where a particular feature (2nd person, 1st person plural, negation) was called for is indicated in the EU row and the actual occurrence of each form is given in the row underneath. Thus, for the pre-instruction informal scenario the students produced a total of 72 occasions where a 2nd person pronoun was required and, of these, 66 instances of *tu* and 6 instances of *vous* were observed. On the formal scenario, on the other hand, 21 possibilities for use of a 2nd person pronoun occurred and of these 16 were appropriately *vous*, but 5 were the informal *tu*. Of the two remaining features, only one instance of an appropriately informal negative form occurred in any of the possible occasions of use. Thus, prior to instruction, the learners showed some inconsistency in their use of the address pronouns using *vous* when *tu* would have been the appropriate form and opting for *tu* when *vous* would have been the better selection. Moreover, the learners

**TABLE 5.4** Student performance on pre- and post-Instruction scenarios (adapted from van Compernolle, 2012)

| | tu | vous | on | nous | Ø . . . pas | ne . . . pas |
|---|---|---|---|---|---|---|
| **Pre-Instruction** | | | | | | |
| **Informal** | | | | | | |
| EU | 72 | | 17 | | 08 | |
| | 66 | 06 | 00 | 17 | 01 | 07 |
| **Formal** | | | | | | |
| EU | 21 | | 19 | | 13 | |
| | 05 | 16 | 00 | 19 | 00 | 13 |
| **Post-Instruction** | | | | | | |
| **Informal** | | | | | | |
| EU | 53 | | 23 | | 14 | |
| | 53 | 00 | 18 | 05 | 10 | 04 |
| **Formal** | | | | | | |
| EU | 12 | | 08 | | 15 | |
| | 02 | 10 | 01 | 07 | 02 | 13 |

*Note:* EU = Environment of Use where each of the features should have been used

showed essentially no sensitivity to the sociopragmatics of negation and 1st person plural pronoun as they categorically used the formal textbook versions of these features.

The post-instruction scenarios show a marked shift in performance. For one thing, *tu* was used consistently, and as planned, by the learners in the informal scenario. The formal address pronoun *vous* was also used more consistently following instruction. Van Compernolle carried out a correlational analysis on the three features and reported moderate, though non-significant, correlations between *tu/vous* and both of the other features; $r = .501$ for *on/nous* and $r = .579$ for negation. However, he did observe a high significant correlation ($r = .943$, $p < .001$) between *on/nous* and negation.

We supplemented van Compernolle's analysis with a chi-square analysis on the data in Table 5.4. It revealed significant pre- and post-instruction differences for all three features in the informal scenarios with no significant differences in the formal scenarios (see Table 5.5). This latter result most likely arises from classroom instructional practices (as noted above), which encourage learners to generalize the formal variants of all but the *tu/vous* distinction, where learners do often practice both forms of address, as illustrated in Susan's comment made during the debriefing phase (see Di Pietro, 1987, for a full discussion of debriefing phase) of the formal scenario:

> Probably you get so used like drilled in your head. Like *ça va? ça va bien. et toi?* 'how are you? Fine and you?' So it was just like it wasn't that I wasn't thinking about it, it was out of habit. It just came out. So that's going to be

**TABLE 5.5**  $\chi^2$ analysis of pre- and post-instruction scenario performance

|  | $\chi^2$ | df | p-value |
|---|---|---|---|
| Informal |  |  |  |
| *tu/vous* | 4.639 | 1 | *.003 |
| *on/nous* | 21.131 | 1 | *.001 |
| negation | 7.071 | 1 | *.007 |
| Formal |  |  |  |
| *tu/vous* | .233 | 1 | n.s. |
| *on/nous* | 2.46 |  | n.s. |
| negation | 1.867 | 1 | n.s |

*Note:* n.s. = non-significant; ★ *p* < .05.

> something I have to think about I'm so so so used to being like *et toi* I've
> been used to saying that.
>
> *(van Compernolle, 2012, p. 129)*

Van Compernolle points out (p. 129) that even though students such as Susan conceptually understood the need to use formal address pronouns in the scenarios, as indicated in her planning phase, the informal response form is heavily practiced in classroom greeting sequences and therefore generated a conflict between orientation/plan and execution of the plan. Another student, Leon, commented that shifting to the informal variant for 2nd person pronoun was fairly easy to accomplish and that he was "slowly beginning to be able to drop" *pas* in negation; however, the shift from *nous* to *on* was more difficult because the latter was "ingrained" in his head (p.123). Van Compernolle also conducted an in-depth microanalysis of each learner's development over the 6-week course of the program. We are unable to document the extremely interesting profiles that emerged from that analysis here.

## STI and L2 Sarcasm

One of the most innovative STI studies carried out to date focused on an aspect of language use that is not manifested in a specific form or set of forms, but is communicated through an array of options that can often be manipulated by speakers (and writers) in subtle ways and with or without humorous intent. The feature is sarcasm, which to our knowledge has not, until the recent completion of Kim's (2013) dissertation, been the object of L2 researchers' attention. Nevertheless, for learners, as expressed by several of the participants in Kim's study, it is very important because not recognizing when an interlocutor is displaying sarcasm can be a very disempowering experience for any newcomer to a languaculture. As with van Compernolle's project we are unable to consider all of the aspects of Kim's study, and will have to settle for pointing out a few of its highlights.

## Defining Sarcasm

Sarcasm is considered to be a sub-category of irony in which a speaker (or writer) produces an utterance that not only contrasts in meaning with what is actually said but at the same time imparts a sense of criticism, insult, and, at times, humor (Kim, 2013, p. 15). Kim pointed out that while most languacultures use irony and sarcasm, the cues used by speakers are not universal; moreover, the intent of sarcastic speech is not the same across communities. Thus, what may mark a sarcastic utterance in one languaculture may not in another and in some communities sarcasm can be used with a humorous effect, but in others it can only convey negative and even hurtful speaker intentions. For instance, Kim points out that in her native language, Korean, sarcasm only carries a negative value, but in English it is often a source of humor, as observed in many American sitcoms and talk shows.

The fact that L2 learners have difficulties recognizing and interpreting sarcasm is documented by Kim (2013) in her analysis of L1 Korean learners of L2 English. In her study, she noted, not surprisingly, that learners used their L1 pragmalinguistic knowledge to recognize and interpret L2 sarcasm. This usually results in failure to detect it in L2 speech and creates problems interpreting it correctly when it was detected (p. 27). In Korean, for instance, word stress and vowel lengthening are the primary indicators of sarcasm and while these cues can be used by English speakers, there are other cues, such as facial expressions, that are not an option in Korean (p. 27). The greatest difficulty reported by Korean learners of English, and where they often differ from L1 speakers, is in interpreting the meaning and intention of sarcastic utterances.

As Kim noted (p. 29), even when Korean learners of English appropriately identified an utterance as sarcastic they generally interpreted it as "insulting, biting and offensive … even among close friends" whereas for L1 English speakers the same utterance could be understood as imparting a humorous or jocular intent, especially when it was used among friends (p. 29). Given this situation, Kim devised an experimental-developmental program to help L1 Korean learners of L2 English identify sarcasm and interpret it accurately. Thus, the focus of the study was not on learner proficiency in producing sarcastic utterances (indeed, some of the participants expressed considerable reluctance at the prospect of producing sarcasm in English) but on detection and comprehension.

## Study Overview

Kim selected her participants on the basis of a pre-test designed to determine learner sarcastic competence. From an original pool of 23 volunteers she selected 10 (one withdrew partially through the project for personal reasons), who also demonstrated sufficient interest and motivation in the topic. Eight of the participants were doctoral students enrolled in different graduate programs of study at Penn State University and one was a post-doc; consequently, they had a high degree of proficiency in written and spoken English. The range of time spent in the U.S. at the time of the study was from 4 months to 4 years.

Kim designed a total of nine instructional sessions lasting 1 hour each preceded by a session in which she interviewed the participants to uncover their pre-understanding of sarcasm in English and in their L1 and to administer the pre-test. One week after the final instructional session Kim administered a post-test and 5 weeks later the participants were given a delayed post-test. The tests were also administered to a group of five native speakers of English for purposes of comparison. Instruction was conducted in Korean to maximize learner understanding and to allow them to more effectively express themselves regarding the subtleties involved in detecting and interpreting sarcasm.

## The SCOBAs

Kim designed eight SCOBAs for her instructional program. Three dealt with the abstract features of sarcasm and five illustrated different body movements often associated with the expression of sarcasm in English. We are unable to include the actual SCOBAs here and will instead describe their content. Of the abstract SCOBAs, the first (p. 54) illustrated the relationship between emotions and speaker use of sarcasm. Affiliated with negative uses of sarcasm are emotions such as contempt, disgust, anger, and jealousy and with positive uses are affection and the desire to bond with another person. Also included in the SCOBA are the goals associated with sarcasm use. On the negative side are: insult, complain, admonish, save face, reduce vulnerability; and on the positive side are: compliment, group solidarity, and improve a relationship. The second abstract SCOBA (p. 55) explained different types of verbal irony, the umbrella concept under which sarcasm is included. Among the features of verbal irony are hyperbole and, its opposite, understatement, double entendre, and, of course, sarcasm.

Based on the research of Yus (1998, 2000) the third abstract SCOBA (p. 60) explained how detection and comprehension of sarcasm occurs, and as such included those features that serve as cues or hints that a speaker intends an utterance to be taken sarcastically. Among the hints are facial expression, gesture, body movements, encyclopedic knowledge of a community, biographical knowledge of the speaker, and lexical cues. There should be incompatibilities between the cues and the expected meaning of what is said for an utterance to be interpreted as sarcastic. For example, if someone says "I really like you" but at the same time rolls their eyes and curls one side of their lips, it is highly likely that the utterance is intended as sarcastic.

Of the five SCOBAs describing body movements associated with sarcasm, one depicts gestures (e.g., arms crossed in front of body, hand touching chin, arms on hips) (p. 58); another describes lip movements (e.g., upper lip curl, unilateral lip corner raise, etc.) (p. 57); a third describes eye and eyebrow positions (e.g., wink,

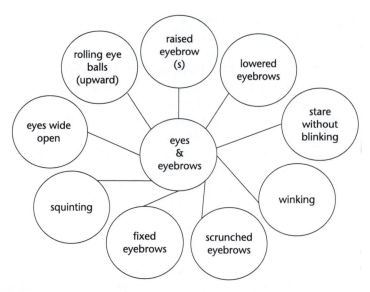

**FIGURE 5.2** SCOBA 4: Potential sarcastic facial expressions (Part II – Eyes and eyebrows) (Kim, 2013, p. 57)

stare without blinking, squinting, raised eyebrow, rolling eyeballs, etc.) (p. 57). As Kim notes, most of the body movement cues of English are not used in Korean to indicate sarcasm; this is especially true with eye and eyebrow movements, although head nods and intonation do at times function as cues in Korean (p. 93). Figure 5.2 illustrates one of the body-movement SCOBAs developed by Kim (p. 57).

## Instructional Program

In this section we will briefly describe the 12-week instructional program implemented by Kim. At the outset she conducted one-on-one interviews with the participants to discover their pre-understanding of sarcasm in English and Korean. We can consider the interviews as communicated thinking sessions where the participants expressed their knowledge of the concept that, according to Kim, was implicit, resulting in difficulties in formulating a clear definition (p. 61). Following instruction, a second interview was carried out where the participants were more able to explain the concept of English sarcasm and compare it explicitly, showing similarities and differences between the L2 concept and the Korean equivalent, *bi-kkom*.

Throughout the program Kim met with the students individually once a week for 1-hour sessions. In these sessions she explained the concept of sarcasm and how it is used in English. She familiarized them with each of the eight SCOBAs beginning with the abstract SCOBAs. Each week thereafter she presented the

SCOBAs that materialized the variety of cues English speakers use to indicate sarcasm. Each tutorial session also included authentic examples of sarcasm use drawn from *YouTube* video clips of television comedy shows, talk shows, political debates, and even cartoons. Prior to each tutorial, the participants were asked to watch a selection of video clips and to write interpretive essays in which they were to analyze the clips for sarcastic utterances, indicating which they felt were sarcastic, identifying the cues they used to detect sarcasm providing an interpretation of the utterances in terms of emotional state of the speaker, the goal of the utterance, and whether it carried a negative or positive valence. According to Kim (p. 64), the essays provided opportunities for dialogic thinking regarding learner understanding of the concept. The participants were also asked to create "movie scripts" in which they were to generate scenes where characters were to appropriately express sarcasm in accordance with the principles and cues manifested in the SCOBAs. The sessions were video-recorded for analysis.

At various points throughout the program the participants met in small groups to engage in specific practice activities. One was designed to imitate the body movements that serve as cues to sarcasm, as described and illustrated in the SCOBAs. These sessions were video-recorded and analyzed by the students guided by the concrete and abstract SCOBAs. The purpose of the activities was not to practice the movements in order to use them when speaking, but to remember them through material movement. Another group activity, which involved all of the students, was a "focus group'" in which they first viewed a video-clip of a TV show and then analyzed it for sarcasm, critiquing and defending each other's interpretations and identification criteria.

## Assessment

The first post-test was administered 1 week following completion of the instructional program and the second post-test was given five weeks later. Each post-test was followed by an individual interview with each participant. Because the goal of the program was not for the students to produce but to interpret sarcastic utterances, the tests were administered in written format. In each test, participants viewed ten video clips (different clips were used for each test) accompanied by a written transcript of the dialogue. Their task was to underline what they identified as sarcastic utterances, check off from the list of cues three that were used by the speaker to signal sarcasm, and explain in writing (in Korean) the meaning of the sarcastic utterances, speaker's communicative goals, and her/his emotional state. To give an example, in a clip from a talk show, a guest is interviewed about the online website, *Ashley Madison*, where married individuals can meet to engage in illicit affairs. When asked to give her opinion on the site by the moderator, the guest says: "well first of all, what a romantic lovely idea that he's come up with you know (sneers with fast nods, head titled, and hands open with palms facing upward) it's just fantastic" (Kim, 2013, p. 144).

The participants' scores improved significantly from the pre- to the post-tests. Kim reported mean scores of 7.4 (sd = 5.25) on the pre-test, 16.6 (sd = 2.96) on the post-test, and 19.7 (sd = 3) on the delayed post-test. The maximum score on all tests was 30. She carried out Wilcoxon signed rank tests comparing the three tests and reported statistically significant differences in each case. Thus, it seems that on the quantitative measures used by Kim, the participants improved their ability to detect and interpret English sarcasm as a consequence of STI.

## STI and Learner Empowerment

STI, because it is grounded in praxis, not only seeks to improve learner performance in practical activity, it is also interested in the effects of developmental education on how learners understand and relate to their social environments. At stake in failing to detect and appropriately interpret sarcastic utterances is a person's emotional equilibrium. Therefore an especially important aspect of Kim's research is her analysis of the consequences of the STI program for learner empowerment.

During Kim's pre-instruction interviews, the commentary of the participant identified as Cho effectively attests to what is at stake for L2 learners:

> When someone uses sarcasm to me in Korean, I can at least show that I am offended by making an angry face or something . . . but in the English-speaking context, I simply become stupid. Even when someone is being sarcastic to me, I will not understand what is actually going on and they will think of me as a stupid person, which is obviously not true. [. . .] Just because of cultural differences and my limited ability to understand the language, I become a stupid person, and I hate that reality.
>
> *(2013, p. 1)*

Following STI, Cho highlighted the fact that her general understanding of sarcasm had changed to the extent that she felt herself empowered in both languages, English and Korean:

> before my interest originated primarily in the frustrated feeling from getting picked on, but now it's at a different level where I can quite accurately figure out what is going on in the situation and further think about whether I should use sarcasm back or not.
>
> *(p. 129)*

Cho also mentioned as a consequence of STI she thought more about sarcasm during conversations (p. 127) and that she even felt more confident in using sarcasm in her "everyday life" in her L1 (p. 126).

Kim (p. 125) pointed out that the changes attested in Cho's comments reflect Vygotsky's (1987, p. 110) argument that study of a foreign language "facilitates mastering higher forms of the native tongue." Moreover, according to Vygotsky (1987), education can also have developmental consequences beyond a specific instructional goal. Kim provided support for this argument in the remarks of another of her participants, Mia, who revealed in the post-instruction interview that because of STI she came to realize

> how there exist actual underlying meanings. And this made me listen and try to understand them more carefully when foreigners (English speakers) say something
>
> *(p. 132)*

and

> the biggest thing is I became better at comprehending speakers' intentions what they really want to say and I'm very happy about that and so I focus on that (intended meaning) first now when I hear things when I communicate with other people ... without those things that we did during class I think I must have lost a lot of those parts that are real important in learning English, I think.
>
> *(p. 133)*

Another participant, Wang, expressed a similar sentiment with regard to his new-found ability to pay closer attention and better interpret what he hears English speakers saying:

> if it was like before I wouldn't have cared much, I would let them all pass. They would just pass by, but now I hear those things that I didn't used to hear and that makes me pay more attention to what people say and go wow they used these expressions to say this? And so English became more fun to me now. It's fun.
>
> *(p. 135)*

A fourth participant, Yoh, effectively captured the relevance of empowerment when he pointed out that some L2 speakers of English, who do not have access to the tools for detecting and interpreting sarcasm provided in the STI program, don't "realize that somebody or some group of people is mocking them" and that if they were to have access to what was provided in the program "they'll be able to say sarcasm back and I believe those things will become power for them" (p. 137).

## Topicalization in Chinese: Testing the Teachability Hypothesis

The final experimental-developmental study to be considered in this chapter is the pilot component of a larger study by Zhang (in progress). The study implemented an STI program to mediate the development of L2 Chinese topicalization by L1 English speaking learners. It was designed to assess Pienemann's (1984, 1989) Teachability Hypothesis (TH), a corollary hypothesis of Processability Theory (PT) (Pienemann, 1998, 2005). To set the stage for our discussion of Zhang's study, we review PT and the TH.

## Processability Theory

PT proposes that some, certainly not all, grammatical and pragmatic features of a language are subject to a sequential processing order that is assumed to be universal for all learners regardless of the contextual circumstances in which a language is acquired. Structures that are assumed to be acquired sequentially include German word order, English question formation, Spanish word order, mood inflection, and noun phrase agreement morphology, and Chinese topicalization, among others. For the reader's convenience we briefly outline the general components of PT. For more detail the reader should consult Pienemann (1998 and 2005).

PT integrates Levelt's (1989) model of speech processing and principles of Lexical Functional Grammar (LFG). The component of Levelt's model that is most relevant for PT is the *Formulator*, which encodes into grammatical form the semantic and functional elements of a message developed in the *Conceptualizer*. Because processing capacity is limited, simpler processes are acquired (i.e., proceduralized) before complex procedures, which then frees up processing capacity for learners to deal with the next, more complex, set of processing procedures.

The LFG process, which is most relevant for PT, is the mechanism of *unification*, a feature-matching process that identifies grammatical information carried by a lexical entry and temporarily stores it for later use in the formulation process (Pienemann, 1998, p. 73). For example, to assign appropriate inflection to a predicate adjective in Spanish a speaker needs to remember information about features of the noun in subject position, as in the following sentence: *Las casas son blancas* 'the houses are white.' To mark the adjective "white" with the correct agreement features, feminine and plural, the speaker needs to store the information that the lemma "house" is feminine and plural and then use this information when processing in the Formulator reaches the adjective. This is assumed to be a more complex process than when the adjective appears in the same phrase as the noun it directly modifies as in *Las casas blancas* . . . 'the white houses.' In the first case the agreement features must be stored and carried across constituent boundaries, whereas in the second the features are assigned within the same phrase.

## Processing Stages

PT posits five processing stages that are implicationally ordered from least to most complex. The first, and simplest stage, is "lemma activation" where learners produce individual words or formulaic chunks. The unification mechanism does not operate at this stage and therefore feature matching is not relevant. At the second stage, the "category procedure" assigns a grammatical feature to a word, such as tense to a verb, or plural to a noun. Again, the unification mechanism is inoperative and therefore information exchange is still not relevant. Consequently, thematic structure is directly mapped onto constituent structure whereby semantic roles, such as agent, are mapped directly onto grammatical positions of constituent structure, giving rise to so-called canonical SVO (subject, verb, object) word order.

The next stage, "phrasal procedure," merges features and with it the capacity to determine positions within phrases appears. Morphologically, plural and gender concord operate but within rather than across constituent boundaries (e.g., *Las casas blancas*). Syntactically the ability to front or post-pose grammatical elements (e.g., adverbs, question words, and prepositional-phrases) appears; however, canonical SVO order is not yet modifiable. For example, in German, adverbs can be moved to initial position, but SV inversion is still not possible, giving rise to ungrammatical strings such as *Heute, **ich gehe** in die Schule* 'Today, I go to school' instead of the grammatically correct *Heute, **gehe ich** in die Schule*. Compound verbs also appear at this stage but in a language such as German they are not separated as required: *Ich habe gekauft ein Buch* 'I have bought a book', instead of *Ich habe ein Buch gekauft* 'I have a book bought.' Because this stage permits movement of elements to initial and post-positions, it also sanctions the appearance of complementizers in phrase initial position resulting in potentially ungrammatical subordinate clauses. Thus, in German, ungrammatical subordinate clauses such as *... dass ich gehe in die Schule* '... that I go to school' emerge and in English inverted indirect questions appear, as in '*... what is his name*' instead of '... what his name is.'

The fourth stage, "S(entence)-procedure," enables unification (i.e., feature matching) across constituent boundaries, which in turn permits modifications in word order as sanctioned by a particular language. Thus, correct word order in German main clauses appears, as in *Heute, gehe ich in die Schule*, 'Today, go I to school', and morphological agreement occurs in Spanish predicative constructions such as *Las casas son blancas*. Also at this stage compound verbs are recognized as such and therefore modal and temporal auxiliaries are appropriately inflected, as in English "does study, is studying, has studied, must study." In German this procedure sanctions separation of inflected auxiliaries from participial verbs as well as separable pre-fix verbs, as in *Ich habe mit der Mann gesprochen* 'I have with the man spoken' and *Ich rufe meine Frau an* 'I call my wife up' 'I telephone my wife.' This stage further sanctions inversion of SV(O) order in German and subject auxiliary inversion in questions in English, as in *Heute, gehe ich in die Schule* and 'What does he study?' However, in embedded clauses, main-clause word order still occurs, as in English '*I don't know what is his name*' and German *... dass ist er in die Schule gegangen* 'that is he in school gone' 'that he has gone to school.'

At the fifth, and final stage, subordination "(S'-procedure)" emerges, which allows for identification of the grammatical function of phrases, including passive versus active voice, etc. Once learners reach stage five they are able to produce grammatically appropriate embedded phrases, which in German entails clause-final finite verbs (e.g., . . . *dass er in die Schule gehen wollte* '. . . that he to school go wanted' '. . . that he wanted to go to school'). It also sanctions non-inversion in English embedded questions, as in 'He asked what John's name is.'

The five stages of processing procedures posited by PT are listed in Table 5.6 below.

Because the focus of PT is on processing capacity, it employs a different criterion for acquisition of a processing stage and its associated grammatical structures than has been accepted practice in the SLA literature. In general SLA literature a new feature is considered to be acquired if it occurs in 80%, or in some cases, 90% of obligatory contexts (see Ellis & Barkhuizen, 2005 for details). In PT, on the other hand, stages are not conceptualized in terms of robustness of occurrence in obligatory contexts but in terms of "a building up of processing prerequisites" that are "considered acquired as soon as the learner produces an analyzed/productive exemplar of the respective structure" (Jansen, 2008, p. 201).

**TABLE 5.6** Five stages of processing procedures in PT

| Stage | Processing Procedure |
|---|---|
| 1. Lemma | Words: no feature matching |
| 2. Category Procedure | Lexical morphology (*casas*, walked): no feature matching<br>Canonical word order: SVO |
| 3. Phrasal Procedure | Intra-phrasal feature matching: *las casas blancas*<br>Fronting and post-positioning of adjuncts: *Heute, ich gehe in die Schule*<br>Adverb SV(O)<br>Compound verbs—auxiliary (modal, temporal) + participle or infinitive<br>Complementizers: *dass ich gehe in die Schule* 'that I go to school' |
| 4. S-Procedure | Interphrasal feature matching: *Las casas son blancas*<br>Non-canonical word order in matrix clauses:<br> *Heute, gehe ich in die Schule.*<br> What does he study?<br>Separation in compound verbs:<br> *Ich habe ein Buch gekauft*<br>Post-position of separable prefixes:<br> *Ich rufe meine Frau an.* |
| 5. S'-Procedure | Distinguish active/passive, indicative/subjunctive mood (subordinate clause)<br>Appropriate word order in embedded clauses:<br> . . . *dass er ist in die Schule gegangen.*<br> . . . what his name is. |

This is because, according to Pienemann (1998, p. 146), spontaneous (unplanned) performance would be impossible in the absence of the necessary processing resources. To enhance the researchers' confidence that performance indeed entails spontaneous and analyzed production rather than planned and memorized chunks, Pienemann (1998, p. 145) recommended setting an emergence criterion whereby at least one occurrence of the relevant features occurs in at least four different obligatory (and optional) contexts.[2] A substantial amount of evidence has been accumulated, in an array of different languages (e.g., German, English, Spanish, Arabic, Chinese, Japanese, Swedish, Italian, Norwegian, and Danish), to support the general claims of PT (see Pienemann, 1998, 2003, 2005, 2007; Mansouri, 2007).[3]

## A Challenge to PT

To our knowledge Liu (1991) is the only study to present evidence that counters the predicted processing sequence of PT. It is a study carried out in an immersion setting rather than under conditions of direct and intentional instruction, as becomes relevant for TH (see below).

In Liu's study (discussed in Tarone & Liu, 1995 and Tarone, 2007), a 5-year-old Chinese-speaking child learning L2 English in Australia was tracked over a 2-year period in three different contextual settings: home, interacting with the researcher; at school, interacting with his teacher; and again at school but this time interacting with other children in desk-work activities (Tarone, 2007, p. 844). As it turns out, the child showed evidence of having acquired stage 4 questions (*wh-* with copula and yes/no questions with auxiliary inversion: "Where is my pencil?" "Is the dog still outside?") and stage 5 questions (*wh-* with auxiliary inversion: "What are you eating?" "When did Mary come home?") in the home setting before stage 3 questions (fronting do, *wh-*: "*Do the man is sleeping?" "*What the kitty is eating?") When this stage did appear it was not in the home setting but in interactions with his classmates in desk-work activities (Tarone & Liu, 1995).

Tarone (2007, p. 844) concluded that "something in these social settings affected Bob's [the child's pseudonym] cognitive processing and internalization of new L2 rules to such an extent that he acquired them out of their so-called universal order." She further pointed out that the findings of Liu's research also offer significant counterevidence to claims that "social setting is irrelevant" (p. 844), as argued for by Long (see Chapter 4).[4] The situation becomes more unsettled when we consider research that has been conducted within the framework of the Teachability Hypothesis, some of which we will consider in the following section.

## The Teachability Hypothesis

TH claims that even though the instructional setting is a different environment from everyday immersion contexts, where learners essentially must rely on their own processing capacities, it will not have any impact on the route of acquisition as predicted by PT. In Pienemann's (1989, p. 57) words, "the acquisition process cannot be steered or modeled just according to the requirements or precepts of formal instruction." A corollary of TH holds that teaching can be effective, with regard to the natural processing hierarchy, only if it takes account of a learner's current stage of development and provides instruction aimed at the very next stage. This so because each stage in the developmental sequence, as we pointed out above, entails increasingly complex processing procedures, and therefore the procedures that operate at each stage are a prerequisite for the procedures that operate at the subsequent stage. To be sure, what Pienemann calls "variable features" of a language (e.g., lexicon, prepositions, phrasal verbs in English) are not subject to natural constraints and therefore instruction need not be concerned with a "learning barrier" (1989, p. 61) presented by TH.

Pienemann and his colleagues conducted several research projects in an attempt to determine if teaching could indeed "overcome" the processing constraints assumed to hold within general PT. The results of this research, reported in several publications (e.g., Felix, 1981; Jansen, 2008; Mansouri, 2007; Pienemann, 1984, 1989, 1998, 2005; Wang, 2011 Zhang, 2001), provided consistent support for TH with regard to the natural order of acquisition posited by PT. Ellis (1989, 2006), also provided evidence in support of TH. Taken together these studies have shown that learners must progress from one processing stage to the next; that learners cannot skip stages; that instruction is only effective if it aims at stage X+1 and not X+2 or higher; that the progress of learners can be plotted on an implicational scale in a stepwise progression from least to most complex processing stage (i.e., Stage 1 to Stage 5); if a learner can produce features at say Stage 4, he or she, implicationally, can also produce features at the three preceding stages.

At first glance, it might appear that TH is to some extent at least, compatible with the SCT concept of ZPD, given Pienemann's (1989, p. 61) claim that instruction aimed at natural sequences can be effectual when learners are "ready," and that in such a circumstance teaching can accelerate development. The difference, however, between TH and the ZPD is that according to SCT, instruction does not need to wait for learners to become developmentally ready; on the contrary, instruction, or more specifically, *obuchenie* (i.e., the teaching–learning dialectic) creates developmental readiness. Thus, in comparing TH and SCT, we confront a situation where the claims of the respective theories can be tested, which is the purpose of Zhang's (in progress) research. Before we move to a discussion of Zhang's research, however, we would like to consider some of the existing studies that challenge TH.

## Challenges to TH: The X+1 Corollary

In this section we will briefly survey four studies that have directly or indirectly tested the two central claims of TH: that formal instruction cannot alter the natural processing sequence predicted by PT and that the only effective instruction is that which is sensitive to learners' developmental readiness; that is, aimed at the next stage in the processing hierarchy.

Two studies, Spada and Lightbown (1999) and Mackey (1999), provided implicit instruction only whereby the former study used input flooding and the latter used negotiated interaction with native speakers to expose learners to English questions. Two studies, Farley and McCollam (2004) and Bonilla (2012), incorporated explicit instruction on features of L2 Spanish that are sensitive to the processing hierarchy into their respective pedagogical approaches.

Although not directly intended as a test of TH, the study by Mackey (1999) included an examination of the effects of different forms of instruction on progress through the processing hierarchy for English question formation. Four differential instructional groups and a control group took part in the quasi-experimental study. Two of the instructional groups are most relevant with regard to TH. One, deemed to be developmentally ready to progress to processing hierarchy Stages 4 and 5, and another, deemed unready, carried out a series of tasks (e.g., picture differences, story completion, picture sequencing) with native speakers of English in which the learners were prompted to ask questions of the NSs. Using a pre-, post-, and delayed post-test procedure, Mackey reported that given the opportunity to engage in negotiated interaction, ready as well as unready learners advanced to higher stages of processing hierarchy. Six of the seven unready learners and five of the seven ready learners produced questions at Stages 4 and 5 on the post-tests; however, the development of the unready group was less systematic than that of the ready group (p. 574).

Spada and Lightbown (1999) also conducted a study on English question formation using implicit instruction with grade 6 intact ESL classes in Quebec. Over a 2-week period, the 144 students participating in the study were given extensive exposure, without explanations, to Stage 4 (i.e., *wh-* with copula, aux inversion in yes/no questions) and Stage 5 (*wh-*questions with aux inversion) questions. According to the researchers, most students pre-tested at Stage 2 (SVO order with rising intonation). Following exposure the majority of this group showed no improvement, while some did improve to Stage 3. Of those pretesting at Stage 3, the majority again showed no development, some even regressed back to Stage 2 and only a small minority moved to Stage 4. Finally, of the students at Stage 4 prior to instruction, none showed improvement to Stage 5, and the majority regressed to Stage 3. Overall, most students (87 out of 144) remained at the processing stage they had been at prior to instruction (Spada & Lightbown, 1999, p. 10).

Spada and Lightbown (1999, p. 14) painted a mixed picture of what the results of the oral production task revealed with regard to TH. On the one hand, they stated that the data "do not provide support" because "students who were ready to advance to Stage 4 [no students pre-tested at Stage 4] tended not to do so, and some who did show progress [the two students who moved from Stage 2 to Stage 4] were at a point where Stage 4 and Stage 5 input would not be expected to prove effective."While the two learners who skipped a stage do seem to provide counterevidence to TH, the fact that students deemed ready to develop failed to do so, does not. TH does not guarantee that learners at a given stage must advance to the next stage, even if instruction targets that stage. The argument is that if a learner advances it can only be to the next stage. Pienemann (1987, p. 92) makes this clear:

> Thus the Teachability Hypothesis defines the possible range of influence of external factors on the SL learning process in a similar way to that in which the Predictive Framework defines the range of possible interlanguage hypotheses. This does not imply that learning is guaranteed by the mechanisms internal to the learner.

On the other hand, the authors concluded, despite the supposed counterevidence, that the oral production data support TH because the learners that did progress did so without skipping stages; that is "most stage 2 learners who progressed, moved to stage 3 (not stage 4) even though the input targeted stage 4 and stage 5 questions" (p. 14).

The two studies that relied on explicit instruction also claimed to have provided evidence counter to the X+1 corollary. Farley and McCollam (2004) framed their research within vanPatten's (1996) Input Processing approach to instruction. They focused on a Stage 4 feature, Spanish personal-*a*, used as a marker of animate direct object NPs (*El gato muerde al perro* 'the cat bites the dog'), and a Stage 5 feature, use of subjunctive mood in subordinate clauses (*El professor duda que los estudiantes salgan bien en el examen* 'the professor doubts that the students will do well on the exam').[5]

Farley and McCollam compared the performance of learners assigned to three different treatment groups (Processing Instruction, Explicit Instruction only, Structured Input only) and a non-instructed control group. While some students from each of the three treatment groups were deemed ready for instruction (i.e., at X+1) with regard to personal-*a*, no student in any of the groups was judged ready for instruction with respect to subjunctive. Statistical analysis of post-test scores showed no significant effect for learner readiness.[6] Following instruction some students deemed unready for subjunctive did meet emergence criterion, and while some students assumed to be ready for personal-*a* indeed met criterion, others failed to do so.

Unfortunately, two problems raise concerns regarding the reliability of Farley and McCollam's findings. Both problems are also noted by Bonilla (2012, p. 56). The first is that the authors did not indicate emergence criterion. We might assume that they followed the criterion set by Pienemann (see above), but we cannot be certain. The second, and perhaps more serious problem, is that the performance required on the respective post-tests for personal-*a* and for subjunctive differed. On the former, learners produced oral descriptions of scenes, whereas on the latter they were asked to "express an opinion about the illustrated scene by selecting one of the two matrix clauses and completing each utterance" (Farley & McCollam, 2004, p. 57). The second task does not appear to meet Pienemann's criterion that performance to assess the status of emergence must be spontaneous.

Bonilla (2012) conducted two studies in university-level Spanish L2 classrooms, one featuring true beginners and the other elementary level students with previous instructional exposure to the language.[7] Both groups received approximately 30 minutes of instruction that included explicit explanations accompanied by teacher-fronted and dyadic practice activities. Some true beginners received instruction on Stage 3 XP-adjunction (e.g., *En dos semanas llega mi abuela* 'In two weeks arrives my grandmother', 'My grandmother is coming in two weeks') and others received instruction on Stage 4 SV Inversion and clitic placement (e.g., *El libro lo compró Roberto*, 'the book it bought Robert', 'The book, Robert bought it'). Some of the more advanced beginners received Stage 4 instruction and others were given instruction on Stage 5, use of subjunctive in subordinate clauses (see above, Farley & McCollam, 2004).[8]

According to Bonilla, learner performance on post-instruction production tests confirmed PT's predictions that processing stages must emerge in the predicted sequence. However, Bonilla reported that instruction "aimed at *next* or at *next* + *x* stages was effective at increasing learners' production of the next stages as well as their current stage" (p. 244, italics in original). According to Bonilla this means that instruction does not have to be targeted at the next processing stage to be effective (p. 245).[9]

A potential problem with Bonilla's study also relates to the elicitation tests. All tests were conducted in a computer lab where students recorded themselves responding to two tasks designed to elicit spontaneous production in Spanish. They were told "not to plan what they wanted to say or pause at any point during the recording or re-do any recordings" (p. 109). This procedure is potentially problematic since we cannot be sure, or at least the reader is not informed by Bonilla, how rapidly the students responded and the extent to which they actually paused, usually assumed to be an indication of planning, as they responded to the test prompts.

With the exception of the two learners reported by Spada and Lightbown, who skipped a level, all four studies provided support for one of the corollaries of TH—that instruction cannot alter the predicted sequence. At the same time, however, they challenged the second corollary—that to be effective instruction must be aimed at the next immediate stage (i.e., X+1). The study by Zhang (in progress), as discussed in the next section, is designed to specifically test the hypothesis that teaching cannot alter the predicted emergence order.

## STI and L2 Chinese: A Challenge to TH

X. Zhang's study (we add his first initial to avoid confusion with Y. Zhang, whose work is also referenced in this discussion), has so far shown that instruction organized in accordance with STI and Vygotsky's theory of educational development can modify the route of emergence of the processing hierarchy, at least with regard to the recently proposed Topic Hypothesis (henceforth, TopH), as it pertains to L2 Chinese. Before discussing the study we will briefly explain the TopH and consider one study that appeared to support its claims.

### The Topic Hypothesis

TopH, proposed by Pienemann, Di Biase, and Kawaguchi (2005), takes into account the fact that speakers make discourse-pragmatic choices with regard to the aspect of an event or state they wish to mark as most prominent and therefore worthy of an interlocutor's attention. Typically in languages with canonical SV(O) syntax, the semantic AGENT is encoded in sentence initial topic position as grammatical SUBJECT. However, speakers can decide to assign topic status to non-subject constituents, as in English *wh*-questions (e.g., "What did you buy at the market?" where OBJECT is topicalized).

TopH states that

> In second language acquisition learners will initially not differentiate between SUBJ and TOP. The addition of an XP to a canonical string will trigger a differentiation of TOP and SUB which first extends to non-arguments and successively to arguments thus causing further structure consequences.
>
> *(p. 239)*

Keep in mind, of course, that in some languages, such as German, as we have in our discussion of PT above, topicalizing an ADJUNCT or an OBJECT still requires the verb to appear in second position; therefore, *Morgan, ich gehe in die Schule* 'Tomorrow, I go to school' and *Das Buch ich habe gelesen* 'The book I have read', both frequently attested in learner language, are ungrammatical.

### Topicalization in Chinese

The examples given in Table 5.7 illustrate the options available for topicalization of ADJUNCTS and OBJECTS in Chinese.[10] Sentence (1) shows canonical order with temporal and locative Adjuncts appearing in default position between SUBJECT and VERB.

According to TopH, L2 learners will progress through three implicationally arranged stages as they acquire the pragmatic options sanctioned by Chinese

**TABLE 5.7** Examples of topicalization in Chinese

---

1. *Wo* (I) *zuotian* (yesterday) *zai fangzi* (at home) *chi–le* (ate) *pingguo* (apples)
   SUBJECT<sub>TOPIC</sub> TEMP LOC VERB ASPECT OBJECT

2. *Zuotian (yesterday) wo* (I) *zai fangzi* (at home) *chi–le* (ate) *pingguo* (apples)
   ADJUNCT<sub>TOPIC</sub> SUBJECT LOC VERB ASPECT OBJECT

3. *Zai fangzi* (at home) *wo* (I) *zuodian (yesterday) chi–le* (ate) *pingguo* (apples)
   ADJUNCT<sub>TOPIC</sub> SUBJECT TEMP VERB ASPECT OBJECT

4. *Pingguo* (apples) *wo* (I) *zuotian (yesterday) zai fangzi* (at home) *chi–le* (ate).
   OBJECT<sub>TOPIC</sub> SUBJECT TEMP LOC VERB ASPECT

---

syntax: $S_{TOPIC}$ (ADJUNCT) V (O) > ADJUNCT$_{TOPIC}$ S V (O) > OBJECT$_{TOPIC}$ S V (Y. Zhang, 2007, p. 154). In terms of PT these correspond to Stages 2, 3, and 4.

Y. Zhang (2007) reported on longitudinal data that traced the progress of three L1 English-speaking students enrolled in a beginning-level university L2 Chinese course in Australia. Using several tasks designed to elicit spontaneous performance (imitation, picture description, story retelling, role-play, monologue), Zhang met with the students a total of nine times (one student missed a session) each over the course of the academic year.

With regard to TopH, Y. Zhang reported that after 50 hours of study the three students met PT emergence criterion (use of the feature in at least four different contexts) for Stage 2, canonical SVO order. Five weeks later, topicalization of ADJUNCTS, Stage 3, met criterion. However, Y. Zhang found that the learners favored temporal over locative adverbs with regard to topicalization, with preverbal (S ADJ V) position favored for locatives (Y. Zhang, 2007, p. 161). Topicalization of OBJECT, Stage 4 in the processing hierarchy, appeared between data sessions 6 and 7 (one learner missed session 6), or between 16 and 19 weeks after Stage 3 emerged. Y. Zhang (2007, p. 163) noted, however, that this feature was "produced in small quantities" even toward the end of the year in sessions 8 and 9. Y. Zhang's (2007) study then appeared to corroborate the TopH and with it to provide additional evidence in support of TH.[11]

## X. Zhang's Study

The full, in progress study, includes 10 participants, 8 of whom are L1 English speakers and 2 of whom are Chinese heritage speakers, who also speak English as a native language. All students were enrolled in an intermediate level Chinese course at a large North American research university. The participants were screened to be sure they were able to produce canonical SVO sentences in spoken Chinese, Stage 2 in the processing hierarchy and Stage 1 in the TopH. For consistency of discussion we will refer to stages in the processing hierarchy only. Thus, the relevant stages are 2 (SVO), 3 (XP-Adjunct), and 4 (OSV). The screening tasks used by X. Zhang included a timed grammaticality judgment, elicited imitation, cartoon description, 10 questions designed to elicit responses with topicalized adjuncts or objects. All of the students who volunteered for the study were at Stage 2 and therefore produced SVO sentences. None of them showed evidence of Stage 3 or 4 structures.

One group of students received instruction on Stage 4 OSV before Stage 3, XP-Adjunct, and the other group was instructed on both stages simultaneously. The heritage speakers were treated as a separate group since they were able to move the object to preverbal position and append the particle *ba-* as a topic marker—a Stage 5 process, according to Gao (2005) and Wang (2011)—but could not process Stage 4 OSV.

Although the instructional program for the full study has been carried out and the post-tests have been administered, X. Zhang has not completed analysis of the data, and we will only be able to discuss one of the participants from the pilot project here. The pilot project was also conducted with university-level learners of Chinese. However, unlike in the full study, the students were selected from among a group of L1 English university students who were at the beginning of a study abroad experience in Guangzhou, China. They were screened using the same tasks as in the main study. Six students were tested but only two were at Stage 2 (SVO), and, of these, only one completed the full course of instruction. The four other students showed evidence of being at Stage 3, XP-Adjunct, and therefore were not selected for participation in the pilot study.

The student and the TR engaged in STI instruction according to the following schedule: 1 hour of instruction on OBJECT topicalization (Stage 4 processing) only. Two days later the second session began with the first post-test. This was followed by an additional hour of instruction on topicalization of Adjuncts (Stage 3 processing). Two days later the third session began with the second post-test that was followed by a 1-hour review of topicalization that included both OBJECT and ADJUNCT. The final, delayed, post-test was administered 2 weeks after the third instruction session.

As with the pre-test, all testing sessions included a timed grammaticality judgment task (GJT), an elicited imitation task, retelling of a short animated cartoon clip, and a question and answer session. Because the GJT is not considered fully appropriate for assessing the emergence criteria of PT, we forego further discussion of this instrument and instead focus on the elicited imitation tasks, the cartoon description (five 1-minute clips from Tom and Jerry cartoons), and the open-ended question task (the researcher asked the participant questions about her experiences living in Guangzhou, China).

X. Zhang developed two SCOBAs for the instructional phase of the study. The first used an animated PowerPoint in which a Chinese sentence was displayed in Chinese characters, English translation, and pictures. A simplified version of the SCOBA is given in Figure 5.3. We do not include the Chinese characters.

Row 1 contains pictures illustrating the Agent, Adjuncts, Action, and Object. Row 2 contains the written version of the sentence using Chinese characters

| 1. | man | clock | house | figure eating | bowl of rice |
|---|---|---|---|---|---|
| 2. | *Ta* | *2-dian* | *zai fangzi* | *chi-le* | *fan* |
| 3. | Man | at two o'clock | at home | ate | rice |
| 4. | S | TEMP | LOC | V | O |

**FIGURE 5.3** PowerPoint SCOBA illustrating Chinese topicalization (based on X. Zhang, in progress)

(we substitute *pinyin*). Row 3 provides the English translation and row 4 indicates the constituent structure of the sentence. In the animation of the PowerPoint, each movable constituent is transposed to sentence initial position along with its picture, Chinese character, and English translation. However, in the first instructional session only Object is shown to move to sentence initial position rendering the example sentence, "Rice he at two o'clock at home ate."

The second SCOBA provided students with the opportunity to verbally and materially manipulate the constituent structure of the sentence. To achieve this, X. Zhang used Cuisenaire rods associated with Silent Way pedagogy (Gattegno, 1963). The arrangement given in Figure 5.4 illustrates the material manipulation process. Each constituent in the sentence is represented by a rod that varied in color and length from the other rods. The labels for the constituents given in the Figure were of course not visibly provided to the students. They only saw the rod display and their task was to manipulate them to produce possible topicalized sentences in Chinese, beginning with Stage 4, OBJECT.

As the students manipulated the rods to create appropriately topicalized sentences, they also verbalized in Chinese the actual sentences they generated as well as the constituent structure for each sentence. Given that the students in the full study as well as the pilot had no prior experience studying or using Chinese there was no issue with pre-understandings that had to be brought to light and changed, as was the case in van Compernolle's studies.

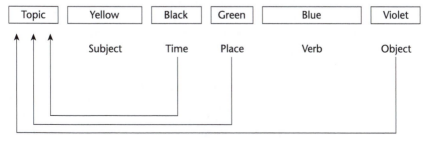

**FIGURE 5.4** SCOBA for material manipulation of sentence constituents (based on X. Zhang, in progress)

**TABLE 5.8** Spontaneous performance of Jane on Post-tests

| Task | Stage | Post-test 1 | Post-test 2 | Delayed Post-test |
|------|-------|-------------|-------------|-------------------|
| EI | 2 | 14/24 | 13/26 | 10/30 |
| | 3 | 00/24 | 03/26 | 14/30 |
| | 4 | **04/24** | 07/26 | 04/30 |
| CD | 2 | 13/19 | 13/24 | 23/43 |
| | 3 | 00/19 | 01/24 | 02/43 |
| | 4 | **04/19** | 08/24 | 14/43 |
| Q&A★ | 2 | 12/17 | 11/16 | — |
| | 3 | 00/17 | 01/16 | — |
| | 4 | **02/17** | 02/16 | — |
| Total | 2 | 39/60 | 37/66 | 33/73 |
| | 3 | 00/60 | 05/66 | 16/73 |
| | 4 | **10/60** | 17/66 | 18/73 |

*Note:* EI = elicited imitation; CD = cartoon description; Q&A = questions and answers
Stages: 2 = SVO; 3 = ADJ+SVO; 4 = OSV
★Q&A not administered on delayed post-test

Table 5.8 provides the data as analyzed by X. Zhang for the pilot study. The pseudonym for the student is Jane. Recall that on the pre-test, Jane was at Stage 2 and therefore produced SVO structures only.

In the first session, instruction focused exclusively on Stage 4 (OSV topicalization). Prior to the start of instruction on Stage 3 (ADJ-topicalization) the following day, post-test 1 was administered. As Table 5.8 indicates, Jane produced a total of 10 out of a possible 60 instances of Stage 4 structures and no instance of Stage 3 structures. At the conclusion of day-two instruction, Jane was given post-test 2 and produced a total of 5 ADJUNCT topic constructions out of 66 possible occasions and slightly increased her use of OBJECT topics to 17 out of 66. In the final instruction session the tutor summarized the concept of topicalization. Two weeks later, Jane took the delayed post-test and, as indicated in Table 5.8, produced almost the same number of ADJ + SVO as OSV structures, which shows that she seemed to have reasonably good control over topicalization in spontaneous performance. Having said this, we highlight the fact that Stage 4 emerged prior to Stage 3 apparently as a consequence of direct STI-based instruction.

X. Zhang also examined Jane's performance during communicated thinking. Toward the end of the first instruction session when tutor and student were working with the Cuisenaire rods, Jane arranged the rods in the following sequence: Subject+temp+loc+verb+object. The tutor asked, "Can you move the verb to the front?" and proceeded to move the blue rod to initial position (see Figure 5.4), to which Jane replied "You said you can't put the verb to the front. I don't think so" (X. Zhang, in progress). The tutor then asked, "Can you move this rod (black rod—temp) to the front?" and Jane again responded, "I don't think you can. Not that I learned in this class" (X. Zhang, in progress). Even though Chinese allows topicalization of temporal adverbs, because Jane had not received instruction that promoted this option, she indicated it was not a possible alternative.

X. Zhang also provided examples of Jane's performance on the post-tests. For instance, on post-test 1 (following OSV instruction) in response to the tutor's question about a cartoon clip, "Where did Jerry see the cat?" (question was produced in Chinese), Jane responded with the correct "Cat, Jerry at home saw." Following the second instructional session on ADJUNCT topicalization, the tutor produced the following sentence during elicited imitation "At school, I don't drink beer" (ADJ+S negV O), which Jane repeated as "At school, Ø don't drink beer"—a grammatically correct sentence, given that Chinese is a pro-drop language. More interesting is that when the tutor intentionally produced an ungrammatical model, Jane corrected it in her imitative response.

> Tutor: *At home, beer, I drink (ADJ+OSV)
>
> Jane: At home, I drink beer (ADJ+SVO)

The following examples show Jane's ability to produce both Stage 4 and Stage 3 sentences on post-test 2, administered after she had received instruction on both stages. In exchange (1), also about a cartoon clip, the tutor asked Jane a question that could elicit an OSV response, which is what she indeed produced:

> Exchange (1)
>
> Tutor: What did the cat open?
>
> Jane: The letter the cat opened. (OSV)

In exchange (2) the tutor asked a question that is followed by a second, adverb focused question, and again Jane responded appropriately:

> Exchange (2)
>
> Tutor: Who is reading the book?
>
> Jane: The cat and mouse read books. (SVO)
>
> Tutor: Where?
>
> Jane: At home the cat and mouse read book. (LOC+SVO)
>
> *(X. Zhang, in progress)*

Following instruction, the tutor asked Jane if she could explain the concept of topicalization in Chinese. Her response was:

> In the normal sentence structure, you have subject, your time, location, then emotions, verb and object. However, if you like to emphasize the object,

you put it in front of the subject and keep everything else in place. Likewise, with the time and location, they can be treated the same as the object.

*(X. Zhang, in progress)*

The tutor also asked Jane for her impressions of the STI experience. She focused on the value of material action with the Cuisenaire rods:

> I tend to be somewhat of a visual learner so having the rods actually represent the parts in the sentence helped me form a sentence when I was speaking it, because I could look at it or I could remember the rods, and it would help me form the sentence.

X. Zhang pointed out that at the beginning of instruction, Jane relied extensively on the rods in forming sentences, often touching them with her finger and moving them systematically as she spoke the words in Chinese.

After Jane improved her fluency and no longer needed to point at or touch the rods during the instruction sessions, the tutor asked her what she thinks about when responding to the various post-test tasks. Jane stated: "I am thinking about the rods to keep the order." She then clarified her remark: "Maybe not thinking about the rods specifically but remembering the order of the words I'm presenting." One of the students in the full study when asked a similar question regarding his own production remarked that he is able to visualize the rods when he speaks and that this helps him produce the appropriate order (X. Zhang, in progress).

We believe that these comments are not only indicative of the value of materialization and material action but also of the fact that Jane's (perhaps the other learner as well) performance emanated from declarative rather than procedural memory. She seemed able to visualize the grammatical structure of the sentences she produced, at least at the early point in her learning experience. However, she did comment that the more she used the language the less she had to think about the order.

Although X. Zhang's pilot study provided evidence from one learner that instruction can affect the route of emergence of processing procedures, we will need to await the outcome of his full study before we can have confidence in the findings of his research. An important aspect of the full study is that Zhang elicited data from the participants with regard to working memory. We suspect that one reason why STI might affect the processing sequence is because the SCOBAs provide external auxiliary support (i.e., mediation) for working memory, which is then internalized through practice. Jane's comments on the effect of manipulating the rods during instruction and thinking about them during the post-tests suggest that this may be the case. In immersion settings where systematic external support is not as forthcoming as in an STI context, learners are not as readily able to create the support for themselves and consequently the processing complexity of each stage in the hierarchy is likely to tax their cognitive resources, including working memory.

## TH and STI: Piagetian vs. Vygotskian Perspectives

A possible reason why previous research on TH failed to change the developmental route is that instruction was either implicit, as in Mackey's (1999) or Spada and Lightbown's (1999) studies, and therefore conditions were similar to natural contexts, where the predictions of PT seem to hold, or when explicit instruction was implemented it was not as well organized and systematic as STI. We cannot be sure in the latter case because, as far as we can determine, TH studies have not provided detailed descriptions of instruction. In the three previous studies that investigated TopH in Chinese (Y. Zhang, 2007; Gao, 2005; Wang, 2011), the instructional practices utilized in each case were not fully delineated.

Looking back at the research on TH, in fact, we find that beginning with Pienemann's (1984) study, where the hypothesis was initially proposed, little detail is provided regarding the teaching approach implemented. We are told that the experiment reported on in the article was "taught as a special class using the teaching material that we had developed" (p. 192). The only other hint as to what actually transpired is that dialogues were apparently "drilled" (p. 195) during instruction. We are not given information on the nature of the explanations provided to learners or even if explanations were part of the instructional program. Even in Bonilla's (2012) study, which included a more detailed pedagogical description than most other studies that address TH, we are not told the explicit content of the PowerPoint explanations provided to the students.

Felix (1981) represents one of the earliest studies to compare naturalistic and classroom learners within the general framework of PT. The study compared the acquisition sequences of classroom learners of L2 English with those of un-tutored learners of this language and found a high degree of overlap between the two sets of learners. From this, Felix concluded that learners make their own contributions to the learning process that are independent of the teaching process and are therefore "apparently not equipped with separate mechanisms to cope with different learning situations" (p. 108), and foreshadowing cognitivist SLA (see Chapter 4) proposed that learners seem to possess "a universal and common set of principles which are flexible enough to be adaptable to the large number of conditions under which language learning may take place" (p. 109). He also per-haps laid the groundwork for what would in a few years become the Teachability Hypothesis (see Pienemann, 1984) with his remark that the "possibility of manip-ulating and controlling the students' verbal behavior in the classroom is in fact quite limited" and if the natural processes are not taken into account "mastery of the L2 will most likely remain unsatisfactory" (p. 109).

In our view, Felix's generalization with respect to the impact of teaching on learner classroom development may have been premature, particularly given that the project did not focus "on the teacher or the method of instruction" (Felix, 1981, p. 89) and therefore decoupled the teaching–learning dialectic (i.e., *obuchenie*) that is vitally important for Vygotsky and Gal'perin. From this perspective the quality of instruction, and hence of the dialectic itself, makes a difference. Spada and Lightbown (1999, p. 14) also suggested that the nature of instruction may be a determining factor. They pointed out (p. 14) that in the studies conducted by Pienemann, instruction was explicit and involved production practice, while instruction in their study was implicit involving exposure to high frequency input.

Given our theoretical framework, we agree with Spada and Lightbown (1999) that quality of instruction should matter. They speculated (p. 14), for example, that explicit instruction might be more effective than implicit instruction if it targets the next developmental stage (i.e., X+1). However, Pienemann disagrees with the contention that the quality of instruction could make a difference with regard to TH. In Pienemann's (1987, p. 86) study on the development of German word order in an instructed learner, he expressly stated that he does not subscribe to the view that "it is crucial to relate the output of the (formal) learner to potentially effective external factors such as the nature of the teaching process before any valid statement about the nature of formal SLA can be made." He supported his stance by pointing out that SLA research "does not indicate that second languages are learned in a completely different mode when developed in a formal context, or when taught with a different method" (p. 86). This orientation, in fact, might explain why in the studies testing TH, detailed descriptions of instructional practices are not provided.

Moreover, Pienemann aligns his stance on TH with Piaget's view of general psychological development, a view that is at odds with Vygotsky's position. In this regard he makes the following statement:

> The approach we have taken in the Predictive Framework of SLA and in the Teachability Hypothesis was inspired by our admiration for Jean Piaget's work on cognitive development. We adopted one concept in particular from Piaget's work, namely the implicational nature of processing prerequisites for the operations possible at the different stages of acquisition.
> *(Pienemann, 1987, p. 92)*

While Vygotsky relied on the early work of Piaget in formulating his own theoretical principles (see Lantolf & Thorne, 2006; van der Veer & Valsiner, 1991), he made it clear that he disagreed with Piaget with regard to the nature of the relationship between development and instruction. Most likely under the influence of his history and training in biology, Piaget argued that for instruction to be effective, children had to be developmentally ready to learn (Egan, 1983), whereas Vygotsky, as we have argued throughout our discussion, proposed that instruction, in the teaching–learning dialectic of *obuchenie*, prepares the way for development.[12] Thus, the contrast between Piaget and Vygotsky is carried into SLA research respectively in Pienemann's PT and TH and in Gal'perin's STI as implemented in our work. We believe this to be an extremely interesting and important contrast to pursue in future research.

## Conclusion

This chapter reviewed three experimental-developmental studies, all of which in some way focused on development of L2 pragmatic capacity. Van Compernolle's and Kim's studies were more robust than Zhang's, in the sense that they included a greater number of participants and were carried out over a longer period of time. Nevertheless, Zhang's pilot study uncovered evidence that, if borne out by his larger study, would represent a significant challenge to the TH. Even so, it would not be unreasonable to suggest that even a single case in which instruction can affect the predicted route of emergence of the processing hierarchy is a problem for TH. Notice that Zhang's evidence is different from what was reported in Spada and Lightbown (1999) where two students skipped a level. In this case, the learners apparently did not acquire a higher stage for English question before a lower stage; they simply acquired a higher stage without acquiring the previous stage. Zhang's pilot participant acquired both stages of Chinese topicalization but in the reverse order of what PT predicts. All three studies supported Vygotsky's (1978, 1987) argument that appropriate cognitive tools are able to provoke development.

Van Compernolle's study, in particular, showed that students' pre-understanding generated during their previous experiences in formal language instruction is difficult, but not impossible, to overcome through appropriately organized instruction. In the next chapter, we will discuss a study on Spanish aspect in which pre-understanding was even more deeply entrenched in learners' knowledge base than was the case in van Compernolle's research.

For her part, Kim provided support for Vygotsky's general educational theory that development in one domain can impact develop in another. Several of her participants indicated that through STI on English sarcasm they gained a deeper understanding of how sarcasm functions in their native language and some even noted that they gained greater confidence in their ability to use this aspect of language use in their L1. Several students also noted that they felt more empowered in L2 English settings because they had developed an ability to at least detect and interpret sarcastic utterances, a common feature of English-speaking interactions that had previously caused them problems.

Given that the three studies were experimental-developmental in nature and following the requirements of the praxis-based theory of development proposed by Vygotsky, the materials and instructional strategies implemented in the three studies must be moved into intact classrooms, where their potential to impact development in the messy environment of the classroom needs to be put to the test. As we will see in the next chapter, however, studies testing the effects of STI intact classrooms have been carried out with a fair degree of success.

## Notes

1　When quoting from the data, we do not indicate all of the diacritic features used by van Compernolle in his transcriptions. We do not believe they are relevant to our immediate purpose of providing an overview of the data.

2　Optional contexts should be included in the criterion given some discourse-level features, such as pro-drop and topicalization, are not grammatically obligatory, as for example, German V-2 is.

3　PT theory has not been without its critics. Jordan (2004), for instance, contends that because its focus is on speech production, the theory fails to account for the full scope of a learner's abstract linguistic competence. Another criticism is that because the theory focuses on emergence of structures and processing capacities, it has not offered any account of how mastery develops (see Zhang, in progress).

4　According to Tarone (2007, p. 844), in a paper that appeared in the *University of Hawaii working papers in ESL* 1998, Long acknowledged that Liu's study provided evidence that "social context might affect the cognitive processes and outcomes of SLA."

5　We categorized the two Spanish features in terms of the general five-stage PT hierarchy given in Table 5.6. Farley and McCollam (2004) followed the hierarchy specifically designed for Spanish by Johnston (1995), according to which personal-*a* is situated at Stage 5 and use of subjunctive in subordinate clauses is located at stage 7.

6　A significant effect was also found for treatment in favor of Processing Instruction; however, this is not the main concern of our discussion and we therefore do not pursue the matter further.

7　Bonilla also carried out a corpus-based study, using the CHILDES data base. Since our concern is with explicit classroom instruction, we forego discussion of this particular study.

8　Bonilla also provided the groups with instruction on Spanish morphology in accordance with Stages 3 through 5; however, because the findings more or less paralleled those for syntax, we will not consider these features here. The only difference, not relevant to our current discussion, was that morphological emergence lagged somewhat behind the emergence of syntax (see Bonilla, 2012, p. 238).

9　Bonilla also reported that, as in Mackey's (1999) study, when learners reached a particular stage, "production of already acquired stages tended to increase" (p. 243). This finding, according to Bonilla, could be relevant for determining "how learners progress toward mastery of features associated with each processing stage" (p. 243).

10　There is another option available for topicalization in Chinese which involves so-called *ba*-structures where an OBJECT is moved to pre-verbal position and the particle *ba-* is attached to the object, as in *ta ba-gongke zuowan le* 'He homework finished.' Some Chinese scholars argue that in such sentences the verb is actually topicalized by moving the object to pre-verbal position. Gao (2005) proposes that *ba*-OBJECT constructions arise at Stage 5, and as such are more complex than OSV constructions. X. Zhang does not include this structure in his study.

11　Another longitudinal study by Wang (2011) on classroom learners of L2 Chinese also confirmed the processing sequence with regard to the TopH and other features of L2 Chinese predicted by PT.

12　For an informative discussion on how their life histories impacted on Piaget's and Vygotsky's theories of cognitive development see Pass (2004).

# 6

# L2 SYSTEMIC THEORETICAL INSTRUCTION

## Intact Classroom Studies

In the present chapter we will consider three studies conducted within Gal'perin's STI framework. One study focused on L2 Spanish, one on L2 Chinese, and a third on L2 English. The Spanish study implemented a complete innovative syllabus designed to seamlessly connect language and literature to empower students to use the language in creative ways in order to express their own meanings. The other two studies integrated a series of lessons using STI into the regular syllabus mandated by the respective instructional programs in Chinese and English. The latter two studies also incorporated post-instruction assessments. In the Chinese study, a comparison was made with students in an intact class at a more advanced level. The English study used pre- and post-tests to assess development. The Spanish project, on the other hand, assessed development on the basis of learners' ability to free themselves from the constraints of traditional rules-of-thumb instruction where performance is judged as correct or incorrect rather than as reflecting a speaker's communicative intentions. We consider the studies in the following order: Spanish, Chinese, and English.

### Spanish Verbal Aspect: Connecting Language and Literature

Yáñez-Prieto (2008) carried out a rich and complex study in a third-year university class in Spanish as a foreign language that served as a bridge between language and literature courses and where focus was on integrating literature and language study through an STI syllabus. The teacher-researcher's (henceforth, TR) goal was to provide instruction to the 13 students enrolled in the class in which literature was considered as an instance of language-in-use. The course was designed to compare and contrast everyday and literary language particularly with regard to concepts such as genre, discourse, metaphor/metonymy (and other tropes), punctuation, etc., and to engage students in activities whereby they could experience directly both types of language use and analyze the connection between them. For example, the students had opportunities to compare the use of metaphor in everyday Spanish with metaphor in literary texts. They also analyzed differences in how grammatical and discursive features of the language were used in everyday and literary genres. In particular, activities that focused on grammar use sensitized students to the fact that in many cases grammar use is not a matter of producing correct and incorrect language but is instead a matter of choice in order to shape meanings that fulfill more effectively a speaker's or writer's communicative intent. This was made especially apparent to learners as the instructor engaged them in analyses of ways in which literary authors manipulate the language in order to evoke particular emotional or aesthetic impressions in readers. To achieve this they often bend if not break the conventions of everyday language use. The TR's goal was to mediate her students so that they could experience something similar in their own use of the language.

To achieve her instructional goal, the TR had to uncover the learners' pre-understanding of features of the language that they had appropriated from their previous educational histories. She also had to confront the students' pre-understanding of language use in general. For instance, at the outset of the course, the students were unwilling to accept the notion that everyday language makes robust use of metaphor and metonymy. The students believed that figurative usage was unique to literary language, while everyday language was literal. Although Yáñez-Prieto's documentation of her struggle to lead the students into a different understanding of figurative usage is very interesting and informative, our focus here is on grammar, in particular, verbal aspect, a traditional problem area for L1 English learners of Romance languages.

### Verbal Aspect: The Literary in Everyday Language

In accordance with Gal'perin's model, TR began her instruction on verbal aspect by presenting learners with a unified SCOBA of the concept.[1] To do this she drew upon the work of cognitive linguists, in particular Turner (1996), who explains aspect in terms of *speaker perspective*, which is fluid and dependent on the component of an event or state that a speaker or writer wishes to bring into focus. Using Salaberry's (2001) and Salaberry and Shirai's (2002) account of lexical aspect, based in part on Vendler's (1967) classic work, TR first explained the difference between situation and viewpoint aspect. In the former, the lexical meaning of verbs is the primary carrier of aspect as a reflection of the temporal character of events and states in the world. In the latter, grammatical aspect imparted through verb morphology in a language such as Spanish, can override lexical aspect (Salaberry & Shirai, 2002, p. 3). Borrowing examples from Salaberry (2001, p. 27), TR explained how a stative verb, such as the Spanish copula *estar* 'to be', inherently non-dynamic, durative, and atelic, when inflected with preterit morphology, becomes an accomplishment, dynamic, durative, and telic, as in *Estuvo en Montevideo en cinco días* 'I made it to Montevideo in five days.'

Figure 6.1 is adapted from the component of Yáñez-Prieto's SCOBA that treated the contrast between preterit and imperfect aspect. For ease of exposition we use prose to describe the events in the SCOBA instead of the images utilized in Yáñez-Prieto's original. Her use of images, in our view, represents an important modification of the heavily verbal flowchart implemented by Negueruela (2003).

**A. Preterit**

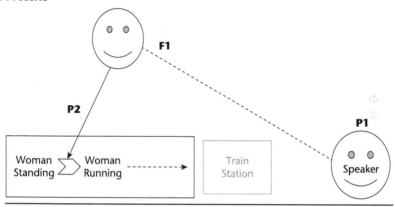

*De repente Jazmín **corrió** hacia la estación de trenes*
(Suddenly, Jazmin set off running toward the train station)

**B. Preterit**

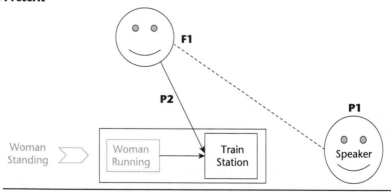

*Jazmín **llegó** a la estación de trenes*
(Jazmin arrived at the train station)

**FIGURE 6.1** SCOBA for Spanish Aspect (based on Yáñez-Prieto, 2008, Appendix B) (Continued)

### C. Preterit

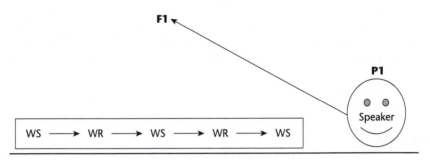

*El año pasado Jazmín corrió todos los días*
(Last year Jazmin ran every day)

### D. Imperfect

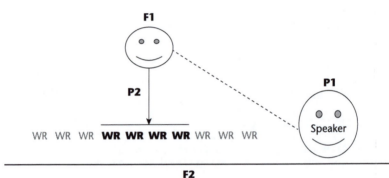

*Ayer Jazmín corría toda la tarde*
(Yesterday Jazmin was running all afternoon)

### E. Imperfect

F1

P2

P1

Speaker

WS →WR   WR →WS   **WS→WR  WR→WS**   WS →WR   WR →WS

F2

*El año pasado Jazmín **corría** todos los días*
(Last year Jazmin ran [used to run] every day)

FIGURE 6.1  SCOBA for Spanish Aspect (based on Yáñez-Prieto, 2008, Appendix B)

In section (A) of the SCOBA, P1 indicates the temporal perspective from which the narrator views the event—a point in time later than the event itself. P2 indicates an imagined temporal perspective that the narrator adopts in order to reposition herself/himself as if viewing the event at the time it occurred. From this perspective the speaker then focuses (F2) on the initiation of the event (i.e., Jazmin setting off running). Even though the entire event in reality is terminated, the speaker wishes to profile only a segment of the event—its onset, which is the bounded segment of the event, indicated by the enclosure. Whether the runner reached the station is not in focus, as is indicated by the light gray letters for 'train station.' In (B), the speaker shifts focus F2 to the conclusion of the event whereby Jazmin arrived at the station. Thus, the onset of the event is not relevant and therefore not profiled. In (C) the speaker's focus (F1) is directly on the bounded event of Jazmin having run on a regular basis last year. Of course, encyclopedic knowledge of the nature of human running activity allows a listener to infer that Jazmin did not run non-stop for an entire year. Finally, in (D) the speaker, again focusing on an event in the past (F1), adjusts perspective to focus (F2) on only one segment of the event and profile it without attention to its onset or end point, as indicated by the gray lettering to the left and right of F2.

After presentation of the SCOBA, TR provided students with excerpts from literary texts to illustrate how aspect can in fact be manipulated to create particular kinds of impressions on a reader. These texts were contrasted with excerpts from Spanish soap operas where aspect was used in accordance with general everyday communicative practice. For instance, background scenes against which the events of a story take place were related with imperfect aspect and the events themselves were narrated with preterit aspect.

An especially effective literary piece used by TR was a short story written by the Argentinian author Julio Cortázar. Instead of using imperfect for background, the author in fact opts to relate the events of the story using this aspect. According to TR the effect is to draw the reader into the events as if they were unfolding before one's eyes. For a full discussion and analysis of the story see Yáñez-Prieto (2008, pp. 221–223). TR's reason for selecting the text was stimulated by comments from the students that they had already taken several language-focused courses where instruction had been repetitious, leading them to wonder "what else could be learned about Spanish?" (p. 225). According to Yáñez-Prieto, the short story then provided a significant opportunity "to break from the student's [sic] conventional history in traditional language courses that mostly focuses on isolated, minimal units, such as words and sentences" (p. 225). Comparing (C) with (E) in the SCOBA reveals that either preterit or imperfect can co-occur in the same utterance referring to an event that took place last year. The difference in meaning, and this is what Cortázar is playing with in his short story, is revealed in the perspectival difference. In the former, the event is profiled as bounded and quite likely terminated, while in the latter no commitment is made to its boundedness and therefore it potentially draws the listener or reader more closely to the event, as if observing it unfolding before one's (imaginary) eye.

## Student Pre-Understanding of Aspect

Following presentation and discussion of the SCOBA and Cortázar's story, TR engaged the students in one-on-one communicated thinking during office hours in order to uncover their pre-understanding of the concept of aspect as well as their understanding of the SCOBA. She discovered that the students had a difficult time appreciating the difference between F1 and F2 and continued to view events only from the perspective of the speech event, F1. In addition, based on what they had internalized in their histories as students of Spanish, they relied on overt linguistic cues and other rules of thumb supplied by textbooks and previous instructors. Consequently, they were puzzled by the use of imperfect aspect in the sentences given in (D) and (E) because they contain adverbials (i.e., yesterday, last year) that supposedly trigger preterit. Referencing the dire warning of Bull and Lamadrid (1971), published more than 40 years ago, Yáñez-Prieto (2008, p. 275) argued that explaining grammar through rules of thumb "may well be tantamount to committing linguistic suicide" (Bull & Lamadrid, 1971, p. 454). Indeed, because rules of thumb, at best, reflect language use in specific empirical contexts, they inhibit more abstract and generalizable thinking, much in the way spontaneous everyday concepts are characterized by Vygotsky (1987). They may be useful and accurate in concrete situations, but they are closely tied to those situations and do not easily recontextualize to other circumstances.

One of the rules of thumb that learners consistently mentioned during communicated thinking was "use preterit for actions that happened once." Yáñez-Prieto (2008, p. 428) pointed out, however, even a one-time event such as one's birth can be rendered in the imperfect: "*Antonio Machado nacía*-imperfect *en Sevilla en 1875*" (Antonio Machado was born in Seville in 1875).

Importantly, students often did not detect contradictions in the rules until they attempted to explain their use of aspect in their essays during communicated thinking. One student, Darcy (pseudonym) when asked by TR why he had used the imperfect in "*la arquitectura parecía*-imperfect *maravillosa*" (the architecture looked wonderful) and the preterit in "*el saber floreció*-preterit *como una charca llena de peces*" (knowledge bloomed like a pond full of fish), became confused as he responded. He began by reciting the rule, which he attributed to his previous instructors, that "with adjectives and descriptions you always use imperfect" (p. 432). When attempting to explain the second sentence, however, he decided that perhaps the preterit was not appropriate and that he should have used imperfect, but he was unable to provide a reason. Pushed by TR, he decided that the sentence described the environment and therefore he switched to imperfect, abandoning his original use of preterit on the grounds that somehow "flowering" was "a start-stop finish" (p. 432). Apparently the start-stop rule is related to the rule which requires preterit for actions that happen quickly (Yáñez-Prieto, 2008, p. 430). Darcy then changed his mind regarding his motive for selecting imperfect in the first sentence from description to on-going event. Imperfect aspect, according to the students, is used for describing emotions, habitual and incomplete actions, and for descriptions of people or objects (p. 431).

Dulcinea (pseudonym) used preterit in a sentence describing weather: "*una noche hizo*-preterit *mucho frío y viento*" (one night it was very cold and windy). However, when asked to explain her choice, she decided that imperfect was more appropriate and cited the rule that imperfect is used for weather descriptions and this should take precedence over completed actions (p. 434). Similarly, another student, Juliet, expressed confusion when she found herself having to think through her motives for aspect selection in the following sentence: "*esto era*-imperfect *la verdad para nuestra heroína*" (this was the truth for our heroine). When asked about her aspect choice by TR, Juliet responded as follows:

> I think … now that I think, I think that it should be "fue" [was–preterit]? … Because I'm talking about the teenage years, but, like, I think I was just thinking about, like, the confusing nature of the years which is more like an emotional thing, which is more like imperfect because it's a state of mind.
>
> *(p. 435)*

Thus, the student changed from her original selection of imperfect to preterit, but upon externalizing the rule for use of imperfect with mental states, decided that perhaps her original choice was appropriate. However, she concluded the interaction with TR with the following comment: "But I would be OK with changing that" (p. 435), presumably an indication that she would be willing to change to "whatever the linguistic 'authority' [TR] considers as correct" (p. 436).

### Toward a New Understanding

After working with the SCOBAs and reading various literary texts for the next several weeks, the students once again engaged in communicated thinking about verbal aspect. This time, we observe the beginnings of a shift in their understanding and a willingness, on the part of some, though not all students, to question their rules of thumb and, with it, their histories as language students. When asked what she now thought about aspect being a matter of choice determined by the meanings one wishes to convey to an interlocutor or reader, Lara (pseudonym) commented (in Spanish but here we provide the English translation only): "I didn't know there were no strict rules with respect to different verbal tenses. It depends on the meaning that the writer wants the necessary tense to indicate. Each of the tenses has a different nuance and concept of time" (p. 438).

Dulcinea, likewise expressed the beginnings of an appreciation for the conceptual way of using aspect. Her comments, however, provided in week seven of the course, exhibit the dialectic tension that emerged in many of the students as their histories collided with a new present:

> This week we learned about aspect and perspective. I feel that I am starting to understand that there are many more uses for the preterit and imperfect

than those introduced in textbooks. It is confusing however to grasp the idea that the preterit can be used to describe something in the past, when we have been taught the "rules" that the imperfect is used for description in the past.

*(p. 440)*

Darcy also expressed confusion accompanied by a note of optimism: "Today I was very confused, because it kind of went against all that I learned before. It will get cleared up though" (p. 439). As we will see shortly, Darcy's optimism was perhaps a bit misplaced, since he, among all of the students, had the most difficult time overcoming his history as he clung to his pre-understanding, despite the contradictory evidence he was presented with.

According to Yáñez-Prieto (2008, p. 439), some students found the fact that personal choice was heavily involved in aspect use creative and very appealing. The following comment from Ulysses (pseudonym) illustrates this:

Ah, the dreaded imperfect–preterit debate. Every person learning Spanish must experience it sometime. However, this time we learned it differently than before. Instead of strict rules, there's more towards the discretion of the writer. It's a neat way to look at the preterit and imperfect. I'm gonna try to have it incorporated into my composition.

*(p. 439)*

When TR engaged another student, Gulliver (pseudonym), in communicated thinking about aspect, his focus was on textbook explanations, which he admitted "doesn't make any sense," with reference to the rule that imperfect is to be used with expression of emotions (p. 458). His next comment indicated that he had begun to appreciate that verbal aspect was a matter of user's choice: "You can write something and it'll be correct one way. You can write it the other way and then it'll also be correct, it all depends on what you mean" (p. 458).

As TR drew the students into close analysis of Cortázar's story as a model exhibiting how manipulation of aspect can affect how readers make sense of the events of the story, many of them began to distance themselves from their pre-understanding based on rules of thumb. They began to perceive the inconsistencies and incomplete nature of the rules. In addition, they began to explore the potential effects of manipulating aspect in their own writing.

### From New Understanding to Performance

One of the course assignments was for students to produce their own story that depicted an emotional or profound event in their own lives. Alice (pseudonym), who early on in the course had dismissed Cortázar's use of aspect "as exceptions to rules" (p. 466), eventually began to explore the effect of playing with aspect in her own writing. Alice wrote about her high-school graduation ceremony, as follows:

> *La música comenzó*-preterit *ocupando los pensamientos de la multitud, y el primer soldado dio*-preterit *un paso hacia adelante. Hombre a hombre. Mujer a mujer. Los soldados entraban*-imperfect *en fila. Saltaban*-imperfect *los flashes de las cámaras como si lucharan*-preterit (subjunctive mood) *contra rayos. Entonces los aplausos llegaban*-preterit.

> [The music started occupying the crowd's thoughts, and the first soldier stepped forward. Man to man. Woman-to-woman. The soldiers came in line. The camera flashes popped as if they fought lightning back. Then the applause arrived.]

Alice explained to TR that she used tense shifts to create "a stop in the action, and make the whole scene appear in slow motion" (p. 469). She even used punctuation to contribute to the effect when she described how the "graduates/soldiers marched in pairs to receive a diploma and to shake the principle's [sic] hand at the graduation ceremony" (p. 469).

Toward the end of the course, Alice commented on her new understanding of aspect:

> It is very confusing but very interesting because I did not know it [aspect] in the past and ... it's almost comforting because I can use it to express something and the reader or a person can interpret my thoughts and words with a word, oh, a word that I use, and it is not cut and dry anymore and it offers many possibilities.
>
> *(p. 470)*

However, as Yáñez-Prieto (2008, p. 471) remarked, Alice was still not completely certain about her new-found understanding of aspect, and asked TR if she would be understood if she used imperfect in speech the way she had used it in her writing. TR assured Alice enthusiastically that she would indeed be understood (p. 471).

In writing about the tragic events of the mass shooting at Columbine High School, in Colorado in April 1999, Lara (pseudonym) wrote: "*necesitaba*-imperfect *encontrar a los niños inmediatamente, pero llegaba*-imperfect *demasiado tarde ...*" (he needed to find the children immediately, but he arrived too late). When asked by TR about her aspect choice, Lara explained that she chose the imperfect instead of the preterit

> because I wanted the perspective to be at that moment in time during this sequence of past events. The woman is telling the story to the man and

recreating the scene. By using the imperfect form, it also creates suspense for the man (the listener) and the reader because it indicates that they don't know what will happen next.

*(p. 474)*

As a final example of use of aspect to intentionally create dramatic effect in student stories, consider the excerpt written by Emma (pseudonym), who related the events of the evening when she and her sisters were informed by their parents that their mother had been diagnosed with breast cancer:

> *Pero esa noche, mi papa no nos molestaba-*imperfect *con sus preguntas y mi mama [sic] ni siquiera levantaba-*imperfect *la vista de su plato. Esa noche, el silencio no era-*imperfect *cómodo; era pesado y fuerte. Llenaba-*imperfect *el cuarto, hundiendo a mi familia, y mis hermanas y yo cruzábamos-*imperfect *miradas preocupadas. Algo no estaba-*imperfect *bien . . . Descendí-*preterit *la escalera lentamente, sin sentir escalones bajo los pies. Con cada paso hacia su cuarto mi corazón latió-*preterit *más alto. Cuando llegué-*preterit *a su cuarto, era-*imperfect *oscuro y callado y mi mamá estaba en la cama, los ojos cerrados.*

*(pp. 478–479)*

[But that night, my dad did not bother us with his questions and my mom did not even raise her eyes from her plate. That night silence was not comfortable; it was heavy and strong. It filled the room, sinking my family, and my sisters and I crossed worried glances. Something was not right . . . I went down the stairs slowly, without feeling the treads under my feet. With each footstep towards her room my heart beat louder. When I arrived at her room, it was dark and quiet and my mom was in bed, with her eyes closed].

*(pp. 478–479)*

Emma was keenly aware of the effect of aspect selection in her story:

> although a lot of my paper could have been written in either imperfect or preterit, I tried to use each tense strategically to convey different meanings. For example, when I was talking about the moments we were in the dining room in silence, I used imperfect to depict everything as if the reader was there in the middle of the action, seeing everything as it was happening . . . When I went to my mom's room to see her after I found out that she was sick, I used preterit for all the verbs. This time I wanted to show each action as a complete act.

*(pp. 478–479)*

According to Yáñez-Prieto (2008, p. 479), Emma's aspect choices are not meaningless reactions triggered by sentence-based contextual cues (finished action, one-time occurrence, description, habitual or non-habitual action). Emma frames her manipulation of aspect in terms of the per-spective ... that she *chooses* to project on the states of affairs occurring at two different times in her narrative.

*(p. 479, italics in original)*

Emma mentioned that her use of aspect was based on her reading of the literary texts included in the course.

This, we argue, is a compelling example of the power of imitation for L2 development. Emma's comments showed that was not arbitrarily using aspect; on the contrary, she had specific motives for her choices and she understood that if she had made other choices, the effect of the text on the reader would have been quite different. Emma's text then illustrates, we believe, what Vygotsky (1987) had in mind when he remarked that "imitation is the source of instruction's influence on development" (pp. 211–212). Emma, and the other students, imitated the meaningful manipulation of aspect of the authors whose works they had studied in the course as well as the conceptual understanding of aspect materialized in the SCOBAs. Recall, however, from our earlier discussion, that imitation is not a mechanistic and thoughtless copying process, but a potentially creative and intentional appropriation of models available in the environment.

Before the end of the course, TR asked the students whether they would use the meaning-based conceptual understanding of aspect or would continue to rely on the rules of thumb provided by their previous experiences in Spanish classes. Essentially, she asked if they had changed their pre-understanding on the basis of their experience in the course. Five of the students indicated that they preferred to rely on the new meaning-based approach to the concept. Two of these students lamented that they had not been presented with the new understanding in their previous courses and one expressed a degree of frustration that her previous classes had required adherence to "strict rules" of use that interfered with "the flow of language" resulting in textbook-like speech (p. 481). Four students thought that the new concept of aspect was complicated for beginning-level students and that it might therefore be better to begin with rules of thumb and then "switch to the concept of aspect at the more advanced stages, even if rules did not work or had too many 'exceptions'" (p. 482). Two other students said that they would probably rely on rules of thumb as well as conceptual knowledge in the future, since some of the rules were valid and as such help clarify things on occasion. Another student appreciated the value of conceptual knowledge of aspect but worried that it might cause problems for him in future courses where he would be expected to produce the correct answer on exams (p. 484). The last of the students interviewed manifested significant resistance to the new way of understanding aspect, despite the persistent attempts of TR to change his orientation throughout the course. This student was committed to the idea that there is always a right and wrong when it comes to grammar, perhaps because he had been a highly successful student (determined by grades) in previous courses that valued this approach to instruction, and "once meaning and choice—with their instability—were introduced into the picture, the means of academic success into which he had been previously habituated crumbled" (p. 450). Thus, most, though not all, of the students either changed their understanding of aspect or were at least willing to entertain the possibility that their pre-understanding needed examination. Engrained history is not an easy thing to overcome even in the face of evidence that contradicts this history.[2]

## The Chinese Temporal System

The next study we will consider was conducted with two intact classrooms of beginning L1 English university learners of L2 Chinese and reported on in Lai (2012). The focus of the study was on development of the Chinese tense and aspect system. Using spatial metaphors of time as discussed in cognitive linguistics (Lakoff & Johnson, 1999), Lai developed a set of SCOBAs that conceptualized tense and aspect in Chinese.

In a language such as English, time metaphors usually conceptualize present time as the spatial location of the observer, while the future is thought of as in front and the past as in back of the observer.[3] An additional metaphor relied on in English is based on the notion of movement through space whereby an event is conceptualized as moving toward the observer, as in *The holidays are coming up*, or the observer is conceptualized as moving toward the event, as in *We're coming up on the holidays*. A third possibility conceptualizes temporal events as sequenced with respect to each other as in *Thanksgiving is before Christmas* and *Tuesday is the day after Monday* (Lai, 2012, p. 95).

Although the sagittal axis is used in a wide array of languages to metaphorize time, they do not all adhere to the English pattern. For example, some, such as Aymara (an indigenous language of the Andean region of Peru, Bolivia, and Chile), situate past time in front of, and future time behind, the observer on the assumption that the past is something that can be perceived because it has already occurred, while the future cannot be, given that it has not yet arrived. According to Lai's analysis, Chinese parallels Aymara in expressing past through the particle *qián* 'front' and future through the particle *hòu* 'back' as in *qián tiān* 'front day' (day before yesterday) and *hòu tiān* 'back day' (day after tomorrow) (p. 134).[4]

Unlike English, Chinese also uses the vertical axis to express time, with the particle *shang* 'up' indicating past, as in *shang libai* 'up week' (last week) and *xia* 'down' indicating future time, as in *xia libai* 'down week' (next week) (p. 106). According to Lai, the vertical axis refers to events that occur in the immediate past or future, while the sagittal axis generally refers to events for which there is an intervening event (p. 139). Thus, last week and next month are rendered respectively as *shang xingqi* (up week) and *xia gu yue* (down month) and 'the day before yesterday' is expressed as *qián tiān* (front-day) and 'the year after next' is rendered as *hòunian* (back-year). There are additional subtleties involved in use of temporal particles that we will not discuss here (pp. 107–108).

Aspect in Chinese is conveyed through particles that are positioned post-verbally. According to Lai (p. 139), two problematic particles for beginning and intermediate learners are the durative marker *–zhe*, as in *Ta zhengzai chi* **zhe** *mian* 'He is eating noodles right now' and the marker for bounded events *–le*, illustrated in the following sentence *Zuotian wo xie* **le** *yi feng xin* 'I wrote a letter yesterday' (p. 140). When *–le* is replicated in the same sentence it expresses a meaning similar to English present perfect aspect, as in *wo kan* **le** *liang ben shu* **le** 'I have read two books (and there are more for me to read)' (p. 142). It can even take on somewhat of a durative function, as in the following example, also from Lai (p. 142): *ta xue zhongwen xue* **le** *san nian* **le** 'He has been studying Chinese for two years.'

## Overview of the Study

Of the two first-semester beginning-level classes included in the study, one ($N = 16$) received instruction on Chinese tense and aspect following principles of STI, and the other ($N = 13$) received instruction on tense only, as was called for in the mandated program syllabus. Instruction in the second class followed procedures outlined in the textbook in which students were provided with a chart listing the four tense particles accompanied by examples and grammatical exercises. Both classes were given the same number of assignments and exams throughout the semester and spent approximately the same amount of time on tense. The STI class also received instruction on aspect. However, because the STI class was required to complete the regular syllabus for the course, the time allotted for instruction on temporal grammar (tense and aspect) was somewhat less for the other class. Both classes were both taught by Lai, the TR. Given that the students in both classes were in their first course in Chinese and were not very proficient in the spoken language, only their performance on written tasks was analyzed with regard to their ability to use temporal markers appropriately.

The program did not explicitly present aspect until the first semester of the intermediate-level course. To draw comparisons with the STI class regarding aspect, a third-semester intermediate-level class ($N = 13$), not taught by Lai, was included in the project. While students in this class had been exposed to aspect in the second semester of their elementary course, they received formal instruction beginning in the third semester.

## Explaining Chinese Tense and Aspect: SCOBAs for Directionality

Lai developed three SCOBAs to conceptualize tense and aspect for the STI class. Two of these are given in Figure 6.2 and the third is described later.

**A. Sagittal Axis Represented as a Train: *qián* 'front', *hòu* 'back'**

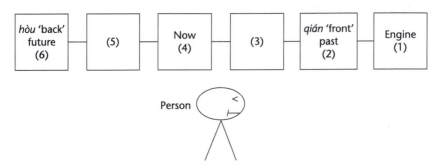

**B. Integration of Sagittal and Vertical Axes**

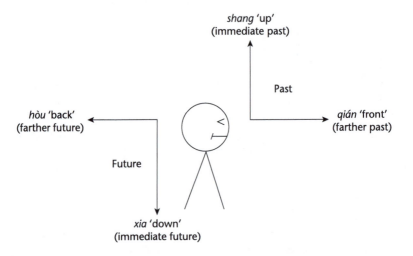

**FIGURE 6.2** SCOBA for Chinese Temporal Grammar. Based on Lai (2012, pp. 135, 138)

Part (A) explains the relationship between the particles for front and back as indicators of past and future events, respectively. The object depicted in the SCOBA is a train, which is moving past the person, who is looking toward the front, the part of the train that has already passed by. The back of the train, or future, has yet to pass the location where the person is positioned, the present. Cars (3) and (5) positioned between (2) and (6) respectively are important features of the train as they indicate that if one unit of time intervenes between the present time and the time period referred to, the front/back particles are used, as in *qián tiān* 'front-day' (day before yesterday) and *hòunian* 'back-year' (year after next).[5] Part (B) of the SCOBA integrates the sagittal and vertical axes, indicating that past is front (far) and up (near) and future is back (far) and down (near).

In the interest of space, we will describe verbally the SCOBA Lai (p. 143) developed for aspect. To indicate durative and stative (i.e., unbounded) aspect, typical of background events indicated with the particle *zhe*, an object is depicted floating in a pond of water. The object then begins to sink to the bottom of the pond, an event described through replication of the particle *le . . . le* to indicate that it is in progress. Finally, the object reaches the bottom of the pond, a completed action signaled through the perfective aspect marker *le*.

## Results of Instruction

To assess the effects of STI on the development of Chinese temporal grammar Lai engaged the students in the STI class in five different tasks, three of these were used to compare the performance of this class with students from the other two classes. The researcher carried out a series of qualitative and quantitative analyses of the tasks. The tasks were administered following instruction. Test items assessing the tense particles were included in the final exam for the STI class and the beginning-level traditional class. Pre-tests were not used because the students enrolled in the beginning classes were true beginners and therefore had no previous instruction on tense particles, and students enrolled in the intermediate-level class had not received previous formal instruction on aspect.

The first task asked students in the two beginning-level classes to write a short essay using as many tense particles as possible. The second task asked the same two classes to complete a fill-in activity in which a set of sentences written in Chinese contained blanks where the appropriate tense particle had to be inserted. The task also asked students to translate entire sentences from English into Chinese. Only the translation tasks were subjected to quantitative analysis. The essay task was analyzed from a qualitative perspective.

The assessment task on aspect, included in the final exam for the course, asked the STI students to write a ten-sentence essay describing university life to a friend. The essay was to incorporate sentences using the aspect particles. The entire exam, which included items other than tense and aspect, was to be completed within a 2-hour time limit. The task for the intermediate-level comparison class was to write a twelve-sentence e-mail or letter to a friend describing an important or unforgettable life experience, which also incorporated aspect particles. Because of objections from the course instructor on including the task in the course exam, the task was completed as an untimed extra-credit homework assignment.

## Analysis of Post-test Scores

On the translation of the eight sentences containing tense particles, students from the STI class produced on average six accurate translations, while those from the comparison class averaged 3.85 accurate translations.[6] Although, not surprisingly, given the differences between Chinese and English, both classes did less well on the vertical (up/down) than on the sagittal (front/back) particles. Nevertheless, the STI class outperformed the comparison class on both categories, scoring a mean of 3.54 for sagittal and 2.46 for vertical particles compared with 1.8 and 1 respectively for the students from the comparison class. Lai (2012, p. 171) subjected the results to a logistic regression analysis (using Generalized Estimating Equations) and reported significant effects for class and particle category. Moreover, an odds ratio analysis showed that the STI class was 5.37 times more likely to accurately translate the relevant items than was the comparison class and that both classes were 3.61 times more likely to translate the sagittal particles more correctly than they were the vertical particles.

With regard to aspect marking, according to Lai (2012, p. 175), a comparison between the STI class and the intermediate-level comparison class revealed that the former class produced slightly more correct instances of aspect than did the latter class (2.06 vs.1.85). However, given that the intermediate class produced more sentences in their essays (12.15) than did the STI class (10.38), the intermediate class actually produced a slightly higher proportion of correct uses (.75) than did the STI class (.71). It turns out, however, that an ANCOVA analysis, with the covariant as the total number of sentences produced, revealed no significant difference between the two classes (p. 176).

The quantitative analysis showed that the traditional practice of segmenting instruction on the temporal system of Chinese into tense and aspect based on proficiency level is problematic and inefficient. Given the significant difference between the beginning-level classes with regard to tense in favor of the STI class and the lack of a significant difference between this and the intermediate-level class, it is quite likely that the temporal system can be effectively taught in a unified way at the elementary level through implementation of an STI instructional program (p. 187). This conclusion is further supported by the extensive qualitative analysis carried out by Lai, in which she reported that a greater number of STI students used temporal expressions more coherently than did the beginning-level comparison class (p. 217). For one thing, many of the STI students were able to consistently distinguish foreground and background information, without over use, while the comparison class students tended to randomly choose temporal expressions as well as to over use the expressions when describing single events (p. 271). Moreover, the STI students incorporated many more self-generated temporal expressions in their essays than did the comparison students, who tended to copy the expressions included in the teaching materials. This is not to say that the STI students did not have problems with the temporal system. For one thing, aspect was not used as accurately as was tense. In particular the perfective particle *le* caused them difficulties, which, according to Lai (p. 228), might have resulted from their inability to fully distinguish tense from aspect.

## Analysis of Learner Verbalization

With regard to the verbalization activities included in the project, it is particularly interesting to note the contrast with some of the students in Yáñez-Prieto's study

(2008) with regard conceptual understanding versus rules of thumb. Even though both studies focused on temporal features of the respective languages, the students' conceptual understanding of Chinese tense and aspect did not compete with rules-of-thumb knowledge simply because they were real beginners. This is not all that surprising, of course; yet, it illustrates that students are able to appropriate and use systematic concepts from the outset of study without the need for rules of thumb, as suggested by some of the students in Yáñez-Prieto's research. Referring to tense marking, one student from the Chinese STI class explained that

> the verbs in a Chinese sentence are not conjugated in any way that would indicate the temporal time of a sentence ... in Chinese temporal aspect markers are used to indicate time in a Chinese sentence. These temporal markers are "yesterday", "today", "tomorrow" etc.

She provided two examples: "*wo* (I) *zuotian* (yesterday) *qu* (go) *tushuguan* (library) [Yesterday, I went to the library]" and "*wo* (I) *mingtian* (tomorrow) *qu* (go) *tushuguan* (library) [Tomorrow, I will go to the library]" (p. 233). With regard to verbal aspect, another student stated that "*zhe* is used to explain that an action is either ongoing or is simultaneous with another action (since no tenses are used)" and gave the example: "*wo zai mang zhe shangwang*"/"I am busy on the internet" (p. 234).

Again, not all of the students were successful in comprehending the meaning of the concept, as is seen in the following erroneous explanation, which confuses aspect and tense: "for past, they use *le* [the perfective aspect marker] and for present they just use the normal form of verb or vocabulary. For the future, I think they use *ba* [a particle used to topicalize verbs]" (p. 234).

Finally, almost all of the students reported that the SCOBAs were very useful in helping them to visually understand the temporal features of Chinese. One student offered the following observation: "pictures definitely help to visualize the concept. It makes it easier to understand and memorize. One still needs explanation to understand but looking at the picture, it reminds you what was taught, in specifically about the topic" (p. 236). The student acknowledges the value of the materialization but at the time recognizes that a verbal explanation needs to be connected to the images, as indeed was proposed by Gal'perin. Another student focused on how the images helped retain the conceptual meaning in memory, once their apparent strangeness was overcome: "They [the pictures] were a little strange at first but they actually did help a lot. It helped explain a basic idea and it stuck in my head so it did help realize the concept of time" (p. 240).

Not everyone found the SCOBAs completely functional, as illustrated in the following comment in which a student remarked that without more explanation things are not completely clear: "They are helpful to give a hint about the time expression. However, the concept behind that is not clearly illustrated and more explanation is needed for someone new in Chinese to understand it" (p. 240).

## English Phrasal Verbs

The final study on an intact classroom was carried out by H. Lee (2012). It reported on a project whose focus was English phrasal verbs, a notoriously difficult concept for L2 learners of the language to control. One of the sources of difficulty arises from the metaphorical meanings imparted by these verbs. That is, verbs such as *stand up, take off, fall down, carry on*, and *fade out* are problematic for learners, the so-called idiomatic forms, because meaning is "not only obscure it is often deceptive because while one expects to be able to figure out the meaning because the words look so familiar, knowing the meaning of the parts does not necessarily aid comprehension" (Celce-Murcia & Larsen-Freeman, 1999, p. 436).

The study was carried out over the final 6 weeks of a 16-week course in ESL for International Teaching Assistants in a large research university. The course is required for all international graduate students whose L1 is not English and who do not score sufficiently high on the program's speaking test, designed to assess their language ability with regard to teaching courses or conducting labs in the student's particular area of graduate education. A total of 23 students were enrolled in the course, all of whom gave consent to participate in the project. The researcher, Lee, was the TR.

Three particles that collocate with verbs were taught during the project: *out, up*, and *over*. One week of instruction was dedicated to each particle and co-occurring verbs. Prior to the start of instruction, students were given an extensive pre-test to assess their knowledge of phrasal verbs formed with the three particles. The test consisted of three parts. The first asked the students to define the three particles and to provide sample sentences illustrating the use of each particle in a phrasal verb construction. Also included was a 32-item multiple choice test where the students had to select from among four options for each item: verb + one of the particles or a bare verb and then indicate whether their choice was based on guessing or not [e.g., *He (held, held out, held up, held over) the child's hand in his*]. The second part contained ten sets of sentences with each set consisting of three to four individual sentences comprised of the same root verb collocated with different particles (e.g., *Many of the demonstrators attacked and burned government buildings; A car this size burns up a lot of fuel; I let the fire burn out*). The aim of this portion of the test was to determine if the students were able to exhibit understanding of the contribution of the particles to the meaning of the verb. The third component of the pre-test contained three sets of sentences consisting of three to five sentences where the same particle was used with different root verbs (e. g., *Who will take over when you retire; The car rolled over and over; I fell and kicked over a vase; The committee agonized over the decision*). As in part 2, the students were asked to explain the meaning of the phrasal verb and what contribution the particle made to its meaning in the context of each sentence.

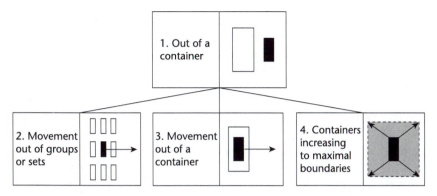

**FIGURE 6.3** SCOBA for English verbal particle *out* (Lee, 2012, p. 85)

To explain the meanings of each of the three particles, Lee developed a set SCOBAs based on the analysis of particles and prepositions provided in Tyler and Evans (2001) and Rudzka-Ostyn (2003). As an example, Figure 6.3 above includes the SCOBA Lee used for the particle *out*.

According to Lee (2012, p. 89) the SCOBA presents both the literal and metaphorical meanings of *out*. The meanings visualized in the SCOBA are illustrated in the following list of sentences with the first sentence in each pair exhibiting a literal meaning and the second a metaphorical meaning.

Examples of verbal particle *out*:

1a. The child's arms were *out* of the blanket, so the mother put them back in.
1b. The man was *out* of his mind with anger.
2a. For some reason that large dog *ran out* of the pack and attacked the stranger.
2b. The professor *singled out* the new theory for special attention.
3a. The boy *jumped out* of the car before it stopped.
3b. How did the FBI agent *figure out* the message hidden in the picture?
4a. The travelers *spread out* the map on the table.
4b. The accountant *filled out* the tax forms.

## Instruction

Lee developed a robust set of instructional activities to develop students' understanding and use of phrasal verbs based on the three directional particles. The first was a "brainstorming" session (Lee, 2012, p. 95), which sought to discover the students' pre-understanding of the meaning of phrasal verbs and if they could distinguish literal from metaphorical meanings. To familiarize students with the concept of metaphor, Lee next presented the CONTAINER metaphor associated with *out* and POSITIVE VERTICALITY associated with *up*. Given that no single overarching metaphor is reflected in the meaning of *over*, Lee explained and illustrated its prototypical meaning as involving movement of an object from one side of a barrier to another.

At appropriate points in the lesson on *over*, she presented specific metaphors associated with particular meanings of the particle. Once the students were familiar with the notion of conceptual metaphors, Lee presented the three SCOBAs and explained and illustrated the meanings reflected in each sub-component of each SCOBA. Next Lee engaged the students in an activity where they had to decide which of a set of collocations occurred with parti-cular particle verbs. For instance, working in small groups students had to determine if the set *coffee, water, beer, tea, feelings of anger, love, frustration, enthusiasm* more appropriately collocated with *pour out, wipe out, sort out, smooth out*, or *throw out* (p. 315). The class next read a series of texts containing phrasal verbs and they were given the task of interpreting and discussing their meanings. They then analyzed the differences between bare and phrasal verbs such as *die/die out, tear/tear up*, etc. As the final activity students were given a writing task where they had to produce as many sentences containing phrasal verbs as possible within a 2-minute time span.

In addition to the activities described above, at the end of instruction on each particle, the students were given a homework assignment consisting of a set of 15 sentences with phrasal verbs containing the relevant particle. They were to verbalize through dialogic thinking (I–me conversation) the meaning of the verb in context and then identify the image from the SCOBA evoked by each verb. The task was carried out in written format and submitted to the instructor for analysis and feedback.

### Assessing Development

Lee used a series of 3- or 4-option multiple-choice pre- and post-tests that were analyzed statistically to determine the effects of STI on learner development. The following is a typical item from the pre-test (Lee, 2012, p. 274): *He sat at his desk and ...... all of the computer printout sheets.* (a. went, b. went out, c. went up, d. went over. Guessed/Did not guess). In addition, the test batteries included several items that asked students to explain the meaning of phrasal and bare verbs used in sentences. These items were analyzed qualitatively only.

The post-tests included the exact questions from the pre-test (33 items) as well as questions comprised of different verb + particle combinations (33 items) than had appeared on the pre-test. In addition, the post-test included items designed to assess if the learners could interpret two new particles (5 items each)—*in, down*—that were not included in the instructional program. This was to determine if the students could transfer their understanding of the principle that particle verbs are motivated by literal and metaphorical meanings of the particles. In other words, if verbs formed with *up* reflect POSITIVE VERTICALITY, would students realize that *down* most likely reflected NEGATIVE VERTICALITY, and that if *out* indicated a position on, or movement to, the outside of a CONTAINER, *in* most likely indicated a position on, or movement to, the inside of a container.

The pre-tests were administrated immediately prior to the beginning of instruction and the post-tests were administered one week following instruction. No delayed post-tests were used. Overall, student scores on the pre- and post-tests showed a statistically significant improvement in performance. This included the repeated items as well as the new post-test items. Each test item also asked students to indicate whether or not they guessed. However, because *in* and *down* were not included in the pre-test, the items assessing performance on these particles were not included in the statistical analysis; rather they were analyzed qualitatively.

Lee conducted four separate analyses on the test items: one that examined performance on separate particles, a second that compared performance on literal versus metaphorical meanings of particle verbs, another that compared changes in performance from pre- to post-test for literal and metaphorical verb meanings, and a fourth that analyzed changes in the guessed/did not guess responses. The analysis of individual particles revealed a significant improvement in student scores from pre- to repeated post-test for *out* (.57 to .74) and *over* (.57 to .74) but no significant change for *up* (.66 to .70), although there was some improvement in this case as well. Student performance on the pre-test for the first two particles was lower than it was for the third and the students also scored higher on the repeated test for *out* and *over* than they did for *up*. The score on the new post-test items for *up* was identical to the pre-test score. While the scores on the new items for *out* (.63) and *over* (.83) where higher than on the pre-test, the difference reached significance only for the second particle. It is worth mentioning that the effect size (ES) for the test comparisons, which were not reported in Lee's study, is large. For *out*, the pre- and repeated post-test ES is ($d = 1.09, r = .480$), and for *over*, ES is ($d = 1.007, r = .450$). The effect size on comparison of the pre-test to the new post-test items is also substantial ($d = 1.576, r = .619$). Unfortunately, Lee offered no explanation for why no significant development was observed for *up*.

With regard to guessing/not guessing responses, Lee reported a significant change favoring not guessing between the pre-test, repeated post-test, and new post-test. We calculated a large to moderate effect size in each case. Between the pre- and repeated post-test we calculated a large ES ($d = 1.363, r = .563$) and between the pre- and new post-test we found a moderate ES ($d = .754, r = .352$). The importance of this difference is that it manifests an increased confidence among the learners in choosing their responses to the multiple-choice items—something we would anticipate with improved understanding of the semantics involved in particle verb formation.

Finally, with regard to differences between literal and metaphorical meanings of the respective particles, it is interesting that on none of the three tests did Lee report a significant difference between learner performance on literal compared with metaphorical test items. Having said this, she did observe significant changes in scores within each of the categories. Performance on literal items significantly improved between the pre- and repeated post-test, with a medium ES ($d = .502$, $r = .243$) and between the pre-test and the new post-test items, also with a moderate ES ($d = .612, r = .292$). For metaphorical items, Lee reported a significant improvement between the pre- and the repeated-items post-test, for which we calculated a medium ES ($d = .689, r = .326$). However, between the pre-test and the new post-test items Lee failed to observe a significant change, although there was a slight difference in scores (from .62 to .64, respectively). Again, this is not too surprising given that metaphorical meanings are usually more difficult to interpret accurately than are literal meanings of phrasal verbs. Be that as it may, when we consider Lee's qualitative analysis, which we will briefly summarize in the next subsection, we see that even though learners may have misinterpreted the metaphorical meanings of some phrasal verbs, they nevertheless understood the conceptual principle that the meanings of such constructions are motivated rather than arbitrary and that metaphorical interpretations are derived from literal meanings.

### Understanding of the Concept: Pre- and Post-Instruction

In order to assess the students' pre-understanding of the meanings of the three particles, Lee asked students on the pre-test to define each particle. The same procedure was repeated as part of the post-test following STI. On the pre-test Lee found that students offered definitions that were contextually limited and often imprecise. One student, Huan (pseudonym) defined *out* as "use all of something" (perhaps, meaning 'run out' of some substance). The same student illustrated a second definition with a drawing of what seems to be a container with a downwardly hooked arrow emerging from it and accompanied by "this means out" (Lee, 2012, p. 145). This student also used a drawing of an arrow pointing toward the top of the page, accompanied by "this means up" to define the particle *up*. Another student, Dongjoon (pseudonym), defined *out* as "move something to other place and then disappear," which includes movement but without any sense that the movement entails exiting a container (Lee, 2012, p. 146). Some students used antonyms to define the particles on the pre-test. For instance, Ru (pseudonym) defined *out* as "the opposite direction of 'in', for example out of the room" (p. 150). Similarly, students also defined *up* and *over* in terms of their opposites, as did Liwei (pseudonym) in "rise in the opposite of down" (p. 152) and Shanyuan in "it's the inverse of 'below'? (not sure)" (p. 153).

Some students provided fairly accurate, though incomplete definitions on the pre-test. Huan, for example defined *over* as "the end, above something, through something, to some place, like come over" (p. 149), and Jia defined the same particle as follows: "cross something: get over that river. Forget or recover from something: I'm over it. End: Game over" (p. 148).

On the post-test the students' definitions, while not always complete or fully accurate, were much more sophisticated and showed a deeper understanding of

1.                     jump over the fence

2. above. The sky over the fence.
3. pass from above. fly over.
4. come to a nearer place. ask the waiter come over.
5. take control. The teacher is watching over us.
6. cover. all over the place
7. bend. Bend over and pick the pocket up. (probably intends pocketbook)
8. Examine. go over the text.
9. Excess. He is over 50.

**FIGURE 6.4** Huan's post-test definition of *over* (Lee, 2012, p. 149)

the literal/metaphorical connection. On the post-test Huan expanded his four-part definition for *over* from the pre-test to reflect the nine-component definition given in the SCOBA during instruction. We provide his full account in Figure 6.4.

Ning defined *out* on the pre-test with an example: "turn out—this turns out to be good news" followed by an explanation: "It makes more sense to me that the phases [sic] with 'out' refers to a certain end of outcome and used in the case whenever there's a result of the event, and sometime means something is used up or all consumed" (p. 155). On the post-test he showed an understanding of the literal/metaphorical connection, using a drawing based on Lee's SCOBA that depicted an object moving from the inside to the outside of a container accompanied by the following commentary: "out of a container, and the container can be real, and can be something imaginary example: Bill Gates dropped out of college. Here 'out' means out of 'college', in which 'college' is the container here" (p. 154).

On the other hand, a few students provided definitions on the pre-test that showed they already had some understanding of the metaphorical meanings associated with the particles. However, even in this case, their post-test definitions were more complete and showed a deeper and more systematic understanding of the potential meanings carried by the particles and related phrasal verbs.

Three students, according to Lee, failed to exhibit much evidence of development in their understanding of the particles as a result of STI. The definitions they provided on the pretest did not appear to change all that much on the post-test. For instance Jisu's (pseudonym) definitions did not seem to reflect an understanding of the meanings of the particles that were based on the SCOBAs. Her pretest account of *over* stated that "if something is more than average or normal, that means over. ex) overcharge overcome → if you have difficult situation, you try to overcome," and her post-test explanation was "something too much, increase than something, move out from normal ex) she get over sick. Come over the problem. I jump over the fence" (p. 163).

Recall that in addition to asking students to complete multiple-choice items, the pre- and post-tests also asked students to explain the meanings of phrasal verbs in the context of sentences. Their performance from pre- to post-test was very informative with regard to development of their ability to provide appropriate interpretations of the verbs. Unfortunately, space only permits us to consider a few examples. For the sentence *The driver was forced to* **hand over** *the car keys and was left standing on the roadside* Shanyuan expressed uncertainty as to the verb's meaning, writing "Hand out?" (p. 167). On the repeated post-test, however, he explained its meaning as "Keys was handed from the driver to others" accompanied by a drawing depicting the prototypical meaning of the particle *over* as seen in Figure 6.4 for Huan. Similarly, Dongjoon used the same drawing on the post-test to explain the meaning of *She* **jumped over** *the edge of the truck, landing lightly on her sandals*, while his explanation on the pre-test indicated the opposite meaning: "get on, board" (p. 169). For the same sentence, Dohyun explained its meaning on the pre-test as "jump and climb up to somewhere"; but on the post-test he explained it as "jump some barrier and reach other place," with a clear understanding of the prototypical meaning associated with the particle (p. 171). Jin-Hua defined **Draw out** *the weekend by taking Monday off* as "something finished and showed" on the pre-test; however, on the post-test his definition clearly and appropriately reflected the meaning evoked by the fourth sub-image in the SCOBA (Figure 6.3 above) for *out*: "making something longer, Out: increasing to maximum" (p. 189).

Finally, we consider a few instances of learner performance on new post-test items. In many, though not all, cases the students were able to use the meanings exhibited in the SCOBAs to appropriately interpret the new phrasal verbs. Jaidee interpreted *The mirror* **clouded over** *as the steam rose from the hot water in the sink* as "became blur [sic] because of steam, 'over' in this case means covering" (p. 209). For the metaphorical meaning of *The police* **pulled** *the speeding motorist* **over** she wrote "forced a motorist to stop at the roadside, I think 'over' in this sentence has the same meaning as 'over' in 'lean over' because it gives a sense of movement like this picture" and she included a drawing of an arrow pointing upward and curved toward the right (p. 209). Hyejin, however, had problems interpreting *The committee* **agonized over** *the decision* and failed to provide a definition. However, for three other sentences with *over* she drew pictures that accurately reflected the meanings of *rules over*, *clouded over*, and *pulled over* (p. 213).

## Transfer to New Particles: In/Down

As for the new particles, *in* and *down*, most of the students provided definitions of phrasal verbs that revealed an understanding that was in some way connected to the meanings of their opposites, *out* and *up*, depicted in the SCOBAs. Given that learner knowledge of the particles was not assessed on the pre-test we cannot be certain that the meanings the students generated for sentences with the new particles demonstrated transfer of learning, but the wording of the explanations is certainly suggestive of this possibility. Jin-Hua, for example, explained the meaning of *Let the stain-remover* **soak in** *for an hour before washing the shirt* as "Making wet totally, In: outside to inside" (p. 190). According to Lee (2012, p. 189), although his definition does not make explicit reference to a container, as did Jin-Hua's explanations for *out* verbs, he most likely had a container in mind in the second part of the interpretation. For the following sentence, *It's not by* **cramming in** *facts and dates that one becomes more intelligent,* Jin-Hua indeed explicitly mentioned a container, "Forcing to put something in container," and followed this with virtually the same statement used in his *soak in* explanation: "In: from outside to inside." Jaidee's definition of the *cramming in* sentence made even more explicit reference to a container: "Pack, learn, memorize. 'in' is used to emphasize movement of knowledge, facts, or dates into container which is brain or memory" (p. 194).

With regard to *down*, some of the learners were able to appropriately interpret its metaphorical use in post-test sentences by linking them to the SCOBA provided for *up*, while others failed to make a connection. Jaidee "realized that physical downward movement can be expanded to abstract movement" as illustrated in her interpretation of the test sentences *They had to* **break down** *many social prejudices to manage to succeed* and *Our cat is so old and ill, so we'll have to ask her vet to* **put** *her* **down** (Lee, 2012, p. 202). The language Jaidee used to interpret the meaning of the phrasal verb in the first sentence emphasized a "decrease of power of social prejudices," and for the second sentence the verb indicated "movement from higher state (being alive) to lower state (death)" (p. 202). This meaning in particular seemed to be linked to the meaning Jaidee assigned to the phrasal verb *sober up*, which she defined as "improving from bad state (being drunk) to better state (being conscious)" (p. 202). While Lihua assigned a more or less appropriate meaning to the *break down* sentence "not exist any more" she appeared to clearly misconstrue the meaning of *put down*, which she understood as "recovery" "not ill any more" (p. 197). Nevertheless, she did connect her interpretation with the directionality of *down* as "a trend of become less" (p. 197) much in the way Lee's SCOBA for *up* included "reaching the highest limit, often suggesting completion" (p. 83).

## Conclusion

The three studies reviewed in this chapter provide clear evidence that STI can be effectively implemented in intact L2 classrooms. As with the experimental-developmental studies reviewed in Chapter 5, two of the projects revealed the challenge presented by learners' pre-understanding of L2 concepts, especially when this understanding is based on empirically restricted rules of thumb.

While H. Lee's (2012) study showed some effects of pre-understanding, in the study by Yáñez-Prieto (2008) it was exceptionally robust. This is not too surprising, given that traditional instruction on English phrasal verbs has generally expected students to memorize verb + particle collocations rather than to rely on a meaning-based approach grounded in principles of cognitive linguistics, while instruction on Spanish aspect has been based on inadequate rules of thumb.

A frequent worry expressed by language teachers is that full coherent explanations of concepts such as temporal systems will be too complex for learners to master. Consequently, instructional programs, including textbooks, usually adopt a reductivist strategy and thereby segment explanations of complex features of a language into small bites that are assumed to be more manageable by learners than is presentation of an entire concept. A common outcome of such an approach is student confusion resulting from the loss of the coherent meaning entailed in a concept. All three studies, and in particular, Lai's (2012), demonstrated that it is indeed possible for learners to effectively develop useful understanding of L2 features through STI without compromising the integrity of the concept and thus avoiding the "linguistic suicide" feared by Bull and Lamadrid (1971).

A problem reported by some of the students who participated in the STI intact studies, and reflected in comments from the students in Yáñez-Prieto's (2008) course, in particular, was that, following instruction, some of the students continued their study of the language in courses organized around traditional methods of instruction; that is, courses where the language was taught in accordance with rules of thumb and where focus was on production of correct and incorrect structures rather than on using the language to express personal meaning in imitation of literary writers. From our perspective the problem resides not in STI but in the traditional curriculum that needs to be modified if not abandoned altogether, especially in light of the newly published report by the National Council on Teacher Quality (2013). We will have more to say about this report in the concluding chapter.

## Notes

1   The SCOBA developed by Yáñez-Prieto was designed to explain the full concept of tense-aspect, including present perfect, past perfect, conditional, conditional perfect, future, future perfect, etc. A thorough discussion of the complete SCOBA along with supporting learner performance data is well beyond our present purpose. The interested reader should consult the full dissertation.
2   Recently, two microgenetic case studies tracing the conceptual and performance development of Spanish aspect in individual learners have been completed. One study traced the progress of a single classroom learner over a period of two academic semesters (Polizzi, 2013) and the other followed a single learner for one academic semester (Garcia, 2012). Each study is quite complex, involving the intersection of several conceptual and performance data sets. To do justice to these studies would require far more space than we are able to devote to them in this book. Nevertheless, we would like to point out that each represents a significant complement to Yáñez-Prieto's

research in that they provide greater detail to the development of conceptual knowledge and the learners' shift away from their inadequate pre-understanding of aspect.

3   It turns out that although English speakers use the sagittal axis when asked to consciously indicate past and future time, when producing spontaneous co-speech gestures they more often rely on the horizontal axis with the left indicating past and the right future time (Casasanto & Jasmin, 2012). Lai did not take this distinction into account when preparing the SCOBAs for her course.

4   As Lai (2012, pp. 100–106) pointed out, there is not universal agreement among linguists on the directionality of time along the sagittal axis in Chinese. Some argue that Chinese parallels English rather than Aymara. Nevertheless, Lai believes the evidence favors her analysis, which formed the basis of her instruction. An analysis of the different interpretations of the sagittal axis is beyond the scope of our discussion.

5   The vertical axis can also be used to refer to an event following or preceding an intervening event. In this case, reduplication is used, as in *shang shang libai* 'up up week' (week before last) and *xia xia libai* 'down down week' (the week after next).

6   It turns out that each class enrolled three native speakers of Korean, who did better on all tasks than did the L1 English speakers, most likely because of the similarity of Korean to Chinese for tense marking. We do not consider these students in the results analyzed here. Lai treated them separately from the English speakers.

# 7

# THE ZONE OF PROXIMAL DEVELOPMENT AND DYNAMIC ASSESSMENT

In the previous two chapters, we considered studies that foregrounded material mediation in the form of SCOBAs as part of STI curricula designed to support learners' internalization of L2 conceptual knowledge and intentional use of this knowledge during communication. In both the experimental-developmental and intact classroom studies, use of these materials was accompanied by interaction between tutor/researchers and learners; that is, learners were not simply provided SCOBAs and asked to complete tasks without additional instruction. As we explained in Chapter 3, Vygotsky understood the social environment to include not only material mediation but also mediation through social interaction, and much work that has proceeded from an SCT perspective has sought to elaborate the relationship between forms of interaction and learner development. In this chapter and the next, we turn our attention to research concerning the ZPD and the related proposal of DA, where the focus is on the potential for social interaction to externalize psychological processes, rendering them available for examination as well as intervention intended to promote development. Our decision to deal with material mediation in Chapters 5 and 6 and social mediation in this chapter and in Chapter 8 is purely for convenience of our discussion and we caution readers not to interpret this division as implying that these forms of mediation operate independently.

To set the stage for how we interpret the ZPD and how it informs our understanding and use of DA in L2 developmental education, we first review the various readings of the ZPD that have influenced research in the general and L2 SCT literature, and consider how these align with the statement and passages from Vygotsky's writings on the concept. Our interest is not in understanding the ZPD as a lens to examine what may or may not occur in a particular educational setting, but in keeping with the notion of praxis and the pedagogical imperative, it is to find ways of optimizing development through appropriate forms of social mediation. We are particularly interested in connecting the ZPD to the work of Reuven Feuerstein and his colleagues on the *Mediated Learning Experience*. We argue that Feuerstein's embrace of a praxis orientation to education is very much in line with Vygotsky's understanding of the ZPD and how, following Luria (1961), the concept has been realized in the practice of L2 DA.

## Interpreting the ZPD

Chaiklin (2003) argued that the ZPD is perhaps Vygotsky's most well known but least understood contribution to psychology and education. Indeed, Miller (2011, p. 366), in describing SCT in general, observed that Vygotsky has become a sort of "mythical figure serving as a kind of totem around which to gather various clans of like-minded believers." This statement has particular resonance for the ZPD, which has been invoked to establish theoretical legitimacy for concepts as varied as scaffolding, assisted performance, reciprocal teaching, and DA. Some lines of ZPD-inspired research represent elaborations of the concept and extend it to domains not explored by Vygotsky. Others, as Miller seemed to warn, distort Vygotsky's ideas by constructing affinities with other theories and practices. In this regard, Wertsch (1984) long ago worried that the ZPD had become so widely used in research, effectively referring to any kind of learning or pedagogical interaction, that the concept risked losing all meaning and explanatory power.

While we share Wertsch's concern and concur that not all forms of interaction or even all types of learning necessarily pertain to the ZPD, we also resist efforts to restrict use of the concept to only those particular contexts and problems specifically mentioned by Vygotsky. Not only does such a move bias against meaningful elaboration of the concept, in our view it also fails to appreciate the ZPD as an expression of Vygotskian praxis. That is, the ZPD offers at once a theoretical account of the relation between interactions with others and the development of new cognitive functions as well as a principled approach to structuring activities that mediate learners into participating in the teaching–learning dialectic, *obuchenie*, in ways that exceed their current abilities. Under-standing the ZPD as an instantiation of the dialectical relation between theory and practice that Vygotsky proposed renders it not only possible but imperative that the concept be extended to contexts in which the development of new capabilities is a concern.

We believe that the ZPD holds considerable promise as a basis for develop-mental education. To be sure, the ZPD has been referenced extensively in the L2 research literature over the past 25 years. Nonetheless, we submit that the potential of this concept for the field has not been fully realized, largely because L2 researchers have not fully committed to the dialectical approach Vygotsky proposed. It is in this respect that the emergence of DA in the L2 field has begun to advance an understanding of how the concept may be used to design pedagogical activities and frame interactions in order to guide learner development. In the next chapter, we present findings from recent studies of L2 DA that showcase how teachers and researchers have taken up this dialectic approach to developmental education. DA overcomes the traditional dualistic relation between teaching and assessment while also offering a powerful theoretical framework that guides and is shaped by practice.

## The Common Conception of the ZPD

Probably the most well known and most frequently cited definition of the ZPD is

> the distance between the actual developmental level as determined by independent problem solving, and the level of potential development as determined through problem solving under guidance or in collaboration with more capable peers.
>
> *(Vygotsky, 1978, p. 86)*

This description is taken from *Mind in Society* (1978), a volume that Vygotsky himself did not produce as a published book but is in fact a compilation of his writings edited by Cole, Scribner, and John-Steiner. Although in the entire corpus of his published writings available in English Vygotsky did not write on the ZPD as extensively as he did on other topics, he did have more to say about the concept than what appears in the 1978 volume. However, Chaiklin (2003) pointed out that that definition is frequently treated as the final word on the topic and is often the only quotation or reference employed in texts that make use of the term. In fact, Chaiklin (p. 41) referred to this definition as the "common conception" of the ZPD, and argued that it is marshaled to substantiate nearly every application of the term in research and practice, even when these diverge sharply from one another. As Miller (2011) cautioned, exclusive reliance on *Mind in Society* results in a diluted understanding of Vygotsky's theorizing.

Given that Vygotksy wrote relatively little on the ZPD it is not too surprising to find a variety of interpretations of the concept appearing in the research literature. Chaiklin (2003) identified three assumptions common to ZPD-based research: *generality assumption*, *assistance assumption*, and *potential assumption*. Holzman (2010) proposed another scheme for categorizing ZPD research according to analytic focus, which overlaps with Chaiklin's taxonomy. Specifically, Holzman referred to *individual*, *dyadic*, and *collective* foci of ZPD work. As we explain below, Chaiklin's potential assumption is brought out strongly in ZPD research that, as Holzman explained, understands the individual as the locus of the ZPD while his assistance assumption is characteristic of research focusing on dyadic interactions. As both of these understandings of the ZPD have received considerable attention in psychological and educational research, we will consider their major tenets and interrogate the extent to which their associated practices adhere to Vygotskian praxis. We then turn to Holzman's favored interpretation of the ZPD as collective activity, which we also believe is most closely aligned with Vygotsky's overall theory of how abilities may be interpreted and promoted. However, we first wish to comment on Chaiklin's generality assumption concerning the ZPD, and in particular the argument he put forth for delimiting use of the term "ZPD."

## Zone of Proximal Learning?

Chaiklin (2003) noted that the above description of the ZPD from Vygotsky (1978), with its reference to "problem solving," has led to a perception of the concept as pertaining to particular problems or tasks that a learner is able to perform "under guidance or in collaboration." At first glance, this view seems perfectly reasonable. Some tasks are sure to be easy for a given individual to complete independently, others will be far beyond his/her current capabilities, and some will be within reach so long as support or expert assistance is provided. As individuals begin to experience greater success with tasks that were previously inaccessible to them, we would appear reasonable to claim that development has occurred. It is in this regard that Chaiklin raised the *generality assumption* on the ZPD, namely whether the concept applies to all instances of learning. Indeed, Chaiklin (2003) cited the work of Wells (1999) and Tharp and Gallimore (1988) as arguing forcefully that the ZPD pertains to any sort of activity in which a skill is mastered or some understanding is gained. A different view, however, emerges from the full array of Vygotsky's writings.

To appreciate this point, it is important to understand the relationship Vygotsky conceived of between learning, on the one hand, and development on the other. As we have already explained (Chapter 2), Vygotsky critiqued many of his contemporaries who viewed learning and development as synonymous. He similarly was aware and critical of the influential proposal put forth by Piaget that we mentioned in Chapter 5, which held that learning could only occur when individuals reached a point when they were developmentally ready to respond to instruction. While Vygotsky shared Piaget's commitment to teaching that is concerned with development (rather than imparting factual knowledge), he reversed the relation between learning and development and assigned a much greater role to the teaching–learning dialectic than did Piaget.

According to Kozulin (1998), the Piagetian influence in Western education systems reinforced the belief that schooling is essentially concerned with *revealing* learner abilities and potentials, assumed to be qualities learners possess independent of instruction. Learners themselves are perceived as autonomous agents, determining and pursuing their own goals, and teachers are careful to avoid getting in the way of education. Following Kozulin (1998), Piaget's proposal stands in sharp contrast to Vygotsky's notion of *obuchenie*. As Vygotsky (1987, p. 12) put it, "Instruction would be completely unnecessary if it merely utilized what had already matured in the developmental process, if it were not itself a source of development." From this perspective, teachers are instrumental in organizing knowledge of the object of study and learning activities that continue to challenge learners while providing appropriate mediation to help them stretch beyond the limits of their current competence (Newman, Griffin, & Cole, 1989).

One of Vygotsky's (1998) favorite descriptions of the ZPD likens it to a garden containing flowers that have already blossomed as well as those that are still only budding; the gardener's responsibility is to both, as the ones that are only budding today will blossom tomorrow. Similarly, for *obuchenie* it is not enough to be concerned with functions that have already fully formed; equal attention must be given to functions that are still developing and that are therefore amenable to instructional intervention. In this regard, Vygotsky (1998, p. 204) stressed that the "great practical significance" of the ZPD to education is in orienting instruction not toward the products of past development, as evidenced in learner *independent performance*, but toward emerging abilities that are manifest in learner participation in joint activity with others. To paraphrase Vygotsky (1978), what a learner can do today in cooperative activity, s/he can do tomorrow independently.

Vygotsky (1987, p. 212) expressed how he conceptualized the ZPD in education in the distinction he made between teaching aimed at imparting "specialized, technical skills" from teaching that is developmental. As examples of skills, Vygotsky mentioned typing and learning to ride a bicycle. To be sure, these are learned, and they may indeed be accompanied by neuro-motor developmental gains (e.g., dexterity, balance, coordination). Learning to type and learning to ride a bicycle, however, do not entail the emergence of new cognitive capabilities, that is, ways of understanding that provide an orienting basis for acting in the world and that go beyond any particular context or problem. In this way, neither typing nor riding a bicycle carry psychological consequences as does, for example, acquiring language.

Before moving on, we wish to stress that while we concur with Chaiklin's (2003, p. 59) assessment that for Vygotsky not all learning is developmental, we do not share his view that "there is no additional scientific value" to using the term ZPD beyond discussion of those cognitive functions referenced in Vygotsky's own empirical work. For Chaiklin,

> It seems more appropriate to use the term *zone of proximal development* to refer to the phenomenon that Vygotsky was writing about and find other terms (e.g., *assisted instruction, scaffolding*) to refer to practices such as teaching a specific subject matter concept, skill, and so forth.
>
> *(p. 59, italics in original)*

At issue here seems to be what counts as development, and in particular development of cognitive abilities. As we discussed at length in Chapters 5 and 6, gaining conceptual knowledge within a field of study alters one's understanding of and capacity to act in the world. Such a shift, in our view, is perfectly in line with Vygotsky's (1987) analysis of formal schooling as a leading activity of development. To be sure, not all content learning prompts conceptual change, as it is possible to "learn," for example, discrete factual information that can be recalled and verbally reported without understanding the conceptual relations behind such facts. If it is this sort of content instruction that Chaiklin discounted, so be it. Like Vygotsky, however, and as we have argued throughout the book, we see education as holding singular potential for the extension of our biological development through artificial, cultural means and this applies to instruction in particular content areas, including language.

## Measurement and the ZPD

Turning to Chaiklin's (2003) *potential assumption* as well as Holzman's (2010) *individual* focus of ZPD research, we see this most strongly represented in the work of assessment specialists reorganizing their test administration procedures in hopes of gaining insights into the abilities of individuals they believe underperform on more conventional measures of IQ and general cognitive abilities (Haywood & Lidz, 2007; Sternberg & Grigorenko, 2002). Much of this work has been framed as DA, although as will be clear later in this chapter, these models represent a significant departure from how the term is used in the work of Feuerstein and how it has generally been applied in the L2 field. Most significant is that the ZPD is construed not as a dialectical framework for diagnosing and promoting learner development but rather as a set of techniques or strategies for revealing and measuring some latent potential, which itself is understood as a "characteristic or property of an individual" (Holzman, 2010, p. 28). In fact, Holzman continues that in such work the ZPD may refer to a set of techniques for eliciting this potential during the test but it may also refer to the potential itself, leading to descriptions of individuals as possessing a "large" or "small" ZPD in much the way that it is widely assumed that an individual's IQ may be high or low relative to a population.

The link between the ZPD and IQ measurement has a long tradition that can be traced to Vygotsky's own research. According to van der Veer and Valsiner (1991), it was within the context of IQ scores and children's performance in school that Vygotsky first discussed the ZPD. Briefly, Vygotsky was confronted with the question of why some children appeared to lose IQ points during their first year of formal schooling while others increased their scores. Beginning from the premise that schooling activity itself has the potential to drive development and therefore influence performance on IQ tests, he reasoned that the problem was that not all children were benefiting equally from the school curriculum.

Specifically, instruction was attuned to some learners' development and therefore promoted their abilities—yielding improved performance on the subsequent IQ test—whereas the children who had initially performed well on the IQ tests had already developed beyond the level where instruction was aimed. The crux of the issue then, was that IQ scores only indicated the products of past development but did not reveal abilities that were currently forming and that would soon come within the child's independent control.

To test his hypothesis, Vygotsky (1987) proposed an alternative procedure for administering the IQ tests wherein children were offered support during problem solving as they experienced difficulties. The result of this process, he argued, would be a developmental diagnosis that included both the fruits of previous development as well as a glimpse into the child's immediate potential level of functioning, that is, their ZPD. According to Vygotsky, the ZPD-based diagnoses did in fact prove a better predictor of the gains children made during their first year of schooling and indicated that enrichment would need to be provided to those individuals with high scores on the initial tests.

In our view, Vygotsky's IQ research is not at odds with his discussion of the ZPD as pointing to where teaching and learning activities may optimally guide development. Indeed, his analysis that a ZPD diagnosis can inform decisions of where to place students in schooling and how a curriculum might be adapted to meet the needs of all learners suggests that from the outset Vygotsky understood teaching and assessing to be in a dialectic relationship. Moreover, this initial formulation of the ZPD occurred not simply as an elegant theoretical construct but was immersed in practical activity. The ZPD offered a theoretical rationale to guide test administration to provide better insights into learner abilities and also yielded immediate recommendations for instruction.

This commitment to praxis, however, is less evident in much of the DA research aimed at measuring learners' hidden potential. Rather, such work appears to have assimilated the ZPD into mainstream psychometric theory, reducing Vygotsky's framework for developmental education to a technical procedure. Poehner (2008b) traces the origins of this shift to the earliest presentation of the ZPD outside of Russia in a paper given by Vygotsky's colleague, Alexander Luria (1961), at a meeting of the American Orthopsychiatric Association. Ironically, Luria's paper was a critique of the inadequacy of traditional psychometric approaches to diagnosing the underlying difficulties experienced by low-performing children in school. Echoing Vygotsky's (1998) indictment of conventional tests as only providing empirical confirmation of what is already self-evident without offering any *prognosis* or basis for remediating difficulties, Luria (1961, p. 5) described "psychometric tests" as having limited utility, noting that they "do not close the problem; they only open the problem." He further explained that by formulating a different approach to assessment, one that broke with psychometric conventions, he and Vygotsky had arrived at a method for identifying the causes of poor academic performance, which they found could be associated with difficult living conditions (e.g., poverty and malnutrition), emotional problems, physical challenges that render learning more difficult, such as hearing impairment, or problems that are biological in nature and that directly impede school success (e.g., brain damage, chromosomal abnormalities).

These points seem to have resonated with many in Luria's audience and proved influential in the emergence of early DA research, most notably the *learning potential* assessments devised by Budoff and his colleagues (Budoff, 1968; Budoff & Friedman, 1964). Budoff's research in turn became a point of reference for subsequent DA models, such the *graduated prompt* approach (Campione, Brown, Ferrara, & Bryant, 1984); the *testing the limits* approach (Carlson & Wiedl, 1992); the *Lerntest* (Guthke, 1992). While the methods employed in these approaches and the populations targeted differ, they share an orientation toward uncovering potential not revealed by conventional testing procedures (see Poehner, 2008b). Elsewhere (Lantolf & Poehner, 2004) we have proposed the term *interventionist DA* to underscore the focus this research places on doing or providing something to individuals for the purpose of gauging their responsiveness.

To be sure, this is not the only tradition within DA. The work of Feuerstein, which we discuss later in this chapter, is an important exception that follows a very different reading of the ZPD. Nonetheless, given the continued prevalence of the line of ZPD research that appears to have drawn inspiration from Luria's report, it is worth considering the account of the ZPD he offered, how this was interpreted by early DA researchers, and the extent to which it may be understood as dialectical activity.

## Interventionist DA

What is immediately striking about Luria's discussion of the ZPD is that it was squarely focused on assessment, with instruction only referenced as a subsequent activity that must take account of the insights gained through the assessment. Luria's model of assessment was a multi-step approach that began by rejecting as inadequate the "first rule of every testing psychologist" of restricting the diagnosis to observations of a learner's independent performance (1961, p. 6). Instead, Luria advocated that by providing assistance in the face of difficulties it is possible to capture what learners are able to do on their own as well as how they respond to help. In addition, Luria proposed that further insights into learner abilities are possible when learners confront parallel tasks and are again asked to perform without assistance, as this reveals the extent to which they benefited from previous support.

As Poehner (2008b) noted, this procedure parallels the classic pre-test–treatment–post-test design of experimental research, and this similarity may have supported—and perhaps shaped—the perception of the ZPD among members of Luria's audience. As mentioned, Budoff's DA research appeared shortly after Luria delivered his paper, and Budoff conceived a very similar multi-stage assessment process. In fact, Budoff's (1968) central argument was that comparisons of pre- and post-test scores allow for the creation of learning profiles, which he maintained are more relevant to claims of learner abilities. Specifically, he grouped individuals as *high scorers* (those with high scores on the pre-test), *gainers* (those who showed improvement from the pre- to post-test), and *non-gainers* (those who failed to improve from the pre- to the post-test). High scorers, Budoff reasoned, will likely continue to be successful because they performed well on an initial test when assistance was not available; these are individuals who would be identified as possessing strong abilities by any assessment. Similarly, non-gainers are those learners who, in spite of the provision of support, fail to improve when the intervention stage is over and they must again function independently. Like high scorers, these individuals turn out to be correctly identified by most assessments. Gainers, in contrast, are those who would be misdiagnosed if we consider only their pre-test performance because, following intervention, they are able to perform at a higher level. Gainers thus possess potential not easily detected by most assessment procedures.

While interventionist traditions of DA have offered an empirical basis for countering policies and practices that disproportionately identify certain populations of learners as having learning difficulties, including immigrant children, learners from low SES backgrounds, and ethnic and racial minorities, this work does not fully embrace the ZPD as a basis for pedagogical praxis. In large part, this is because assessment and instruction remain only loosely connected. Interventionist DA has generally been within the purview of educational psychologists rather than teaching and curriculum specialists. Perhaps revealing in this regard is the title of Sternberg and Grigorenko's (2002) book on the subject, *Dynamic Testing*, which connotes a further delimiting of DA practices by favoring the word 'testing' to 'assessment.' In that work, the authors suggested that dynamic testing may be differentiated from dynamic assessment as the former is concerned with the more modest goal of exploring individuals' potential to benefit from subsequent instruction while the latter aims to promote change over the course of the procedure. Sternberg and Grigorenko appeared to recognize the ZPD's potential as dialectical, transformative activity but had little to say about it, preferring instead to remain close to a psychological measurement orientation.

The framework espoused by Sternberg and Grigorenko (2002) continues to separate assessment from instruction. A dynamic test in this framework is usually administered by a trained professional, typically a school psychologist, and the results, often reduced to a single score or set of scores, are then passed on to stakeholders, including teachers, learners, and administrators. The extent to which such reporting leads to changes in classroom practice that can promote learner development is, at best, unclear. As Haywood and Lidz (2007) pointed out, teachers are often only minimally involved in the assessments and are not prepared to act on specific recommendations from testers, if indeed there are any.

As we explain later in this chapter, Feuerstein's DA research has followed a decidedly non-measurement trajectory and, in our view, more accurately captures the notion of praxis as intended by Vygotsky's understanding of the ZPD. However, before turning to Feuerstein's research we will discuss another important tradition of ZPD-inspired work, namely research that emphasizes mediated interaction and learner development.

## ZPD as Learning Prosthesis

Holzman (2010, p. 29) observed that the majority of studies that invoke the ZPD do so in the context of dyadic interactions, wherein the ZPD is "reduced to a two-person unit," usually an adult (presumed "expert") and a child ("novice") working together to complete a task. Wertsch (1991) suggested that the expertise brought to such interactions functions as a *learning prosthesis*, enabling learners to benefit from knowledge and experience beyond their own. In principle, a learning prosthesis that allows individuals to perform beyond the limits of their current capabilities may well be compatible with an understanding of the ZPD as dialectical activity that leads development. However, as Holzman (2010) contended, there has been a strong tendency in ZPD-based research examining dyadic interactions to neglect the question of development in favor of highlighting successful task completion. Here we see considerable overlap with Chaiklin's (2003) discussion of the *assistance assumption* on the ZPD, which he argued effectively reduces the ZPD to a sort of common-sense recommendation that offering learners "help" will enable them to do better.

Returning to Miller's (2011) analysis of the effect of *Mind in Society* on English-speaking audiences, it is not difficult to appreciate how the ZPD, with its emphasis on "guidance" and "collaboration with more capable peers," would have represented a sophisticated and appealing antidote to educators seeking to move away from practices that favored solo activity, such as note-taking and memorization, and toward greater recognition for the value of interaction in teaching and learning. Beginning in the late 1970s and continuing at least through the 1980s, a proliferation of research appeared referencing the ZPD and advocating the need for *scaffolding* (Wood, Bruner, & Ross, 1976) and *assisted performance* (Tharp & Gallimore, 1988). Here we see an emphasis on what is offered *to* learners and on the outcome relative to the task at hand. Less clear is whether the experience entails developmental consequences; that is, whether learners are in a stronger position to assume greater responsibility for such tasks in the future (Poehner & Lantolf, 2005). In this regard, we note a parallel with the tradition in DA research of conceptualizing mediation as a fixed treatment or intervention that can be provided to individuals. In such DA work, the aim is to broaden diagnoses of learner abilities according to how they respond to the treatment, while in scaffolding and assisted performance models, the goal is to determine whether or to what extent learner performance can be improved as a result of intervention.

The more important question, from the perspective of the ZPD, is whether such interactions guide learner development, and this is often not addressed explicitly. As a result, mediation offered under such circumstances may align with an individual's developmental needs, but it would do so only serendipitously rather than by design (Torrance & Pryor, 1998).

To illustrate clearly the difference between what we might term task-oriented and development-oriented interactions, we consider two examples both reported by Wertsch (Wertsch, 1984; Wertsch, Minick, & Arns, 1984). The first of these concerns the hypothetical case of a young child learning basic arithmetic and who, when told precisely which numbers and symbols to write, completed complex derivations in calculus. Wertsch (1984) explained that although a successful outcome was produced as a result of interaction, this did not likely carry any developmental consequences for the child, who was simply following directions to put marks on a page without an understanding of the concepts and relations they represent. To this we would add that the "assistance" described in Wertsch's example did not appear to mediate the child's engagement in a developmental activity but rather allowed him to carry out a task, which from the child's point of view more than likely required little thought. In this case, the task-orientation did not overlap with a development-orientation but rather ran counter to it (see also Stone, 1993).

A more detailed account of these differing orientations and how they impact the quality of interaction and potential for promoting development was provided in Wertsch and colleagues' (Wertsch et al., 1984) study of pre-school-aged children and their mothers working together to complete puzzles. The authors reported that the dyads were drawn from two distinct populations, mothers from urban environments, who had attended school, and those from rural backgrounds, who had little or no schooling. Analysis of the dyads' interactions revealed that these backgrounds shaped the mothers' perception of the activity and that this in turn impacted how they engaged with their children. Specifically, urban mothers were generally less concerned with completing the puzzles than they were with helping their children learn how to approach puzzles. They encouraged their children to be actively involved in the puzzle tasks and expected that the children would make mistakes and require multiple attempts before putting the pieces together correctly. These mothers also tended to engage in dialogue with their children about the activity, discussing how they might begin, ways of identifying the appropriate place for a given piece, features of different pieces that could give clues as to how they fit together, etc. In contrast, rural mothers were more inclined to attempt to complete the puzzles as efficiently and accurately as possible. They were quick to intervene when they saw their child about to make a mistake and frequently provided verbal directives, effectively taking over the task and expecting the child to quietly observe the process. As the authors explained, the rural mothers' emphasis on efficiency in completing the puzzles they were given meant that their children, unlike those of the urban mothers, did not have the same opportunities to learn how to complete puzzles and were less well prepared to approach other puzzles in the future.

The point of all this is that one cannot assume that a task-orientation during interaction will guide learner development. As we have explained, Vygotsky proposed the ZPD's significance as educational activity that leads development, and this occurs as psychological processes are externalized during interaction. This allows mediator and learner to jointly examine these processes and together move forward. To be sure, a development orientation entails a shift in how mediation is conceived as well as the forms of contribution that are possible. We will have more to say about the quality of mediator–learner interaction when we consider Feuerstein's DA framework. First we wish to conclude this section with some comments concerning Holzman's (2010) collectivist interpretation of the ZPD. This view of the ZPD entails a form of cooperative engagement, wherein participants work toward a common goal and contribute as they are able, which closely parallels Feuerstein's understanding of DA and Vygotsky's vision for ZPD in developmental education.

## ZPD as Co-Regulated, Collective Activity

While much has been made in educational research of the ZPD as a lens for understanding pedagogical activity, it is important to recall that Vygotsky (1978) also wrote of the ZPD's significance during the pre-school years, when the primary driver of development, he argued, is play. As Bodrova and Leong (2007) explain, Vygotsky's definition of play did not encompass all forms of activity typically described as play but instead centered on activities in which children create imaginary situations, adopt and enact roles, and follow rules that direct how they should perform their roles. In contrast to other notable scholars interested in childhood play, including Erickson and Piaget, Vygotsky argued that children do not engage in such activity in order to escape from reality but rather to further access the social world (Elkonin, 1998).

Vygotsky began from the premise that, unlike in pre-industrialized societies, where children may participate in the social world of adults from a young age, modern societies require long periods of schooling and vocational or professional education prior to becoming full participants. In such societies, children play at being doctors, firefighters, soldiers, teachers, and parents, things they cannot yet be in real life. Creating an imagined world allows them to imitate these roles and functions. As Elkonin (1998, p. 150) summarized, the purpose behind such play is to learn to "act like an adult." For this reason, Karpov (2005) suggested the term *socio-dramatic play* to refer to Vygotsky's particular conception of play.

While Vygotsky was concerned with play as a leading activity of development prior to the start of formal schooling, Holzman (2010) argued that such activity holds enormous potential for promoting development throughout the lifespan. She based her position on the observation that socio-dramatic play requires a collective orientation in which all participants come together and function as a social unit. It is this collective functioning that allows for the creation of new potential among members of the group in which individuals take on new roles, contribute to the group's endeavor as they are able, and perform in ways they previously had not. Holzman (2010) reported that approaching the ZPD as an activity that creates an environment of collective behavior as well as an outcome of individual and group development informs her own practice in psychotherapy.

While we appreciate Holzman's commitment to extending socio-dramatic play beyond early childhood contexts and we concur that the potential for such activity to support development across the lifespan should be explored, what we find particularly compelling about her work is the understanding of the ZPD as activity in which individuals function collectively, working toward a shared object and wherein forms of participation and contribution may shift as new capabilities are formed. The idea of development as a potential that emerges and is created through collective engagement nicely captures Vygotsky's premise of the social genesis of psychological functions, and this pertains not only to play but also to education, which he similarly regarded as a primary driver, or leading activity, of development.[1]

For Vygotsky development is provoked by the tension between what an individual is capable of and what that person is not yet capable of. If and how this tension is resolved is the key to understanding the activity that unfolds in the ZPD. The activity clearly is not unidirectional from more capable to less capable individuals but involves mutual cooperation, or what Fogel (1991) called *co-regulation*. It is through co-regulation that individuals appropriate and ultimately internalize the forms of mediation available in a social environment and in this way eventually attain self-regulation (i.e., agency).[2]

Co-regulation centers on the idea that learners themselves are in fact active in regulating mediator behavior, through both verbal and non-verbal means and in ways that may be quite explicit or much more implicit. In this way, the contingent nature of mediation reflects not merely a mediator's interpretation of learner behavior but also how the mediator him/herself is guided by the learner. Fogel (1991) illustrated this idea with the example of a parent helping an infant into a seated position, and suggested that rather than simply propping the child into the desired position both participants may cooperatively engage in the activity of sitting up. This occurs as the child is prompted to grasp the parent's fingers and both exert force in opposite directions, resulting in the child's body moving from a horizontal to a vertical orientation. The end result of the upright child is no different than if the parent had propped the child into that position; nevertheless, by functioning as a participant in the activity, the child experiences him/herself as an agent rather than an object. The child may also enjoy a sense of satisfaction at having achieved success, especially if the parent overtly praises the accomplishment (e.g., "We did it!" accompanied by applause).

This example also underscores that to be effective, mediation must be contingent upon learner needs (see also Aljaafreh & Lantolf, 1994). Viewing the ZPD as co-regulated activity compels us to understand mediation not as a treatment that can be administered to individuals to move them from one level of development to another but rather as interaction that must remain attuned to learner needs and changes in learner contributions over time. A great deal of responsibility is thus placed on teachers, or mediators, to optimally involve learners in determining how to approach tasks, set goals, select strategies, evaluate outcomes, and reformulate plans and actions.

Achieving appropriate collaborative functioning requires that mediation be sufficiently explicit to be of value to learners but not so explicit that it limits learners from fully contributing to the activity. For instance, mediation that learners require to participate at the outset of an activity may quickly become unnecessary as they gain greater control over those features of performance, in which case mediation that had been necessary to support development becomes a potential obstacle to continued development. This is documented in ZPD research with elder populations (Calero & Navarro, 2004; Navarro & Calero, 2009), which showed that mediation not aligned with individuals' shifting needs may result in loss of agency and autonomy.

It is also the case that the ZPD necessarily entails a level of challenge to learners, as they strive to push beyond what they are capable of achieving comfortably. This challenge can produce feelings of discomfort and frustration on the part of learners to which mediators must also be sensitive. The child in Fogel's example, if s/he is to develop, must continually be challenged to take over more and more of the activity until eventually parental support is no longer required. At that point, there will of course be other activities that will require cooperation for the child to achieve. Thus, the process of development, because of its dialectical nature, is potentially unending.

As we explain in the next section, co-regulation is also an essential characteristic of Feuerstein's approach to DA that captures the spirit of Vygotsky's real-world praxis in education and in improving the lot of individuals suffering from psychological disorders (see Vygotsky, 1990). In the next chapter, we consider how Feuerstein's framework has influenced L2 DA.

## Feuerstein's Mediated Learning Experience as a Framework for DA

Miller (2011, p. 54) remarks, "If anyone deserves the Vygotsky mantle it is surely Feuerstein whose work in all its aspects represents the further development and application of Vygotsky's ideas." Miller enumerated points of commonality between Vygotsky and Feuerstein including the fact that both authors understood that psychological difficulties may be biological in origin or may arise as a result of cultural responses to disabilities; their common recognition of the fundamental role of mediation for the development of psychological tools for thinking; and that Feuerstein's ongoing development of the *Mediated Learning Experience* (MLE) bears remarkable similarities to the view of ZPD as collective activity.

Despite these similarities, and our agreement with Miller's evaluation of the strong affinity between Vygotsky's and Feuerstein's commitment, it must be pointed out that Feuerstein maintains that he developed his theory and approaches with no knowledge of Vygotsky (see Burgess, 2000).[3] Kozulin and Gindis (2007) mused that the similar practical problems facing Vygotsky and Feuerstein may help to account for the similarities in their work. Indeed, just as much of Vygotsky's theory was formed in the context of his practical work meeting the needs of diverse learners in the early days of the Soviet public schools, Feuerstein began to develop his theory through his work with young children who had survived the Holocaust and had little or no formal schooling.

Kozulin (1998, 2003), a noted Vygotsky scholar who is also research director at Feuerstein's International Center for the Enhancement of Learning Potential (ICELP) in Israel, has further explicated the parallel and complementary nature of both theorists' contributions. Kozulin further explicated, on the one hand, Feuerstein's emphasis on the development of basic cognitive functions necessary for school learning (e.g., categorical thinking, spatial organization, comparative and contrastive relations, syllogistic reasoning), and, on the other hand, Vygotsky's analysis of development through formal schooling, arguing that both approach development as the internalization of psychological tools that individuals use to organize and regulate their mental world.

As our interest is in DA as a realization of the ZPD, we focus only on this aspect of Feuerstein's agenda. Specifically, we overview his theory of *Structural Cognitive Modifiability* (SCM) as a perspective on human beings that motivated his proposal of mediated learning as a basic explanatory principle of development. As we will see, his perspective has driven the design of MLE as a set of practices for modifying learner abilities through social interaction. At the same time, and in keeping with Vygotsky's understanding of praxis, MLE has continued to be elaborated through its extension to different populations and to address different kinds of problems. As Feuerstein himself explained, "It is our fundamental position that one needs both theory and practice. How we develop concepts guides our practices, and what we do (our practices) contributes to the shaping of our theory" (Feuerstein et al., 2010, p. 5).

## Cognitive Modifiability for All Individuals

Feuerstein traced the development of his DA framework to his efforts to diagnose and remediate children who had survived the Holocaust and were relocated to the newly formed state of Israel (Feuerstein et al., 2010). According to Feuerstein, many of these children not only lacked any experience of formal schooling but the tragedy of their lives meant that they had missed more typical kinds of caregiver–child experiences. Specifically, Feuerstein, like Vygotsky, argued that human beings' relation to the world is fundamentally mediated, typically by others in our environment (Kozulin, 1998). Feuerstein, Rand, and Hoffman (1979) elaborated that, in contrast to the classic stimulus–response model of behaviorism, human experiences are in fact marked by our relations to others, who mediate our experience of reality by drawing attention to certain features of phenomena, interpreting the meaning of objects and events, and making connections across phenomena and experiences. However, in extreme circumstances these mediated learning experiences either do not occur or are not sustained or frequent enough for individuals to develop basic cognitive functions required for subsequent learning. These functions include "correct perception, proper data collection, sensitivity to problems, properly identifying and defining situations to be responded to, solving those problems, and making rational, grounded decisions" (Feuerstein et al., 2010, p. 3).

According to Feuerstein, Rand, and Rynders (1988), individuals who have not yet mastered the means to mediate or regulate their own perception of the world or their actions in it exist in an 'unmediated', or direct, relation to the world. As a result, they have only an episodic grasp of reality, meaning that they are not able to assign meaning to events and objects and are unable to connect one experience with another. Feuerstein referred to such individuals as *culturally deprived*, signaling that they have not gained access to the mediational means of development afforded by any human culture. Feuerstein's analysis of cultural deprivation parallels Vygotsky's (1990) proposal of *cultural primitivism*, which referred to the effects of systematically withholding mediating artifacts and experiences from individuals with special needs, typically as a result of societal taboos (Kozulin & Gindis, 2007). For Vygotsky, this represented a *secondary defect* that was cultural in origin rather than biological but that could be equally if not more damaging.[4] Just as Vygotsky argued that such difficulties could in fact be remediated through cultural means, Feuerstein proposed the MLE as a practical means of determining the source of an individual's difficulties, how responsive s/he is to mediation, and the forms of mediation that appear most helpful.

Feuerstein, Feuerstein, and Falik (2010) explained that the basic motivation behind MLE is a conviction that an individual's manifest performance is not a final or absolute indication of his/her potential for future development. Rejecting conventional definitions of intelligence, Feuerstein, Rand, and Hoffman (1979) proposed the notion of *learning propensity*, or *learning potential*, which may be understood as openness to mediation. A key distinction they drew between learning potential and intelligence is that the former accepts today's performance only as a starting point for efforts to remediate abilities and not as a final verdict on an individual's future. In fact, Feuerstein maintains throughout his writings that human abilities, including learning potential, do not exist as objects or stable traits but may be more appropriately construed as "dynamic" states that are "unstable and responsive to the person's need" for mediation as they "adapt to situations and cope with them successfully" (Feuerstein et al., 2010, p. 17). Put another way, all psychological functions are modifiable through mediation.

Tzuriel and Alfassi (1994) offered a particularly compelling illustration of this point. In a study of the effects of Feuerstein's cognitive education program (discussed below), the authors diagnosed children's learning potential via DA prior to enrolling them in an enrichment program at Feuerstein's ICELP. Following 2 years of instruction, parallel versions of the original assessments were administered. Tzuriel and Alfassi reported that some of the children identified as "low learning potential" at the start of the program actually outperformed children originally rated at a higher level of learning potential who had not participated in the program. Moreover, some of these initially low learning potential children also performed better on tests evaluating cognitive abilities that had not been the subject of instruction. That is, the children's cognitive gains were not limited to those that were explicitly addressed in the program but extended to other domains as well. Following Tzuriel and Alfassi (1994), this suggests that the children's overall ability to benefit from mediation had improved; they had, in essence, become more effective learners.

This perspective compels a reconsideration of the meaning that can be attributed to assessment performance. That is, the conventional view of assessment performance is that it gains validity according to how well it generalizes beyond the assessment context and allows for claims about likely functioning in the future. For Feuerstein and colleagues, such generalizations make little sense because psychological functions are assumed to be in continual flux and therefore highly amenable to intervention and guidance. Feuerstein and colleagues have frequently employed the term *retarded performers* rather than *retarded individuals* to underscore the point that deficiencies are attributes of a given performance and not of individuals. Poor performance is interpreted only according to the "manifest repertoire of the individual," a repertoire that may be modified through appropriate mediation (Feuerstein et al., 1979, p. 95).

More recently, Feuerstein has begun to argue that his position on cognitive modifiability also has a sound basis in neuroscience. Feuerstein, Feuerstein, and Falik (2010) noted that the emergence of technologies for observing brain activity, such as fMRI, CAT, and PET scans, have made it possible to investigate the effects of mediated learning in a way that was previously not possible. Relying on brain scans of individuals during sessions with mediators as well as those of individuals who have participated in extensive remediation programs, they reported that mediated learning leads not only to changes in behavior and cognition but also to changes in neural structures and activity. They concluded, "it is now no exaggeration to state that *the neural system is modified by the behavior, no less than the behavior is determined by the neural system*" (p. 134, italics in original)

## *Feuerstein's Proposal for Praxis: Mediated Learning Experience*

Feuerstein regards mediated learning as the driving force of the development of psychological functions. More than an explanatory principle, this view is also the basis for practical activity intended both to gauge an individual's propensity for cognitive change and to bring about such change through intensive MLE. During MLE a mediator engages jointly with learners to complete tasks that would otherwise be beyond their level of ability (Feuerstein et al., 1988). Mediators do not place any limitations on how they interact with learners so long as learners are optimally involved in the activity. Mediators often encourage learners to take the lead in completing the tasks relatively independently but they may also intervene when necessary to provide feedback, ask leading questions, point out salient features of the task, or make suggestions. Moreover, during MLE mediators themselves frequently model effective problem-solving behavior, including speaking aloud as they note their own perceptions of the task and its requirements, developing a plan, and evaluating their progress through the task and upon its completion. Such modeling is also employed relative to more affective dimensions of performance. These include verbalizing feelings of frustration and anxiety and how these may be managed as well as expressing reactions to success and conveying more positive perceptions of self. Within Feuerstein's theory of SCM, there is a mutually influential relationship between the affective and the cognitive, wherein nearly all functioning encompasses both elements. The affective element is the *driving force* that explains why individuals act or choose not to act while the cognitive element in turn allows for emotion to be regulated and controlled during activity (Feuerstein et al., 2010).

## *MLE and L2 DA*

We wish to call attention to two MLE features that have proved particularly important for L2 DA theory and practice: *reciprocity* and *transcendence*. While considerable work has explored how mediator efforts may render MLE effective (Feuerstein, Falik, Rand, & Feuerstein, 2003; Feuerstein et al., 1988), both reciprocity and transcendence are squarely focused on learners. Reciprocity in particular may be considered as the complement to mediation. Lidz (1991), working within a Feuersteinian framework, originally proposed the term to refer to ways in which learners respond to mediation during DA, noting in her own clinical work that responses are often not so straightforward as simply correct or incorrect, improved or unimproved. Rather, learners may respond in unpredicted ways, creating different kinds of errors or asking questions that in turn are central to informing a mediator's next move.

In the L2 field, Poehner (2008a) extended this line of reasoning to suggest that learner reciprocity may be understood as a process of negotiating mediation. In some cases this may involve simply responding to a hint, prompt, or leading question that is offered; in others, learners themselves may initiate the exchange by asking for particular forms of support, requesting clarification from the mediator, or seeking approval of performance. This account of reciprocity aligns with the notion of co-regulation in the ZPD as discussed earlier in this chapter. In practice, reciprocity broadens the forms of learner participation in DA that teachers and assessors may encounter and opens the door to what these behaviors might signal in terms of learner development.

The concept of transcendence concerns the durability of developmental gains from MLE and subsequent intervention. In Feuerstein's approach to DA, MLE is only the initial step toward remediating cognitive functions. During MLE, mediators carefully note the forms of mediation that proved most effective, learners' degree of responsiveness to mediation as well as reciprocating behaviors, and any insights gained into the likely underlying causes of poor performance. This information is then summarized as a learner profile around which an intervention program is designed, typically in the form of what Feuerstein (Feuerstein et al., 1988) described as *Instrumental Enrichment* (IE). This term refers to the set of "instruments" including problems and materials organized according to difficulty level and aimed at promoting the development of basic psychological functions (e.g., analogical reasoning). The instruments are "enriched" in that they provide a focus for ongoing mediator–learner engagement, wherein they function collectively and continue the work begun during MLE.

IE programs may continue for weeks, months, or even years, depending upon the amount of cognitive ground to be covered. While interactions in these sessions parallel those during MLE, it is of course expected that as learners come to develop relevant capabilities they will function more independently. It is for this reason that the problems within each of the 'instruments' are graded according to increasing complexity and difficulty. Learners are then able to move through the relevant instruments and continue to experience challenge that will necessitate engagement with a mediator until requisite abilities are developed. Throughout IE and upon its conclusion, learners are challenged to extend their new capabilities beyond the problems they have previously encountered and to new ones, as well as to new domains. For Feuerstein (Feuerstein et al., 1988), transcending the here-and-now demands of a given task is what differentiates psychological development from task-specific training, and it resonates with his conceptualization of the power of mediated learning.

Transcendence then serves theoretically as a marker of development as well as a principle for organizing tasks within the IE program and ongoing diagnoses of learner abilities. Indeed, Tzuriel and Alfassi's (1994) investigation of the effects of IE on individual's learning potential, discussed earlier, is a revealing example of transcendence as learners made gains not only with respect to the psychological functions that had been the focus of the program but their improved performance extended to other domains as well. In this regard, transcendence concerns more than moving from less difficult to more difficult tasks of a given kind, although that is also important evidence of development. Rather, Tzuriel and Alfassi's study emphasized transcendence as positioning individuals to become better learners in the future.

Given its importance for understanding development, transcendence has been a prominent feature in L2 DA research. According to Poehner (2007), transcendence underscores connections across DA interactions by drawing attention to changes in mediation, learner performance, and the nature of the tasks carried out from one session to the next. This, he noted, is because unlike many other assessments DA does not occur over a single session that disrupts or concludes instructional sequences but is rather a framework for ongoing classroom interaction. In this regard, Poehner suggested that transcendence might be a more helpful concept for teachers than traditional notions of generalizability that have emerged from the psychometric research literature as the latter requires predicting learner performance in future situations on the basis of limited observations while transcendence allows teachers to systematically track learner performance across contexts.

Most L2 DA studies to date have explicitly included transcendence in the design of their procedures by introducing tasks at the end of an enrichment program that require learners to apply concepts and principles they studied to new situations (e.g., Ableeva, 2010; Lantolf & Poehner, 2013; Poehner, 2008b). Typically this has meant that learners must rely on their new understanding of relevant components of the L2 as they perform in a different communicative modality or that the tasks themselves require learners to apply concepts while simultaneously attending to other dimensions of the task and controlling other language features. Often these are referred to as *transfer tasks*, following the terminology employed in the *graduated prompt* approach to DA (Campione et al., 1984). That model sets before learners a series of tasks that depart increasingly in a stepwise fashion from those used in the instructional program. Tracing learner performance on *near, far,* and *very far transfer tasks* indicates how well they are able to extend, or to recontextualize, their abilities. We will have more to say about learner performance of transfer tasks in L2 DA in the next chapter.

## MLE in Action

In this section we briefly consider two recent projects that showcased several important features of Feuerstein's DA framework. The first concerns the work of Tzuriel, a colleague of Feuerstein who has been working steadily since the early 2000s to develop what he has termed the Peer Mediation for Young Children (PMYC) program (Shamir & Tzuriel, 2004; Tzuriel, 2011; Tzuriel & Shamir, 2007). Continuing a tradition established by Feuerstein of providing instruction for parents to help them better function as mediators for their children at home and thereby support work being done with the children at the ICELP, Tzuriel's program seeks to extend this instruction to school settings, where MLE-based strategies can be taught to children to help them serve as mediators to one another, or *peer mediators*.

Referencing explicitly both the ZPD and MLE, Tzuriel (2011, p. 125) argued that the PMYC program is based on the premise that "teaching for peer-mediation will both elicit better mediating skills from the tutors and improve cognitive skills in both tutees and tutors." The focus of PMYC is not on any particular academic subject but on helping children develop a *mediating teaching style* that includes sets of strategies applicable to any content area. The lack of attention to a specific content is justified, in part, by the population of young primary-grades learners with whom Tzuriel works, as their class work often blends content from several subjects. The MLE features that are drawn upon in PMYC concern attention to the demands of the task at hand, searching for task features or dimensions that are similar to ones previously encountered, inhibiting guessing in favor of developing plans, and reviewing and evaluating outcomes.

In a series of studies, Tzuriel and colleagues examined the psychological benefits to being trained as an effective mediator. A particularly interesting hypothesis, based on Feuerstein's discussions of MLE, is that learning to be a mediator opens individuals to being more receptive to mediation themselves because the training leads to flexibility in their thinking that is conducive to engaging in MLE interactions. In one study, Tzuriel and Shamir (2007) followed two groups of children, one of whom had completed PMYC in addition to the regular school curriculum while the other group received only regular school instruction. At the end of the PMYC program, both groups of children were dynamically administered an assessment of analogical reasoning, which included a standard pre-test phase followed by an interactive mediation phase and a post-test. Although the PMYC program did not address analogical reasoning but instead dealt with problem solving in general, Tzuriel and Shamir reported that statistically significant differences were found between the two groups, with the children who had participated in PMYC outperforming those who had not on the analogies pre-test. Moreover, the authors noted that the children trained as peer mediators were more active during the mediation phase and made greater gains than the other children on the post-test administration of the analogical reasoning measure.

Tzuriel (2011) concluded that while additional research is needed to fully understand the effects of PMYC, the findings of the peer mediation study suggest that learning to function as a mediator may indeed help individuals benefit from mediation in different contexts and aimed at various abilities. To this, we would add that PMYC may offer insights to classroom teachers interested in dyadic and small group work. Such modes of participation have become increasingly common in educational settings, including in L2 classrooms, and yet it is not at all clear whether the quality of these interactions is optimal for supporting learner development. The PMYC model may provide a starting point for considering how L2 learners can be taught to effectively mediate other learners as well as themselves.

The other line of MLE research we wish to comment upon is Kozulin's work with adult immigrants to Israel (e.g., Kozulin 2009, 2011). Our interest here is in the challenge Kozulin posed to widely accepted notions concerning the lack of cognitive modifiability among adult learners. Indeed, Feuerstein et al. (2010) explained that MLE stands in direct opposition to critical age period models, which hold that if certain cognitive abilities do not develop by a given age subsequent instructional and remediation efforts will be unsuccessful. While Kozulin (1998) acknowledged that Feuerstein's work has been conducted primarily with children, he emphasized that Vygotsky and Luria did not restrict their research to children because they recognized that development can occur throughout the lifespan of individuals provided that appropriate forms of mediation are accessible (e.g., Luria, 1973, 1976; Vygotsky, 1990). This is particularly important for the L2 field, where much research is conducted with adults in formal learning environments.[5]

Drawing on a series of recent studies, Kozulin (2009) investigated the degree of cognitive modifiability among Ethiopian and Russian immigrants to Israel, many of whom had little formal education prior to their arrival, and who found themselves in secondary school or vocational education settings. Thus, in addition to content that may be either academic or technical, depending upon an individual's course of study, many of the immigrants also had to overcome language challenges and cope with the demands of a structured learning environment. Relying on DA sessions to gain preliminary insights into learners' receptiveness to mediation, an adapted version of Feuerstein's IE program was employed to target particular abilities that were identified during the assessment.

An important finding that emerged from Kozulin's work is that while the adult participants managed to make impressive development gains, these gains often came only after prolonged participation in IE. These *culturally different* adults appear to parallel the *culturally deprived* children with whom Feuerstein works, in the sense that both groups require more than a single MLE session to develop. As we discuss in the next chapter, L2 DA research to date has similarly found that while gains may be made over very short periods of time, more robust and sustained changes are more likely when principles of mediated learning are integrated as an ongoing feature of classroom activity.

## Conclusion

In this chapter we have argued that the ZPD is a powerful expression of Vygotsky's view of praxis as it represents a profound theoretical perspective for understanding the relationship between engagement in practical activity and development while at the same time provoking that development. In our view, casting the ZPD either in terms of a latent trait possessed by individuals that may be revealed during interaction or as forms of assistance that help learners complete tasks more efficiently impoverishes Vygotsky's proposal. While we acknowledge that work such as Budoff's has made contributions to our understanding of the potential DA has to provoke development, we do not believe that it has realized the full potential of the ZPD as a framework for developmental education. Specifically, this work has not lived up to Vygotsky's (1998) view of the ZPD as a means to diagnose development that includes abilities that have already emerged and those that are in the process of emerging. Furthermore, Vygotsky's approach requires the mediator to uncover the sources of difficulty that may prevent individuals from developing and through co-regulated interaction the mediator and learner are "bowed over the same task" (Feuerstein et al., 1979, p. 102) and striving to help the learner "become what he [sic] not yet is" (Bronfenbrenner, 1977, p. 528, citing A. N. Leontiev).

The similarities between Vygotsky's understanding of the ZPD and Feuerstein's proposal of the MLE framework for DA are indeed striking. Both are based on the conviction that all individuals are capable of developing beyond their current abilities so long as appropriate forms of mediation are made available. Both frameworks unify instruction and assessment as indispensable components of the same process and both have been brought directly into practical educational activity.

Feuerstein's efforts have focused almost exclusively on remediating general cognitive functions of young children and learners with special needs to prepare them for subsequent school learning. However, other members of Feuerstein's ICELP, most notably Kozulin, have extended DA work to adults including those with cultural and linguistic differences that have been obstacles to their full integration into society. Vygotsky and his colleagues from the outset have focused their ZPD-informed educational efforts on general psychological development as well as on specific school subjects.

Most of the initial content-specific DA work informed by Vygotsky's theory has dealt with areas such as math, science, social studies, and L1 literacy, rather than foreign and second languages. Research on L2 DA did not begin until Poehner (2005) and Lantolf and Poehner (2004). Since that time an increasing number of L2 DA studies have been carried out and as with STI some of this work has followed the experimental-developmental format and some of it has been conducted in intact classrooms. The next chapter reviews several of the key studies that illustrate the range of ways learner L2 development may be mediated according to DA principles.

## Notes

1   For Vygotsky (1998) the third leading activity of development that emerges in adult life is work. Since our interest is in education as a leading activity, we will not pursue further the effects of work activity on development. For a discussion of development in the work place see Scribner (1997).

2   Vygotsky used other-regulation to describe the period of development where individuals are influenced and guided by others. Unfortunately, the English term carries

a sense of unidirectionality leaving the impression that the individual who is other-regulated is passive and plays no role in the developmental process. For this reason we prefer Fogel's term—co-regulation.

3 The fact that these two men developed such parallel views of human abilities and their development and that they are marked by a dedication to praxis is likened by Miller (2011) to the independent creation of calculus by both Newton and Leibniz.

4 Recall our discussion in Chapter 3 of the psychological consequences suffered by Deaf children deprived of full access to language because they were educated in "oral" schools.

5 Kozulin (1998) pointed out that Feuerstein has remained relatively silent on the question of how development may continue for adolescents and adults once they enter school. Vygotsky, in contrast, understood formal schooling as a leading activity of development.

# 8
# DYNAMIC ASSESSMENT AND L2 DEVELOPMENT

In the present chapter, we turn to the growing DA research literature concerned with L2 development. We wish to note from the outset that L2 DA has followed a markedly different trajectory from DA research in general education and psychology. The DA practices that have evolved in those fields have tended to be designed by measurement specialists tasked with identifying (and often labeling) special needs learners. The L2 field, in contrast, has been introduced to DA only relatively recently. Indeed, DA was not included in discussions of either L2 assessment or teaching prior to a string of publications by the present authors (Lantolf & Poehner, 2004; Poehner, 2007, 2008b; Poehner & Lantolf, 2005). However, an influential paper that employed the ZPD to examine the quality of interaction between a tutor and tutee (Aljaafreh & Lantolf, 1994) provides an important touchstone for more recent L2 DA research. While Aljaafreh and Lantolf do not explicitly reference DA, their study elaborated important principles concerning the use of mediation in dialogic interaction in order to understand the extent to which learners are able to control the L2 and the forms of support they require to maintain and extend that control.

DA, like the L2 STI studies reviewed in Chapters 5 and 6, extends SCT research in a crucial direction as it moves beyond a theoretical lens for understanding development and provides a framework for practical activity. This shift towards Vygotskian praxis has meant that the lion's share of L2 DA research has been implemented not in formal testing situations but in intact classroom and experimental-developmental contexts, where learner development is an intended outcome. This work has emphasized the dialectic integration of assessment with teaching through teacher–learner interactions during which mediation is negotiated for learners to optimally contribute to activities and for mediators to gain insights into learner abilities necessary to guide their efforts to move development forward. This does not mean, however, that we believe DA's relevance to L2 education should be limited to classroom settings. Indeed, later in this chapter we present recent efforts to apply DA principles developed in classroom studies to the design of computer-based DA (C-DA) procedures.

This chapter reviews three key L2 DA studies that showcase efforts to diagnose and promote learner development through adherence to a framework of co-regulated activity informed by the ZPD and Feuerstein's MLE. We do not provide full analysis of all L2 DA research, and interested readers are referred to relevant publications for further discussion (Lantolf & Thorne, 2006; Lantolf & Poehner, 2008; Poehner, 2008b; Poehner & Rea-Dickins, 2013). Comprehensive bibliographies of DA publications in the general education literature (www.dynamicassessment.com) and the L2 field (http://calper.la.psu.edu/dyna_assess.php?page=articles) are recommended as additional resources.

The aim of our discussion here is twofold. We consider how processes of L2 development have, in dialectical fashion, been brought to light through first-order (social) mediation. At the same time, we address how the issues raised in this work have required the continued conceptual development of an L2 DA framework. That is, we point to how Vygotskian theory has driven L2 DA practice as well as how the demands of this practice have further elaborated the framework itself. Although DA has not been readily accepted by everyone working in L2 assessment, we argue that one of the problems has been the difficulty people have in overcoming the dualistic approach to scientific research (see Chapter 2), especially as it separates instruction from assessment. We begin our discussion by situating social mediation, the key element of DA, in relation to ongoing discussions in the field of SLA concerning the value of feedback and error correction for L2 development. Later in the chapter, we address critiques directed specifically at DA.

## Quality of Mediation in L2 DA

In his review of the SLA research literature on corrective feedback, Ellis (2008) observed that there has been extensive and ongoing discussion of whether L2 development is best supported through implicit or explicit feedback. He explained that in implicit feedback, as for instance with recasts, a central question concerns whether learner repetition of a corrected form in fact advances acquisition. Learners may simply repeat a teacher's corrected utterance without understanding why it is correct or even necessarily noting the correction. Explicit feedback attempts to erase this ambiguity by calling learner attention to errors, providing a correction, and, in some cases, offering an explanation grounded in metalinguistic knowledge of the L2. In this respect, explicit feedback would appear to be advantageous, an argument also advanced by Carroll and Swain (1993), who suggested that a weakness in implicit feedback is that it requires learners to infer both the site and nature of the error. While Ellis also advocated explicit feedback, postulating that it may support learner comparison of their errors with teacher corrections, he concluded that studies directly comparing the effects of explicit and implicit correction remain difficult to interpret. For one thing SLA researchers have not always agreed on what constitutes implicit and explicit correction and, for another, studies have been carried out across a range of tasks, including mechanical exercises as well as communicative activities (see Ellis, Loewen, Elder, Erlam, Philip, & Reinders, 2009).

From the perspective of the ZPD we developed in the preceding chapter, discussions of implicit and explicit feedback are problematic both in terms of how learners are construed and the intended outcome of feedback. The ZPD is not concerned with assisting learners to efficiently move through tasks but with promoting learner agency, a process that involves co-regulation. This means that mediation is not a prescribed set of behaviors or comments delivered to learners but rather is a dynamic process in which mediators align their moves with learner needs and difficulties, learners contribute as they are able, and they form a functional unit. Active learner participation in this process runs counter to feedback as a simple message sent from teacher to learner. The question is not which form of feedback, implicit or explicit, is inherently better but which is most appropriate in the context of a particular interaction.

The study by Aljaafreh and Lantolf (1994) offered perhaps the first in-depth analysis of how mediation may be conceived as an emergent feature of L2 ZPD activity. The authors followed a mediator engaged in one-to-one tutoring sessions with ESL learners struggling to control particular features of English grammar as they prepared compositions for an intensive writing class. Rather than scripting mediation in advance, the tutor was free to respond according to his interpretation of learner needs as these emerged during interactions. According to their understanding of the ZPD, Aljaafreh and Lantolf argued that mediation appropriately attuned to learner development must be graduated, negotiated, and contingent. Specifically, learners should have maximal opportunity to attempt to self-regulate, with mediator intervention occurring only when necessary. In addition, mediation should be minimally intrusive in the learner's attempt to self-regulate. In other words, mediation should be only as explicit as it needs to be to prompt an appropriate response from the learner. If one form of support is not effective, then mediation may become more explicit, but beginning at a more explicit level would risk losing insights into which aspects of learner control over the language are ripening. The process of determining appropriate mediation is one that is negotiated with learners, as mediation must attune to learner responsiveness and needs as these are made known. Finally, mediator efforts must be contingent and therefore withheld when learners show signs of functioning without them. This struggle to self-regulate is essential for learner development, and if mediation continues to be offered when not required it may in fact inhibit development.

Aljaafreh and Lantolf (1994) reported that analysis of the tutoring sessions revealed a range of mediator moves that positioned learners to function

0. Tutor asks the learner to read, find the errors, and correct them independently, prior to the tutorial.
1. Construction of a "collaborative frame" prompted by the presence of the tutor as a potential dialogic partner.
2. Prompted or focused reading of the sentence that contains the error by the learner or the tutor.
3. Tutor indicates that something may be wrong in a segment (e.g., sentence, clause, line)—"Is there anything wrong in this sentence?"
4. Tutor rejects unsuccessful attempts at recognizing the error.
5. Tutor narrows down the location of the error (e.g., tutor repeats or points to the specific segment which contains the error).
6. Tutor indicates the nature of the error, but does not identify the error (e.g., "There is something wrong with the tense marking here").
7. Tutor identifies the error ("You can't use an auxiliary here").
8. Tutor rejects learner's unsuccessful attempts at correcting error.
9. Tutor provides clues to help the learner arrive at the correct form (e.g., "It is not really past but some thing that is still going on").
10. Tutor provides the correct form.
11. Tutor provides some explanation for use of the correct form.
12. Tutor provides examples of the correct pattern when other forms of help fail to produce an appropriate responsive action.

**FIGURE 8.1** Regulatory scale—implicit (strategic) to explicit (Aljaafreh & Lantolf, 1994, p. 471)

independently. Importantly, these were not scripted in advance and followed in a lock-step format but emerged as the mediator endeavored to respond to learner behavior according to the principles explained above. The authors insisted that these moves should not be viewed as a prescription for how to engage in mediating activity but instead provide documentation of the process of mediator–learner co-regulation. The full inventory of mediating moves identified by Aljaafreh and Lantolf is provided in Figure 8.1.

L2 DA studies have continued to provide insights into processes of co-regulation. This work further specifies that appropriate mediation varies along three planes: individual (different individuals struggling with the same feature of the L2 may not respond in the same way to a given form of mediation and may require different forms of support to overcome the issue), time (the same individual may require more explicit mediation to address a problem at one point in time than another), and L2 feature (an individual may require only a recast to perceive and correct a phonological problem but may require more extensive support to overcome a difficulty in discourse-level grammar). Thus, the modifier *dynamic* in DA refers as much to the view of learner abilities as to the activity of co-constructing a ZPD with learners.

With regard to outcomes, explicit feedback may offer a level of efficiency for dealing with errors, but this comes at the cost of gaining insights into learner abilities. For instance, if one opts to employ only explicit correction, the opportunity to diagnose emerging abilities is lost. Developmental insights are effectively limited to the determination that independent performance was not successful and correction was needed. For assessment purposes, this blurs distinctions among learners who, for example, are quite close to successfully functioning independently, those who continue to struggle with only a particular aspect of the language, and those for whom the task is well beyond their current capabilities. A "one-size-fits-all" reliance on explicit feedback thus runs counter to formative purposes of assessment, as teachers do not gain the necessary understanding of learner capabilities on which to base instruction. Moreover, exclusive use of explicit feedback risks creating learner dependence rather than promoting self-regulation because answers and explanations are provided regardless of learner needs. In L2 DA, negotiating mediation with learners is the basis for diagnosing their abilities and promoting their autonomous use of the language.

## DA in an Intact Elementary L2 Spanish Classroom

The first DA project we consider involved collaboration between the researchers and a practicing L2 teacher, who implemented DA in her elementary school L2 Spanish classroom (see Lantolf & Poehner, 2011a). The teacher was not concerned with L2 research but was interested in finding ways to better meet the needs of her students and believed that DA offered an appropriate means to do so. The project was notable because the teacher did not attempt to follow a prescribed DA protocol; rather in collaboration with the researchers she designed her own framework and set of procedures for implementing DA in her unique teaching environment. At the same time, and in true dialectic fashion, the project generated insights that enhanced the researchers' appreciation for how DA can be brought to bear in real-world classrooms.

Recognizing that a theory grounded in praxis requires the dialectic unity of theoretical principles and practical activity, we developed *A Teachers Guide* to DA (see Lantolf & Poehner, 2006). The aim of this work was not merely to inform teachers how to implement DA in their instructional activities, but to serve as a vehicle for teacher–researcher collaborations. Such collaboration allows for deeper insights into the affordances offered by DA as well as constraints on its use in language classrooms while at the same time helping teachers in their efforts to improve student learning in those classrooms.

The *Guide* includes a monograph-length introduction to SCT principles and how these are brought to bear in DA. It also presents different models of DA that have been formulated for different educational purposes. It contains close analyses of excerpts from actual L2 DA interactions on negotiating appropriate levels of mediation, eliciting learner verbalizations of how learners approach a task, and identifying the points where learners encounter difficulties in carrying out specific language tasks. The video appendices provide detailed commentary on actual mediator–learner interactions that illustrate various procedures that can be utilized in implementing DA. A new edition of the *Guide* (Lantolf & Poehner, 2011b) incorporates the findings of the intact L2 Spanish classroom project described below. The *Guide* therefore serves as an artifact that mediates researcher and teacher understanding of the potential for the theory–practice unity embodied in DA to help learners. This has implications for teacher education, a topic we return to in Chapter 9.

## Teacher-Designed DA

The teacher (Tracy, a pseudonym) was the sole Spanish teacher in her school and was responsible for delivering 15-minute instructional lessons each day to classes of roughly 20 children aged eight to eleven. Tracy designed her own curriculum around thematic units intended to introduce the students to formal properties of the language as well as cultural information about Spanish-speaking countries in age-appropriate contexts. For instance, at the time she integrated DA into her class activities the children were learning about Peruvian habitats and wildlife. In this context, relevant vocabulary and grammatical points, such as substantive-modifier concord, were introduced. Tracy made frequent use of game activities such as the one analyzed below, where learners are individually called upon to roll a cube that bears the image of a different rainforest animal on each side. The child is then challenged to produce a description in the L2 of the animal whose image is facing up when the cube comes to a stop.

In an effort to render her interactions with learners as systematic as possible, Tracy scripted in advance precisely how she would try to mediate her students as they participated in the game activity. Drawing inspiration from the regulatory scale outlined by Aljaafreh and Lantolf (1994) included in the *Guide*, Tracy planned her supporting moves along a continuum of most implicit to most explicit. When a learner produced an error, for instance, she would first pause to create an opportunity in the interaction for the learner to consider his/her utterance, determine whether a mistake had been made, and attempt a correction. If the learner did not note the error or was unable to correct it, Tracy repeated the learner's utterance with a questioning intonation, signaling that she wished to confirm that this was indeed what the learner intended. The mediating moves become increasingly explicit and culminate in the teacher identifying the correct answer and offering an explanation of why it is correct.

An important difference between Tracy's use of mediating prompts and Aljaafreh and Lantolf's (1994) regulatory scale is that the latter represented the researchers' identification of mediating behaviors through grounded analysis of the interactions. Tracy, in contrast, planned in advance precisely how she would approach mediation during a given lesson. While she recognized that this necessarily imposed constraints on how she might support learners and on her ability to accurately diagnose their development, she believed that scripting mediation would minimize the possibility that she would overtly correct learners

---

1 Pause
2 Repeat the whole phrase questioningly
3 Repeat just the part of the sentence with the error
4 Teacher asks, "What is wrong with that sentence?"
5 Teacher points out the incorrect word
6 Teacher asks either/or question (negros o negras?)
7 Teacher identifies the correct answer
8 Teacher explains why

---

**FIGURE 8.2** Tracy's inventory of mediating prompts (from Lantolf & Poehner 2011a)

when this was not necessary and thus undermine the very process she was attempting to provoke. In addition, the precise content of some of the prompts Tracy used varied according to the focus of the activity. For example, in the lesson we discuss here, the focus was on learners' control of substantive-modifier concord as they employed number and color terms to describe the rainforest animals pictured on the cube. The inventory of mediating prompts Tracy designed for this lesson is given in Figure 8.2.

## Implementing the Design

To demonstrate Tracy's use of the inventory to structure her interactions with the students, consider the following interaction between Tracy (T) and Vicente (V), who was the first student in the class to take a turn at rolling the cube. The image Vicente needed to describe was that of a *lechuza* (owl). Tracy (T) attempted to facilitate Vicente's description of the owl by first calling attention to its ears:

T:  1. *¿Cuántas orejas?* 'how many ears?'
V:  2. *tiene dos orejas* 'it has two ears'
    (long pause, points at the image on the cube, then looks at Tracy)
    3. *café* 'brown'
    (looks out to the class, then back to the teacher)
    4. *café* 'brown'
    (then looks back at the cube)

Vicente responded to Tracy's question by correctly stating in Spanish that the owl has two ears and has added the additional detail that they are brown in color. While the modifier *café* is an exception in most varieties of the language by not marking agreement, this is not universally the case, and so Tracy prompted Vicente to reconsider his utterance. Following her inventory, she began by repeating his construction with a questioning intonation to determine whether this would alert him to the error (line 5). When Vicente reaffirmed his initial response, Tracy then repeated only the problematic segment of his utterance—the word *café* (line 7):

T:   5. *¿Tiene dos orejas \*café?* 'it has two \*brown ears?'
V:   (looks at the cube again and points at it twice with his finger)
      6. *sí dos orejas . . . . . . \*café* 'yes two \*brown ears'
T:   7. *¿\*Café?* 'brown?'
V:   8. *¿Amarillo?* 'yellow?'
T:   9. *'Café' es correcto pero ¿dos orejas <u>café</u>?* (brown is correct but two <u>brown</u> ears?)
V:   10. (no response, turns his body to face the class, looks at cube then out at class and back to cube)
T:   11. shhh (directed to another student murmuring something off camera)
      12. *Hay un problema . . . con la palabra café.* 'There is a problem with the word brown'.
V:   13. (Vicente does not respond but another student in the class says "oh" and raises her hand)
T:   14. (looks toward the other student and then back to Vicente)

Vicente's response was to switch to another color term that he had learned, *amarillo* (yellow). This suggests that his attention was on identifying the appropriate color term rather than on to the need to mark number concord between the color term and the plural noun *orejas*. Tracy attempted to shift Vicente's attention in line 9 as she accepted his use of *café* but by stressing that word in her speech and employing a rising intonation, she implicitly pointed to the agreement problem. This move was apparently sufficient for other learners in the class observing this exchange, as evidenced by the off-camera murmuring from the class and another learner raising her hand to volunteer the correct formulation. While Tracy could have recruited participation from others in the class at this point, she instead continued her exchange with Vicente. While this might not have been the most efficient way to reveal the correct structure, it was necessary to fully diagnose Vicente's level of understanding of this L2 feature, and that, after all, was Tracy's goal. Finally, Tracy resorted to offering Vicente a choice between the form he had produced for her and what was the correct formulation of the structure.

T:   15. *¿Es \*café or cafés?* 'is it \*brown sg. or brown pl.?'
V:   16. *Cafés* 'brown pl.'
T:   17. *Sí muy bien tiene dos orejas cafés muy bien excelente Vicente* 'Yes very good it has two brown ears very good excellent Vicente'

At the conclusion of the interaction, Vicente produced the appropriate form, marking the modifier "brown" to agree in number with "ears"; but he accomplished this only with extensive mediation. Specifically, Tracy worked stepwise through her mediating inventory and reached level 6, providing an either/or question. Additional insights could have been gained had Tracy elicited from Vicente whether he understood why the addition of an −*s* to *café* was necessary. This would have allowed Tracy to determine whether Vicente had simply guessed correctly between the two choices she offered, or if he had genuinely understood the grammatical feature. At any rate, important diagnostic information about Vicente's understanding of noun–modifier concord was obtained through this interaction. He required extensive mediation and did not appear to be attuned to this feature of the language, something that differentiated Vicente's performance from some of the other students who required far less mediation. This leads to two important points, one concerning the benefit to Vicente of having engaged in first-order mediation with Tracy and the other pertaining to opportunities created for promoting development of others in the class through their observation of the interaction between Tracy and Vicente.

With regard to Vicente, we argue that while his interaction with Tracy indicates that he was far from controlling the agreement rule on his own, his struggle created an opportunity for him to engage with the teacher in the process of marking agreement. What is important is not that Vicente finished by producing the correct form but rather the quality of their collaboration, which may have impacted his understanding of how to mark agreement. Although we cannot claim that this exchange in itself propelled Vicente to more autonomous control of the language, we note that his performance a week later, when he was confronted with the same construction was markedly different. While playing a game in which learners took turns guessing animals described by their partners, Vicente offered a description of a *chinchilla* that included mention of both its ears and eyes:

*V:*  1. *Tengo* …. (looks at photo he is holding in his hands) *dos . . . orejas . . . cafés*
   'I have two brown ears'
*T:*  2. *Dos orejas cafés ¿y?* 'two brown ears and?'
   (Vicente looks at the teacher)
   3. *¿Qué más?* 'What else?'
   (Vicente looks at the photo)
*V:*  4. *Orejas* 'ears'
*T:*  5. *Sí, dos orejas cafés. Sí.* what else? *¿qué más? Y . . . . ¿De qué color es la boca?*
   6. *¿o los ojos? Or* [sic] *las piernas* 'What color is the mouth? Or the eyes? Or the legs?'
*V:*  7. *Ojos* 'eyes'
   8. *Y? y dos ojos* 'and? and two eyes'
   9. *Y dos ojos* 'and two eyes'
*T:*  10. *Dos ojos ¿de qué color?* 'Two eyes, What color?'
   (Vicente looks at the teacher, who points to the picture)
   11. *¿De qué color son los ojos? dos ojos . . .?* 'What color are the eyes? Two eyes?

V:   12. *Ah, negros* 'ah, black'
T:   13. *Negros. Perfecto. ¿Yo soy?* 'Black perfect. And I am. . .?

Vicente began his description by orienting to the animal's ears, producing precisely the construction that had been the topic of his earlier interaction with Tracy (*dos orejas cafés*). Of course, this could be taken as an indication that he simply remembered the earlier "correction." However, when prompted by Tracy to describe another feature of the chinchilla, Vicente stated that the animal had two black eyes (*dos ojos negros*), marking agreement appropriately. This suggests that, far from remembering *dos orejas cafés* as a fixed, unanalyzed expression, Vicente was on his way to controlling nominal concord accord in Spanish. Looked at from the perspective of the ZPD, the change in his performance was not entirely surprising as the process of accurately diagnosing abilities, as we saw in Tracy's first interaction with Vicente, requires cooperatively mediating learners and this in turn supports development.

Returning to that earlier episode, after Vicente described the picture of the owl that he had rolled on the cube, there was time for two other members of the class to take a turn at the game. In order to maintain a record of how the learners performed, Tracy used a grid with each learner's name listed on it where she noted the level of mediation (represented numerically, 0 to 8) learners required during their performances. In this way, Tracy maintained a running record of the interactions and was able to trace learner development over time as well as variability from one learner to another within the class. An example of Tracy's interaction grid is reproduced in Figure 8.3.

As can be seen, the two other learners who participated in the description game following Vicente, Gabriela and Amora, both required fewer prompts than Vicente. Analysis of the activity reveals that a clear progression is discernable, with Vicente engaging in a lengthy process with Tracy, Gabriela requiring far less support during her turn, and Amora in fact performing the task independently of overt teacher mediation.

| NAME | INTRCT. 1 | INTRCT. 2 | INTRCT. 3 | COMMENTS |
|---|---|---|---|---|
| GABRIELA | 3 | | | *dos ala gris* |
| MANUEL | | | | |
| VICENTE | 6 | | | *dos orejas café* |
| ROBERTO | | | | |
| AMORA | 0 | | | *dos ojos negros* |
| RAQUEL | | | | |

**FIGURE 8.3** Example of L2 DA interaction grid (from Lantolf & Poehner 2011a)

Poehner (2009b) noted that while it is possible that these differences in the learners' understanding of Spanish concord may have existed prior to the lesson, another possibility is that the learners were able to benefit from the exchanges that preceded their turn. That is, both Gabriela and Amora were able to follow Vicente's discussion with Tracy, potentially benefiting from the mediation Tracy offered as *secondary interactants* in the exchange. Similarly, Amora was a witness to Gabriela's turn at the task and was therefore particularly well placed when she attempted it herself. This view of secondary interactants might also help to explain the change observed in Vicente's performance the following week, as he also saw his classmates work through the process of determining how and when to mark concord. Poehner (2009b) argued that mediation that is directly addressed to one learner but that occurs in a social space where other learners may also be engaged in the process, albeit in a more indirect or secondary way, offers potential to create a group ZPD. Also, recall the discussion of imitation through observation in Chapter 3 whereby individuals are able to vicariously experience a learning event by eavesdropping rather than by directly participating in it.

From the perspective of a group ZPD, any given mediating move may be more or less explicit than particular individuals require, but so long as the activity itself is beyond what any learner in the group can accomplish independently but within the reach of all if provided mediation, then there is potential to promote the development of all. As Poehner (2009b) suggested, this involves moving the group forward in its abilities by focusing directly on individuals' development. Of course, other approaches to engaging in ZPD activity with groups of learners may be possible and much more work is needed to explore how this may be orchestrated (see Kuk & Kellogg, 2007). We wish to emphasize, however, that this project, which was in fact motivated by the teacher's desire to better meet her learners' needs in her day-to-day practice, also furthered the development of the conceptual model underlying DA by pointing toward possibilities for following the same theoretical principles but expanding the scope of interaction beyond dyads to include groups of individuals.

We wish to conclude our discussion of this project by noting an unintended consequence of this teacher–researcher collaboration. Upon completion of the project, the classroom teacher, Tracy, enrolled in a doctoral program in order to continue to learn about L2 theory and research so that she would be better positioned to help her students learn. Eventually, she carried out her own dissertation project, which involved collaboration with a classroom teacher and focused on DA. While we do not discuss the details of that project here, we note that Tracy's transition from practitioner to researcher-teacher, and subsequently to teacher educator resonates with Vygotsky's praxis-based theory. Tracy's classroom practice was re-oriented as a result of her engagement with the *Guide*, and this in turn prompted her to begin to pursue her own investigations into L2 theory and research but these remain guided by questions of practice and are responsive to the demands of real classrooms.

# DA and L2 Listening Comprehension: An Experimental-Developmental Study

Ableeva (2010) carried out an experimental-developmental DA study on listening comprehension in L2 French. An experienced teacher, Ableeva developed significant expertise in SCT during her doctoral studies and decided to devote her thesis to exploring how DA might be employed to support the development of learners' L2 listening abilities, an area that is often overlooked in classroom instruction and that Ableeva, because of her experience, recognized as challenging for learners to master. As with Tracy's study, Ableeva's approach was not prescribed but was responsive to her instructional interest, including the language proficiency and curricular focus of the courses she normally taught at university.

Ableeva's study was conducted with seven volunteers from a fourth-semester undergraduate university French language course designed to develop students' conversational abilities. The problem, as identified by Ableeva, was that such courses usually focus on the speaking component of conversations and do little to help learners with the comprehension side of interactions. The sequencing of material and selection of texts and tasks were primarily determined by a supervising faculty member, although individual instructors had some degree of latitude in day-to-day classroom activities.

The study is an important contribution to our understanding of learner participation in DA and to the relevance of co-regulation in supporting learning development. In particular, Ableeva's analysis revealed a range of learner reciprocating (i.e., co-regulating) behaviors that yielded insights for the mediator to capitalize on when attuning her mediation to the learners. These included the sources of their difficulties and how near they were to independent performance. We underscore that the study was not undertaken to further theorize the concept of learner reciprocity. Ableeva's interest was in how her efforts to support the development of learners' listening abilities could be enhanced by structuring her interactions with learners according to DA principles. The contributions from this work to the theoretical concepts underlying DA, namely learner reciprocity, is another instance of the sort of praxis that Vygotsky envisioned and that we have argued for throughout this book.

## Description of the Study

Ableeva's (2010) study occurred over an 8-week period and began with a one-to-one assessment of learners' listening comprehension, which offered a baseline diagnosis of their abilities. This initial diagnosis consisted of two parts: a conventional assessment during which learners listened to an authentic, unaltered French audio text twice and recalled orally in their L1 (English) as much of the text as they could; a parallel version of this task in which the mediator dialogically interacted with the learners during the repetitions and recall. The aural texts themselves were created by Ableeva and comprised interviews with native speakers of French around a range of topics (e.g., cuisine, politics, cinema) in order to elicit a wide sample of spoken language. The interview passages employed during the assessment and enrichment sessions were coded according to Johnson's (1970) notion of pausal units, a propositional analysis system frequently employed in comprehension research. This enabled Ableeva to assess learner comprehension on the basis of the number of pausal units they recalled after listening to the texts. In addition, these insights were supplemented through analysis of the mediator–learner dialoguing during the dynamic administrations. Ableeva noted how successfully learners comprehended the texts as well as the source of difficulties they experienced, mediation they required, and their reciprocating behaviors with regard to mediation. Her analysis revealed that learners encountered comprehension problems arising from phonology, sentence-level and discourse-level grammar, and lexical and cultural knowledge.

Following the initial diagnosis, Ableeva conducted enrichment sessions with the learners. The sessions focused on those areas that were most problematic as revealed by the diagnosis. The learners then participated in an additional series of listening comprehension tasks both in independent and DA format. Included among the new series of tasks were three levels of transfer, or transcendence (Poehner, 2007). Transfer tasks involved texts arranged by complexity level on the basis of topic, grammatical complexity, vocabulary, lack of redundancy, and articulation rate. The near transfer texts were similar to the original texts used during the pre-enrichment sessions where native speakers of French discussed French and American cuisine. The far transfer text was a partially scripted TV documentary on the controversial topic of smoking in French restaurants, and the very far transfer text was a fully scripted 20-second radio commercial for a Belgian restaurant chain. While the first two transfer texts included visual images of the speakers, the radio commercial did not and this greatly increased its level of difficulty for the learners. In addition, because of the time constraint of commercials, it was delivered at a high articulation rate and without the redundancies and pauses normally encountered in spontaneous talk.

Our major interest in discussing Ableeva's research is with its innovative analysis of learner responsiveness, or reciprocity, to the mediator that occurred during co-regulation in the DA sessions. We consider this topic following a brief analysis of learner performance on the pre- and post-enrichment tasks, with special attention to the transfer tasks.

## Transfer

Table 8.1 presents the descriptive statistics for learner performance on the pre- and post-enrichment tasks used in Ableeva's study. It includes the mean recall units for the learners' independent performance rather than their performance during the DA sessions. The statistics therefore reflect the effects of the DA sessions

**TABLE 8.1** Descriptive statistics for independent performance on listening tasks (based on Ableeva, 2010)

| | Pre-Enrichment | | Post-Enrichment | | Transfer | | |
|---|---|---|---|---|---|---|---|
| | Pre-DA | Post-DA | Pre-DA | Post-DA | NT | FT | VFT |
| IUs per text | 32 | 27 | 21 | 25 | 22 | 25 | 6 |
| MUR | 2.85 | 6.14 | 05 | 7.14 | 07 | 5.57 | 0.57 |
| | (09%) | (23%) | (24%) | (29%) | (32%) | (22%) | (10%) |
| SD | 1.67 | 1.86 | 2.88 | 1.21 | 2.94 | 3.99 | 0.97 |

*Notes:* IU = Idea Units; MUR = Mean number of Idea Units Recalled; NT = Near Transfer (similar text as pre-DA); FT = Far Transfer (TV documentary on restaurant smoking); VFT = Very Far Transfer (20-second radio commercial)

and the enrichment program on the actual level of learner development with regard to listening comprehension. Most relevant among these is the learners' independent performance during the transfer tasks used by Ableeva. These show the extent to which the learners were able to generalize what they appropriated during mediation to new and increasingly complex tasks. A full analysis of learner performance on all tasks (independent and mediated) is found in Ableeva (2010) and in Ableeva and Lantolf (2011).

Ableevas's inferential statistical analyses showed several instances where learner performance improved significantly as a result of DA. The analyses also revealed cases where performance failed to show significant improvement. Prior to enrichment, learner performance showed significant improvement from the initial independent task to the post-DA task. Following enrichment, Ableeva also reported significant improvement from the pre- to the post-DA task. Finally, she found a significant change in performance between the initial pre-DA task administered prior to enrichment and three of the tasks administered following enrichment: pre-DA, post-DA, and near transfer.

While Ableeva did not find a significant difference between the pre-DA task given during pre-enrichment and either the far or very far transfer tasks, she reported that when the performance of individual learners is examined, three of the them did relatively well on the far transfer task, recalling 7, 10, and 11, idea units, respectively. However, one learner scored a 0 on the far transfer task. Ableeva and Lantolf (2011, p. 144) commented that this type of evidence confirms that development in the ZPD is not the same for all learners at the same point in time. Even though all of the learners received mediation during the 8-week project, they did not all appropriate it in the same way. This is not to say that the learner who was unable to transfer mediation to the more complex task was incapable of developing. The same learner did well on the near transfer task. Consequently, his developmental trajectory evolved more slowly than that of some of the other participants. This type of developmental outcome has been reported in other ZPD projects going back to Aljaafreh and Lantolf's (1994) study.

It is clear that the very far transfer task was problematic for all of the learners, as they recalled, on average, less than 1 idea unit. This task then represented the upper limit of their microgenetic development (Ableeva & Lantolf, 2011, p. 144). Again, this does not represent an end to their development. It means that the effect of first-order mediation, as it was carried out during the 8-week study, could only take the learners so far and that additional time and mediation would be required to move their development beyond the level it had achieved at the conclusion of Ableeva's project.

### Responsiveness and Reciprocity During Co-Regulation

An especially interesting aspect of Ableeva's (2010) study is how she conceptualized learner contribution during DA. Although DA researchers have traditionally focused their analyses on the quality and effect of mediation provided to learners, Ableeva argued that it is also important to distinguish between responsiveness to mediation in terms of development and the various forms of reciprocity learners manifest during the co-regulation that takes place in DA. With regard to responsiveness, Ableeva proposed a distinction between *progressive moves* to refer to learners' responses to mediation that represent a correction of the problem that the mediation addressed and *regressive moves* that occur when learners either repeat the same problem or address it unsuccessfully, producing other errors. Ableeva used this distinction to monitor learner progress across sessions throughout the 8-week program. By recording the overall number of progressive and regressive moves during a session as well as the specific focus (e.g., making a choice or deciphering a pattern), it was possible to capture a dimension of learner behavior beyond independent performance. That is, she was able to capture the extent to which learners benefited from mediation during a given session as well as to monitor how their performance was affected when new challenges were introduced during transfer.

Ableeva (2010) also documented reciprocating patterns of participation in the DA sessions, which she grouped as follows: *requesting a replay of a text, using the mediator as an evaluator, using the mediator as a resource, imitating the mediator, incorporating feedback, accepting mediator assistance,* and *rejecting mediation.* Unlike responsiveness, reciprocating behaviors were not found in every session nor were they observed with every learner. This is because they were not a direct reaction to the mediator's efforts to intervene in the comprehension process; rather they represented learner questioning and negotiation with the mediator that was fostered by the cooperative atmosphere of the sessions.

To provide a sense of how reciprocity occurred in the DA sessions, we discuss two data fragments reported by Ableeva (2010, pp. 302–303) that illustrate two of the above reciprocal moves: using the mediator as a resource and imitating the mediator. In the first excerpt (mediator as resource), Michel (a pseudonym) had already listened to an interview with a French speaker commenting on various foods. At one point, the speaker used the construction *ça a pas forcément de goût* (it doesn't have much taste). During interaction, the mediator (R) realized that Michel (M) had not comprehended the meaning of this utterance and therefore replayed it for him. She then repeated the line herself. Interestingly, in line 2 M initiated a discussion of the negative construction, and in particular the fact that the pattern displayed here—the inclusion of the negative particle *pas* but the absence of the particle *ne*—deviated from the pattern for forming negatives in writing, where *ne* and *pas* always co-occur (see the discussion of van Campernolle's study in Chapter 5).

Excerpt 1: Mediator as resource

R:  1. did you hear it? *ça a pas?* it doesn't have. . . *ça a pas forcément de goût* . . . 'it doesn't have much taste'

M:  2. I forgot what you told me. . . they drop the ne. . . (rising intonation)

R:  3. yes. . . they drop the *ne*. . . all the time. . .

M:  4. . . . *ça a pas?* 'it doesn't have?'

R:  5. . . . *ça a pas* . . . it's not . . . *ça n'a pas* . . . it's . . . *ça a pas* . . . he says. . . *ça a pas*
6. *forcément de goût* . . . 'it doesn't have much taste'
7. basically this is sort of classic French . . . *ça n' a pas* but they drop this *ne*
8. all the time in spoken French. . .

M:  9. they do it all the time? =

R:  10. = yes . . . I mean in spoken French . . . when they speak . . . not when they write. . .
11. when they write they tend to use this *ne* though . . .

The mediator had previously mentioned differences in forming negative constructions in written and spoken French. However, it is apparent that Michel did not fully recall the explanation and was not able to use it to interpret the utterance at hand. He mentioned this in line 2, expressing his uncertainty with rising intonation, and again in line 4 he repeated the construction *ça a pas* as a question. In this way, the learner elicited an explanation from the mediator and followed this up with a question (line 9) regarding how frequently he might expect to encounter similar constructions.

We see in this example recognition on the part of the learner that even though the primary focus of the session was to comprehend the interview he had heard, the presence of the mediator created possibilities for interaction and for learning that extended beyond the here-and-now demands of the task. In other words, the learner was seeking not simply to get through the present task but to improve his L2 abilities and as such recognized the mediator as an important resource.

Dan, another participant, struggled during the first DA session with some of the food vocabulary used by one of the native speakers. Consequently, in line 1, in excerpt 2 below, the mediator began to render some of the terms in English. Dan (D) mentioned poultry in line 2, which was in fact produced by the speaker during the interview (*la volaille*). It is not clear whether D recognized this word while listening to the interview or has inferred that poultry was discussed after R mentioned chicken and turkey. At any rate, he attempted to produce the word for poultry in French in line 4 but then pointed out that he did not know the word.

Excerpt 2: Imitating the mediator
R: 1. so . . . when it's about chicken and turkey . . .
D: 2. . . . poultry
R: 3. ok poultry . . . do you know the word poultry?
D: 4. is it *volan? . . . uhm . . . I don't know the word . . .
R: 5. it's *la volaille* (R writes this word for D)
D: 6. aaa-ah . . . *la volaille*
R: 7. *la volaille* means poultry . . .
D: 8. Ok . . . *la vo-laille* . . . (slowly repeats the word after R)

Rather than simply acknowledging that R had provided the French term *la volaille* in both spoken and written form, in line 6, D repeated the item aloud and did so again in line 8, only this time uttering the word slowly and carefully enunciating both syllables. Ableeva (2010) described this in relation to Vygotsky's (1978) account of imitation as an important driver of development (see our discussion in Chapter 3). Dan's imitation is an intentional move on his part to support internalization of the word and its pronunciation.

In the full study, Ableeva (2010) provided numerous examples of learner reciprocating behaviors. The value of attending to such reciprocity, in our view, is twofold. Important insights into learner development are afforded by looking beyond their responsiveness to mediation and examining their active engagement with the mediator, particularly with regard to their efforts to understand relevant principles or to gain practice using L2 structures, lexical items, or phonological segments. In addition to the diagnostic value of examining learner reciprocity, it is difficult to overstate the importance for learner development of this kind of open-ended, joint exploration of the L2. Such interaction is very much in the spirit of Feuerstein's MLE and the commitment of ZPD activity to go beyond particular tasks and to orient to learner development. We take up this point in the next section, where our discussion centers on applications of DA for more formal assessment purposes.

## L2 DA Beyond the Classroom

Torrance (1995), in a critical review of classroom-based assessment practices, argued that a challenge to determining the appropriateness and value of such teacher-driven assessments is that they are frequently judged according to criteria established for large-scale psychological and educational measurement. Particularly troubling for Torrance is the assumption that the sophisticated statistical methods used for validating standardized tests should be relevant and applicable to classroom assessments intended to serve pedagogic functions. In the L2 field, a similar position was put forth by Teasdale and Leung (2000), who suggested that while there may be important connections between psychometric principles and classroom formative assessments, these have yet to be elaborated, and so it remains an open question whether the latter forms of assessment should—or can—be expected to conform to standards set for the former. Moss (2003) noted that despite such protests, as well as growing recognition of the divergent goals of these activities and assumptions about learner abilities that drive them, classroom assessment practices continue to be shaped by standardized testing. She pointed to the widespread perception that psycho-educational testing offers an objective and scientific means of uncovering the truth about individuals' abilities as an explanation for why it continues to exert influence over more pedagogically-oriented assessments. Whatever the reason, work in L2 DA has followed a markedly different trajectory. That is, rather than modeling classroom assessment according to what is held to be effective in testing contexts, L2 DA has proceeded in the opposite direction.

The majority of L2 DA studies to date have resulted from collaborations with teachers motivated to employ DA as a framework to help them more effectively understand and respond to learner needs. It is only now that efforts are underway to explore how the principles for supporting development through DA might be leveraged for the design of more formal assessment activities. Of course, this does not reflect an assumption that DA is somehow more relevant to classrooms than other contexts. Indeed, in Chapter 7 we discussed research documenting the use of standardized approaches to DA that have been implemented to obtain alternate indicators of learner abilities.

We critiqued that work on the grounds that it generally did not fully embrace Vygotsky's commitment to a view of teaching and assessment as dialectic activity. The standardization of mediation in *interventionist* DA reduces the chance that the interaction will be sensitive to learner emergent needs, and in this regard *interactionist* DA, such as Feuerstein's MLE, has a distinct advantage. However, *interventionist* DA more readily lends itself to large-scale formats of test administration, such as computer-based testing. Indeed, a challenge for L2 DA has been to determine how it may be conducted on a scale with large numbers of individuals without losing the responsiveness of mediation to learner behaviors that has been characteristic of its use in dyads and in intact classrooms.

The two studies we discuss in this section are different components of the same project undertaken with precisely this aim in mind. Building on previous L2 DA research, the project sought to integrate mediation into L2 assessments that could be administered to multiple learners simultaneously. The advantage of such an approach is that while designing the assessment procedure is a labor-intensive process, once the assessments are prepared there is no longer the need for a co-present human mediator. In classroom settings, the number of learners concerned is generally more manageable and it is feasible to approach DA in either a one-to-one or group format as we have discussed earlier in the chapter. In other assessment contexts, this is not a realistic possibility.

Antón (2009) described the use of DA to inform placement decisions in a university L2 Spanish program. Her study provided clear evidence that insights into learner abilities obtained through individualized DA sessions frequently led to more appropriate placement decisions than if only the learners' independent performance had been taken account of. The total number of students applying to the program described by Antón, however, was relatively small. As she acknowledged, the approach to DA would need to be modified if there were dozens—or hundreds—of applicants each of whom needed to be assessed for placement purposes. Poehner (2009a) argued that applications of DA to very large populations of learners should be pursued and understood as operating in tandem with classroom-based DA, as together these represent a new assessment "culture" that is essential for developmental education.

Our project, discussed in detail elsewhere (Poehner & Lantolf, 2013), concerns the use of DA in a computerized format (C-DA). In C-DA, the assessment instrument is delivered via computer and dialogic mediation is replaced by scripted prompts that are provided to learners either upon request or when an error is produced. To our knowledge, three earlier computer-based initiatives were pursued by DA researchers: Guthke and Beckmann (2000), Jacobs (2001), and Tzuriel and Shamir (2002).

Clearly, moving from an approach in which mediation is dialogic to one where it is scripted in advance limits the potential to engage learners in ZPD activity because assumptions need to be made regarding the source of learner difficulty when designing mediation and it is not possible to react to unpredicted responsive moves on the part of the learner. Moreover, learner reciprocity and co-regulation are removed from the assessment equation. For example, mediation that is designed to make an L2 text more accessible by providing prompts and explanations relevant to selected lexical items and grammatical structures found in the text will be of little help to a learner who is struggling because of insufficient cultural knowledge. In this case the learner might require several prompts before arriving at the correct response, and the resultant diagnosis will misrepresent his/her development. In addition, the learner will not receive the cultural information that impeded full comprehension of the text. Consequently, the success of C-DA hinges upon preparing mediation that is as responsive to learner needs as is feasible in the absence of co-regulation.

## Three C-DA Programs

Each of the three C-DA programs mentioned above follows a different approach to integrating mediation into the testing procedure. Perhaps the most sophisticated approach is that of Guthke and Beckmann (2000), who created a series of tutorials presented to learners when they produce an error during the test. These authors designed tasks to assess general cognitive abilities, with each task connected to an underlying construct. When a learner answers a test item incorrectly, the test is paused and a tutorial begins to provide instruction, examples, and practice employing concepts and principles relevant to that task. After the tutorial concludes, the test resumes and learners are permitted to re-attempt the task. This is a one-size-fits-all approach to mediation in that there is only one tutorial per assessment task. It is also true that learners are only allowed a single attempt to improve their performance as a result of the tutorial, and therefore the diagnosis only reveals whether a learner required the intervention and if it led to an improved performance. It is not possible to determine whether more or less support would have been sufficient for a given individual and whether the learner in fact gained something from the tutorial but did not improve sufficiently to successfully execute the task. Nonetheless, Guthke and Beckmann's model is noteworthy because it embeds teaching and learning activities in the assessment, and this may benefit learners beyond the confines of the test. To our knowledge, the authors have not published other studies on their approach.

Jacobs (2001) followed a similar approach in her design of KIDTALK, a computerized assessment of pre-school children's language aptitude. The test begins with an introductory video featuring puppets that teach children the basic rules of an imaginary language, *kidtalk*. The children are then presented with a series of samples from the language and asked to determine, for instance, the word in kidtalk that should come next or the appropriate order for the words. Whenever a child answers incorrectly, the test is paused and the relevant portion of the introductory video is replayed. The child is then given the opportunity to answer again. If s/he is still unsuccessful, that part of the video is replayed and the child is permitted a third attempt before moving on. While the diagnosis reveals which features of the language were difficult for particular learners and keeps track of the number of attempts required to answer each question, mediation is once again very limited. In fact, the content of the mediation did not vary at all but was simply repeated such that if the initial instruction failed to help learners meet the demands of the tasks, the repetitions were not likely to have much value.

This point is recognized by Tzuriel and Shamir (2002), who advocate what we might term a hybrid approach to C-DA. That is, in their approach mediation is delivered via computer but a human mediator is also co-present to provide additional support when computerized mediation is insufficient. Their C-DA program, which focuses on young children's seriational thinking abilities, makes use of scripted prompts arranged from most implicit to most explicit. The authors note that while computerized mediation leads some learners to overcome problems during the assessment, others require dialogue with a mediator to help reframe the assessment tasks and to help them reflect on unsuccessful performances. While we empathize with Tzuriel and Shamir's position that computerized mediation may be most effective when coupled with human interaction, such an approach limits the functionality of C-DA in assessment contexts with large numbers of learners.

## L2 C-DA

The goal of the project was to develop tests of computer-based tests of listening and reading comprehension in three different languages (Chinese, French, and Russian) that followed a DA format. As an initial step, we developed the test instruments themselves. These were modeled after other widely used comprehension measures in those languages. A multiple-choice rather than an open-ended format was selected because it more readily lends itself to standardization of mediation. Moreover, research comparing the two formats reported correlations of measures obtained through both methods to be as high as .95 (see In'nami & Koizumi, 2009). In addition, the test questions and mediating prompts that accompanied the questions were in English, thus avoiding the possibility that learner performance would reflect difficulty comprehending not only the reading or listening passage but the questions and prompts as well. The listening passages in all three languages consisted of short texts that were played twice before learners were directed to answer the multiple-choice questions. In the case of reading, the texts in Chinese and Russian were also short; however, longer texts were used in French as it was determined that learners of L2 French at the targeted proficiency level, intermediate, were able to better handle longer texts than were learners of the other two languages.

The test items themselves each targeted particular constructs relevant for comprehension. In the case of listening this involved lexis, grammar, phonology, discourse, and culture. The reading test items target each of these with the exception of phonology. Each test item is also accompanied by a series of mediating prompts that are made available to learners when they respond incorrectly. In order to maximize the number of potential prompts, each question includes a correct choice and four distracters. The prompts are designed not simply to lead learners to the correct answer but are intended to be relevant to the construct underlying a particular item.

Mediation for each test item was determined by administering a paper-based version of the instruments in an individualized, open-ended, DA format with six learners of each language. The interactions between mediators and learners were audio and video recorded. The recordings were analyzed in order to identify recurring difficulties experienced by the learners and mediation patterns that proved most effective. This informed the creation of the standardized mediation included in the C-DA program.

The first study we discuss emerged from the individualized dialogic administration of the French reading comprehension test. The second concerns analysis of scores obtained through initial piloting of the computerized versions of the test. Both studies involved dynamic approaches to administering formal L2 tests, and both have produced important insights into the effects of DA on L2 development, including co-creation of learning opportunities that do not bear directly on the task at hand (i.e., opportunities that emerge spontaneously from learner responsiveness and reciprocity) and the generation of nuanced developmental profiles that offer teachers useful information on learner strengths and weaknesses.

## Individualized DA in French Reading Comprehension

In the one-on-one administrations of the C–DA tests, learners read or listened to the L2 texts and then independently attempted the comprehension questions that followed. As each multiple-choice question contained five options, learners had a maximum of four attempts after which it would be clear that the remaining option was correct. A mediator was present throughout the test; however, s/he did not interact with the learners when they made their initial attempt to respond to each item. The initial response for each item was assumed to constitute the learners' actual level of development. Following the initial learner response and regardless of whether it was correct or incorrect, the mediator engaged the learner. If the learner had responded correctly, the mediator sought to understand the reasons behind the learner's choice in order to ascertain whether it reflected an appropriate understanding of the text, or if it had been a guess. If a response was incorrect, the mediator offered support to determine the feature(s) of the text that impeded learner comprehension and to gauge learner responsiveness to mediation. The initial mediation offered was always implicit. Learners were then given a second opportunity to respond to the test item. If learners did not answer correctly, the process continued with mediation becoming increasingly explicit until either the learner selected the correct response or the mediator explained why the remaining option was preferable.

Following close analysis of one-to-one administrations of the French reading comprehension test, Poehner and van Compernolle (2011) noted that these interactions included the mediator offering prompts, making suggestions, providing leading questions, responding to learner questions, reminding learners of features of French language and culture that the learner had likely previously encountered, and generally discussing the texts with learners. The aim of this analysis was to identify the kinds of mediation that could inform the design of standardized support for use in the final, computerized version of the test.

Poehner and van Compernolle's analysis also yielded insights relevant to how mediation may be further conceptualized in DA. Specifically, they found that mediator and learner moves at times maintained a close focus on the demands posed by the assessment task while at other times these moves signaled a departure from the test, an exploration of aspects of the language and culture that were not explicitly relevant to successfully responding to a given test item. The researchers proposed that these occasions constituted distinct but interrelated 'frames of interaction.' They described *collaborative* interactions as seeking to determine the quality of mediation learners require to understand relevant portions of the reading passages and to ascertain which features of the texts were problematic. They contrasted these interactions with frames that they termed *cooperative*, characterized as involving more wide-ranging discussions of lexico-grammatical features of the L2, pragmatic variation, or knowledge of the target culture.

While in a collaborative frame the mediator directs learners to reread texts or particular portions of texts and may provide English equivalents of unfamiliar L2 lexical items, in a cooperative frame the mediator provides additional information concerning structures found in the text, explicates cultural references, and helps learners to draw connections among ideas to deepen their comprehension. A cooperative frame then can allow for both a more nuanced understanding of the text as well as greater knowledge of the L2 that will better position learners to comprehend texts in the future. Moreover, Poehner and van Compernolle argued that DA interactions allow for flexibility such that mediator and learner may step out of a collaborative frame to discuss issues of language and culture more broadly before returning to the immediate task. In this way, it is possible to trace how, over the course of a DA interaction, particular mediator moves create opportunities to both diagnose and intervene in processes of learner L2 comprehension.

Poehner and van Compernolle (2011) offered an example of the shifting focus of mediation in an exchange between a mediator (M) and a learner, Victoria (V). The interaction occurred after V had successfully responded to a comprehension question concerning a reading passage in which the author recounted weekends during his childhood spent in the country with his grandparents. The question asked what the author most liked about his time in the country and V correctly concluded that the best response option was the time together with his grandfather. In some sense, then, the assessment task itself had been completed. However, before moving on to the next text M attempted to create a cooperative frame with V by asking whether she had any questions about this passage. This offered an opportunity for the learner to take the lead in exploring linguistic and cultural features of the text that may serve to deepen her understanding of the passage or simply be an opportunity to learn something new. This opportunity became a moment of teaching-learning, but it also gave rise to an important correction to the diagnosis of V's comprehension.

We enter the exchange after V had responded to M's question by asking about a phrase in the text that was unfamiliar to her, *les bruits de la ville* (the noises of the city).

Excerpt 3: Teaching–learning following task completion
*M:*  1. the noises?
*V:*  2. oh okay

*M:* 3. the sounds *les bruits de la ville* 'the sounds of the city'

*V:* 4. okay

*M:* 5. right okay so you didn't understand that cause that was

6. the calm in the country (one of the response options) it was supposed to –

*V:* 7. yeah

*M:* 8. okay

Initially M responded by rendering *les bruits* as noises in English, and he noted (line 5) that V had failed to understand an important line from the text in which the author expresses how much he enjoyed the tranquility of the countryside, as it was far from the noises of the city to which he was accustomed. In part, this information is relevant because one of the distracters for this particular question mentions the appeal of the calm countryside. An interesting question is whether V would have selected this option had she understood that phrase in the text. While we cannot know for certain, this brief exchange, which would not have occurred in most assessment contexts, was intended to support learner comprehension of the text and in fact provided M with additional relevant diagnostic information about V's comprehension.

A moment later in their discussion, M pursued the matter, asking V how she interpreted the word *calme*, an obvious English–French cognate.

Excerpt 4: Refining the diagnosis of learner abilities

*V:* 1. I figured it just was like um it was uh a cal-calm um area like away from

2. the like I got that it was kind of like a place that wasn I thought like

3. like I took as being a place like in the country?

*M:* 4. mhm did you see did you see country in here?

*V:* 5. no but just I saw animal

*M:* 6. uhhuh

*V:* 7. and

*M:* 8: what about *c'était à la campagne loin de tous les bruits de la ville* 'it was in the countryside far from all the sounds of the city'

9. do you remember *la campagne?* 'the countryside'?

*V:* 10. I thought it was like country area but=

*M:* 11. =yeah it's the countryside

*V:* 12. okay

V's response in line 1 revealed that she in fact failed to recognize *la campagne* (the countryside), which was crucial for accurate comprehension. While she correctly inferred that the author is talking about 'country area' (line 10), she did so on the basis of another cognate, *animal*.

From the perspective of DA's assessment function, this interaction revealed that although the learner had completed the task successfully, her performance did not reflect an accurate understanding of the text. To be sure, in this particular case V may have guessed the correct answer as a result of the multiple-choice format of the test. Indeed, elsewhere Poehner and van Compernolle (in press) argued that an important contribution of DA interactions in formal assessment settings may lay in uncovering the process through which learners arrive at their responses to test items, thus identifying instances of guessing and cases when learners arrive at a correct answer but for erroneous reasons. The point here is that this instructional interaction, framed as a follow-up to the assessment itself, served as a continuation of the assessment process as the mediator was able to identify and remediate comprehension difficulties the learner had experienced and that would have otherwise gone unnoticed.

In the full study, Poehner and van Compernolle (2011) contrast this episode with examples in which mediator–learner attention is focused squarely on considering a particular test question and its accompanying response options. This collaborative interactional frame foregrounds the diagnostic function of DA by pinpointing the forms of mediation required for learners to access ideas in the text. The more explicit the mediation, the further the individual is from comprehending such texts independently. While a collaborative frame brings assessment into focus, the authors point out that the mediation offered to learners has an instructional quality that may support their comprehension of L2 texts in general. For instance, providing a gloss of an L2 lexical item, suggesting that the learner reread portions of the text where relevant information may be found, and calling attention to discursive features of the text that create particular relations among ideas, may impact how learners approach subsequent texts. Just as the cooperative interaction considered above may have foregrounded learning but still provided diagnostic information, collaborative frames also maintain the dialectic unity of teaching and assessment that characterizes DA. Indeed, Poehner and van Compernolle (2011) argued that even if the focus of mediation shifts over the course of a DA interaction, both interactional frames can be relevant for learner development.

This final point is worth bearing in mind as we turn now to the phase of the project in which mediation was standardized and delivered via computer. At first glance, it may appear that prompting learners as they respond to test questions is simply a matter of scaffolding them through the task and that without opportunities for a cooperative frame such support is unlikely to affect their development. In our view, the difference is that in both the one-to-one and computerized DA administrations of these tests the comprehension tasks themselves were not the object of mediator–learner activity but rather they provided a vehicle for understanding and promoting learners' L2 reading abilities. The prompts were designed with an instructional intent such that learners may require less support later in the test because they have benefited from mediation provided during the process of working through earlier items. This is true even during the fully computerized version of the tests, when mediation was scripted and standardized.

For instance, the mediation that accompanies the French reading test item discussed above is based on analysis of the mediator's individualized sessions with each of the learners. It was found that with all learners, it was helpful to narrow the search space in the text by directing learner attention to increasingly smaller fragments of the passage with each prompt. This is done consistently with all the test items.

Mediation on the final version of the tests also includes prompts that direct learners to consider how particular statements in the passage might be connected to one another, English glosses of French words that might be unfamiliar to learners, and explanations of complex discourse-level features of the texts. With regard to the French text we have discussed, a construction that proved particularly challenging for learners to understand and that is crucial for accurate comprehension of the passage is the author's statement that it is not the animals that he loved most about his time in the country but rather the quiet evenings spent with his grandfather. The mediation in the final version of the test includes an explanation of this construction.

We also wish to mention that, just as important instances of mediated learning were found to occur in the one-to-one administrations after learners successfully completed a task, the computerized versions offer learners the chance to view a statement in English that explains why a particular response option is the best choice and that cites specific details from the text relevant to understanding this. In this way, a learner who answers an item correctly, whether on her first or third attempt, but who does so without an appropriate understanding of the passage (as occurred with V in the example discussed earlier) still has the opportunity to more fully comprehend a text and perhaps to learn more about the L2. Finally, and in keeping with earlier DA work, transfer items are included in the C-DA tests. Examining learner performance of transfer items offers additional information about their development, namely, how successfully they are able to move toward more difficult tasks and the level of mediation they require. We will have more to say about this below.

## Profiling Development in C-DA: Learning Potential Scores

C-DA holds much potential for contexts in which it is necessary to diagnose the development of large numbers of learners. Our use of C-DA to address L2 listening and reading comprehension represented an initial step in what we hope will be a new direction for language assessment specialists. Each of the tests has been piloted and is available online for use by L2 learners, teachers, and program administrators (go to www.language.la.psu.edu). We discuss some of the findings of the pilot data in what follows. A detailed discussion of pilot results is found in Poehner and Lantolf (2013). Here we focus a potentially informative approach to profiling L2 development that simultaneously takes account of learner independent functioning and responsiveness to mediation. To be sure, taking account of learner performance under these two conditions is a defining feature of DA that sets it apart from other assessments. What has received far less attention is how these sources of information may be combined to generate what Kozulin and Garb (2002) have termed a *learning potential score* (LPS).

Kozulin and Garb (2002), building on the work of Budoff (1987), sought to differentiate learners according to the change profiles they observed when comparing individuals' scores on dynamic and non-dynamic administrations of reading tests. Examining learner abilities in a range of domains, Budoff proposed a taxonomy to distinguish learners whose initial scores (without mediator inter-vention) are already high from two other groups of learners: those whose scores show marked improvement following an intervention stage in the assessment and those who exhibit little or no change. Kozulin and Garb's (2002) study followed a similar format, wherein learners completed a traditional reading test before taking part in an enrichment program designed to improve their comprehension. After the program, a parallel version of the original test was administered. Comparing the two sets of scores the authors noted significant negative cor-relations between initial, or unmediated, and mediated scores, meaning that the latter varied independently from the former. In other words, learners' initial scores did not offer a strong basis for predicting their scores following the enrichment program. This in itself is an important finding as predictions of learners' future success on tests of language aptitude, for example, are generally made exclusively on the basis of independent test performance. Moreover, the authors reported that individuals who earned the same initial unmediated score sometimes received different mediated scores. In line with Vygotsky's (1987) discussion of the ZPD, these findings offer evidence that individuals can be simultaneously the same and different, that is, they can manifest similar levels of actual development but differ with regard to the range of abilities that are in the process of forming.

To better understand the relation between learner unmediated and mediated performance, Kozulin and Garb proposed the formula for generating a LPS, given in Figure 8.4. This allowed the researchers to organize learners into three groups: high scorers (LPS $\geq$ 1.0), mid-range scorers (.88 $\geq$ LPS $\geq$ − .79), and low scorers (LPS $\leq$ .71).[1]

An LPS of 1 or more means that the score improved by one standard deviation, and any score of less than one signals a change of less than a standard deviation. The value of including an LPS in profiling learner development is that it supplements the information revealed through unmediated and mediated scores and indicates the degree of change observed. If this change is understood as a sign of an individual's openness to mediation, then it raises interesting possibilities regarding how LPS might contribute to assessment decisions, such as placing learners in a program of study. For instance, a learner whose initial score is relatively high and who benefits little from mediation will have a lower LPS than one who performs poorly on the initial assessment but improves dramatically following mediation. We would therefore predict that each individual would

$$LPS = \frac{(S\ post\text{-}mediation - S\ actual)}{Max\ S} + \frac{S\ post\text{-}mediation}{Max\ S}$$

Abbreviated as follows:

$$LPS = \frac{2(S\ post\text{-}mediation) - S\ actual}{Max\ S}$$

**FIGURE 8.4** Formula for Learning Potential Score (Kozulin & Garb, 2002, p. 121)

respond differently to a similar instructional program and that each might better benefit from being placed in different instructional programs. This claim requires careful testing, but it has potentially important consequences for the organization of educational programs.

In our piloting of the L2 C-DA reading and listening tests, we employed the same LPS formula and procedure for grouping learners into categories as Kozulin and Garb. As an example of how learners' actual and mediated scores function together with their LPS to create a profile of their development, Table 8.2 presents the results from the pilot of the Chinese listening comprehension test. The table also includes scores from the transfer items. Because the transfer items target the same dimensions of comprehension as other test items but are more demanding, then how well learners do on the transfer items relative to their performance on the rest of the test is indicative of any development that may have occurred during C-DA. Poehner and Lantolf (2013) offered additional analyses of our piloting of the tests as well as more detailed interpretation of the results.

**TABLE 8.2** Individual actual and mediated scores, LPSs and transfer scores—Chinese listening test (Poehner & Lantolf, 2013)

| Learner | Actual* | Mediated | LPS | Transfer** |
|---|---|---|---|---|
| 1 | 8 | 40 | 1.20 | 16 |
| 2 | 40 | 54 | 1.13 | 12 |
| 3 | 48 | 57 | 1.10 | 24 |
| 4 | 40 | 53 | 1.10 | 16 |
| 5 | 40 | 52 | 1.07 | 28 |
| 6 | 16 | 40 | 1.07 | 16 |
| 7 | 28 | 44 | 1.00 | 12 |
| 8 | 32 | 46 | 1.00 | 12 |
| 9 | 28 | 43 | 0.97 | 12 |
| 10 | 36 | 46 | 0.93 | 8 |
| 11 | 24 | 40 | 0.93 | 8 |
| 12 | 24 | 34 | 0.73 | 12 |
| 13 | 16 | 20 | 0.70 | 8 |
| 14 | 16 | 28 | 0.67 | 8 |

*Note:* *Maximum score = 60
**Maximum score = 32

The actual and mediated scores in Table 8.2 are in line with what one would expect from the perspective of the ZPD: individuals' independent functioning may vary separately from their performance with mediation. For example, Learners 1, 6, and 11 each earned a mediated score of 40 although their independent scores are dramatically different (8, 16, and 24, respectively). Similarly, we see that regardless of their actual score, some learners benefited little from mediation. In the case of Learner 3 (actual score of 48, mediated score of 57), it may be that the initially high score left less room for improvement through mediation (i.e., an individual ceiling effect). Learner 13, in contrast, improved only from 16 to 20 with mediation, suggesting that the tasks may have been beyond his/her current developmental level (i.e., an individual floor effect).

Turning to the transfer scores, we see that these are not predictable on the basis of actual scores. For example, some individuals with lower actual scores than other learners earn the same transfer score (see Learners 1 and 4 or Learners 10 and 14). Such individuals may have started the assessment at one place developmentally but then improved as a result of working through the process of responding to test items, including the explanations provided for each item. An interesting question that arises here is whether the LPS correlates with transfer scores. That is, if LPS does in fact signal openness to mediation as theorized, then it may predict learning during the C-DA procedure, as indicated by performance on the transfer items.

As an initial investigation into this possibility, we grouped individuals into the High, Mid, and Low LPS categories. We then examined the transfer scores within each group. Table 8.3 presents the means and standard deviation of the transfer scores for each of the LPS groups on three of the C-DA tests. There were no scores available in the low range for either the Chinese reading or French listening tests. We performed a Mann–Whitney U to determine whether statistically significant differences existed between the transfer scores of the LPS groups. The Chinese Listening test revealed significant differences between the high and mid ranges ($z = 3.94$; $p < .05$) and also between the high and low ranges ($z = 3.05$; $p < .05$). Comparing the mid and low ranges for that test, we see a slightly higher

TABLE 8.3 Mean and standard deviation of transfer scores grouped by LPS range (Poehner & Lantolf, 2013, Table 4)

| LPS Range | Chinese Listening | Chinese Reading | French Listening |
|---|---|---|---|
| High | $\bar{x} = 18.27$ (8.56) $n = 30$ | $\bar{x} = 12.22$ (5.72) $n = 55$ | $\bar{x} = 12.75$ (5.31) $n = 16$ |
| Mid | $\bar{x} = 8.38$ (4.54) $n = 20$ | $\bar{x} = 8.30$ (5.49) $n = 20$ | $\bar{x} = 9.61$ (4.56) $n = 5$ |
| Low | $\bar{x} = 9.67$ (3.17) $n = 12$ | — | — |

mean score in the low group but the difference was not significant ($z = -.84$). The Chinese Reading test similarly revealed a significant difference between the high and mid LPS ranges ($z = 2.53; p < .05$). Analysis of the French listening test did not reveal statistically significant differences between the high and mid-range transfer scores ($z = 1.11; p > .05$). While these results are quite preliminary in nature, we believe they suggest that LPS may hold promise for predicting changes in learner performance during the C-DA itself. As more learners take each of the C-DA tests that are currently available, we expect to gain a better understanding of the predictive power of LPS.

An interesting question that remains is whether LPS is able to predict performance beyond the C-DA itself, especially with regard to classroom contexts. While we oppose the use of LPS to deny learners (particularly those with a low LPS) the opportunity to continue language study, it will be important to investigate whether, as the theory predicts, individuals with a higher LPS will be more responsive to classroom instruction and will advance more quickly and with less support from the teacher. Of course, the theory does not predict that individuals with a low LPS cannot develop; it predicts that they most likely require a more intensive investment of instructional support. A formal application of DA used to place learners into a classroom environment in which teachers work to align instruction to their emerging capabilities on an ongoing basis would represent, from our perspective, a particularly powerful approach to promoting L2 development for all learners (see Lantolf & Poehner, 2013).

## Concluding Remarks and Ongoing Challenges

In this chapter we have elaborated how the view of DA as an activity oriented toward diagnosing and promoting learner development has been pursued in the context of L2 education. Each of the DA studies we have considered began as a project to address practical concerns in L2 education, such as aligning instruction with learner needs and systematically tracking development in a group setting, helping learners access authentic aural L2 texts, and designing an online procedure useful for marking student achievement and determining appropriate placement decisions for large numbers of learners. Each of these projects required careful planning to implement DA principles in a manner appropriate to the goals and conditions of a particular context. For example, the use of DA in the elementary school L2 Spanish program reflected the classroom teacher's understanding of how mediation may be organized as hierarchically arranged prompts as well as her awareness of the need to maintain the children's attention and to move through the curriculum during her temporally constrained fifteen-minute instructional sessions. Similarly, the C-DA project employed scripted mediation that focused learner attention on relevant excerpts in the text and provided support in interpreting complex structures and unfamiliar lexical items. This decision derived both from the practical concern to develop a system of mediation embedded in tests that can be administered on a large scale as well as from analyses of forms of support that proved helpful to learners during dialogic DA administrations of the tests.

At the same time, we have argued that while these projects each represent a theoretically motivated approach to addressing practical problems, the practical work itself has allowed for elaboration of concepts underlying DA. In the case of the elementary school L2 Spanish program, the systematic approach the teacher devised to recording the number of mediating prompts each learner required on a given day provided a means for tracing the development of individual learners as well as the whole class over time. Moreover, her integration of DA with whole class game activities allowed her to offer mediation to individuals while simultaneously provoking development of others through attentive observation and possibly vicarious imitation. While analysis of this class suggests that DA may indeed have functioned to support individual learners directly and the entire class indirectly, much more work is needed to understand possibilities for constructing group ZPDs with classes.

In a similar vein, the actual and mediated scores yielded by the C-DA exams created the possibility to investigate a new construct in the L2 field, learning potential. The commitment to a social ontology entails a commitment to the view that learning potential is not a fixed and immutable capacity of individuals but is instead a consequence of their access to appropriate forms of first-order (and as argued in Chapters 5 and 6, second-order) mediation. There exists the possibility that the construct of learning potential and learning potential scores might be misused (as happened with IQ tests and language aptitude measures) to provide access to educational opportunities for some and deny access to others. However, if conceived as an openness to mediation, then learning potential can provide important information to teachers and program directors seeking to place learners at a level of study where instruction is most likely to promote continued development. Again, we see this as an area ripe for praxis-oriented investigations.

Given the range of L2 contexts and problems to which DA has been applied as well as the robust psychological theory that underlies DA, it is perhaps not entirely surprising that DA has, over a relatively short span of time, attracted the attention of researchers concerned with a range of assessment and instructional topics. As we have seen, DA poses a theoretically motivated challenge to the accepted view that insights gained into learner functioning through observations of independent performance fully capture the range of their abilities as well as their learning potential. DA provides a systematic and principled approach to classroom and non-classroom assessment that allows for a nuanced understanding of learner capabilities while simultaneously offering instruction attuned to learner needs in order to move development forward. DA's commitment to mediation as co-regulation requires that assistance and support must be sufficiently explicit to prompt an appropriate response from learners but not so explicit that the mediator ends up assuming most of the responsibility for carrying out an activity. In our view, this offers an original contribution to debates in SLA over the desirability of explicit or implicit corrective feedback.

However, DA has not been accepted by all in the L2 field, and in particular by those with a decidedly psychometric orientation to assessment. Outside the L2 domain, DA has long been criticized for not adhering to psychometric principles of standardization for both administration procedures and scoring of performances. According to this view, the stated goal in DA of intervening in psychological processes and promoting their development as an essential part of the assessment undermines the relatively stable nature of abilities that is assumed in conventional psycho-educational measurement (e.g., Büchel & Scharnhorst, 1993; Glutting & McDermott, 1990). This stability is understood to be necessary if interpretations of an individual's performance during the assessment can be thought to provide any valuable insights into his/her likely performance in other contexts.

Such critiques have prompted different responses from DA practitioners. While the *interventionist* DA framework does in fact advocate standardization in its procedures, Feuerstein, for his part, has consistently argued that it is through open-ended dialogue with learners that one can most successfully diagnose and promote development, a view that we believe is fully supported by SCT. Poehner (2011) acknowledged that while the technical approaches to validity frequently employed in large-scale testing are problematic in DA, particularly in its inter-actionist format, this does not mean that DA is not concerned with establishing arguments regarding the appropriateness of interpretations of learner abilities. Poehner proposed that validity in DA might be conceived to operate at a micro and macro level. The former, he explained, concerns particular mediator moves during interaction and examines the appropriateness of the interpretation of learner abilities that motivated the move. That interpretation is accepted, refined, or rejected according to how the leaner responds to the mediator's move (p. 257). Macro validity, on the other hand, pertains to the effectiveness of the interaction as a whole at providing diagnostic insights into learner abilities. Particularly important for the macro validity of DA is whether the interaction appeared to provoke learner development, as this indicates that mediator and learner attention was indeed focused on abilities that were ripening (p. 259).

## Responding to Critiques of L2 DA

Within the L2 field, the most frequent critique of DA has been aimed at how the framework may be implemented in contexts involving large numbers of learners. This issue pertains as much to formal assessment settings as well as to classrooms, where teachers are frequently responsible for 20 to 30 learners, and some-times many more. This is a legitimate concern, and one that must be addressed if DA's contributions to L2 education are to be fully realized. We point to both the elementary school L2 Spanish program and the C-DA exams discussed in this chapter as viable starting points for exploring how DA can move beyond the dyadic interactions that characterize the early studies. Additional efforts are, of course, needed to understand how learners may be engaged in ZPD activity in classrooms with large numbers of students as well as in formal testing situations, and we hope L2 researchers will pursue projects in this area.

Another challenge to DA we have encountered is that it is nothing new but is merely "good teaching." This point was made by Fulcher (2010), whose misunderstanding of the general theory of SCT we discussed in Chapter 3. With regard to DA, Fulcher (2010, p. 75) insisted that the process of co-constructing a ZPD is indistinguishable from "what teachers normally do in classrooms to get learners to notice their mistakes." On his view DA invokes complex theoretical terms from SCT to describe what teachers are already doing. While we concur that DA is indeed "good teaching" in that it guides learner development by attuning to their ripening capabilities, we are not at all convinced that this is what teachers normally do. In fact as we have seen, a fundamental debate continues in the field of SLA over whether corrective feedback ought to be implicit or explicit. Teachers are likely to be offered different recommendations in this regard depending upon the SLA research they read.

Moreover, irrespective of the approach to corrective feedback that teachers might adopt, it is not at all clear that their preferred approach to feedback will in any way influence their assessment practices or that their teaching interactions with learners will be taken into account as a form of assessment. Indeed, it has been widely noted that much classroom-based assessment is fashioned after large-scale, standardized testing and adheres to principles including prohibiting interaction with the teacher or other students, imposing time constraints, and restricting access to supporting materials (see Moss, 2003 and our discussion of Perkins, 1993 and Nickerson, 1993 in Chapter 4). When more interactive kinds of formative assessment are used by teachers, feedback to learners can be unsystematic and ad hoc. The resultant records of learner performance are often impressionistic, with the consequence that learner abilities are either over- or under-estimated (Rea-Dickins & Gardner, 2000). Moreover, as Torrance & Pryor (1998) documented, teachers frequently reward and praise students for making an effort (e.g., 25% of a final grade is based on class attendance and on participating actively in class), and often miss opportunities to provoke development. It is this state of affairs that has led many to decry the lack of a theoretical basis to guide classroom assessment practice (e.g., Teasdale & Leung, 2000), a point acknowledged by Fulcher (2010) himself.

Our own experience with DA and working with teachers to help them consider how to reframe their practices further convinces us that DA is not something teachers typically do in a consistent and systematic way. To be sure, teachers vary with regard to how perceptive they are of their learners' needs and how facile they are in attempting to adapt their instruction to meet these needs. However, without theoretical principles to direct their attention to particular cues from learners and to guide their decision-making, even veteran teachers miss insights into learner functioning and opportunities to intervene in their development. Attending to learner responsiveness and reciprocity and altering mediation accordingly as an activity unfolds moment-to-moment is highly demanding, and in our collaborations with teachers we find that their efforts to move toward a DA framework are greatly supported by jointly discussing and analyzing recorded DA sessions followed by considerable practice implementing DA with their own learners and reflecting on those experiences. In other words, what is required is, as we have argued from the outset of the book, a dialectical unity of theory and practice so that theory guides and informs practice and practice guides and informs theory. As Vygotsky (1987) reminded us, practice without theory is mindless activity, but theory without practice is verbalism.

Fulcher (2010), however, raised a more fundamental critique of DA, one that concerns the purpose of doing DA in the first place. He (p. 75) asserted that because mediator and learner function together during DA this means that in practice "anything learned from DA is only meaningful in context; with these particular participants, these particular tasks, at this particular time." Consequently, he argued that DA has no meaning that can be generalized "beyond the instance of occurrence" (p. 75). In Fulcher's view this shortcoming derives from a lack of a theoretical basis to guide DA. He claimed that terminology from SCT is invoked in DA studies only to describe what occurs, not to function the way theory ought to in research. In particular, he referred to a lack of attention to "variables" in DA and how their presence, absence, or strength impacts outcomes and may therefore be used to evaluate the explanatory power of the theory. This led Fulcher (2010, p. 79) to conclude that "DA appears to be based on a theory that is not testable, but is self-validating in each new context."

As we have argued throughout our discussions, the purpose of DA is to promote learner development, not merely to describe what occurs during a single interaction. In Chapter 7 we argued for a view of ZPD activity as an instantiation of Vygotsky's genetic method, with careful attention to how learner abilities may be understood and promoted through interactions in which their engagement is mediated. Analysis of DA sessions is therefore very much concerned with the presence, absence, and quality of mediation that is available to learners and how they respond to it because this provides insights into their emerging capabilities. This is why, for example, the elementary school L2 Spanish DA program traced the level of prompting individuals required over time and used this information in making instructional decisions. Within the context of a single administration of a test, the C-DA program also tracks the amount of mediation learners require across test items in order to better understand the dimensions of listening and reading comprehension that are most problematic for learners. The fact that most L2 DA programs, and indeed DA programs concerned with general cognitive development (see Campione et al., 1984; Feuerstein et al., 2010), also include transfer tasks further underscores the importance of looking beyond a single interaction to understand and guide processes of L2 development. Indeed, the C-DA tests and also Ableeva's (2010) approach to diagnosing L2 listening comprehension discussed in this chapter are both examples of the value, from a DA perspective, of examining how learners respond to more challenging tasks, including the degree to which they are able to self-regulate or require external mediation to perform. Moreover, Vicente's performance in the second description game in the elementary school L2 Spanish classroom must also be interpreted as an indication of transfer and therefore evidence of real development. In fact, Lantolf and Poehner (2011a) made this precise argument.

As for whether DA is based on an untestable, "self-validating" theory, Fulcher seemed to be raising the question of whether development would occur if either no mediation or a different form of mediation were offered. As we have explained, the quality of mediation is a paramount concern in DA and is the reason, for example, that considerable effort was expended conducting and analyzing one-on-one DA sessions with learners prior to designing the scripted mediation for the C-DA exams. Indeed, a potential drawback to any DA program in which mediation is scripted and inflexible is that it may not be sensitive to the difficulty an individual learner is experiencing; in dialogic forms of DA, this is less likely to occur because the interaction typically draws out the processes behind learner performance. Even in such cases, however, it may not be immediately apparent to a mediator what the source of difficulty is, a point made by Poehner (2008b) in his discussion of a prolonged interaction between mediator and learner as they complete an oral narration task in the L2. In what Poehner described as a misinterpretation or misdiagnosis of learner performance, the mediator began a process of offering increasingly explicit support to address what he believed was confusion over verbal aspect only to realize after several minutes that the learner had simply overgeneralized a pattern for forming past participles.

Another example of the importance of appropriate mediation for supporting development came from a small-scale study by Nassaji and Swain (2000). These authors set out to investigate whether mediation attuned to learners' emerging needs was more effective in promoting development than mediation that was not. Beginning with the regulatory scale outlined by Aljaafreh and Lantolf (1994), Nassaji and Swain paired a tutor with two ESL learners. The tutor engaged with one of the learners in the same way as described by Aljaafreh and Lantolf, beginning with implicit mediation and becoming only as explicit as necessary; with the other learner, the tutor offered the mediating moves in a completely randomized order (i.e., that is, mediation was offered but no effort was made to align it with learner needs). According to Nassaji and Swain, the learner for whom mediation was negotiated and contingent upon his needs had actually performed worse on the initial assessment of independent writing than the learner in the randomized condition. Nonetheless, unlike the learner in the randomized condition, the learner who had received negotiated mediation showed consistent improvement across the sessions and outperformed the randomized condition learner on the final assessment of independent writing. Similarly, comparisons may be made of diagnoses of learner abilities based on independent performance with those derived from DA. One may seek to ascertain, for instance, which diagnosis better predicts learners' future performance. Such direct comparisons are quite common in the general DA literature (see Haywood & Lidz, 2007; Lidz & Elliott, 2000; Sternberg & Grigorenko, 2002) and in fact provide the empirical basis for the argument that DA allows one to glimpse future independent functioning through interaction in the present. Such studies will certainly be worth undertaking as more programs like the C-DA tests we have discussed become available in the L2 field and as more classroom teachers adopt and adapt procedures along the lines of those formulated by Tracy.

The point that we must not lose sight of, however, is that DA is based on a materialist psychology of mind, and so it requires moving beyond observation and contemplation toward active intervention that attempts to understand the object of study by changing it. In the case of L2 DA, this means providing forms of mediation that are believed to be helpful in guiding learner development, monitoring learner responsiveness, and altering mediation accordingly. In our view, the unification of assessment and teaching as a development-oriented activity is DA's greatest strength, and it must not be compromised for the sake of adhering to principles of controlled experimentation and theoretical assumptions borrowed from the natural sciences. On this point, Vygotsky's (1978, 1987) position is clear.

## Note

1   In Kozulin and Garb's study, no participant earned an LPS between .71 and .78 or between .89 and .99, which is why these ranges are missing from the categories they developed for grouping learners by LPS. In our L2 C-DA project, while we followed Kozulin and Garb's formula for calculating LPS as well as their logic of grouping learners according to high, mid, and low score ranges, our low-range began with .71, mid-range scores extended from to .99 through .72, and high scorers were 1.0 and above.

# 9
# CONCLUSION

Throughout this book we argued in favor of reconceptualizing the relation between theory/research and L2 educational practice, maintaining that practitioners (in this case, language educators) must not be mere consumers of research and nor should they be left to derive their own practices solely on the basis of intuition and experience. The theory–practice dialectic demanded by a Vygotskian perspective understands practice as the ultimate test of theory, and in this sense the L2 classroom becomes the site not simply for the application of theory but for its requisite elaboration and development. Classroom teachers therefore assume a primary, and ultimately more agentive, role in this enterprise than is possible when theory and practice remain separated. This is because disconnecting theory from practice either positions teachers as technicians who apply ready-made methods in a prescribed manner with no need to understand the theoretical principles or assumptions behind the methods or it negates the value of professional expertise altogether and substitutes intuition for conceptual understanding. A praxis orientation, in contrast, is contingent upon teachers' theoretical classroom activity—that is, their use of theoretical principles to orient classroom practices— and this, of course, is only possible if teachers have a well-developed theoretical understanding of their content (language) and of learner development.

Having said this, as we saw in Chapter 5, experimental-developmental research is also an important component for testing various aspects of the theory and is itself a form of praxis, albeit with limitations. For example, and as we alluded to in Chapter 4, testing the contributions of the various components of STI (i.e., materialized and material action, external speech, as communicated and dialogic thinking) is more readily achieved in experimental-developmental settings than in intact classrooms. Talyzina (1981), for instance, reported on extensive experiments that demonstrated that limiting explanations to verbal information only and eliminating the materialized or material stage in STI in an array of school subjects had negative consequences for development. For one thing, the students were able to recite the information provided verbally but they were unable to use the information in solving problems, unless the researcher continually repeated the information and reminded them to use it (p. 121). Moreover, omitting the external speech stage "inhibits the process of abstraction from nonessential properties, without which an action cannot be translated into conceptual form" (p. 127). Omitting both materialized knowledge and external speech stages completely blocked action and development of conceptual knowledge (p. 121). Clearly, it is much easier to make and assess the effects of such modifications to the framework under laboratory conditions. However, as we argued in Chapter 5, the findings of this research must ultimately be tested in intact classrooms. Talyzina (p. 325) recognized this requirement as well and in fact asserted that "an activities-oriented approach to the learning process and an understanding of the social nature of the relevant principles have simplified considerably the transition from laboratory experiments to school practice."

The theory of developmental education elaborated throughout the book represents our response to the perceived theory/research–practice gap that many SLA researchers and practitioners have been concerned with almost from the inception of the field of applied linguistics. Keep in mind that the theory is not one that is independent of practice. It is a theory that simultaneously informs and responds to practice; that is, as Vygotsky (1997a) insisted in his response to the crisis in psychology it is a theory grounded in praxis. In Chapter 1 we stated that a major goal of this book was to address R. Ellis's (2010) misconstrual of the theory with regard to the gap. Recall that Ellis (2010, p. 186) characterized the SCT position as untenable because teachers and researchers have different interests and inhabit different discourse worlds, one where theory, at best, is implicit and "action based" and another where theory is explicit and formulated in "technical knowledge." In an effort to bridge these worlds, Ellis (and others, including Long and Erlam) has proposed sets of principles based on the findings of SLA research and theorizing designed to inform and help teachers improve their pedagogical efforts. We singled out three of these principles to consider in our project: that instruction must be directed at implicit knowledge, that it must respect the learner's built-in syllabus, and that it requires extensive/rich input.

With regard to the principles, we argued in Chapter 4, on the basis of SCT as well as research in cognitive neuroscience, that in tutored settings properly organized explicit instruction can be an effective means of promoting learner development, and in fact, for older learners it may be the only means of guiding development. In Chapters 5, 6, and 8, we provided empirical evidence from experimental-developmental and intact classroom projects to support our argument. In Chapter 5, we considered evidence from a pilot study (and we recognize that caution is in order in this case until the full study is complete) that challenged the need to take account of learners' built-in syllabus. In this regard we argued, based on Vygotsky's theory of developmental education and the empirical STI research we discussed, that while rich and extensive input is required for language development to occur, well organized explicit instruction that integrates conceptual understanding of a language with practice offers particularly rich and extensive L2 knowledge.

The realization of Vygotskian praxis is ultimately contingent upon the activity of teachers, and therefore we believe it is appropriate to devote our final chapter to the implications of praxis for L2 teacher education. In fact, while Vygotsky's contributions to theory and to our understanding of child development are well established, it is less well known that he was also keenly interested in teacher education. Much of the work that occupied him from the mid-1920s onward was concerned with rendering the results of his psychological investigations accessible to an audience of public school teachers, whom he saw as playing a pivotal role in the re-imagining of Russian schools and, consequently, Russian society (Davydov, 1997).

## The Role of Teachers in Developmental Education

In *Educational Psychology*, which Vygotsky (1997c) intended as a textbook for "the rank-and-file teacher," he stated that his intent was to "promote the development of a rational understanding of the educational process in light of the most recent results of the science of psychology" (p. xvii). Vygotsky's view of education as scientifically grounded and of teachers as both practitioners and scientists themselves, is repeated throughout the text, as is his commitment to education as an activity concerned not with transferring knowledge from teacher to student but with creating special environments for learner development to occur: "For present day education, it is not so important to teach a certain quantity of knowledge as it is to inculcate the ability to acquire such knowledge and to make use of it" (p. 339). He also remarked that the teacher's role in this activity is different from how it has been previously conceived, as now the teacher "has to become the director of the social environment, which, moreover, is the only educational factor" (p. 339). Indeed, Davydov (1997) remarked that for Vygotsky development is a consequence of the teacher's ongoing efforts to create an appropriate environment and to mediate that environment to learners. According to Davydov, this vision of educational environments and of the role of the teacher sets Vygotsky's proposals apart from previous thinking while also challenging contemporary views of schooling.

In a chapter entitled "The psychological nature of the work of the teacher," Vygotsky identified and rejected two widely held beliefs about successful teaching, both of which are still prevalent today. The first portrayed the teacher as a fountain of knowledge whose responsibility is to act "as a simple pump, filling up the students with knowledge" (1997c, p. 339). Vygotsky's response was that such a teacher "can be replaced with no trouble at all by a textbook, by a dictionary, by a map, by a nature walk" because when a teacher simply lectures at students "he is only partially acting in the role of teacher" (p. 339). That is, the teacher was doing nothing more than providing bits of information but was not mediating a learner's engagement in educational activity—the source of development. As we explained in Chapter 4, it is this sort of instruction that leaves knowledge in verbal form only, disconnected from practical activity.

The other view of teachers that Vygotsky critiqued was that of a coach whose primary responsibility is to motivate students and offer affective support. In Vygotsky's view this greatly devalues the role of the teacher, emphasizing his personality over his professional expertise. From such a perspective "what is required of the teacher is enthusiasm, and it is with such inspiration that the teacher may nourish the students" (1997c, p. 341). While he acknowledged the importance of learner interest in the topic of study and the centrality of teacher–student relations, he maintained that these derive from the teacher's engagement with the learner in the social environment they have created, and not from the teacher's personality:

> Whether someone is an inspiring teacher is not the point in the least. Nor is the problem the fact that this inspiration does not always reach the student. The real point is that the student must be made to become enraptured by the very same thing.
>
> *(p. 343)*

The ultimate aim of education for Vygotsky is for students to become their own inspiration, and this occurs as they take on increased responsibility for their own learning, guiding their own involvement in the activities of schooling. However, this development is most likely to happen when the teacher mediates their engagement with the social environment of the school following scientific principles.

Vygotsky's repeated mention of science in his discussion of teacher activity revealed his commitment to the potential for education to drive learner development as well as his understanding of what is required for effective teaching. He proposed the term *scientific pedagogics* to capture this orientation to teaching, asserting that "what is required of the teacher is enhanced knowledge of the subject, and enhanced knowledge of the methodology of his craft" (1997c, p. 345). Vygotsky conceived of teachers not as tools or instruments of the educational process but as scientists in their own right. This position aligns with the argument we have made in this book for L2 developmental education. To recall our discussion in Chapter 1 of Vygotsky's dialectical understanding of the relation between theory and practice, rooted in Marx's *Eleventh Thesis on Feuerbach*, the teachers-as-scientists that Vygotsky envisioned are guided in practical activity by a theoretical orientation to both the subject matter and the learners, but at the same time their activity is essential to the scientific enterprise itself because it provides the necessary grounding and validation for the science.

This notion of scientific pedagogics may also be cast in terms of Vygotsky's distinction between spontaneous and scientific concepts, which we discussed in Chapter 4. In the case of L2 education, all teachers undoubtedly develop knowledge about language and learning from their experiences as L2 learners themselves as well as from noting what other teachers do and forming opinions about what appears "to work" in their particular context. Systematic, abstract conceptual understandings are (or should be, as we argue in this chapter) the subject of formal study in teacher education programs. Full conceptual understanding, which in this case we might refer to as a teacher's professional expertise, develops as teachers employ theoretical principles to guide their classroom practice, a theoretical re-orientation of practical activity. In fact, a theory–practice dualism, in contrast, works against teachers' development of professional expertise, privileging instead their knowledge gleaned from direct experience or advocating that abstract conceptual understanding is not relevant to their practical work, a position argued for by some scholars in applied linguistics (see Chapter 1). To be sure, teachers may arrive at theoretical principles on their own, but as we discussed in Chapter 4 in the context of learners' conceptual knowledge of language, it cannot be assumed that such knowledge will simply form on its own. Even if this were to happen, an exploratory discovery-based method is clearly less efficient than explicit presentation of concepts (see also Karpov, 2003).

Unfortunately, it is not at all clear that either practicing teachers or those currently enrolled in teacher education programs are developing the kind of expertise that underlies Vygotsky's scientific pedagogics. In the next section, we consider current trends in teacher education, including the *pre-service* preparation of future language teachers as well as the ongoing *in-service* professional development of current teachers. In both instances, we highlight work undertaken from a Vygotskian perspective that we believe helps move teachers toward a praxis-based orientation that is developmental education. As will be clear in our discussion, the context we are most familiar with is that of language teacher education in the U.S., and while we of course recognize that important differences exist among education systems around the world, experience suggests that the U.S. is not unique in its approach to preparing teachers and its assumptions about the kinds of knowledge teachers should possess. Similarly, some of our comments pertain specifically to the preparation of foreign language rather than ESL teachers. Here again, we recognize that these disciplines have different histories and that foreign language and ESL teachers do not necessarily follow similar career paths. Be that as it may, we contend that our arguments regarding the availability of opportunities for developing professional expertise apply to both populations. Readers will judge for themselves the extent to which our arguments hold for their particular contexts. Finally, we wish to emphasize that our intent is not merely to critique existing practices in teacher education. Indeed, a review of both the L2 and general education research literatures offers many examples of programs that heighten teacher awareness of their decision-making and help them to move beyond simple implementation of textbook exercises or test-driven curricula. Our position is that such efforts may be enhanced when the forms of expertise discussed above are made available to teachers. Put another way, the scientific pedagogics envisioned by Vygotsky overcomes the theory–practice dualism and places teachers in the strongest position possible to implement educational practices that unite theory and practice and where the teaching–learning (*obuchenie*) dialectic maximizes the development of all learners.

## L2 Teacher Education

In her overview of trends in L2 teacher education, Johnson (2009) situated contemporary models as reflective of broad epistemological shifts in the social sciences and humanities over at least the last 30 years. She observed that as these fields moved away from positivist traditions and toward a more interpretive orientation, teacher education has similarly departed from its long held commitment to identifying behaviors and practices of 'effective' teachers (i.e., teachers whose learners were successful, as indicated by test scores or other products or performances) for the purpose of scaling up such practices. Following Johnson, the assumption here was that teacher and student behaviors as well as features of the classroom, learner background, etc. could all be treated as variables, as in the tradition of controlled experimental research. A practice that was found to produce positive outcomes, however defined, in one classroom context should be transferrable to others. Johnson (2009, p. 8) explained that this research generally failed to improve educational practices, in part because the preference for controlled research designs effectively neutralized social, political, and historical dimensions of real classrooms, and consequently generated findings that tended to be "simplistic, almost commonplace."

Teacher education research in the L2 field, as in other areas, has turned increasingly toward interpretive approaches to understanding the reasons behind teacher practices and how these are shaped by the social contexts in which teachers operate. Johnson (2009, p. 9, emphasis added) characterized this change as "a shift from observational studies of *what* teachers do to ethnographic descriptions based on observation, description, and interviews with teachers about *why* they do what they do." In step with this re-orientation, both pre-service and in-service teacher education programs have come to emphasize teachers' active role in their own professional development. Increasingly, teachers are expected to construct their own knowledge about highly localized practices, often with the support of a community of practitioners (Darling-Hammond, 2006). For pre-service teachers, this community is comprised of those enrolled in courses devoted to pedagogical teaching methods. Under guidance of a course instructor, pre-service teachers engage in classroom observations of practicing teachers, one-to-one tutoring, and practice instructional sessions with peers.

Reflection on these experiences, during in-class discussions, daily journals, or other formal writing assignments, is often given a premium as a vehicle for knowledge construction.

With regard to in-service teacher education, Cochran-Smith and Lytle (2009) pointed out that professional learning communities remove teachers from the isolation of their individual classrooms and allow them to connect with others for the purpose of sharing experiences and collaborating on solutions to problems of practice. While in-service teacher education traditionally relied heavily on readings, workshops, and lectures to present teachers with abstract ideas that they might then apply to their own instructional contexts, the move toward teacher construction of localized knowledge has emphasized creating "a mediational space for teachers to engage in on-going, in-depth, systematic, and reflective examinations of their teaching practices and their students' learning" (Johnson, 2009, p. 95). In the general education literature, this orientation to teacher education has been referred to broadly as *inquiry-based* or *reflective teaching* (e.g., Allen & Blythe, 2004; Joyce & Showers, 1995; Schon, 1987).

Teacher inquiry models are marked by a process that generally involves identification and documentation of a problem of practice, sharing the documentation with colleagues, and discussion to examine the problem from multiple perspectives, thereby emphasizing the pooling of expertise within a community of practitioners to explore questions of curriculum sequencing, designing instructional material, assessing student progress, and evaluating new methods of instruction (Darling-Hammond, Hammerness, Grossman, Rust, & Shulman, 2005). As with pre-service teacher education, reflection is again framed as the necessary catalyst to ensure that the activities help participants arrive at new understandings of issues in their own practice and possibly generate new courses of action. Darling-Hammond et al. (2005) explain that reflecting on their experiences helps teachers to maintain a critical perspective on their practice, continuing to question what they do and how it may be done differently. Whether reflection occurs individually, as with teacher journals, or through dialogue within the community of practitioners, its broader aim is to help teachers develop a commitment to professional lifelong learning, and this includes recognizing the value of mentoring other teachers as well as turning to their colleagues as a resource for their own continued professional development (Dana & Yendol-Hoppey, 2009).

From the perspective of scientific pedagogics, our concern is that such approaches are not likely to consistently yield the intended professional outcomes for teachers unless requisite expertise, both in terms of the object of study (language in this case) and a coherent theory of development, is present in the group. Without such expertise, teachers have little to guide their instructional decisions aside from "tricks" and strategies offered by other teachers or formed on the basis of their own experiences. Our perspective on praxis leads us to conclude that experiential knowledge of this sort is not without value, but it must exist in relation to generalized, scientific knowledge if teachers are to have an appropriate orienting basis for their practice.

Consider, for instance, the knowledge required for teachers to engage in the two important lines of L2 educational praxis we discussed in previous chapters, Systemic Theoretical Instruction and Dynamic Assessment. It is difficult to imagine a teacher pursuing either of these sets of practices without an understanding of key principles of Vygotskian theory. In fact, even convincing teachers that L2 education can be developmental activity, that is, that studying an L2 can lead to new ways of thinking rather than simply to knowledge about the L2, can be challenging. For teachers to appreciate this point, they need a theory that presents a unified account of development and its relation to activity in the world, including schooling. Similarly, pursuing either STI or DA requires specialized knowledge of language. Both assign a central role to designing mediation to support learner L2 development, and mediation for this purpose presupposes a sophisticated understanding of the capabilities that learners are to develop. In the case of STI, teachers themselves need to understand important linguistic concepts and how these are realized in the particular language they are to teach. Otherwise, they are not likely to move beyond the rule-of-thumb presentation of grammar provided in language textbooks. Similarly, while DA offers a powerful framework for supporting learner development, it is not likely to be as effective if the language curriculum itself is oriented toward following simple grammar rules to produce a desired form. Such a curriculum, with an emphasis on correct answers in very narrow contexts, may certainly present opportunities to scaffold learners as they work to select an answer, but this is clearly different from developing an understanding of how the language presents resources for constructing and interpreting meanings. In the next section we consider more carefully pre-service teacher education programs and how these may be reconceived to more effectively orient teachers to function as scientists in the classroom, as Vygotsky put it. We then consider the implications of this perspective for ongoing, in-service teacher professional development.

## Developing Expertise in Pre-Service L2 Teacher Education

### Scientific Understanding of Learner Development

Vygotskian scientific pedagogics requires sophisticated understanding of both the dynamics of learner development as well as one's content area, in this case language. With regard to a theory of development, we are not suggesting a survey of various perspectives in psychology that have influenced educational practices, as often occurs in introductory-level university courses in educational psychology. A superficial treatment of several theories may well provide nothing more than a set of terms teachers can use to describe—rather than challenge—their existent beliefs and practices, and it is not likely to provide the depth of understanding of a coherent theory that can be drawn upon to guide decision-making in the classroom. As we have argued, Vygotsky provides us with such a theory and demands that we test and elaborate it through practice. Unfortunately, few texts currently available offer this kind of in-depth treatment of theory for pre-service teachers, particularly at an undergraduate level. That said, there are to our knowledge three notable exceptions that we wish to briefly comment on here. Each introduces key Vygotskian concepts in language designed to be accessible to undergraduate university students and each draws connections to teaching practices.

Bodrova and Leong's (2007) *Tools of the Mind: The Vygotskian Approach to Early Childhood Education*, now in a second edition, offers an excellent and highly readable discussion of the theory and how teachers may use it to guide classroom activity in support of learner development. While this book is not concerned with L2 development but with general cognitive development among pre-school children, we include it here because it is the earliest text to our knowledge that is commercially available and that specifically targets pre-service teachers for the purpose of introducing Vygotskian concepts and principles. Moreover, the organization of the book creates considerable potential to orient pre-service teachers to understanding how they may establish social environments in their classrooms that promote learner development. In the first few chapters Bodrova and Leong draw on Vygotsky's own writings as well as those of his immediate colleagues to present the theory itself, including explicit discussion of lower and higher psychological functions, mediation, leading activities of development, and the ZPD. Subsequent chapters then use these concepts to lead readers through interpreting instances of learner development and its relation to their engagement in pre-school activities as well as extended illustration of classroom practices that have been developed with these principles in mind. Among these are forms of play and storytelling that may engage pre-school children in developmental activities.

Bodrova and Leong's exclusive focus on early childhood education limits the book's relevance to pre-service L2 teachers, which is regrettable because the L2 field has not produced a text quite like *Tools of the Mind*. Bodrova and Leong's text thus has the advantage of demonstrating how the theory accounts for recognized phenomena in child development and then arguing for how the theory can lead this development through activity. Two books that present Vygotskian theory as a basis for L2 educational practice are *Methods for Teaching Foreign Languages: Creating a Community of Learners in the Classroom* by Hall (2001) and Swain, Kinnear, and Steinman's (2011) *Sociocultural Theory in Second Language Education: An Introduction Through Narratives*.

As announced by its title, Hall's (2001) text is not concerned with explicating Vygotskian theory per se but rather provides pre-service teachers with a background in several areas relevant to L2 pedagogy. Thus the first chapter serves to orient teachers to the object of study and argues for potential goals of L2 education by introducing notions of communicative and intercultural competence while the second chapter overviews a Vygotskian perspective on L2 development. With this as background, the remainder of the book is devoted to exploring how learner L2 abilities may be developed through organizing classroom activities that allow for a range of communicative practices. These activities are heavily influenced by standards for both language learning and language teacher education outlined by the American Council on the Teaching of Foreign Languages (ACTFL). As such, individual chapters are devoted to *interpersonal, interpretive,* and *presentational modes of communication* as foci for the L2 capabilities learners should be developing and the kinds of activities required for that development. A strength of the book, then, is its commitment to classroom activity.

Hall articulated a clear vision for L2 education around meaningful communication in the target language and offered concrete proposals for how teachers may realize this vision in their day-to-day practice. What is not always clear is how this vision is itself rooted in Vygotskian theory or how the exemplar activities described in the book are informed by the theory. Indeed, the ACTFL principles themselves make no reference to Vygotskian theory or to any other theory of development, and it is these that seem to most explicitly shape the L2 classroom community that Hall described. Terms such as ZPD, internalization, and private speech are introduced in the book and their use in interpreting L2 phenomena is illustrated through references to the research literature, but how practices may be organized on the basis of these concepts is less explicit. Similarly, there is no discussion of how the theory itself may be elaborated through teacher practice, and this is of course a crucial point from the perspective of praxis. Of course, as the text is intended for a course devoted to methods of language teaching, it may be the responsibility of the course instructor to help pre-service teachers make these connections, particularly as they move into practice teaching experiences in actual classrooms.

The link between teachers' own practices and experiences and Vygotskian theory is more prominent in Swain, Kinnear, and Steinman's (2011) *Sociocultural Theory in Second Language Education: An Introduction Through Narratives.* This text places the theory itself as the centerpiece for understanding L2 development and how this is shaped by social and cultural means. The text relies on narratives drafted by L2 teachers and learners to illustrate Vygotskian concepts, and the narratives themselves provide an immediate context to help teachers appreciate how the concepts offer insights into challenges learners experience and how these may be addressed pedagogically. Each chapter takes up a key feature of SCT, such as mediation, the ZPD, and scientific concepts. Chapters include an explanation of the central concept; presentation of the narrative; the authors' interpretation of the narrative and how it showcases the concept in question; discussion of related theoretical concepts; and finally comments concerning the concept's relevance to research and practice. These last two sections are particularly important. By helping readers draw connections among concepts in the theory, and in some cases ideas that have been proposed from outside a Vygotskian framework, the authors avoid a piecemeal presentation of theory as a collection of disconnected parts from which teachers may pick and choose. This increases the potential for teachers to find in the theory a basis to orient their educational work. Finally, the link back to both research and practice that concludes each chapter pushes teachers not only to consider implications for day-to-day classroom activity but also to interrogate their own assumptions about language, learners, and L2 development.

The three texts we have described, and there may be others that are devoted to different theoretical perspectives, offer opportunities for pre-service teachers to arrive at an understanding of development and how it may be guided through educational activity. In this way, the texts help teachers to appreciate the significance of their role in L2 education. However, our own experiences working with in-service and pre-service foreign language and ESL teachers lead us to believe that it is exceptional for L2 teachers to have a sophisticated understanding of development and its relation to pedagogy. More common is the course that surveys multiple theoretical perspectives, often leaving pre-service teachers confused over the differences and similarities among theories and their relevance to the classroom (e.g., what does it matter whether one subscribes to an innatist or cognitivist account of L2 abilities? Are i + 1 and ZPD the same concept or do they mean different things for classroom practice?). As we see in the next section, there are similar challenges for teachers to develop the other form of professional expertise necessary for a scientific L2 pedagogy, namely, knowledge about language.

### Scientific Understanding of Language

It goes without saying that a requisite level of proficiency in the target language is generally mandated and is either marked by native speaker status or measured by a formal language test (e.g., the ACTFL Oral Proficiency Interview and Written Proficiency Test, the TOEFL, the IELTS, etc.). While proficiency is undoubtedly a necessary part of a teacher's expert knowledge, it is not, in itself, sufficient for L2 developmental education. As we hope the reader can appreciate following our discussion in earlier chapters, it must not be assumed that as individuals develop proficiency in the L2 they spontaneously arrive at systematic, abstract knowledge of the language that will be helpful in teaching it to others. Similarly, we are not referring to whether teachers can recite, for instance, verb conjugations or rules for employing one preposition over another. As we explained in earlier chapters, rules of thumb, a staple of language instruction, are at best limited to particular instantiations of language in specific contexts, and, at worst, wrong. For teachers, what is more helpful is a conceptual understanding of the target language, and this kind of expertise is most likely to arise through university courses devoted to linguistic analysis.

Our argument here echoes discussions in the general teacher education research literature around *pedagogical content knowledge* (Shulman, 1987). Pedagogical content knowledge concerns not merely knowledge of one's discipline but, crucially, knowledge of how the discipline may be rendered accessible to learners. Following Shulman (1987), the notion of pedagogical content knowledge does not itself signal a commitment to a particular theory of development, but it does recognize that effective instruction is not merely transmitting knowledge from an expert to novices through a traditional lecture. Instead, pedagogical content knowledge comprises an understanding of how important concepts and principles in a discipline may be sequenced in a logical manner and represented by models and charts as well as how classroom tasks and dialogic interaction may be enlisted to support learner engagement with the material. In the case of L2 teachers, this kind of knowledge presupposes a sophisticated understanding of linguistic concepts and the relations among them with the goal of guiding learners to develop the ability to use the language as a tool to participate in and regulate concrete communicative events. A conceptual understanding of the language enables teachers to go beyond a form-focused, rule-based approach to instruction and to focus instead on language as a system of concepts that foregrounds the ways in which particular meanings may be created through intentional use of forms.

In Chapter 4, we argued strongly in favor of the relevance of cognitive linguistics[1] for L2 education. Cognitive linguistics not only lends itself well to the kinds of visual representations of language concepts that are required in STI, but it is itself predicated upon a view of language that assigns a central role to meaning as motivating the structural features of language that may be created and manipulated by users to meet their communicative needs. This understanding of language offers an especially relevant base of expert knowledge for teachers to draw upon in rethinking the content and sequencing of their language curriculum, the design of pedagogical materials, the planning and implementation of instructional activities, and the sorts of connections across features of the L2 as well as between the L2 and the L1 that may be made implicitly and explicitly during daily classroom interactions. The question we must consider, however, is the likelihood that pre-service L2 teachers will develop such an understanding of language. This is vitally important, because as Talyzina (1981, p.41) reminded us, "education and training are specially organized forms of joint activities of members of the older and of the younger generations that permit the latter to assimilate the experience of the preceding generations." Therefore, a great deal hinges on the quality of teacher knowledge of language developed by the generation they represent.

## Language Curriculum for Pre-Service Teachers

While the precise content of courses for pre-service teachers at any university is sure to reflect the background and expertise of faculty members, university programs that prepare students for a license to teach foreign languages in U.S. public schools must adhere to standards set by the relevant state Department of Education. Moreover, these programs typically submit to regular review and accreditation by national professional organizations. As a result, it is not difficult to determine the kinds of knowledge that are believed to be important for L2 educators. Indeed, most programs in the U.S. are influenced to some degree by the *ACTFL Standards for the Preparation of Foreign Language Teachers* (2002). The *Standards* comprise six core competencies that ACTFL, as the preeminent professional organization for foreign language educators in the U.S., has determined are necessary for pre-service teachers to develop if they are to be successful in the classroom.

Only two of the standards are concerned directly with classroom-relevant content: Standard 1—language, linguistics, comparison, and Standard 2—cultures, literatures, and cross-disciplinary concepts. The remaining four standards reflect a pedagogical orientation. The third standard, for example, addresses knowledge of theoretical perspectives on SLA and how it may ground instructional decisions, and the others each address dimensions of teachers' professional practice (i.e., methods of teaching and assessing). While Standard 2 focuses on literature and culture, a point we return to below, only Standard 1 is explicitly concerned with language itself. The document further specifies that Standard 1 comprises both "a high level of proficiency in the target language" (ACTFL Foreign Language Teacher Standards Writing Team, 2002 p. 3) as well as knowledge of "the linguistic features of the target language system" (p. 10). It is emphasized that pre-service teachers should

> understand and can describe how words are formed (morphological rules), how sentences are put together (syntactic patterns), and how meaning is conveyed (semantics). They [pre-service teachers] understand and can describe the rules for word and sentence formation such as those pertaining to the verb system (time, aspect, mood), agreement (nouns and adjectives/ articles, verbs and subjects), word order, the pronominal system, use of key prepositions/postpositions, and interrogatives.
>
> *(p. 10)*

It is worth pointing out that despite advances in the field of linguistics and more recent approaches to understanding the relation between form and meaning, as we discussed in Chapter 4, the above description of linguistic knowledge expected of pre-service teachers clearly emphasizes rules and structures (i.e., form) over meaning. The extent to which this more traditional kind of linguistic knowledge positions teachers to design materials and activities that help learners internalize conceptual knowledge about language is an open question. Our concern is that dissociating meaning and form and privileging the latter is not conducive to developing functionally useful conceptual knowledge.

To understand the role afforded to linguistics and language analysis in foreign language pre-service teacher education programs at U.S. universities, we commissioned a survey of the websites of a total of 222 universities in the U.S.[2] These universities included private, liberal arts colleges, small teaching-oriented public institutions, and large research universities. In line with trends in L2 offerings in U.S. public schools, the languages offered most frequently include Spanish, French, and German, with some universities advertising programs in Latin, Russian, and Italian as well as Mandarin, the popularity of which has increased dramatically in American schools in recent years.

Among the universities that display their full language curriculum online, certain courses are readily identifiable as they carry titles such as *Introduction to Linguistics*. Not surprisingly, descriptions of such courses, when available, suggest a survey approach to linguistics, with particular readings and class meetings devoted to syntax, phonology, morphology, etc. It is not universally the case that teacher education programs require such an introductory course; in some programs this kind of course is offered as an elective, while in other programs there are no linguistics courses included in the curriculum. Less common still are programs offering courses devoted to specific areas of linguistics (e.g., a course on Spanish phonology), and even among such programs none of those surveyed requires students to complete a full sequence of courses in all areas of linguistics. We do not wish to suggest that the language curricula we examined do not offer other opportunities for pre-service teachers to study language itself. In fact, most programs list advanced grammar courses among their requirements. Unfortunately, in most cases these more often than not entail a rehash of the rules of thumb that are propagated in language programs and even when they do not follow this tradition, these courses are normally addressed to all students specializing in the language for whatever reason and therefore do not take account of the conceptual needs of those wishing to become language teachers. Programs in French frequently offer courses in *stylistiques*, and while they may be useful for their analytical focus, they too do not meet the pedagogical standards we are arguing for.

In contrast to the relatively marginalized role of linguistics and language analysis courses in U.S. university foreign language teacher preparation programs, the same survey revealed considerable curricular offerings in literature courses. This may be partly attributed to the collective expertise of faculty in those departments, where literary scholars are far more prevalent than linguists. Stern (1983) explains that historically in the U.S. the purpose for studying other languages, especially European languages, was linked to philology (i.e., the study of written texts) as the literature associated with a particular nation or cluster of nations was viewed as representative of the best of that culture. Studying French, for instance, was understood as a means to access great works of literature and philosophy with which educated people should be familiar. While the 20th Century saw a marked shift toward language study to increase economic opportunities, and in the U.S. for off-and-on national security needs (see Lantolf & Sunderman, 2001) especially as English asserted itself as the language of a global market place, the bent toward literary and cultural studies remains the goal in many foreign language programs. Consequently, pre-service foreign language teachers in the U.S. are likely to find that once they have passed through introductory courses the remainder of their study is dominated by courses in literature, history, and culture.

While we do not dispute the value of studying literature or any discipline within the human sciences, we do question the privileged status of literary knowledge in programs that ostensibly prepare language teachers. Again, we are not arguing that the study of literature should be removed from teacher education programs; recall Yáñez-Prieto's (2008) study discussed in Chapter 6. We are, however, arguing for opening up more space in the curriculum for in-depth and pedagogically viable knowledge of the language. We stress these two components because courses that survey various theories of language are highly unlikely to provide in-depth knowledge and courses that provide in-depth knowledge are not always concerned with its pedagogical viability. The survey turned up both types of courses in teacher education programs. Unfortunately, we were unable to identify any programs that included significant course work on language of the type we are proposing.

## In-Service L2 Teacher Education Through Praxis

To date, the most fully developed example of partnering with L2 classroom teachers to both guide instructional practice and further refine the theory has centered on DA. As an initial step in this line of work, we developed the *Teachers Guide* (Lantolf & Poehner, 2006) to DA. To recall our discussion from Chapter 8, the *Guide* features a monograph-length manuscript introducing the ZPD and leading models of DA as well as video of mediator–learner interactions to diagnose and promote L2 development. Suggested readings, discussion questions, and enrichment activities invite teachers to consider connections between the ideas presented and their own experience, to form their own interpretations of data and examples presented, and to begin to plan ways in which the principles may be brought into their instructional settings.

Now in its second edition (Lantolf & Poehner, 2011b), the *Guide* has been revised to include two of the DA projects described in Chapter 8, namely its use to diagnose listening comprehension (Ableeva, 2010) and to structure classroom interactions in an elementary school L2 setting (Lantolf & Poehner, 2011a). A strength of the *Guide* is that it does not provide a prescriptive approach to implementing DA but rather presents the theoretical rationale and principles that help teachers understand how providing mediation to learners as they engage in cooperative tasks can both diagnose their L2 abilities while simultaneously supporting ongoing development. The precise forms of action that this theoretical position leads to are the result of dialogue and planning with the teachers rather than a pre-determined intervention or experiment designed for research purposes alone. In the case of Tracy, the elementary school Spanish teacher, an unintended outcome of this partnership was that it motivated her to pursue doctoral studies in the L2 field and to undertake her own research–practice collaborations with teachers focused on DA.

This manner of functioning collectively with teachers to re-orient L2 classroom practices and to understand its relation to ZPD activity is the primary focus of a project currently underway to produce a *Casebook* of DA (Poehner, in preparation). Intended as a companion to the *Guide*, the *Casebook* documents the experiences of language teachers as they come to understand Vygotskian principles of mediation, internalization, and the ZPD and employ these to reformulate classroom activities to more effectively guide learner L2 development. Each of the cases is distinguished by the L2 in question, the age and level of learners, and the teacher's curricular goals. For instance, one of the cases emerges from a collaboration with another teacher in the same Spanish elementary program as Tracy that we discussed in Chapter 8. This teacher, Anne (a pseudonym), also conducted 15-minute lessons each day following a curriculum she organized around thematic units, usually showcasing countries or geographic regions where Spanish is spoken. Anne was introduced to DA through the *Guide*, and she developed an interest in attempting to follow a DA approach to help her more effectively track her students' progress and determine when additional instruction is necessary. She saw DA as particularly relevant to lessons focused on language forms, as her curriculum, while thematically organized, emphasized features of Spanish grammar such as verb conjugation and tense, noun–adjective agreement, and definite and indefinite articles. We point out that Anne did not have the linguistic preparation of the kind we are proposing, which emphasizes meaning, and the *Guide* is not intended to provide this knowledge. Like Tracy, Anne began by scripting mediating prompts that she would employ during lessons focused on grammar, and she devised a grid for tracking the level of prompting individuals required during the lessons.

The details of Anne's use of DA are beyond the scope of the present discussion but are reported in full by Davin (2011). What is of interest here and is the focus of the *Casebook* description is how her engagement with DA represented a form of professional development for Anne that produced changes in her perception of the kinds of language activities that are beneficial to learners as well as the merits of engaging in dialogue with students when challenges arise. Anne cooperated with a team of researchers (Poehner & Davin, 2013) and invited them to observe and record her lessons both prior to, during, and following the 2-week period during which she explicitly used DA. This allowed the researchers to document changes to Anne's practice, which were then discussed in interviews with her.

Anne expressed that DA fulfilled her intent to provide more individualized feedback and support to learners by determining the precise level of prompting required rather than simply offering explicit corrective feedback. More interesting was that at the end of the 2-week period, she reported that the interventionist approach she had followed constrained her ability to tailor her interactions with learners and for that reason she ceased scripting prompts in advance and instead employed an interactionist DA approach. As Anne herself explained, "I felt sometimes I wasn't always responding to the students' zone of proximal development ... maybe they didn't need to go through this whole thing or maybe they needed a different prompt to kind of help them" (Poehner & Davin, 2013, p. 12). She further stated that the process of aligning mediation with learner needs based on their responsiveness happened "naturally" for her as she developed her abilities as an effective mediator. In Anne's words, "I think you kind of start to internalize the things that the students might need to get them to where you want them to be" (p. 12).

According to Poehner and Davin (2013), these remarks were borne out in the quality of Anne's interactions with learners, which frequently involved a greater overall number of turns-at-talk than during the period preceding her use of DA and were also marked by the provision of various kinds of prompts that increased in their level of explicitness but were not precisely the same for every learner, reflecting differences in learner needs as well as the more open-ended and dialogic nature of her exchanges with learners. We would add that Anne's experience is in line with the position elaborated earlier regarding the importance of teachers' understanding of a theory of development to orient their practice. As Anne internalized Vygotskian principles, she became adept at structuring her interactions with learners accordingly rather than simply adhering to a set script. That is, she gained control over the tool (in this case, a system for prompting learners) rather than allowing the tool to control her.

Related to the change in quality of Anne's interactions with her class, Poehner and Davin (2013) uncovered shifts in the kinds of language tasks she used with her learners. While L2 forms continued to enjoy a central role in the curriculum, the tasks put before the students became much more open-ended, allowing for more than right-or-wrong or single-word responses and instead requiring learners to use the language more creatively and for personal expression. For example, fill-in type exercises that required learners to merely mark adjective agreement with nouns for number and gender were replaced with an activity in which learners were asked to describe their favorite sports teams, including details of the players' uniforms. To be sure, noun–adjective agreement frequently surfaced during the activity as an area where learners made mistakes and required mediation, but the object of the activity shifted from controlling L2 forms to expressing meanings in the L2. In an interview, Anne acknowledged this change of focus and accounted for it this way:

> It [DA interaction] helps the students to build their confidence and allow them to make meaning on their own terms, and use the language on their own terms ... it gives them a better understanding [of] how the language

works and as we said they kind of internalize that process and use it when they're creating on their own.

*(Poehner & Davin, 2013, p. 19)*

In our view, Anne's remark underscores our argument that while DA principles might be called into service to support learners regardless of the focus of an L2 curriculum, DA will most likely realize its full potential to promote learner development when it is employed in tandem with a view of language that emphasizes resources for constructing and interpreting meaning. Of course, in Anne's case, her use of DA was not to rethink her understanding of L2 curricula but had to do with tracking and supporting learner progress through the established curriculum. Similarly, the researchers had not planned this collaboration for the purpose of altering Anne's understanding of the value of different kinds of classroom language tasks. Rather, Anne's shift toward activities that place a greater emphasis on meaning was a spin-off (see Wertsch, 1998) of her use of DA and in particular her thinking through with learners how language forms create possibilities for expressing meaning.[3]

Negueruela (2011) proposes a model for understanding the relationship between teacher beliefs and actions that is helpful in interpreting the changes observed in Anne's practice. Proceeding from a Vygotskian dialectical perspective, Negueruela argued that intentionally mediating in-service teacher reflection on classroom activity has the potential to bring their everyday beliefs about language learning and teaching into contact with L2 theory and research. In dialectical terms, Negueruela understands the former as the *thesis* that functions as the teachers' current orienting basis for action and the latter as an *anti-thesis*. By bringing these together in discussions of problems of practice, it is possible to support connections between them, helping teachers to understand theory through its relevance to their practice but also prompting them to regard, and modify, their practice anew through a theoretically informed lens.

In his work with in-service L2 teachers, Negueruela pointed out these experiences allow teachers to formulate a new orienting basis, a *synthesis* that reflects both their everyday experiences and their knowledge of theory. This new basis for action allows teachers to move beyond models that emphasize reflecting on the past or imagining possible futures and to instead begin to take theoretically-grounded actions that allow them to construct a new future in the here-and-now. Negueruela's (2011) recommendations align nicely with the arguments we have made regarding the implications of Vygotskian praxis for teacher education. Of course, it is not only teachers who stand to benefit from such activity but also their students as well as others interested in understanding what it means to develop abilities in an L2 and how these processes can be shaped through education. To echo Vygotsky's (1997a) analysis of the *Crisis in psychology*, which ultimately concluded that practical psychology is the future of all psychology, conceived as a unified scientific discipline, we submit that the future of L2 developmental studies lies in the activity of teachers and learners.

## Notes

1   We acknowledged in Chapter 4 that other theories of language, such as Systemic Functional Linguistics and Integrational Linguistics, also foreground meaning and therefore may provide viable linguistic conceptual knowledge. Thus, other linguistic theories may prove superior to cognitive linguistics; we are not wedded in perpetuity to this theory. It is for us an attractive option because of its commitment to meaning, its materialization of concepts, its commitment to general cognitive principles rather than innate modular knowledge, and its usage-based commitment, which for us, means that language is a tool shaped by users in service to their concrete communicative goals.

2   We are indebted to Kimberly Buescher, a doctoral student in applied linguistics and an RA in the Center for Language Acquisition at Penn State, for her invaluable work in compiling the survey.

3   We critique our own work for not yet having produced a *Guide* for STI or one that integrates DA with STI, and we hope to redress this shortcoming in the near future. The task of producing a *Guide* for STI, however, is complex given the importance we attribute to in-depth conceptual knowledge of an L2. Although some examples of STI lessons can be included in a *Guide* to illustrate how the procedures and stages can be implemented, this would not be sufficient. What is needed are L2 STI curricula infused with appropriate conceptual explanations and materializations of these concepts for individual languages and at all levels of instruction. We encourage others in the field with requisite knowledge of specific languages to undertake this enterprise.

# REFERENCES

Ableeva, R. (2010). *Dynamic assessment of listening comprehension in L2 French.* Unpublished Ph.D. dissertation. The Pennsylvania State University, University Park, PA.

Ableeva, R., & Lantolf, J. P. (2011). Mediated dialogue and the microgenesis of second language listening comprehension. *Assessment in Education: Principles, Policy & Practice, 18,* 133–149.

ACTFL Foreign Language Teacher Standards Writing Team. (2002). *American Council on the Teaching of Foreign Languages (ACTFL) program standards for the preparation of foreign language teachers.* Available at www.actfl.org. Retrieved November 19, 2008.

Agar, M. (1994). *Language shock. Understanding the culture of conversation.* New York: Morrow.

Aljaafreh, A., & Lantolf, J. P. (1994). Negative feedback as regulation and second language learning in the Zone of Proximal Development. *The Modern Language Journal, 78,* 465–483.

Allen, D., & Blythe, T. (2004). *The facilitator's book of questions: Tools for looking together at student and teacher work.* New York: Teachers College Press.

Allwright, D. (2005). From teaching points to learning opportunities and beyond. *TESOL Quarterly, 39,* 9–31.

Antón, M. (2009). Dynamic assessment of advanced language learners. *Foreign Language Annals, 42,* 576–598.

Arbib, M. A. (2002). The mirror system, imitation, and the evolution of language. In K. Dautenhahn & C. L. Nehaniv (Eds.), *Imitation in animals and artifacts (Complex adaptive systems)* (pp. 229–280). Cambridge, MA: MIT Press.

Arievitch, I. M., & Haenen, J. P. P. (2005). Connecting sociocultural theory and educational practice: Gal'perin's approach. *Educational Psychologist, 40,* 155–165.

Arievitch, I. M., & Stetsenko, A. (2000). The quality of cultural tools and cognitive development: Gal'perin's perspective and its implications. *Human Development, 43,* 69–92.

Atkinson, D. (2002). Toward a sociocognitive approach to second language acquisition. *Modern Language Journal, 86,* 525–545.

Atkinson, D. (2012). Introduction: Cognitivism and second language acquisition. In D. Atkinson (Ed.), *Alternative approaches to second language acquisition* (pp. 1–23). Oxford: Routledge.

Baddeley, A. D., & Hitch, G. J. (1974). Working memory. In G. H. Bower (Ed.), *The psychology of learning and motivation* (Vol. 8, pp. 47–89). New York: Academic Press.

Bakhurst. D. (1991). *Consciousness and revolution in Soviet philosophy. From the Bolsheviks to Evald Ilyenkov*. Cambridge: Cambridge University Press.

Baldwin, J. M. (1915). *Mental development in the child and the race*. New York: Macmillan.

Belcher, D. (2007). A bridge too far? *TESOL Quarterly, 41*, 396–399.

Bodrova, E., & Leong, D. J. (2007). *Tools of the mind. The Vygotskian approach to early childhood education* (2nd ed.). Upper Saddle River, NJ: Pearson/Merrill Prentice Hall.

Boers, F., & Lindstromberg, S. (2008). From empirical findings to pedagogical practice. In F. Boers & S. Lindstromberg (Eds.), *Cognitive linguistic approaches to teaching vocabulary and phraseology* (pp. 375–394). Berlin: Mouton de Gruyter.

Boivin, N. (2008). *Material cultures, material minds. The impact of things on human thought, society and evolution*. New York: Cambridge University Press.

Bonilla, C. (2012). *Testing processability theory in L2 Spanish: Can readiness or markedness predict development?* Unpublished doctoral dissertation. University of Pittsburgh, Pittsburgh, PA.

Bronfenbrenner, U. (1977). Toward an experimental ecology of human development. *American Psychologist, 32*, 513–531.

Brooks, L., & Swain, M. (2009). Languaging in collaborative writing: Creating of and response to expertise. In A. Mackey & C. Polio (Eds.), *Multiple perspectives on interaction. Second language research in honor of Susan M. Gass* (pp. 58–89). New York: Routledge.

Büchel, F. P., & Scharnhorst, U. (1993). The Learning Potential Assessment Device (LPAD): Discussion of theoretical and methodological problems. In J. H. M Hamers, K. Sijtsma, & A. J. J. M. Ruijssenaars (Eds.), *Learning potential assessment: Theoretical, methodological and practical issues* (pp. 83–111). Amsterdam: Swets & Zeitlinger.

Budoff, M. (1968). Learning potential as a supplementary testing procedure. In J. Hellmuth (Ed.), *Learning disorders. Vol. 3*. Seattle, WA: Special Child.

Budoff, M. (1987). The validity of learning potential assessment. In C. S. Lidz (Ed.), *Dynamic assessment: An interactional approach to evaluating learning potential* (pp. 53–81). New York: Guilford Press.

Budoff, M., & Friedman, M. (1964). "Learning potential" as an assessment approach to the adolescent mentally retarded. *Journal of Consulting Psychology, 28*, 434–439.

Bull, W. E., & Lamadrid, E. E. (1971). Our grammar rules are hurting us. *Modern Language Journal, 55*, 449–454.

Burgess, R. V. (2000). Reuven Feuerstein: Propelling the change, promoting continuity. In A. Kozulin & Y. Rand (Eds.), *Experience of mediated learning: An impact of Feuerstein's theory in education and psychology* (pp. 3–20). Oxford: Pergamon Press.

Bygate, M. (2005). Applied linguistics: A pragmatic discipline, a generic discipline? *Applied Linguistics, 26*, 568–581.

Calero, M. D., & E. Navarro. (2004). Relationship between plasticity, mild cognitive impairment and cognitive decline. *Archives of Clinical Neuropsychology, 19*, 653–660.

Campione, J. C., Brown, A. L., Ferrara, R. A., & Bryant, N. R. (1984). The zone of proximal development: Implications for individual differences and learning. In B. Rogoff & J. V. Wertsch (Eds.), *Children's learning in the 'Zone of Proximal Development'* (pp. 77–91). San Francisco: Jossey-Bass.

Carlson, J. S., & Wiedl, K. H. (1992). Principles of Dynamic Assessment: The application of a specific model. *Learning and Individual Differences, 4,* 153–166.

Carroll, S., & Swain, M. (1993). Explicit and implicit negative feedback: An empirical study of the learning of linguistic generalizations. *Studies in Second Language Acquisition, 15,* 357–386.

Casasanto, D., & Jasmin, K. (2012). The hands of time: Temporal gestures in English speakers. *Cognitive Linguistics, 23,* 643–674.

Celce-Murcia, M., & Larsen-Freeman, D. (1999). *The grammar book: An ESL/EFL teacher's course* (2nd ed.). Rowley, MA: Newbury House.

Chaiklin, S. (2003). The zone of proximal development in Vygotsky's analysis of learning and instruction. In A. Kozulin, B. Gindis, V. S. Ageyev, & S. M. Miller (Eds.), *Vygotsky's educational theory in cultural context* (pp. 39–64). Cambridge: Cambridge University Press.

Chapelle, C. (2007). Pedagogical implications in TESOL Quarterly? Yes, please. *TESOL Quarterly, 41,* 404–406.

Clark, A. (2008). Where brain, body, and world collide. In C. Knappett & L. Malafouris (Eds.), *Material agency* (pp. 1–18). Boston: Springer.

Clarke, M. A. (1994). The dysfunctions of theory/practice discourse. *TESOL Quarterly, 28,* 9–26.

Cochran-Smith, M., & Lytle, S. L. (2009). *Inquiry as stance: Practitioner research in the next generation.* New York: Teachers College Press.

Cole, M. (1996). *Cultural psychology. A once and future discipline.* Cambridge, MA: Belknapp Press.

Cole, M. (2009). The perils of translation: A first step in reconsidering Vygotsky's theory of development in relation to formal education. *Mind, Culture, Activity: An International Journal, 16,* 291–295.

Cole, M., Levitin, K., & Luria, A. (2006). *Autobiography of Alexander Luria: A dialogue with the making of mind.* Mahwah, NJ: Lawrence Erlbaum Associates.

Corder, S. P. (1973). *Introducing applied linguistics.* New York: Penguin Books.

Corder, S. P. (1978). Learner language and teacher talk. *Audio-Visual Language Journal, 16,* 5–13.

Courtin, C. (2000). The impact of sign language on the cognitive development of Deaf children. The case of theories of mind. *Journal of Deaf Studies and Deaf Education, 5,* 266–276.

Crookes, G. (1998). On the relationship between second and foreign language teachers and research. *TESOL Journal, 7*(3), 6–11.

Dana, N. F., & Yendol-Hoppey, D. (2009). *The reflective educator's guide to classroom research: Learning to teach and teaching to learn through practitioner inquiry* (2nd ed.). Thousand Oaks, CA: Corwin Press.

Darling-Hammond, L. (2006). *Powerful teacher education: Lessons from exemplary programs.* San Francisco: Jossey-Bass.

Darling-Hammond, L., Hammerness, K., Grossman, P., Rust, F., & Shulman, L. (2005). The design of teacher education programs. In L. Darling-Hammond & J. Bransford (Eds.), *Preparing teachers for a changing world: What teachers should learn and be able to do* (pp. 390–441). San Francisco: Jossey-Bass.

Davin, K. J. (2011). Group Dynamic Assessment in an early foreign language learning program: Tracking movement through the Zone of Proximal Development. Unpublished Ph.D. dissertation, The University of Pittsburgh, Pittsburgh, PA.

Davydov, V. V. (1997). Introduction: Lev Vygotsky and educational psychology. In *Educational psychology*, L. S. Vygotsky (pp. xxi–xxxix). Boca Raton, FL: St. Lucie Press.

Davydov, V. V. (2004). *Problems of developmental instruction. A theoretical and experimental psychological study*. Moscow: Akademiya.

DeKeyser, R. M. (1998). Beyond focus on form: Cognitive perspectives on learning and practicing second language grammar. In C. J. Doughty & J. Williams (Eds.), *Focus on form in second language acquisition* (pp. 42–63). New York: Cambridge University Press.

DeKeyser, R. M. (2003). Implicit and explicit learning. In C. J. Doughty & M. H. Long (Eds.), *Handbook of second language learning* (pp. 313–348). Oxford: Blackwell.

DeKeyser, R. M. (2007). Skill acquisition theory. In B. VanPatten & J. Williams (Eds.), *Theories in second language acquisition. An introduction* (pp. 97–114). Mahwah, NJ: Erlbaum.

DeKeyser, R. M., & Criado, R. (2013a). Automatization, skill acquisition, and practice in second language acquisition. In C. A. Chapelle (Ed.), *The encyclopedia of applied linguistics*. London: Blackwell. doi: 10.1002/9781405198431.wbeal0067.

DeKeyser, R. M., & Criado, R. (2013b). Practice in second language instruction. In C. A. Chapelle (Ed.), *The encyclopedia of applied linguistics*. London: Blackwell. doi: 10.1002/9781405198431.wbeal0925.

Di Pietro, R. J. (1987). *Strategic interaction. Learning languages through scenarios*. Cambridge: Cambridge University Press.

Egan, K. (1983). *Education and psychology: Plato, Piaget, and scientific psychology*. New York: Teachers College Press.

Elkonin, D. (1998). Epilogue. In R. W. Rieber (Ed.), *The collected works of L. S. Vygotsky. Vol. 5. Child psychology*. New York: Plenum.

Ellis, N. (2009). Optimizing the input: Frequency and sampling in usage-based and form-focused learning. In C. Doughty & M. H. Long (Eds.), *The handbook of language teaching* (pp. 139–158). Malden, MA: Wiley-Blackwell.

Ellis, R. (1989). Are classroom and naturalistic acquisition the same? A study of the classroom acquisition of German word order rules. *Studies in Second Language Acquisition*, *11*, 303–328.

Ellis, R. (1997). SLA and language pedagogy: An educational perspective. *Studies in Second Language Acquisition*, *19*, 69–92.

Ellis, R. (2005a). Measuring implicit and explicit knowledge of a second language. A psychometric study. *Studies in Second Language Acquisition*, *27*, 141–172.

Ellis, R. (2005b). Principles of instructed language learning. *System*, *33*, 209–224.

Ellis, R. (2006). Modeling learning difficulty and second language proficiency: The differential contributions of implicit and explicit knowledge. *Applied Linguistics*, *27*, 431–463.

Ellis, R. (2008). *The study of second language acquisition* (2nd ed.). Oxford: Oxford University Press.

Ellis, R. (2010). Second language acquisition, teacher education, and language pedagogy. *Language Teaching*, *43*, 182–201.

Ellis, R. (2012). *Language teaching research and language pedagogy*. West Sussex: Wiley-Blackwell.

Ellis, R., & Barkhuizen, G. (2005). *Analysing learner language*. Oxford: Oxford University Press.

Ellis, R., Loewen, S., Elder, C., Erlam, R., Philp, J., & Reinders, H. (2009). *Implicit and explicit knowledge in second language learning, testing and teaching*. Bristol, UK: Multilingual Matters.

Erlam, R. (2008). What do researchers know about language teaching? Bridging the gap between SLA research and language pedagogy. *Innovations in Language Learning and Teaching, 2,* 253–267.

Evans, G. W., & Schamberg, M. A. (2009). Childhood poverty, chronic stress, and adult working memory. *Proceedings of the National Academy of Sciences, 106*(16), 6545–6549.

Farley, A., & McCollam, K. (2004). Learner readiness and L2 production in Spanish: Processability theory on trial. *Estudios de lingüística aplicada, 40,* 47–69.

Felix, S. W. (1981). The effect of formal instruction on second language acquisition. *Language Learning, 31,* 87–112.

Ferreira, M. (2005). *A concept-based approach to writing instruction: From the abstract concept to the concrete performance.* Unpublished doctoral dissertation, The Pennsylvania State University, University Park, PA.

Feuerstein, R., Falik, L., Rand, Y., & Feuerstein, R. S. (2003). *Dynamic assessment of cognitive modifiability.* Jerusalem: ICELP Press.

Feuerstein, R., Feuerstein, R. S., & Falik, L. H. (2010). *Beyond smarter: Mediated learning and the brain's capacity for change.* New York: Teachers College, Columbia University.

Feuerstein, R., Rand, Y., & Hoffman, M. B. (1979). *The dynamic assessment of retarded performers: The learning potential assessment device, theory, instruments, and techniques.* Baltimore: University Park Press.

Feuerstein, R., Rand, Y., & Rynders, J. E. (1988). *Don't accept me as I am. Helping retarded performers excel.* New York: Plenum.

Fogel, A. (1991). *Developing through relationships: Origins of communication, self, and culture.* Chicago: University of Chicago Press.

Fulcher, G. (2010). *Practical language teaching.* London: Hodder Education.

Gallego, M., & Vasquez, O. A. (2011). Praxis-in-dis-coordination. In P. R. Portes & S. Salas (Eds.), *Vygotsky in 21st century society. Advances in cultural historical theory and praxis with non-dominant communities* (pp. 214–228). New York: Peter Lang.

Gal'perin, P. Ya. (1957). An experimental study in the formation of mental actions. In B. Simon (Ed.), *Psychology in the Soviet Union* (pp. 213–225). London: Routledge and Kegan Paul.

Gal'perin, P. (1967) On the notion of internalization. *Soviet Psychology, 5,* 28–33.

Gal'perin, P. Ya. (1969). Stages in the development of mental acts. In M. Cole & I. Maltzman (Eds.), *A handbook of contemporary Soviet psychology* (pp. 249–272). New York: Basic Books.

Gal'perin, P. Ya. (1970). An experimental study in the formation of mental actions. In E. Stones (Ed.), *Readings in educational psychology. Learning and teaching* (pp. 142–154). London: Methuen.

Gal'perin, P. Ya. (1979). The role of orientation in thought. *Soviet Psychology, 18,* 19–45.

Gal'perin, P. Ya. (1989). Mental actions as a basis for the formation of thoughts and images. *Soviet Psychology, 27*(2), 45–64.

Gal'perin, P. Ya. (1992). Stage-by-stage formation as a method of psychological investigation. *Journal of Russian and East European Psychology, 30*(4), 60–80.

Ganem-Gutierrez, G. A., & Harun, H. (2011). Verbalisation as a mediational tool for understanding tense-aspect marking in English: An application of Concept-Based Instruction. *Language Awareness, 20,* 99–119.

Gao, X. D. (2005). *Noun phrase morphemes and topic development in L2 Mandarin Chinese: A processability perspective.* Unpublished doctoral dissertation, University of Wellington, Victoria, NZ.

Garcia, P. (2012). *Verbalizing in the second language classroom: The development of the grammatical concept of aspect.* Unpublished doctoral dissertation, University of Massachusetts, Amherst, MA.

Gass, S. M., & Mackey, A. (2007). Input, interaction, and output in second language acquisition. In B. VanPatten & J. Williams (Eds.), *Theories in second language acquisition. An introduction* (pp. 175–200). New York: Routledge.

Gass, S. M., & Mackey, A. (Eds.). (2012). *The Routledge handbook of second language acquisition.* New York: Routledge.

Gattegno, C. (1963). *Teaching foreign languages in schools: The silent way.* New York: Educational Solutions.

Gergen, K., & Gergen, M. (2002). Toward a cultural constructionist psychology. In M. Hildebrand-Nilshon, C-W. Kim, & D. Papadopoulos (Eds.), *Kultur in der Psychologie* (pp. 47–64). Heidelberg, Germany: Asanger Verlag.

Gibbs, R. W., Jr. (2005). *Embodiment and cognitive sciences.* Cambridge: Cambridge University Press.

Gillon Dowens, M., Vergara, M., Barber, H. A., & Carreiras, M. (2009). Morphosyntactic processing in late second-language learners. *Journal of Cognitive Neuroscience, 22*(8), 1870–1887.

Glutting, J. J., & McDermott, P. A. (1990). Principles and problems in learning potential. In C. R. Reynolds & R. W. Kamphaus (Eds.), *Handbook of psychological and educational assessment of children. Intelligence and achievement* (pp. 277–295). New York: Guilford.

Goldman, A. I. (2005). Imitation, mind reading, and simulation. In S. Hurley & N. Chater (Eds.), *Perspectives on imitation. From neuroscience to social sciences. Volume 2. Imitation, human development, and culture* (pp. 79–94). Cambridge, MA: MIT Press.

Greenwood, J. (2003). Wundt, *Völkerpsychologie*, and experimental social psychology. *Historical Psychology, 6*, 70–88.

Guthke, J. (1992). Learning tests—The concept, main research findings, problems, and trends. *Learning and Individual Differences, 4*, 137–151.

Guthke, J., & Beckmann, J. F. (2000). The learning test concept and its applications in practice. In C. S. Lidz & J. G. Elliott (Eds.), *Dynamic assessment: prevailing models and applications* (pp. 17–69). Amsterdam: Elsevier.

Haenen, J. (1996). *Piotr Gal'perin: Psychologist in Vygotsky's footsteps.* New York: Nova Science Publishers.

Haenen, J. (2001). Outlining the teaching–learning process: Piotr Gal'perin's contribution. *Learning and Instruction, 11*, 157–170.

Hall, J. K. (2001). *Methods for teaching foreign languages: Creating a community of learners in the classroom.* Upper Saddle River, NJ: Pearson.

Han, Z. (2007). Pedagogical implications: Genuine and pretentious. *TESOL Quarterly, 41*, 387–393.

Harré, R. (2009). Saving critical realism. *Journal for the Theory of Social Behaviour, 39*, 129–143.

Hatch, E. (1978). Apply with caution. *Studies in Second Language Acquisition, 2*, 123–143.

Haywood, H. C., & Lidz, C. S. (2007). *Dynamic assessment in practice. Clinical and educational applications.* New York: Cambridge University Press.

Holme, R. (2009). *Cognitive linguistics and language teaching.* Basingstoke: Palgrave Macmillan.

Holmes, J., Gathercole, S. E., & Dunning, D. L. (2009). Adaptive training leads to sustained enhancement of poor working memory in children. *Developmental Science, 12*(4), F9–F15.

Holodynski, M. (2013). The internalization theory of emotions: A cultural historical approach to the development of emotions. *Mind, Culture, and Activity: An International Journal, 20,* 4–38.

Holzman, L. (2009). *Vygotsky at work and play.* New York: Routledge.

Holzman, L. (2010). Without creating ZPDs there is no creativity. In M. C. Connery, V. P. John-Steiner, & A. Marjanovic-Shane (Eds.), *Vygotsky and creativity: A cultural-historical approach to play, meaning making, and the arts* (pp. 27–40). New York: Peter Lang.

Hopper, P. (1997). Discourse and the category 'verb' in English. *Language & Communication, 17,* 93–102.

Hulstijn, J. H. (2002). Towards a unified account of the representation, processing and acquisition of second language knowledge. *Second Language Research, 18,* 193–223.

Hurley, S., & Chater, N. (2005a). Introduction: The importance of imitation. In S. Hurley & N. Chater (Eds.), *Perspectives on imitation. From neuroscience to social sciences. Volume 2. Imitation, human development, and culture* (pp. 1–52). Cambridge, MA: MIT Press.

Hurley, S., & Chater, N. (Eds.). (2005b). *Perspectives on imitation. From neuroscience to social science. Volume 1: Mechanisms of imitation and imitation in animals. Volume 2: Imitation, human development, and culture.* Cambridge, MA: MIT Press.

Hutchins, E. (1995). *Cognition in the wild.* Cambridge, MA: MIT Press.

Ilyenkov, E. (1977). *Dialectical logic. Essays on its history and theory.* Moscow: Progress Press.

Ilyenkov, E. (2012). Dialectics of the ideal (2009). *Historical Materialism, 20,* 149–193.

In'nami, Y., & Koizumi, R. (2009). A meta-analysis of test format effects on reading and listening test performance: Focus on multiple-choice and open-ended formats. *Language Testing, 26,* 219–244.

Jacobs, E. L. (2001). The effects of adding Dynamic Assessment components to a computerized preschool language screening test. *Communication Disorders Quarterly, 22*(4), 217–226.

Jakobovits, L. A., & Gordon, B. (1974). *The context of foreign language teaching.* Rowley, MA: Newbury House.

Jansen, L. (2008). Acquisition of German word order in tutored learners: A cross-sectional study in a wider theoretical context. *Language Learning, 58,* 185–231.

John-Steiner, V. (1985). The road to competence in an alien land: A Vygotskian perspective on bilingualism. In J. V. Wertsch (Ed.), *Culture, communication, and cognition. Vygotskian perspectives* (pp. 348–371). Cambridge: Cambridge University Press.

John-Steiner, V., & Mahn, H. (1996). Sociocultural approaches to learning and development: A Vygotskian framework. *Educational Psychologist, 31,* 191–206.

Johnson, K. E. (2009). *Second language teacher education. A sociocultural perspective.* New York: Routledge.

Johnson, R. E. (1970). Recall of prose as a function of the structural importance of the linguistic units. *Journal of Verbal Learning and Verbal Behavior, 9,* 12–20.

Johnston, M. (1995). *Stages of acquisition of Spanish as a second language.* University of Western Sydney, Macarthur. The National Languages and Literacy Institute of Australia, Language Acquisition Research Centre.

Jordan, G. (2004). *Theory construction of second language acquisition.* Amsterdam: John Benjamins.

Joyce, B., & Showers, B. (1995). *Student achievement through staff development: Fundamentals of school renewal.* New York: Longman.

Karpov, Y. V. (2003). Vygotsky's doctrine of scientific concepts: Its role for contemporary education. In A. Kozulin, B. Gindis, V. S. Ageyev, & S. M. Miller (Eds.), *Vygotsky's educational theory in cultural context* (pp. 65–82). Cambridge: Cambridge University Press.

Karpov, Y. V. (2005). *The neo-Vygotskian approach to child development.* Cambridge: Cambridge University Press.

Karpov, Y. V., & Haywood, H. C. (1998). Two ways to elaborate Vygotsky's concept of mediation. *American Psychologist, 53,* 27–36.

Kim, J. (2013). *Developing conceptual understanding of sarcasm in a second language through concept-based instruction.* Unpublished doctoral dissertation, The Pennsylvania State University, University Park, PA.

Klein, K., & Boals, A. (2001). The relationship of life event stress and working memory capacity. *Applied Cognitive Psychology, 15,* 565–579.

Klingberg, T. (2010). Training and plasticity of working memory. *Trends in Cognitive Science, 14,* 317–324.

Kozulin, A. (1998). *Psychological tools: A sociocultural approach to education.* Cambridge, MA: Harvard University Press.

Kozulin, A. (2003). Psychological tools and mediated learning. In A. Kozulin, B. Gindis, V. S. Ageyev, & S. M. Miller (Eds.), *Vygotsky's educational theory in cultural context* (pp. 15–38). Cambridge: Cambridge University Press.

Kozulin, A. (2009). New reference points for Dynamic Assessment (DA): A commentary on Karpov and Tzuriel. *Journal of Cognitive Education and Psychology, 8,* 242–245.

Kozulin, A. (2011). Learning potential and cognitive modifiability. *Assessment in Education: Principles, Policy & Practice, 18*(2), 169–181.

Kozulin, A., & Garb, E. (2002). Dynamic assessment of EFL text comprehension of at-risk students. *School Psychology International, 23,* 112–127.

Kozulin, A., & Gindis, B. (2007). Sociocultural theory and education of children with special needs: From defectology to remedial pedagogy. In H. Daniels, M. Cole, & J. V. Wertsch (Eds.), *The Cambridge companion to Vygotsky* (pp. 332–361). Cambridge: Cambridge University Press.

Krashen, S. (1981). *Second language acquisition and second language learning.* New York: Pergamon Press.

Krashen, S. (1982). *Principles and practice in second language acquisition.* New York: Pergamon Press.

Kuk, I., & Kellogg, D. (2007). The ZPD and whole class teaching: Teacher-led and student-led interactional mediation of tasks. *Language Teaching Research, 11,* 281–299.

Lai, W. (2012). *Concept-based foreign language pedagogy: Teaching the Chinese temporal system.* Unpublished doctoral dissertation, The Pennsylvania State University, University Park, PA.

Lakoff, G., & Johnson, M. (1999). *Philosophy in the flesh: The embodied mind and its challenge to Western thought.* New York: Basic Books.

Lantolf, J. P. (2006). Sociocultural theory and L2. State of the art. *Studies in Second Language Acquisition, 28,* 67–109.

Lantolf, J. P. (2008). Praxis and L2 classroom development. *ELIA: Estudios de lingüística inglesa aplicada, 8,* 13–44.

Lantolf, J. P. (2009). Dynamic assessment: the dialectical integration of instruction and assessment. *Language Teaching, 42,* 355–368.

Lantolf, J. P., & Appel, G. (1994). Theoretical framework: An introduction. In J. P. Lantolf & G. Appel (Eds.), *Vygotskian approaches to second language research* (pp. 1–32). Norwood, NJ: Ablex Press.

Lantolf, J. P., & Beckett, T. (2009). Research timeline for sociocultural theory and second language acquisition. *Language Teaching, 42,* 459–475.

Lantolf, J. P., & Poehner, M. E. (2004). Dynamic Assessment: Bringing the past into the future. *Journal of Applied Linguistics, 1*(1), 49–74.

Lantolf, J. P., & Poehner, M. E. (2006). *Dynamic Assessment in the foreign language classroom. A teachers guide.* Center for Advanced Language Proficiency Education and Research, The Pennsylvania State University, University Park, PA. [149 pp. & video DVD. Version 1.0]

Lantolf, J. P., & Poehner, M. E. (2008). Introduction to sociocultural theory and the teaching of second languages. In J. P. Lantolf & M. E. Poehner (Eds.), *Sociocultural theory and the teaching of second languages* (pp. 1–32). London: Equinox Press.

Lantolf, J. P., & Poehner, M. E. (2011a). Dynamic assessment in the classroom: Vygotskian praxis for L2 development. *Language Teaching Research, 15,* 11–33.

Lantolf, J. P., & Poehner, M. E. (2011b). *Dynamic Assessment in the foreign language classroom. A teachers guide* (2nd ed.). Center for Advanced Language Proficiency Education and Research, The Pennsylvania State University, University Park, PA. [200 pp. & video DVD]

Lantolf, J. P., & Poehner, M. E. (2013). The unfairness of equal treatment: Objectivity in L2 testing and Dynamic Assessment. *Educational Research and Evaluation, 19,* 141–157.

Lantolf, J. P., & Sunderman, G. (2001). Foreign languages in the school curriculum: The struggle for a place in the sun. *Modern Language Journal, 85,* 5–25.

Lantolf, J. P., & Thorne, S. L. (2006). *Sociocultural theory and the genesis of second language development.* Oxford: Oxford University Press.

Lapkin, S., Swain, M., & Knouzi, I. (2008). French as a second language: University students learn the grammatical concept of voice: Study design, materials development, and pilot data. In J. P. Lantolf & M. E. Poehner (Eds.), *Sociocultural theory and the teaching of second languages* (pp. 228–255). London: Equinox.

Larsen-Freeman, D. (1990). On the need for a theory of language teaching. In J. E. Alatis (Ed.), *Georgetown University round table on language and linguistics. Linguistics, language teaching and language acquisition: The interdependence of theory, practice, and research* (pp. 261–270). Washington, DC: Georgetown University Press.

Larsen-Freeman, D., & Cameron, L. (2008). *Complex systems and applied linguistics.* Oxford: Oxford University Press.

Lave, J., & Wenger, E. (1991). *Situated learning: Legitimate peripheral participation.* Cambridge: Cambridge University Press.

Lee, H. (2012). *Concept-based approach to second language teaching and learning: Cognitive linguistics-inspired instruction of English phrasal verbs.* Unpublished doctoral dissertation, The Pennsylvania State University, University Park, PA.

Leontiev, A. A. (1981). *Psychology and the language learning process.* London: Pergamon.

Levelt, W. J. M. (1989). *Speaking: From intention to articulation.* Cambridge, MA: MIT Press.

Lidz, C. S. (1991). *Practitioner's guide to dynamic assessment.* New York: Guilford.

Lidz, C. S., & Elliott, J. G. (2000). *Dynamic assessment: Prevailing models and applications.* Amsterdam: Elsevier.

Lightbown, P. (1985). Great expectations: Second language acquisition research and classroom teaching. *Applied Linguistics, 6,* 173–189.

Lightbown, P. (2000). Anniversary article: Classroom SLA research and language teaching. *Applied Linguistics, 21,* 431–462.

Littlemore, J. (2010). *Applying cognitive linguistics to second language learning and teaching.* Houndsmills, UK: Palgrave.

Liu, G. (1991). *Interaction and second language acquisition: A case study of a Chinese child's acquisition of English as a second language.* Unpublished doctoral dissertation, LaTrobe University, Melbourne, Australia.

Long, M. H. (2007). *Problems in SLA.* Mahwah, NJ: Erlbaum.

Long, M. H. (2009). Methodological principles for language teaching. In M. H. Long & C. J. Doughty (Eds.), *The handbook of language teaching* (pp. 373–394). Malden, MA: Wiley-Blackwell.

Long, M. H., & Doughty, C. J. (2003). SLA and cognitive science. In C. J. Doughty & M. H. Long (Eds.), *Handbook of second language acquisition* (pp. 866–870). Malden, MA: Blackwell.

Luria, A. R. (1961). Study of the abnormal child. *American Journal of Orthopsychiatry. A Journal of Human Behavior, 31*, 1–16.

Luria, A. R. (1973). *The working brain.* New York: Basic Books.

Luria, A. R. (1976). *Cognitive development. Its cultural and social foundations.* Cambridge, MA: Harvard University Press.

Luria, A. R. (1979). *The making of mind: A personal account of Soviet psychology.* Cambridge, MA: Harvard University Press.

Luria, A. R. (1982). *Language and cognition.* New York: John Wiley and Sons.

Luria, A. R., & Vygotsky, L. S. (1992). *Ape, primitive man, and child: Essays in the history of behavior.* Orlando, FL: Paul M. Deutsch Press.

Mackey, A. (1999). Input, interaction and second language development: An empirical study of question formation in ESL. *Studies in Second Language Acquisition, 21*, 557–587.

Magnan, S. (2007). Gauging the scholarly value of connecting research to teaching. *TESOL Quarterly, 41*, 400–404.

Mahn, H. (2009). Vygotsky's methodological approach. A blueprint for the future of psychology. In A. Toomela & J. Valsiner (Eds.), *Methodological thinking in psychology: 60 years gone astray?* (pp. 297–323). Charlotte, NC: Information Age Publisher.

Mansouri, F. (Ed.). (2007). *Second language acquisition research: Theory-construction and testing.* Newcastle, UK: Cambridge Scholars Publishing.

Marx, K. (1978a). The *Grundrisse.* In R. C. Tucker (Ed.), *The Marx–Engels reader* (2nd ed., pp. 221–293). New York: W. W. Norton.

Marx, K. (1978b). Theses on Feuerbach. In R. C. Tucker (Ed.), *The Marx–Engels reader.* (2nd ed., pp. 143–145). New York: W. W. Norton.

Marx, K., & Engels, F. (1978). *The Marx-Engels reader* (2nd ed.) R. C. Tucker (Ed.). New York: W. W. Norton.

Meltzoff, A. N. (2002). Elements of a developmental theory of imitation. In A. N. Meltzoff & W. Prinz (Eds.), *The imitative mind: Development, evolution, and brain bases* (pp. 19–41). New York: Cambridge University Press.

Meltzoff, A. N., & Gopnik, A. (1989). On linking nonverbal imitation, representation, and language learning in the first two years of life. In G. E. Speidel & K. E. Nelson (Eds.), *The many faces of imitation in language learning* (pp. 23–52). New York: Springer Verlag.

Mezzacappa, E., & Buckner, J. C. (2010). Working memory training for children with attention problems or hyperactivity: A school-based pilot study. *School Mental Health, 2*, 202–208.

Miller, R. (2011). *Vygotsky in perspective.* New York: Cambridge University Press.

Mitchell, R., & Myles, F. (1998). *Second language learning theories.* London: Edward Arnold.

Mitchell, R., & Myles, F. (2004). *Second language learning theories* (2nd ed.). London: Edward Arnold.

Mitchell, R., & Myles, F. (2013). *Second language learning theories* (3rd ed.). London: Routledge.

Moll, H., & Tomasello, M. (2007). Cooperation and human cognition: The Vygotskian intelligence hypothesis. *Philosophical Transactions of the Royal Society of Britain, 362,* 639–648.

Moss, P. A. (2003). Reconceptualizing validity for classroom assessment. *Educational Measurement: Issues and Practice, 22*(4), 13–25.

Nassaji, H., & Swain, M. (2000). A Vygotskyan perspective towards corrective feedback in L2: The effect of random vs. negotiated help on the acquisition of English articles. *Language Awareness, 9,* 34–51.

National Council on Teacher Quality. (2013). *Teacher prep review: A review of the nation's teacher preparation programs.* http://www.nctq.org/dmsStage/Teacher_Prep_Review_ 2013_Report.

Navarro, E., & Calero, M. D. (2009). Estimation of cognitive plasticity in old adults using Dynamic Assessment techniques. *Journal of Cognitive Education and Psychology, 8*(1), 38–51.

Negueruela, E. (2003). *A sociocultural approach to the teaching and learning of second languages: Systemic-theoretical instruction and L2 development.* Unpublished doctoral dissertation, The Pennsylvania State University, University Park, PA.

Negueruela, E. (2008). Revolutionary pedagogies: learning that leads (to) second language development. In J. P. Lantolf & M. E. Poehner (Eds.), *Sociocultural theory and the teaching of second languages* (pp. 189–227). London: Equinox.

Negueruela, E. (2011). Beliefs as conceptualizing activity: A dialectical approach for the second language classroom. *System, 39,* 359–369.

Newman, D., Griffin, P., & Cole, M. (1989). *The construction zone: Working for cognitive change in school.* Cambridge: Cambridge University Press.

Nickerson, R. S. (1993). On the distribution of cognition: Some reflections. In G. Salomon (Ed.), *Distributed cognitions. Psychological and educational considerations* (pp. 229–261). Cambridge: Cambridge University Press.

Novack, G. (1978). *Polemics in Marxist philosophy. Essays on Sartre, Plekanov, Lukacs, Engels, Kolakowsi, Trotsky, Timpanaro, Colletti.* New York: Pathfinder.

Ohta, A. S. (2001). *Second language acquisition processes in the classroom: Learning Japanese.* Mahwah, NJ: Erlbaum.

Palincsar, A. S., & Brown, A. L. (1984). Reciprocal teaching of comprehension-fostering and comprehension-monitoring activities. *Cognition and Instruction, 1,* 117–175.

Palincsar, A. S., Brown, A. L., & Campione, J. C. (1993). First-grade dialogues for knowledge acquisition. In E. A. Forman, N. Minick, & C. A. Stone (Eds.), *Contexts for learning: Sociocultural dynamics in children's development* (pp. 43–57). New York: Oxford University Press.

Paradis, M. (2009). *Declarative and procedural determinants of second languages.* Amsterdam: John Benjamins.

Pass, S. (2004). *Parallel paths to constructivism. Jean Piaget and Lev Vygotsky.* Charlotte, NC: Information Age Publishing.

Perkins, D. N. (1993). Person-plus: A distributed view of thinking and learning. In G. Salomon (Ed.), *Distributed cognitions. Psychological and educational considerations* (pp. 88–110). Cambridge: Cambridge University Press.

Pienemann, M. (1984). Psychological constraints on the teachability of languages. *Studies in Second Language Acquisition, 6,* 186–214.

Pienemann, M. (1987). Determining the influence of instruction on L2 speech processing. *Australian Review of Applied Linguistics, 10,* 83–113.

Pienemann, M. (1989). Is language teachable? Psycholinguistic experiments and hypotheses. *Applied Linguistics, 10,* 52–79.

Pienemann, M. (1998). *Language processing and second language development: Processability theory.* Amsterdam: John Benjamins.

Pienemann, M. (2003). Language processing capacity. In C. Doughty & M. H. Long (Eds.), *The handbook of second language acquisition* (pp. 679–714). Malden, MA: Blackwell.

Pienemann, M. (Ed.). (2005). *Cross-linguistic aspects of processability theory.* Amsterdam: John Benjamins.

Pienemann, M. (2007). Processability theory. In B. VanPatten & J. Williams (Eds.), *Theories in second language acquisition: An introduction* (pp. 137–154). Mahwah, NJ: Erlbaum.

Pienemann, M., Di Biase, B., & Kawaguchi, S. (2005). Extending processability theory. In M. Pienemann (Ed.), *Cross-linguistic aspects of processability theory* (pp. 199–252). Amsterdam: John Benjamins.

Pienemann, M., & Kessler, J-U. (2011). *Studying processability theory: An introductory textbook (Processability approaches to language acquisition research & teaching).* Amsterdam: John Benjamins.

Pineda, J. A. (Ed.). (2010). *Mirror neuron systems. The role of mirroring processes in social cognition.* New York: Humana Press.

Poehner, M. E. (2005). *Dynamic assessment of advanced L2 learners of French.* Unpublished doctoral dissertation, The Pennsylvania State University, University Park, PA.

Poehner, M. E. (2007). Beyond the test: L2 Dynamic Assessment and the transcendence of mediated learning. *The Modern Language Journal, 91,* 323–340.

Poehner, M. E. (2008a). Both sides of the conversation: The interplay between mediation and learner reciprocity in Dynamic Assessment. In J. P. Lantolf & M. E. Poehner (Eds.), *Sociocultural theory and the teaching of second languages* (pp. 33–56). London: Equinox Publishing.

Poehner, M. E. (2008b). *Dynamic assessment: A Vygotskian approach to understanding and promoting second language development.* Berlin: Springer.

Poehner, M. E. (2009a). Dynamic Assessment as a dialectic framework for classroom activity: Evidence from second language (L2) learners. *Journal of Cognitive Education and Psychology, 8*(3), 252–268.

Poehner, M. E. (2009b). Group Dynamic Assessment: Mediation for the L2 classroom. *TESOL Quarterly, 43*(3), 471–491.

Poehner, M. E. (2011). Validity and interaction in the ZPD: Interpreting learner development through L2 Dynamic Assessment. *International Journal of Applied Linguistics, 21*(2), 244–263.

Poehner, M. E. (in preparation). *Dynamic Assessment: A casebook.* Center for Advanced Language Proficiency Education and Research, The Pennsylvania State University, University Park, PA.

Poehner, M. E., & Davin, K. (2013). Learning to teach 'reactively' through Dynamic Assessment. Annual Meeting of the American Association for Applied Linguistics. Dallas, TX. March.

Poehner, M. E., & Lantolf, J. P. (2005). Dynamic assessment in the language classroom. *Language Teaching Research, 9,* 233–265.

Poehner, M. E., & Lantolf, J.P. (2013). Bringing the ZPD into the equation: Capturing L2 development during computerized Dynamic Assessment. *Language Teaching Research*, *17*(3), 323–342.

Poehner, M. E., & Rea-Dickins, P. (Eds.). (2013). *Addressing issues of access and fairness in education through dynamic assessment*. London: Routledge (special issues as books program).

Poehner, M. E., & van Compernolle, R. A. (2011). Frames of interaction in Dynamic Assessment: Developmental diagnoses of second language learning. *Assessment in Education: Principles, Policy and Practice*, *18*(2), 183–198.

Poehner, M. E., & van Compernolle, R.A. (in press). L2 development around tests. Learner response processes and Dynamic Assessment. *International Review of Applied Linguistics*.

Polizzi, M-C. (2013). *The development of Spanish aspect in the second language classroom: Concept-based pedagogy and dynamic assessment*. Unpublished doctoral dissertation, University of Massachusetts, Amherst, MA.

Ratner, C. (2002). *Cultural psychology. Theory and method*. New York: Kluwer/Plenum.

Ratner, C. (2006). *Cultural psychology: A perspective on psychological functioning and cultural reform*. Mahwah, NJ: Lawrence Erlbaum.

Ratner, C. (2012). *Macro cultural psychology. A political philosophy of mind*. New York: Oxford University Press.

Rea-Dickins, P., & Gardner, S. (2000). Snares and silver bullets: disentangling the construct of formative assessment. *Language Testing*, *17*, 215–243.

Rieber, R.W., & Robinson, D. K. (2004). Problems of the theory and history of psychology. *Crisis in psychology*. In R. W. Rieber & D. K. Robinson (Eds.), *The essential Vygotsky* (pp. 221–225). New York: Kluwer/Plenum.

Rizzolatti, G. (2005). The mirror neuron system and imitation. In S. Hurley & N. Chater (Eds.), *Perspectives on imitation. From neuroscience to social science. Volume 1: Mechanisms of imitation and imitation in animals* (pp. 55–76). Cambridge, MA: MIT Press.

Rudzka-Ostyn, B. (2003). *Word power: Phrasal verbs and compounds. A cognitive approach*. Berlin/New York: Mouton de Gruyter.

Salaberry, M. R. (2001). *The development of past tense morphology in L2 Spanish*. Amsterdam: John Benjamins.

Salaberry, M. R., & Shirai, Y. (2002). L2 acquisition of tense-aspect morphology. In R. Salaberry & Y. Shirai (Eds.), *Tense-aspect morphology in L2 acquisition* (pp. 1–20). Amsterdam: John Benjamins.

Saville-Troike, M. (1988). Private speech: Evidence for second language learning strategies during the 'silent period.' *Journal of Child Language*, *15*, 567–590.

Schon, D. (1987). *Educating the reflective practitioner*. San Francisco: Jossey-Bass.

Schumann, J. H., Crowell, S. E., Jones, N. E., Lee, N., Schuchert, S. A., & Wood, L. A. (2004). *The neurobiology of learning. Perspectives from second language acquisition*. Mahwah, NJ: Erlbaum.

Scribner, S. (1997). *Mind and social practice: Selected writings of Sylvia Scribner*. Eds. E. Tobach, R. J. Falmange, M. B. Parlee, M. M. W. Martin, A. S. Kapelman. New York: Cambridge University Press.

Scribner, S., & Cole, M. (1981). *The psychology of literacy*. Cambridge, MA: Harvard University Press.

Shamir, A., & Tzuriel, D. (2004). Children's mediational teaching style as a function of intervention for cross-age peer-mediation. *School Psychology International*, *25*, 58–97.

Shulman, L. S. (1987). Knowledge and teaching: Foundations of the new reform. *Harvard Educational Review*, *57*(1), 1–22.

Silverstein, M. (2003). Indexical order and the dialectics of sociolinguistic life. *Language and Communication, 23,* 193–229.

Slobin, D. I. (1996). From 'thought and language' to 'thinking for speaking.' In S. Gumperz & S. Levinson (Eds.), *Rethinking linguistic relativity* (pp. 70–96). Cambridge: Cambridge University Press.

Slobin, D. I. (2003). Language and thought online: Cognitive consequences of linguistic relativity. In D. Gentner & S. Goldin-Meadow (Eds.), *Advances in the study of language and thought* (pp. 157–192). Cambridge, MA: MIT Press.

Sowell, T. (2009). *Intellectuals in society.* New York: Basic Books.

Spada, N., & Lightbown, P. M. (1999). Instruction, first language influence, and developmental readiness in second language acquisition. *Modern Language Journal, 83,* 1–22.

Speidel, G. E. (1989). Imitation: A bootstrap for language to speak ? In G. E. Speidel & K. E. Nelson (Eds.), *The many faces of imitation in language learning* (pp. 151–180). New York: Springer Verlag.

Speidel, G. E., & Nelson, K. E. (1989). A fresh look at imitation in language learning. In G. E. Speidel & K. E. Nelson (Eds.), *The many faces of imitation in language learning* (pp. 1–22). New York: Springer Verlag.

Steele, C. M., & Aronson, J. (1995). Stereotype threat and the intellectual test performance of African Americans. *Journal of Personality and Social Psychology, 69,* 797–985.

Stern, H. H. (1983). *Fundamental concepts of language teaching: Historical and interdisciplinary perspectives on applied linguistics research.* Oxford: Oxford University Press.

Sternberg, R. J., & Grigorenko, E. L. (2002). *Dynamic testing. The nature and measurement of learning potential.* Cambridge: Cambridge University Press.

Stetsenko, A. (2010). Teaching–learning and development as activist projects of historical becoming: Expanding Vygotsky's approach to pedagogy. *Pedagogies: An International Journal, 5,* 6–16.

Stetsenko, A., & Arievitch, I. M. (2004). Vygotskian collaborative project of social transformation. History, politics, and practice in knowledge construction. *International Journal of Critical Psychology, 12,* 58–80.

Stetsenko, A., & Vianna, E. (2009). Bridging developmental theory and educational practice. Lessons from the Vygotskian project. In O. A. Barbarin & B. H. Wasik (Eds.), *Handbook of child development and early education* (pp. 38–54). New York: Guilford Press.

Stewart, T. (2006). Teacher–researcher collaboration or teachers' research? *TESOL Quarterly, 40,* 421–430.

Stone, C. A. (1993). What's missing in the metaphor of scaffolding? In E. A. Forman, N. Minick, & C. A. Stone (Eds.), *Contexts of learning: Sociocultural dynamics of children's development* (pp. 169–183). New York: Oxford University Press.

Sutton, J. (2008). Material agency, skills and history: Distributed cognition and the archaeology of memory. In C. Knappet & L. Malafouris (Eds.), *Material agency* (pp. 37–55). Boston: Springer.

Swain, M. (2006). Languaging, agency and collaboration in advanced language proficiency. In H. Byrnes (Ed.), *Advanced language learning: The contribution of Halliday and Vygotsky* (pp. 95–108). London: Continuum.

Swain, M., Kinnear, P., & Steinman, L. (2011). *Sociocultural theory in second language education: An introduction through narratives.* Bristol: Multilingual Matters.

Swain, M., & Lapkin, S. (2007). The distributed nature of second language learning: A case study. In S. Fotos & H. Nassaji (Eds.), *Focus on form and teacher education: Studies in honor of Rod Ellis* (pp. 73–84). Oxford: Oxford University Press.

Swain, M., Lapkin, S., Knouzi, I., Suzuki, W., & Brooks, L. (2009). Languaging: University students learn the grammatical concept of voice in French. *Modern Language Journal, 93*, 5–29.

Talyzina, N. (1981). *The psychology of learning. Theories of learning and programed instruction.* Moscow: Progress Press.

Tarone, E. (2007). Sociolinguistic approaches to second language acquisition research—1997–2007. *Modern Language Journal, 91*, 837–348.

Tarone, E., & Liu, G. (1995). Situational context, variation, and second language acquisition theory. In G. Cook & B. Seidlhofer (Eds.), *Principle and practice in second language acquisition* (pp. 107–124). Oxford: Oxford University Press.

Tarone, E., Swain, M., & Fathman, A. (1976). Some limitations to the classroom applications of current second language acquisition research. *TESOL Quarterly, 10*, 19–32.

Teasdale, A., & Leung, C. (2000). Teacher assessment and psychometric theory: A case of paradigm crossing? *Language Testing, 17*(2), 163–184.

Tharp, R. G., & Gallimore, R. (1988). *Rousing minds to life: Teaching, learning and schooling in social context.* Cambridge: Cambridge University Press.

Thorne, S. L., & Lantolf, J. P. (2006). A linguistics of communicative activity. In S. Makoni & A. Pennycook (Eds.), *Disinventing and reconstituting languages* (pp. 170–195). Clevedon: Multilingual Matters.

Tomasello, M. (1999). *The cultural origins of human cognition.* Cambridge, MA: Harvard University Press.

Tomasello, M. (2003). *Constructing a language: A usage-based theory of language acquisition.* Cambridge, MA: Harvard University Press.

Tomasello, M., Carpenter, M., Call, J., Behne, T., & Moll, H. (2005). Understanding and sharing intentions: The origins of cultural cognition. *Behavioral and Brain Sciences, 28*, 675–735.

Torrance, H. (1995). Teacher involvement in new approaches to assessment. In H. Torrance (Ed.), *Evaluating authentic assessment* (pp. 44–56). Buckingham, UK: Open University Press.

Torrance, H., & Pryor, J. (1998). *Investigating formative assessment: Teaching, learning and assessment in the classroom.* Buckingham, UK: Open University Press.

Tulviste, P. (1991). *The cultural-historical development of verbal thinking.* Commack, NY: Nova Science Publishers.

Turner, M. (1996). *The literary mind. The origins of thought and language.* New York: Oxford University Press.

Tyler, A. (2012). *Cognitive linguistics and second language learning: Theoretical basics and experimental evidence.* New York: Routledge.

Tyler, A., & Evans, V. (2001). Reconsidering prepositional polysemy networks: The case of *over. Language, 77*, 724–765.

Tzuriel, D. (2011). Revealing the effects of cognitive education programmes through Dynamic Assessment. *Assessment in Education: Principles, Policy & Practice, 18*(2), 113–131.

Tzuriel, D., & Alfassi, M. (1994). Cognitive and motivational modifiability as a function of the Instrumental Enrichment (IE) program. *Special Services in the Schools, 8*, 91–128.

Tzuriel, D., & Shamir, A. (2002). The effects of mediation in computer assisted dynamic assessment. *Journal of Computer Assisted Learning, 18*, 21–32.

Tzuriel, D., & Shamir, A. (2007). The effects of peer mediation with young children (PMYC) on children's cognitive modifiability. *British Journal of Educational Psychology, 77*, 143–165.

Ullman, M.T. (2005). A cognitive neuroscience perspective on second language acquisition: The Declarative/Procedural Model. In C. Sanz (Ed.), *Mind and context in adult second language acquisition: Methods, theory, and practice* (pp. 141–178). Washington, DC: Georgetown University Press.

Ullman, M. T. (2012). The declarative/procedural model. In P. Robinson (Ed.), *The Routledge encyclopedia of second language acquisition* (pp. 160–164). New York: Routledge.

Ur, P. (2012). Grammar teaching: Theory, practice and English teaching education. In J. Huttner, B. Mehlmauer-Larcher, S. Reichel, & B. Schiftner (Eds.), *Theory and practice in EFL teacher education. Bridging the gap* (pp. 83–99). Bristol: Multilingual Matters.

Valsiner, J. (2012). *A guided science. History of psychology in the mirror of its making.* New Brunswick, NJ: Transaction Publications.

Valsiner, J., & van der Veer, R. (2000). *The social mind. Construction of the idea.* Cambridge: Cambridge University Press.

van Compernolle, R. A. (2012). *Developing sociopragmatic capacity in a second language through concept-based instruction.* Unpublished doctoral dissertation, The Pennsylvania State University, University Park, PA.

van der Veer, J., & Valsiner, J. (1991). *Understanding Vygotsky: A quest for synthesis.* Oxford: Blackwell.

VanPatten, B. (1996). *Input processing and grammar instruction.* Norwood, NJ: Ablex.

Vendler, Z. (1967). *Linguistics in philosophy.* Ithaca, NY: Cornell University Press.

Veresov, N. N. (1999). *Undiscovered Vygotsky. Etudes on the pre-history of cultural-historical psychology.* Frankfurt-am Main: Peter Lang.

Vocate, D. (1994). Self-talk and inner speech: Understanding the uniquely human aspects of intrapersonal communication. In D. Vocate (Ed.), *Intrapersonal communication. Different voices, different minds* (pp. 3–32). Hillsdale, NJ: Erlbaum.

Voloshinov, V. N. (1973). *Marxism and the philosophy of language.* Translated by L. Matejka & I. R. Titunik. Cambridge, MA: Harvard University Press.

Vygotsky, L. S. (1935). The question of multilingual children. In L. S. Vygotsky (Ed.), *Mental development of children in the process of schooling.* Moscow-Leningrad: State Publishing House. [Republished in Vygotsky (1997b, pp. 253–259).]

Vygotsky, L. S. (1971). *The psychology of art.* Cambridge, MA: MIT Press.

Vygotsky, L. S. (1978). *Mind in society. The development of higher psychological processes.* Cambridge, MA: Harvard University Press.

Vygotsky, L. S. (1986). *Thought and language.* Translation newly revised and edited by A. Kozulin. Cambridge, MA: MIT Press.

Vygotsky, L. S. (1987). *The collected works of L. S. Vygotsky. Volume 1: Problems of general psychology, including the volume Thinking and speech.* R. W. Rieber & A. S. Carton (Eds.). New York: Plenum.

Vygotsky, L. S. (1990). *The collected works of L. S. Vygotsky. Volume 2: The fundamentals of defectology (abnormal psychology and learning disabilities).* R. W. Rieber & A. S. Carton (Eds.). New York: Plenum.

Vygotsky, L. S. (1994a). The development of academic concepts in the school-aged child. In J. van der Veer & J. Valsiner (Eds.), *The Vygotsky reader* (pp. 355–370). Oxford: Blackwell.

Vygotsky, L. S. (1994b). The problem of the environment. In J. van der Veer & J. Valsiner (Eds.), *The Vygotsky reader* (pp. 338–354). Oxford: Blackwell.

Vygotsky, L. S. (1997a). *The collected works of L. S. Vygotsky. Volume 3: Problems of the theory and history of psychology.* R. W. Rieber & J. Wollock (Eds.). New York: Plenum.

Vygotsky, L. S. (1997b). *The collected works of L. S. Vygotsky. Volume 4: The history of the development of higher mental functions.* R. W. Rieber (Ed.). New York: Plenum.

Vygotsky, L. S. (1997c). *Educational psychology.* Boca Raton, FL: Nova Science.

Vygotsky, L. S. (1998). *The collected works of L. S. Vygotsky. Volume 5: Child psychology.* R. W. Rieber (Ed.). New York: Plenum.

Vygotsky, L. S. (1999). *The collected works of L. S. Vygotsky. Volume 6: Scientific Legacy.* R. W. Rieber (Ed.). New York: Plenum.

Vygotsky, L. S. (2004/1926). The historical meaning of the crisis in psychology: A methodological investigation. In R. W. Rieber & D. K. Robinson (Eds.), *The essential Vygotsky* (pp. 227–344). New York: Kluwer/Plenum.

Wang, X. (2011). *Grammatical development among Chinese L2 learners: From a processability account.* Newcastle: Newcastle University, UK.

Wells, G. (1994). The complementary contributions of Halliday and Vygotsky to a "language-based theory of learning." *Linguistics and Education, 6,* 41–90.

Wells, G. (1999). *Dialogic inquiry: Towards a socio-cultural practice and theory of education.* Cambridge: Cambridge University Press.

Wertsch, J. V. (1984). The zone of proximal development: Some conceptual issues. In B. Rogoff & J. V. Wertsch (Eds.), *Children's learning in the "zone of proximal development."* (pp. 7–18). San Francisco: Jossey-Bass.

Wertsch, J. V. (1991). *Voices of the mind: A sociocultural approach to mediated action.* Cambridge, MA: Harvard University Press.

Wertsch, J. V. (1998). *Mind as action.* Oxford: Oxford University Press.

Wertsch, J. V., del Rio, P. & Álvarez, A. (1995). Sociocultural studies: history, action, and mediation. In J. V. Wertsch, P. del Rio, & A. Álvarez (Eds.), *Sociocultural studies of mind* (pp. 1–36). Cambridge: Cambridge University Press.

Wertsch, J. V., Minick, N., & Arns, F. J. (1984). The creation of context in joint problem solving. In B. Rogoff & J. Lave (Eds.), *Everyday cognition: Its development in social contexts* (pp. 151–171). Cambridge, MA: Harvard University Press.

Widdowson, H. G. (1990). *Aspects of language teaching.* Oxford: Oxford University Press.

Williams, J. N. (2012). Working memory and SLA. In S. M. Gass & A. Mackey (Eds.), *The Routledge handbook of second language acquisition* (pp. 427–441). New York: Routledge.

Williams, R. (1977). *Marxism and literature.* Oxford: Oxford University Press.

Wood, D., Bruner, J., & Ross, G. (1976). The role of tutoring in problem solving. *Journal of Child Psychology and Psychiatry, 17,* 89–100.

Wundt, W. (1904a). *Principles of physiological psychology. Volume 1.* London: Sonnenschein.

Wundt, W. (1904b). *Völkerpsychologie: eine Untersuchung der Entwicklungsgesetze von Sprache, Mythus und Sitte.* Leipzig: Wilhelm Engelmann.

Yáñez-Prieto, M. C. (2008). *On literature and the secret art of invisible words: Teaching literature through language.* Unpublished doctoral dissertation, The Pennsylvania State University, University Park, PA.

Yus, F. (1998). Irony: context accessibility and processing effort. *Pragmalinguistica, 5–6,* 391–411.

Yus, F. (2000). On reaching the intended ironic interpretation. *International Journal of Communication, 10,* 27–78.

Zhang, Y. (2001). *Second language acquisition of Chinese grammatical morphemes: A processability perspective.* Unpublished doctoral dissertation, The Australian National University, Canberra, Australia.

Zhang, Y. (2007). Testing the topic hypothesis: The L2 acquisition of Chinese syntax. In F. Mansouri (Ed.), *Second language acquisition research. Theory-construction and testing* (pp. 173–198). Newcastle upon Tyne, UK: Cambridge Scholars Publishers.

Zhang, X. (in progress). *The teachability hypothesis and concept-based instruction: Topicalization in Chinese as a second language.* Unpublished doctoral dissertation, The Pennsylvania State University, University Park, PA.

# INDEX

Note: 'N' after a page number indicates a note; 'f' indicates a figure; 't' indicates a table.

abbreviation 62
Ableeva, R. 181–186, 204
abstractions. *See* scientific concepts
abuse 41
*ACTFL Standards for the Preparation of Foreign Language Teachers* 218
actions, types of 62
adults, cognitive modifiability of 167
African Americans 41–42
Agar, M. 11
Alfassi, M. 162, 164–165
Aljaafreh, A. 43, 170, 172–173
allostatic load 38n7
Allwright, D. 3
Álvarez, A. 59
Antón, M. 188
Appel, G. 45
applied linguistics 1
apprenticeship model 55n1
Arbib, M. A. 51
Arievitch, I. M. 5, 64
Aristotle 5
Aronson, J. 41–42
artifacts. *See* tools
*Ashley Madison* website 97
assessment: Budoff's model of 153–154; formative 202; implicit vs. explicit

feedback 171–174; vs. instruction 154; IQ scores 151–152; of learning potential 153; Luria's model of 153; and ZPD 151–153. *See also* computerized dynamic assessment (C-DA); dynamic assessment (DA); L2 dynamic assessment (DA)
assisted performance 155
Atkinson, D. 38n5, 39
*Aufhebung* 20–21, 23
Australia 10
auxiliary stimuli: Cuisenaire rods 111, 112, 114; examples of 8–9, 25–26; in experimental-developmental method 82. *See also* Schema of a Complete Orienting Basis of an Action (SCOBA); tools

Baddeley, A. D. 34
Bakhurst, D. 21
Baldwin, J. M. 50
Beckmann, J. F. 189
Behne, T. 50
Belcher, D. 2, 3
Boals, A. 35
Bodrova, E. 157, 214
Boers, F. 70

Boivin, N. 38n4

Bonilla, C. 105–107, 115, 118nn7–9

brain: development of 22; dialectics of 22–24; mirror neurons in 50, 51, 52; scans of 162. *See also* cognitive processing

brain damage 38n4

Bronfenbrenner, U. 168

Brooks, L. 67

Brown, A. 58

Budoff, M. 153–154, 196

Buescher, K. 224n2

Bull, W. E. 124

Bygate, M. 1

Call, J. 50

capitalism 33–34

Carpenter, M. 50

Carroll, S. 171

*Casebook* of DA (Poehner) 221

category procedure 101

Celce-Murcia, M. 136

Chaiklin, S. 147, 148–151, 155

Chapelle, C. 2

Chater, N. 50, 51

children: and auxiliary stimuli 25–26; cultural development of 9–10; deaf 44, 169n4; environment's role in development of 40–43; and first-order mediation 58; and imitation 50, 51; and internalization 48; as mediators 165–166; planning ability in 12; and play 157–158; and prior knowledge 68–69; and working memory (WM) 35–36. *See also* education; human development

Chinese language 108–117, 118nn10–11, 130–135

CL. *See* Cognitive Linguistics (CL)

Clark, A. 38n4

Clarke, M. A. 3

Cochran-Smith, M. 212

Cognitive Linguistics (CL) 224n1; and L2 research 70; and pre-service education 217; and Systemic Theoretical Instruction (STI) 71–72; and visual representations as cognitive maps 72

cognitive modifiability 160–162, 167

cognitive processing: effects of social change on 28–31, 36; and language acquisition 43–44; and mediated learning experiences 161. *See also* psychology; working memory (WM)

Cole, M. 11, 31, 57

communicated thinking 66–67, 96, 124–126

computerized dynamic assessment (C-DA) 188–199; collaborative vs. cooperative interactions 192, 194; KIDTALK 189; profiling development in 195–199; and study in French reading comprehension 191–195

Concept Based Instruction (CBI). *See* Systemic Theoretical Instruction (STI)

concepts: and effective SCOBAs 65; and prior knowledge 68–69; spontaneous vs. scientific 60–61, 64–65. *See also* tools

conceptual thinking 30–31

consciousness: and environment 48–49, 49f; language as 22; origins of 56

constructivism 53–54, 63

conversations, and ZPD 12–13

Corder, S. P. 1

co-regulation 158, 164, 173, 181, 184–186

Cortázar, Julio 123

Courtin, C. 44

Criado, R. 73

crisis. *See under* psychology

Crookes, G. 1

Cuisenaire rods 111, 112, 114

cultural deprivation 161, 167, 169n4

cultural primitivism 161

culture: dialectics of 22–24; effects of, on perception 10; effects of, on psychology 33–34, 49, 49f; institutions of, as third-order mediation 61. *See also* environment; macro cultural psychology; tools

Darling-Hammond, L. 212

Davin, K. J. 222

Davydov, V. V. 65, 208

Declarative/Procedural Model (DPM): implications for instruction 79; and

implicit/explicit divide in SLA 77–79; as model of adult language acquisition 74–75
deduction 30–31
DeKeyser, R. M. 73–74
del Rio, P. 59
Descartes, R. 17
development. *See* human development
developmental education. *See* education
developmental readiness 104, 116–117, 149. *See also* Teachability Hypothesis (TH). *See* Schema of a Complete Orienting Basis of an Action (SCOBA); visual representations
dialectical materialism: definition of 16; and pedagogical imperative 7. *See also* Vygotsky, L. S.
dialectics: of brain and culture 22–24; example of 20–21; overview of 19–20
dialogic thinking 66–67
Di Biase, B. 108
Di Pietro, R. J. 84, 90
dis-coordination 69
Doughty, C. J. 39
DPM. *See* Declarative/Procedural Model (DPM)
dualism: vs. dialectic approach 5–6; of mind-body 18–19, 37; and Western psychology 14
dynamic assessment (DA): computerized (C-DA) 188–199; extending beyond classrooms 187–188; in general vs. L2 research 170; graduated prompt approach 153; interventionist 153–155, 187; large-scale 201–202; *Lerntest* 153; and Spanish program placement 188; teachers' experience of 221–223; testing the limits approach 153; and transcendence 165; transfer tasks 165. *See also* L2 dynamic assessment (DA)
*Dynamic Testing* (Sternberg and Grigorenko) 154

East Side Institute 43
education: and cognitive processing 28–31; as developmental process 11; Gal'perin's theory of developmental 63–68; of L2

teachers 210–224; as leading activity 151, 169n5; and play 157–158; and prior knowledge 68–69; role of, in development 37; and socioeconomic status 43–44; task- vs. development-oriented interaction in 156–157; teachers' role in developmental 208–211; Vygotsky on 56; and ZPD 12–13. *See also* children; Systemic Theoretical Instruction (STI)
*Educational Psychology* (Vygotsky) 208
*Eleventh Thesis* 27, 37, 209
Elkonin, D. 157
Ellis, R. 82; on corrective feedback 171–172; on DeKeyser's position 73; and explicit/implicit L2 knowledge 78; on implicit knowledge 79; on L2 research studies 82; misconstrual of SCT 4–5, 207; on SLA 2; and Teachability Hypothesis (TH) 104; on theory/research–practice gap 3–4
empowerment 98–99, 172
emulation 55n2
Engels, F. 20
English language 136–143
environment: the ideal as aspect of 43–44; role of, in development 40–43, 48–49, 49f. *See also* culture
Evans, G. W. 35–36
Evans, V. 137
event-related potentials (ERPs) 77
experimental-developmental method 25, 82, 206
experimental-developmental studies: L2 sarcasm 93–99; sociopragmatics of L2 French 83–93; topicalization in Chinese 108–117
explicit/implicit interface 72–74, 77–79. *See also* knowledge

Falik, L. H. 161, 162
Farley, A. 105–107, 118n5
Fathman, A. 2
feedback 171–174. *See also* assessment
Felix, S. W. 115–116
Feuerbach, L. 19
Feuerstein, R. 159–168, 160, 160–162, 201

Feuerstein, R. S. 161, 162
first-order mediation 58
Firth, J. R. 47
Fogel, A. 158
French language 83–93, 181–186, 191–195
Fulcher, G. 53–54, 202, 203

Gallimore, R. 149
Gal'perin, P. Ya. *See* Systemic Theoretical Instruction (STI)
Ganem-Gutierrez, G. A. 67
Gao, X. D. 110, 118n10
gap. *See* theory/research–practice gap
Garb, E. 196
Gass, S. M. 2
generalization 62
genetic method 24–26, 52–53
Gergen, K. 55
Gergen, M. 55
German language 101–102, 108
Gillon Dowens, M. 77
Gindis, B. 160
Goldman, A. I. 50, 52
Gopnik, A. 51
Gordon, B. 3
Graduate Record Examination (GRE) 41–42
Greenwood, J. 15
Grigorenko, E. L. 154
grouping task 28–30
Guthke, J. 189

Haenen, J. 63–64, 66
Hall, J. K. 214–215
Han, Z. 2
Harré, R. 54
Harun, H. 67
Hatch, E. 2
Haywood, H. C. 58, 59, 154
Head Start 43
Hegel, G. 20
Heraclitus 5, 19
historical analysis. *See* genetic method
*The Historical Meaning of the Crisis in Psychology* (Vygotsky) 14
Hitch, G. J. 34

Hoffman, M. B. 161
Holme, R. 70
Holmes, J. 35
Holocaust 160
Holodynski, M. 45–46, 48
Holzman, L. 148, 151, 155, 157–158
Hopper, P. 47
Hulstijn, J. H. 73
human development: as collective activity 158; education's role in 56; elasticity of 161–162; environment's role in 40–43, 48–49, 49f; and instruction 63; and language acquisition 43–44; in teachers' pre-service education 213–216; teachers' role in 208–211; Vygotsky's view of, vs. learning 149–151; and ZPD 150–151. *See also* children
Hume, D. 5
Hurley, S. 50, 51

the ideal 43–44
idealism 17–18
IE. *See* Instrumental Enrichment (IE)
Ilyenkov, E. 18–19, 32
imitation: as basis of ZPD 50; and children 50, 51; definition of 50; vs. emulation 55n2; observation as form of 52; role reversal 51; and secondary interactants 180; in study of Spanish verbal aspect 129
immersion environments 77, 81n1
implicit knowledge. *See* explicit/implicit interface; knowledge
indexicality, orders of 84–85
in-growing. *See* internalization
inner speech. *See* internalization
Input Processing approach 106
inquiry-based teaching 212
institutions. *See* culture
instructional practice: and Declarative/Procedural Model (DPM) 79; and development 63; quality of 116; and SLA 1–3. *See also* practice; theory/research–practice gap
Instrumental Enrichment (IE) 164
intention reading 55n3

interiorization. *See* internalization
internalization: vs. apprenticeship model
  55n1; and children 48; definition of
  44–45; as inner speech 67–68; locus of
  control in 48; meaning vs. sense 45–46;
  and mental actions 63; and
  psychological grammar 46–47; in STI
  67–68
IQ scores 151–152

Jacobs, E. L. 189
Jakobovits, L. A. 3
Jansen, L. 102
Johnson, K. E. 182, 211
John-Steiner, V. 81n1
Johnston, M. 118n5
Jordan, G. 118n3

Kant, I. 5, 17
Karpov, Y. V. 58, 59, 157
Kawaguchi, S. 108
KIDTALK 189
Kim, J. 93–99
Kinnear, P. 214, 215
Kirghizia 28–31
Klein, K. 35
Klingberg, T. 35
Knouzi, I. 67
knowledge: automatized 73–74; declarative
  73–77; explicit vs. implicit in L2
  learning 72–74, 77–79; and memory
  75–77; procedural 73–77. *See also*
  memory
Korean language 94
Kozulin, A. 34, 149, 160, 166, 169n5,
  196
Krashen, S. 63, 73
Krupskaya, N. 38n3

L2 dynamic assessment (DA):
  computerized dynamic assessment
  (C-DA) 190–199; criticisms of 201–205;
  mediation quality in 171–174; study in
  listening comprehension 181–186; study
  of elementary Spanish classroom
  174–180

L2 learning: childhood as optimal time for
  75; and Cognitive Linguistics (CL)
  71–72; and cognitive modifiability 167;
  and declarative memory 76; and
  Declarative/Procedural Model (DPM)
  79; as developmental 213; and
  empowerment 98–99; and immersion
  environments 77; and prior knowledge
  68; and procedural memory 75–77; and
  Processability Theory (PT) 115;
  profiling development in 195–199; and
  sociocultural theory (SCT) 70–71;
  teachers' role in 210; verbal actions
  incorporated in 66–67. *See also* research
  studies
Lai, W. 130–135, 144, 145nn3–4
Lamadrid, E. E. 124
"languaculture" 11
language: figurative 120; inner vs. social
  46–47; scientific understanding of
  216–220; and sociocultural theory 9–10;
  of speech vs. thought 46; as unit of
  analysis 22; Vygotsky on 22. *See also*
  sociocultural theory (SCT)
language acquisition: and cognitive
  processing 43–44; usage-based theory of
  51
language pedagogy, and SLA theory 57
languaging 22, 38n2, 67
Lantolf, J. P.: on apprenticeship 55n1; and
  exclusion of SCT from psychology 15;
  on inner speech 45; and mediation in
  dialogic interaction 170; on person-solo
  concept 81n2; and SCT in L2 research
  6; and social interaction mediation 43;
  and sociocultural research on L2 70;
  study on medication in L2 ZPD activity
  172–173
Lapkin, S. 67
Larsen-Freeman, D. 57, 59, 136
Lave, J. 55n1
leading activities 61, 168n1, 169n5
learners: cognitive modifiability of
  160–162, 167; empowerment of 98–99,
  172; Piagetian vs. Vygotskian view of
  149–150; and reciprocity 163–164

learning. *See* education; L2 learning; teaching–learning–development
learning potential 153, 161–162, 164
learning potential score (LPS) 196, 199
learning prosthesis 155–157
Lee, H. 136–143
lemma activation 100–101
Leong, D. J. 157, 214
Leung, C. 187
Levelt, W. J. M. 100
Lewin, K. 5
Lexical Functional Grammar (LFG) 100
LFG. *See* Lexical Functional Grammar (LFG)
Lidz, C. S. 154, 163
Lightbown, P. 2, 105–106, 115, 116
listening comprehension 181–186
Littlemore, J. 70
Liu, G. 103
Long, M. H. 1, 4, 39
LPS. *See* learning potential score (LPS)
Luria, A. R.: on assessment 153; on conceptual thought 30; on indigenous Australian languages 10; on internalization 44–45; on psychometric tests 152–153; research in mediation 28; research on brain damage 38n4; research on cognitive processing 28–31; research on education 11; research on planning 12
Lytle, S. L. 212

Mackey, A. 2, 105, 115
macro cultural psychology: overview of 32–34; and working memory (WM) 34–36
Magnan, S. 2
Mahn, H. 22
Marx, K. 7, 19–21, 27
Marxism 17–18
mastery 62, 76
material actions 62
materialism: definition of 17; and mind-body relationship 18–19; and mirror analogy 18; overview of 17–19. *See also* dialectical materialism

materialist psychology. *See* psychological materialism
McCollam, K. 105–107, 118n5
meaning: knowledge as having 71; vs. sense 45–46; *znachenie* and *smysl* 45–46, 47, 72, 84
measurement. *See* assessment
Mediated Learning Experience (MLE): Instrumental Enrichment (IE) 164; learning potential 161–162; overview of 163; reciprocity 163–164; similarity to ZPD 160; transcendence 163–165
mediation: collaborative vs. cooperative interactions 192, 194; as co-regulated, collective activity 158–159; definition of 8; effects of, on brain activity 162; first-order mediation 58; in L2 ZPD activity 172–173; Luria's research on 28; and memory 26; orders of 57–61; Peer Mediation for Young Children (PMYC) program 165–166; quality of, in L2 DA 171–174; secondary interactants 180; second-order mediation 58–61; social interaction as 146, 161; in study of elementary Spanish classroom 175–176; third-order mediation 61. *See also* auxiliary stimuli; social interaction; tools
Meltzoff, A. N. 51
memory: and auxiliary stimuli 25–26; declarative 75–77, 81n6, 81n7; eidetic 23; mediated 26; procedural 75–77, 81n6; voluntary 23; working 34–36, 114–115
mental actions: SCOBA as cognitive map 64–65; in STI 62–63
metacognitive mediation 58
*Methods for Teaching Foreign Languages* (Hall) 214–215
Miller, R. 57–61, 69, 147, 148, 155, 159
mind/body relationship 18–19, 37
*Mind in Society* (Vygotsky) 148
mirror analogy 18
mirror neurons 50, 51, 52
Mitchell, R. 70, 81n4
Moll, H. 50, 55n3
Moss, P. A. 187
Myles, F. 70, 81n4

Nassaji, H. 204
Negueruela, E.: and dialogic thinking 66; on in-service teacher education 223; overview of research by 6; and prior knowledge 69–70; and SCT-L2 research 70
Nelson, K. E. 52
neuroscience research 75–77
Nickerson, R. S. 60
non-interface position 73–74, 77
Novack, G. 5, 17–18

*obuchenie* 57, 104, 116–117, 150, 211
other-regulation 168–169n2

Paradis, M. 73, 74–77
pedagogical content knowledge 217
pedagogical imperative 6–8
peer mediation 165–166
Peer Mediation for Young Children (PMYC) program 165–166
pencil example 20–21
perception, as mediated 10
perceptual actions 62
Perkins, D. N. 59–60
person-solo 59–60, 81n2
phrasal procedure 101
phrasal verbs 136–143
Piaget, J. 116, 149–150
Pienemann, M. 37, 53, 55n4, 63; on Processability Theory (PT) 103; and quality of instruction 116; on Teachability Hypothesis (TH) 106; Teachability Hypothesis (TH) 104, 115; Topic Hypothesis 108. *See also* Processability Theory (PT)
Pineda, J. A. 51
planning 11–12
Plato 5, 17
play 157–158
Poehner, M. E.: computerized dynamic assessment (C-DA) 191–192; on DA 188, 194, 201; on group ZPD as mediation 180; on Luria's paper 152, 153; overview of research by 6; on reciprocity 163; on teacher as researcher 222; on transcendence 165

poverty, and working memory (WM) 35–36
practice: concept of 5–6; as research 7–8. *See also* instructional practice
praxis: implications of, for teacher education 208; and in-service education 220–224; and psychological materialism 27; as theory–practice unity 6, 27
pre-understanding. *See* prior knowledge
prior knowledge: overview of 68–69; in study of English phrasal verbs 140–142; in study of sociopragmatics of French 86–87; in study of Spanish verbal aspect 124–126
Processability Theory (PT) 37, 53; challenges to 103, 118n3; five stages of processing procedures 102t; overview of 100–103. *See also* Teachability Hypothesis (TH)
Pryor, J. 202
psychological materialism: goals of 24; overview of 21–22; and praxis 27; research methodology of 24–26; and theory/research–practice gap 37. *See also* sociocultural theory (SCT)
psychology: crisis in 15–17; culture's effects on 33–34; modern vs. macro cultural 32; SCT categorized under 15; as sociocultural phenomenon 49, 49f. *See also* cognitive processing

Rand, Y. 161
ratchet effect 52
Ratner, C. 7; on brain/culture link 36; on constructivism 54–55; on macro cultural psychology 32–34; on third-order mediation 61
reciprocal teaching 58
reciprocity 163–164, 181, 184–186
reflective teaching 212
research: practice as 7–8. *See also* theory; theory/research–practice gap
research methodology: experimental-developmental method 25, 82; genetic method 24–26, 52–53; of psychological materialism 24–26

research studies: Chinese temporal grammar 130–135; English phrasal verbs 136–143; experimental-developmental 83–117; intact classroom 119–143; L2 sarcasm 93–99; sociopragmatics of L2 French 83–93; Spanish verbal aspect 119–130; topicalization in Chinese 108–117

Rizzolatti, G. 50

role reversal imitation 51

Rudzka-Ostyn, B. 137

rules of thumb: in Chinese temporal grammar study 134–135; and pre-service education 216; in Spanish verbal aspect study 124–125, 129–130

Rynders, J. E. 161

Salaberry, M. R. 120

sarcasm 93–99

Saville-Troike, M. 51

scaffolding 155

scenarios 90–91

Schamberg, M. A. 35–36

Schema of a Complete Orienting Basis of an Action (SCOBA): in Chinese temporal grammar study 131–133, 135; in Chinese topicalization study 110–111; in English phrasal verb study 137; overview of 64–65; in study of L2 sarcasm 95–97; in study of sociopragmatics of French 85–86; in study of Spanish verbal aspect 120–124; as visual representation 72

Schumann, J. H. 38n4, 81n6

scientific concepts 60–61, 64–65, 68–69, 210

SCOBA. See Schema of a Complete Orienting Basis of an Action (SCOBA)

Scribner, S. 11, 31

SCT. See sociocultural theory (SCT)

secondary interactants 180

second language acquisition (SLA): cognitivist view of 39; Ellis on 2; and explicit/implicit interface 72–74; implicit/explicit divide 77–79; and instructional practice 1–3; and language

pedagogy 57; Pienemann's Processability Theory of 37. See also L2 learning

second-order mediation 58–61

the self, concept of 33

self-regulation 58. See also co-regulation

sense 45–46

Shamir, A. 166, 189

Shirai, Y. 120

Shulman, L. S. 217

signification: definition of 22; and sociocultural theory 9–10. See also language

Silent Way pedagogy 111

Silverstein, M. 84–85

SLA. See second language acquisition (SLA)

Slobin, D. I. 11

smysl 45–46, 47, 72, 84

social interaction: dyadic 155–156; macro-level structure of 12; as mediation 146, 161; secondary interactants 180; task- vs. development-oriented 156–157

sociocultural theory (SCT): auxiliary stimuli in 8–9; definition of 7, 8; Ellis's misconstrual of 4–5, 207; Fulcher's misconstrual of 53–54; and L2 learning 70–71; and language 9; mediation in 8–9; overview of 8–13; and planning 11–12; as psychological 14–15, 52. See also Vygotsky, L. S.; Zone of Proximal Development (ZPD)

Sociocultural Theory in Second Language Education (Swain et al.) 214, 215

socio-dramatic play 157–158

socioeconomic status 42–43

Socratic dialogue 19

Sowell, T. 27

Spada, N. 105–106, 115, 116

Spanish language 100–101, 106–107, 119–130, 174–180

speed 34

Speidel, G. E. 51–52

S-procedure 101

Stalinist regime 28, 38n3

Stanford University 41–42

Steele, C. M. 41–42
Steinman, L. 214, 215
stereotype threat 41–42
Sternberg, R. J. 154
Stetsenko, A. 5, 6, 63, 71; on environment's
    role in development 40
Stewart, T. 3
STI. *See* Systemic Theoretical Instruction
    (STI)
stress: and allostatic load 38n7; and
    working memory (WM) 35
strong interface position 73–74
Structural Cognitive Modifiability (SCM)
    160–162
subject-verb (object) (SV[O]) syntax 108
subordination (S'-procedure) 102
superordinate categorization 28–30
Sutton, J. 38n4
Swain, M. 2, 38n2, 66–67, 171, 204, 214,
    215
syllogisms 30–31
Systemic Theoretical Instruction (STI)
    65–67; and Cognitive Linguistics (CL)
    71–72; educational praxis 63–68; and
    explicit/implicit interface 72–74; inner
    speech 67–68; and learner
    empowerment 98–99; mental actions
    62–63; Schema of a Complete
    Orienting Basis of an Action (SCOBA)
    64–65, 72; and teaching–learning–
    development 63; verbal actions 65–67;
    and visual representations as cognitive
    maps 64–65, 72. *See also* research studies

Talyzina, N. 206–207, 217
Tarone, E. 2, 103, 118n4
taxonomic classification 28–30
Teachability Hypothesis (TH): challenges
    to 104–107; and developmental
    readiness 104–105; overview of
    103–104; Piagetian vs. Vygotskian views
    115–117; vs. Zone of Proximal
    Development (ZPD) 104. *See also*
    Processability Theory (PT)
teachers: and DA experience 221–223;
    education of, for L2 learning 210–224;
    implications of praxis for 208; in-service

education 220–224; language
    curriculum for pre-service 217–220;
    pre-service education 210–220; as
    researchers 206, 209; role of, in
    developmental education 208–211
*Teachers Guide* (Lantolf and Poehner)
    220–221
teaching–learning–development: concept
    of 57; and developmental readiness 104,
    116–117; and L2 teachers 211; and STI 63
Teasdale, A. 187
temporal events 130–131, 145nn3–5
*TESOL Quarterly* 2–3
Tharp, R. G. 149
theory, concept of 5–6
theory/research–practice gap: closing of
    37, 206–207; Ellis on 3–4; proposed
    solutions for overcoming 3–5; and
    *TESOL Quarterly* 2–3. *See also* praxis
*Thinking and Speech* (Vygotsky) 14, 21, 60
third-order mediation 61
Thorne, S. L. 6, 15, 55n1, 70; on person-
    solo concept 81n2
Tomasello, M. 50, 51, 52, 55n3
tools: and actions 62; Cuisenaire rods 111,
    112, 114; and effective SCOBAs 65;
    scientific concepts as 60–61; and
    second-order mediation 58–61; and
    taxonomic classification 29–30. *See also*
    auxiliary stimuli
*Tools of the Mind* (Bodrova and Leong) 214
Topic Hypothesis 108–117
Torrance, H. 186–187, 202
transcendence 163–165
transfer tasks 165, 182–184
Tulviste, P. 11, 31
Turner, XX 120
Tyler, A. 70, 71, 72, 137
Tzuriel, D. 162, 164–166, 189

Ullman, M. T. 74–77, 81n7
Ur, P. 57
Uzbekistan 28–30

Valsiner, J. 6, 11, 151
van Compernolle, R. A. 83–93, 191–192,
    194

van der Veer, J. 151
vanPatten, B. 106
Vendler, Z. 120
verbal actions 62, 65–67
verbal aspect 119–130
verbs, phrasal 136–143
Veresov, N. N. 14
Vianna, E. 5, 6, 40, 63
visual representations: and Cognitive Linguistics (CL) 72; SCOBA as cognitive map 64–65. *See also* Schema of a Complete Orienting Basis of an Action (SCOBA)
Voloshinov, V. N. 21
Vygotsky, L. S.: on brain development 22–23; on childhood multilingualism 81n1; on education 56; *Educational Psychology* 208; on experimental-developmental method 25; on genetic method 24–26; *The Historical Meaning of the Crisis in Psychology* 14; on the ideal 43; on imitation 50, 129; on inner vs. social speech 46–47; on language as consciousness 22; on learning vs. development 149–151; on meaning vs. sense 45; *Mind in Society* 148; and mirror analogy 18; and natural sciences 53–54; on perception as mediated 10; on practice as research 7–8; on praxis 27–28; on prior knowledge 68; psychological materialism 21–22; on relationship of individuals and environment 40; on speech vs. thought 46; on teachers' role in development 208–209; theoretical origins of 6; *Thinking and Speech* 14, 21, 60; on verbalism 71; on ZPD 148. *See also* dialectical materialism; psychology, crisis in; sociocultural theory (SCT); Zone of Proximal Development (ZPD)

Wang, X. 110, 118n11
weak interface position 73–74
Wells, G. 8, 62, 81n3, 149
Wenger, E. 55n1
Wertsch, J.V. 59, 60, 81n2, 147, 155, 156
Whorf, B. 10–11
Widdowson, H. G. 8, 27, 57
Williams, J. N. 34, 36
work 168n1
working memory (WM): in children 35–36; and Chinese topicalization study 114–115; and macro cultural psychology 34–36; and poverty 35–36; and stress 35. *See also* memory
Wundt, W. 15

Yáñez-Prieto, M. C. 119–130
Yus, F. 95

Zhang, X. 108–117
Zhang, Y. 109
*znachenie* 45–46, 47, 72, 84
Zone of Proximal Development (ZPD): assistance assumption 155; common conceptions of 148–149; and conversations 12; as co-regulated, collective activity 157–159; as developmental 150–151; as garden 150; generality assumption 149; imitation as basis of 50; interpretations of 147–148; and learner empowerment 172; as learning prosthesis 155–157; and measurement 151–153; and mediation 172–173; potential assumption 151; secondary interactants 180; vs. Teachability Hypothesis (TH) 104
zoopsychology 38n6
ZPD. *See* Zone of Proximal Development (ZPD)